MAXWELL AIN

To my son, Max,
Have a great Naval Medical
Career — the best of both
worlds — I'm very proud
of you,

Dad

Ship's Doctor

Ship's Doctor

Capt. Terrence Riley
Medical Corps, U.S. Navy

Naval Institute Press
Annapolis, Maryland

Library of Congress Cataloging-in-Publication Data
Riley, Terrence L.
    Ship's doctor / Terrence Riley.
        p. cm.
    ISBN 1–55750–721–X
    1. Riley, Terrence L. 2. Ship physicians—United States—
Biography. 3. United States. Navy—Medical care. I. Title.
RC986.R54 1995
616.9'8024'092—dc20
[B]   95–8186

Printed in the United States of America on acid-free paper ∞

02 01 00 99 98 97 96 95   9 8 7 6 5 4 3 2
First printing

Although I have tried to portray the true life of the aircraft carrier, and
to honestly describe the life of the medical department, no real people
living or dead are depicted in this story. All characters and all medical
cases are either fictional or composites of several personalities or other
cases. Even the composites are altered in little ways. I want to authentically
recreate the tempo, stress, and adventure of life on the ship, but also to
protect the privacy and dignity of my shipmates and patients.

   The opinions and events in this book are entirely the opinions and
experiences of the author, and they do not represent those of the
Department of the Navy or the Bureau of Medicine and Surgery.

To my mother,
Clarissa Riley

Contents

Prologue

The nosewheel sliced up horizontally after it snapped and flew straight toward the island. It first hit the two aircraft handlers, who made loud, crunching sounds as they flew up against the island. Metal fragments like burning shrapnel hit four other people after the wheel ricocheted off two tractors.

The plane bounced twice on the orphan oleo strut and snapped the arresting cable under max tension. The cable whipped the skin right off Lieutenant Carson's legs while they were snapping, tore off his left wrist, and cracked his skull like a walnut on the hot nonskid.

"Call the wing surgeons to the flight deck and get Dr. Hardy and anesthesia set up now!" I yelled over my shoulder on my way up to the flight deck BDS.

Thirty seconds later, I threw one innocent bystander out of the way to get into the BDS. Carson's legs looked like fresh-skinned drumsticks, with the skin slipped down like loose stockings around his ankles. Blood pumped out of the stump of his wrist. He wasn't breathing. Bill cranked in two large-bore IVs, and I slipped in the endotracheal tube. Van, the surgeon, arrived just then, clamped down the bleeding stump, and handled the loose skin. While Van took over, I called the bridge, "We need the deck edge elevator now!"

"He's arrested!" Rob called, "No pulse."

V-fib.

"Stand back!" Three hundred joules. Sinus.

"We got a pulse. Bill, more fluid."

"Activate the blood bank!" Van called. "Let's get to the OR."

Behind the island, two other guys' legs were snapped like twigs by the cable when it whipped back. The flight surgeons were triaging the six guys injured from the broken wheel and the metal fragments. One

1

of them had a gash across the left side of his face that tore open his sinus and left eye; another was unconscious. Deftly covering the open wounds, the team started the IVs, immobilized the spines, and got the casualties into shelter.

In less than two minutes, the casualties were clear and the handlers pulled the broken F-14 out of the way. We still had thirteen airplanes to recover.

Introduction

This is the personal story of a ship's doctor, a flight surgeon on an aircraft carrier. It's mostly going to be true. I might ramble on here and there, but I'll tell the truth mostly. It may help for you to know a little background first, a little about what military and ships and airplanes and doctors have in common. You can read my story without this part if you want, but I'd like to set the stage for you.

It would surprise a lot of people that military and naval sciences were so far ahead of medicine for the first millennium that they almost didn't cross paths until the time of the Reformation. Nobody knew what caused diarrhea, pneumonia, or plague. If the scourges of disease crumbled a city (or disabled an army), it had to be attributed simply to fate or maybe to conjurers casting spells. Those few aspects of medicine that had any scientific basis at all—and there weren't many—were not demonstrably any more effective for the individual patient or for populations than were spiritual remedies. Of course, a lot of people would argue that's still true today.

After metal, gunpowder, and sailing ships reached certain pinnacles around the 1500s, their progress slowed a bit. Maybe it was one of those technological plateaus or paradigm shifts we hear so much about these days. Arts and the study of nature were catching up with warfare and the study of machines. In this era, Michelangelo, da Vinci, and other artists and scholars began to dissect human bodies. So professors of medicine were more or less forced to look at cadavers too, to try to keep up with the artsy crowd. When they looked they began to learn that not only were there a number of discrete parts inside the body, but that, surprisingly, these parts seemed to fit together in pretty much the same way in everybody. This being the case, one could study how those parts functioned in healthy folk and how they

3

looked different in sick or dead ones. Thus was medicine reluctantly dragged into the realm of scientific thought.

Although the scientific method has been sometimes capriciously applied in medicine, once introduced it quickly became downright fashionable. As medicine and surgery began to produce results, armies had to take surgeons along. They couldn't at first really heal many soldiers, but a few could be bandaged up and sent back to the front. Just saving as many lives of the other wounded as possible was critical, even if they couldn't return to the fight, because the populace was beginning to take note of how many died. Even if an amputee couldn't return to the front line, if he survived to go home his fellow villagers would be less angry than if he died.

Medicine and seafaring finally collided in scientific parity around 1617, the year John Woodall wrote the first text for ship's doctors. Woodall, the surgeon general for the East India Company, was an accomplished physician in his day. He evidently spent a lot of time at sea, as his treatise speaks of the rigors of sea travel and the effects of loneliness, danger, and hardship on those who sail. In *The Surgion's Mate,* Woodall extols the importance of behaving like an officer and gentleman, as expected of the physician on a ship. It is unclear whether Woodall left the East India Company because, as was known, he felt poorly paid for his level of renown, or because he ripped off the company and the junior ship's "surgions" by forcing them to buy expensive supply trunks and inventories from his personal side market.

Arguably warfare grew more complex in the century after Woodall; it certainly grew more international . . . at least more colonial. Britain, France, and Spain all sent forces to America and Africa, warring with one another and the aborigines. Ship's surgeons didn't all come from academic backgrounds like Woodall's. In fact, many were sailmakers or sailors too old and decrepit or too drunk for their original trades who simply apprenticed with an incumbent sawbones at sea. Hygiene and nutrition became as important to the surgeons as the treatment of wounds and diseases. The simple acts of quarantine and isolation were the only real tools for fighting disease, though. The scientific armamentarium at sea languished for a century.

Aviation began a century later with the first balloons, and physicians, always eager to dabble in somebody's good idea, sneaked into the vanguard. Dr. John Jeffries, an American physician, was the first to cross the English Channel in a balloon, and also the first to bring the value of biological perspective to the cockpit. He saved his gondola from crashing by dumping overboard all unnecessary weight: his clothes and about six pounds of urine he figured he could spare. In that same year, a French physician, Pilatre de Rozier, employed the unique kind of scientific ingenuity for which the medical profession is famous. He reasoned that if hot air could create lift and hydrogen (they called it "flammable air") could create lift, then hot hydrogen should be twice as good! His ingenuity went cruelly unrewarded, alas. When he lit the match to the burner to heat up the hydrogen, Pilatre suddenly discovered why it was called "flammable air." Thus a doctor became the first recorded aviation fatality.

Although naval medicine progressed very little in the two centuries after Woodall, in the nineteenth century the medical revolution came. The biggest changes affected infectious disease, surgery, and psychiatry, the areas most important to doctors who treated soldiers and sailors. The U.S. Navy's first hospital ship, the *Red Rover,* was commissioned in the Civil War. While America was preoccupied by the war, aviation kept moving on elsewhere, with lighter-than-air craft and gliders. In the 1870s, a French physician named Paul Bert pioneered studies of gas pressures at altitude.

Within thirty years, it became clear that balloons weren't particularly well suited for purposeful travel. Aircraft needed to be powered and controllable. Hence the airplane. When airplanes were evolving at an accelerating pace, their first practical applications seemed to be for the military. The Navy was involved from the beginning, though rather tentatively at first. In November 1910, Eugene Ely made the first takeoff from a flight deck, one built on the scout cruiser *Birmingham.* Four months later he had another first—the first arrested landing—this one on the cruiser *Pennsylvania.* For the next ten years, though, airplanes remained pretty flimsy and short-ranged, so the Navy had little interest in them.

World War I, however, woke us up. Airships were bombing London, and airplanes were proving major weapons in the war. Thousands of young Americans wanted to fight in the war as pilots. The Army Surgeon General's Office designed a set of physical standards, and in 1918 the War Department sent doctors from the Air Service Medical Research Laboratory to France to help the squadrons. Doctors became integral members of the flying and fighting organizations to protect the health of the aviators.

The U.S. Navy started an air force but had no initial facilities for equipment or training, so the first Navy pilots had to go to Canada to train. One of the first was a young Princeton graduate named James V. Forrestal. The son of an Irish immigrant, Forrestal had overcome the barriers against his Catholic, middle-class background to become a rising star on Wall Street. One of the brightest flight students, Forrestal was not an adept stick-and-rudder man but good enough to graduate. He became Naval Aviator #154. His greatest skills apparently were as a staffer, so he never flew much and never left the States. He stayed on duty a couple of years after the war, but soon returned to Wall Street and a very lucrative career. The Navy would see him again later.

After the war, the nation wanted to return to normalcy (which was a good thing for Warren Harding) and the admirals wanted to get back to basics, namely battleships. Gen. Billy Mitchell was court-martialed for his insubordinate insistence that airplanes could wreck fleets, and the Navy was able to limit its commitment to airborne submarine patrols and airships. Only after being goaded by the more innovative British did the Navy launch its first aircraft carrier, the *Langley*, CV-1, in 1922. (All Navy ships are designated by type, class, and sequence. Carriers are "C," fixed-wing aircraft are "V," and *Langley* was the first of its type, hence "CV-1.") That year the Navy sent five doctors—the first naval flight surgeons—to the Army School for Flight Surgeons on Long Island. Carriers would need doctors.

Aviation and ships grew more complex and more capable. The Navy built the *Saratoga* and the *Ranger*. Higher G forces, higher altitudes, more psychological stress—all made the medical needs of the aviator more demanding. The Navy opened a school for flight surgeons at its medical school in Washington in 1927, just before Lindbergh flew across the Atlantic. In 1932, a Navy doctor working at Harvard, Lt. Cdr. John Poppen, designed the first antigravity suit (G suit) to cope with G-induced complications of dive-bombing in naval aircraft.

Since the Army was bigger and had been doing aviation medicine longer, there were pressures to let it continue to train naval flight surgeons. The Navy needed something different from its flight surgeons, though. For one thing, the flying missions were a little different. But it was the sea that really made the difference. The ships. A naval flight surgeon had all the same medical and physical concerns that the Army doctor did, but he had to practice on a ship. He wasn't just a doctor for the aviators; he also had to take care of a lot of other people in that enclosed but isolated place, and there was no station hospital for him to fall back on as there was for the Army flight surgeon. The isolation and rigors at sea imposed entire dimensions of medical complexity.

The Brotherhood of the Sea was a force in this, too. Already familiar with that special value of the brotherhood, being a "shipmate," naval aviators wanted their "docs" to be part of the brotherhood—this time, the Brotherhood of the Air. If they were real members, maybe they could take better care of us, kind of like Errol Flynn did in *Dive Bomber* when he was a naval flight surgeon. From the beginning of the Navy School of Aviation Medicine at Pensacola, in 1939, all student naval flight surgeons had to pass all the swimming and survival courses right along with the aviators. But what set them apart from Army Air Corps flight surgeons was that they had to learn to fly. For those who graduated there were wings of gold, just as cherished among doctors as the Wings of Gold among pilots. If you passed all the courses but didn't learn to fly, you would be designated an aviation medical examiner, not a flight surgeon. Good job . . . but no wings.

The role of aircraft carriers really began to take form in the 1930s. Airships had a period in the limelight, too, but didn't make the final cut. This was the Flash Gordon and Buck Rogers era, so America loved it when great, bullet-shaped airships like the *Macon* could actually perform as *flying* aircraft carriers. The *Macon* could actually land biplane fighters by snaring them with a dangling trapeze and then launch them out as necessary to fight off marauders. By 1935, though, both the *Macon* and its sister ship, the *Akron,* had crashed, with Admiral Moffett, the father of naval aviation, among the fatalities. Although airships and blimps would continue to be used as patrol craft to hunt submarines, they would never again carry other aircraft. CVs were another matter altogether. In the late 1930s, the United States began to develop aircraft carriers and early concepts of naval air warfare. This seemed particularly suitable for the Pacific, where distances, isolation, and logistical trails seemed designed for a flexible, maneuverable air asset.

When the Japanese carrier *Akagi* led the surprise attack on Pearl Harbor, the role of the aircraft carrier would never be questioned again. Within five months, the U.S. carrier *Hornet* launched Lt. Col. Jimmy Doolittle's Army B-25s over mainland Japan. Within a month came the Battle of the Coral Sea, the first major naval battle fought primarily in the air. Capt. William Davis, the senior medical officer (SMO) of the *Yorktown,* was commended for gallantry in the battle as he treated casualties in fires and in areas with explosions. On the *Lexington* the SMO was Cdr. Arthur J. White. Blown against a bulkhead by the explosion from the first of several torpedo hits, Commander White continued to treat casualties despite a broken clavicle and two badly sprained ankles. When his "surgery" (what we would now call the ER) was blown up he carried patients on his shoulder through hatches and scuttles to get them to safe areas. The *Lexington* eventually went down that day, but

White kept treating patients for three hours after the first torpedo and later received the Navy Cross. Although usually considered a standoff, Coral Sea was the prelude for the Battle of Midway, the first major naval engagement in which the adversaries were beyond sight of each other and the turning point of the war in the Pacific.

The Navy had been forced to adapt quickly to this new form of warfare. One of the driving forces was the man who had become the first undersecretary of the Navy when the post was created in 1940, Naval Aviator #154, James V. Forrestal. The secretary, a very old Republican named Frank Knox, had left most of the details and budgetary battles to the brilliant young Forrestal, and as the war progressed and Knox grew more feeble, Forrestal took over more and more of the functions of the department. Known for genius, driven patriotism, and inexhaustible energy, Forrestal was credited by many with virtually reinventing the Navy. A dedicated liberal, he made the desegregation of the Navy one of his highest goals. Human issues were as important to him as efficiency and winning. Strong in his opinions, perhaps even lofty, he was said to dislike what he considered the dirty side of politics—the compromises, the give-and-take.

There was a haunting, dark side to Forrestal also. His marriage had long been difficult. His wife drank a lot. She made vulgar statements and scenes in front of high society and the general public alike. After a brief hospitalization she was diagnosed as suffering from schizophrenia, but she refused further treatment and Forrestal complied with her choice to leave the hospital. Most people thought she was simply an eccentric alcoholic. Whatever the case, the record doesn't show Mr. Forrestal to have eased her torment in any way. At any rate, he continued to work eighteen-hour days throughout the war, worrying about the role of politics in government and suppressing his personal life. When Knox died of heart failure in 1944, Forrestal took over as secretary of the Navy.

The Navy's postwar adjustments were as demanding as the war had been. Forrestal sparred with the chief of naval operations, Adm. Ernest King, a difficult man who chafed at the idea of civilian control. Forrestal had to fight for power over the budget and against the unavoidable reductions in the size of the Navy. On the other hand, while overseeing proper force reductions with the Navy Line, he helped President Truman fight to preserve readiness in the nuclear age in the face of Communist expansion. Along with George Kennan, Clark Clifford, and a few others, he made up a clique that urged containment and vigilance regarding China and the Soviet Union. The concepts of nuclear capability and deterrence were in their infancy, and Forrestal was one of the godfathers. In 1947 the individual military services lost their lofty cabinet positions and were reduced to subaltern status in a single Department of Defense (DOD). The War and Navy Departments, along with the new Air Force, were now just branches of the DOD. This was a bitter experience for many generals and admirals at the time. President Truman chose Forrestal, now one of his main advisors, to be the first secretary of defense.

The year 1948 brought a maelstrom to the DOD that had striking parallels to the one faced in the mid-1990s. The most fundamental views of warfare were shaken by recent changes in the world order and by the atom bomb and the jet engine. Yet at the same time, the populace and the politicians demanded drastic cuts in force structure and budget. A Democratic president who had promised economic recovery was being pummeled by Congress and was losing popularity faster than a chaperon at a drive-in movie. Forrestal realized that although we had to decommission most of the thirty-three aircraft carriers, ironically we still needed a bigger one. In the hazardous new world, a deck big enough for a plane that could carry atom bombs for long strategic strikes was necessary. A supercarrier, perhaps as big as 60,000 tons, would be needed by the 1950s, when Russia and China could feel their oats. (For comparison, the then-newest carriers like *Franklin Delano Roosevelt* and *Coral Sea* were about 45,000 tons.) The Air Force argued then, as now, that their long-range bombers could strike any target the nation would need; ships were obsolete. Gen. Curtis LeMay was a persuasive advocate. Congress had no stomach for the big price tag on a supercarrier. Other challenges Forrestal faced were arguments over bases in the Pacific or in Europe and racial integration of the services.

Forrestal continued to be a star in the Truman cabinet until, in 1949, something seemed different. He appeared to be fatigued. His concentration began to falter, and he overlooked detail. His staff and the others in the cabinet worried that his wife's illness or the unabated frenzy of high office for nine years was wearing him out. Finally, President Truman asked for his resignation. Depleted, emotionally threadbare, and with no solace available in his marriage, Forrestal was eventually admitted to the National Naval Medical Center in Bethesda. One day, he cajoled or ordered the corpsman on duty to go on some errand, then jumped to his death from his sixteenth-floor window.

The supercarrier was finally built. The keel was laid in July 1951 for CV-59, and in 1954 it was christened USS *Forrestal*. With its slanted deck, huge size, and dazzling speed, it drew a lot of press. I remember seeing reports about its sea trials completely filling newsreels at the movies in 1955. The crew's motto was "*First In Defense*," so the big ship was nicknamed the FID.

When I was a neurology resident at Bethesda in 1974, all of us new doctors were tauntingly taken to see a stain on the pavement in front of the hospital, the infamous spot "where Forrestal hit." That was all most of us knew about him, the stain. Like most legends about Forrestal, that too was wrong. He didn't hit the sidewalk at all. He struck the roof of the X-ray department in the three-deck south wing that sticks out from the tower.

The fact is, he remains both a titan and a tragic figure. Though wounded and suffering, he left behind the strongest and most adaptable navy in history. His namesake supercarrier continued the paradox. During flight operations on "Yankee Station" off Vietnam on 29 July 1967, a Zuni rocket was fired accidentally and ignited an A-4 Skyhawk attack jet. Within minutes the flight deck and most of the after half of the ship was in flames. That day 134 *Forrestal* shipmates died and 164 more were injured. The heroism of those who died and their shipmates is a naval legend. The Navy had long filmed all flight operations, so most of the conflagration and the fighting of the fire are on film. Most people in the Navy, certainly all who go to sea, study those films in a universal training classic called *Trial by Fire*. The film is intended to be a training tool in fire fighting and damage control. To people in the sea services, though, it's more than that. It's an example of what sailors do and what shipmates do for one another.

Many in the Navy know of CV-59 only from *Trial by Fire*, so the ship is sometimes called "The Forrest Fire," or "USS Zippo." You will never hear a FID sailor call her that. They don't even joke about the fire among themselves nearly thirty years later.

In the eighties I received orders to the *Forrestal*. "Report in July for duty in a flying status, to serve as Senior Medical Officer. Duty as Department Head." I read the book *Supercarrier*, by George Wilson, about a deployment of the USS *John F. Kennedy*. Intimidated as I was by the book, I discovered that my friend Monty Aumin had been the SMO on the cruise described in that book. I asked him a few questions. Yes, it was about the hardest job he ever had . . . but it might have been the best, too. I asked him about his experiences with the executive officer in *Supercarrier;* after reading the book, I was afraid of what it could be like to work for a guy like that. "Yeah, he was tough," Monty said. "He was kind of hardheaded, and he could be a screamer, but, you know, in his way he was fair. That makes up for a lot. He was smart, too." Monty is a known mellow guy. Maybe he could take it, but with all the other challenges, I hoped I wouldn't have to work for a screamer. That wasn't why I'd come back into the Navy.

"One thing," he told me, "when I had a really bad day . . . when it was over, I'd go out to the fantail and stand there a while, and tell myself, 'only fourteen people in the world have this job.'"

Chapter 1

Coming to the Forrestal

At 30,000 feet, with nothing to see but ocean and perfect blue sky, it can be very lonesome, knowing you are somewhere over the absolute middle of the Indian Ocean. At that altitude you can see the edges of the planet, and there's not one speck of soil or human all the way to those edges.

I was sitting in the back of a US-3 with four other passengers en route from the island of Diego Garcia to the USS *Forrestal*, somewhere in the north Arabian Sea. My cranial was too tight. The cranial is a kind of hard hat used by people who work on carrier hangar decks and flight decks. There are three hard plates that cover the forehead, top, and back of the head, and large, hard, cup-shaped earpieces to protect the ears. It's all held on by a big, sweaty chin strap. These are better than industrial hard hats because they're lighter and fit the contour of the head. Since you have to wear them all day, the cloth composition makes them more comfortable, and to keep them from blowing off in the wind and jet exhaust on the flight deck, they must fit firmly against the head. They didn't have a large size, so I had to make do with a medium, and it was beginning to be uncomfortable, especially over my ears. In fact, it had been worsening for about half an hour.

The S-3 is a fixed-wing antisubmarine jet aircraft that usually takes a crew of four: a pilot, a copilot, an enlisted sonar operator, and a tactical command officer (TACO)—a naval flight officer. Fleet replenishment squadrons usually use the venerable C-2, a large, two-propeller aircraft, for carrier onboard delivery (COD) missions. However, at times like this, when the ship would be operating beyond the range of the C-2, the US-3, with its longer range, had to do COD chores. The ship-based S-3 was designed to spend very long hours at sea flying grid after grid hunting for submarines. Its utility version is the US-3.

Because I was most senior on the airplane, I was allowed to sit in the front line of the seats so I could look through the windscreen and speak with the pilot and copilot. We were going to be flying a total of five hours that day, and since we were traveling at about 300 miles per hour or faster, I reckoned we had well over 1,000 miles to go, mostly due north.

About an hour and a half into the flight, my ears and cheeks started hurting from the tightness of the cranial, and I began to realize it was going to be a very long five hours. Also, I'd had a lot of coffee that morning, and I became aware that there would be other reasons for five hours to get uncomfortable.

It was too loud in the US-3 to carry on a conversation with my fellow passengers. We mostly made hand signals, and I had on my lap a copy of the book *Supercarrier*. Even though I'd read it once before, I thought I should brush up on it a little bit just in case I had to deal with similar situations or people.

There was a kind of bulkhead immediately behind the seat of the pilot on the left and the copilot on the right, leaving an opening about eighteen inches wide through which I could look out the windscreen or into the cockpit. I had to crane my neck around a little to the right, but I was willing to do that because there were no windows in the fuselage otherwise. I was a little bit surprised to see the copilot with the *New York Times* spread out over his lap and control yoke, completely covering all the instruments in the cockpit. He was eating a boxed lunch absentmindedly while he read, much like any ordinary employee on a lunch break.

I noted with a little bit of dismay, perhaps jealousy, that they had not provided us passengers with a boxed lunch, but told us, "Well, you'll be able to eat when you get to the ship." I craned my neck a little bit further so I could see the pilot and ask him a question or two. He also had a newspaper spread out over the yoke and was reading it. The control panel was completely covered, including the gyroscopes and compass, and neither of them had their hands on the wheel. Then I looked up again and glanced over the control panel to notice that we were still pretty high. I couldn't tell how high because the altimeter was covered, but clearly the horizon was very far away, and the ocean was so far below that all you could tell was that it was a deep blue. We were high enough that you couldn't see the waves. Not a cloud to be seen and, of course, no islands. If there was any way to know we were lost, no one would be able to tell it. What the hell, I thought. If you're lost at sea anyway, what good is it to be in control?

To the best of our knowledge, Amelia Earhart had her hands on the control yoke, and it didn't do her any good.

After eight years longing to be back in the Navy, I was finally fully engaged. My promise to Ann and the girls—that by returning to active duty I would have more time to spend at home—was not very convincing at the moment, especially since I couldn't really tell them exactly where on the planet I might be right now.

There is a global positioning system (GPS) on the control panel which would help us to navigate, of course, but since the aircraft was on autopilot and both our pilots were busy reading the news, there was no way of knowing we were really on course that way either. I guess I figured we were going more or less north, but I couldn't see the sun at all, so there was no way to judge that.

I tried to read the book, but I found it hard to concentrate because of the pain in my ears, the effort it was taking me to remain nonchalant about the two guys reading the newspaper, and that other problem from the coffee. Finally I asked the third crew member, the loadmaster, if there was a relief tube. He pointed to the back of the aircraft, spoke into the internal communications system (ICS) to the pilot, and turned back to me and gave me a thumbs-up signal. Although this is a very powerful aircraft, it's small enough that weight and balance need to be kept in line when people move around. He had to ask another person, who was seated somewhat further back, to move forward, and he had to move a bag of mail forward.

Just as promised, in the back of the aircraft, where a person had to bend down somewhat, there was a conical, funnel-shaped device stuck to a large rubber tube clamped up against the bulkhead. I was able to use it properly to relieve one nagging problem I had, but when I went back to my seat the two pilots were still browsing through their newspapers and nibbling at their lunches, and my ears started to hurt even more in the cranial one size too small.

It wouldn't do to let anybody think I had less than complete trust in the modern naval aviator, or to show that I had any worry about personal safety, while we were at 30,000 feet on a five-hour flight over the middle of the ocean. If you get a map or globe and look directly south from the Arabian Peninsula, perhaps a little bit east, you may or may not find the Maldives, a group of islands more or less halfway between India and Africa and equally far south of the Arabian Peninsula. In fact, they're so small and so far from any other land that they don't even appear on some maps. There wasn't a runway anywhere to be seen if we ran out of fuel. Reflecting on how often in flying my small airplane across the Midwest I had become treacherously low on gasoline, I remembered the time I had to radio a runway, announcing that I had just run out of fuel, and had to glide into a landing because the engine had stopped. There I was patted on the back by some of my fellow pilots for a "great job" but received some disapproving stares from older flight instructors, who pointed out that running out of gasoline was not conducive to great longevity.

The one thing I had done besides work during the eight years out of the Navy was fly. Instruments, multiengine, aerobatics—I did as much as I could. I hadn't had much spare time all those years, but when I could eke out a free hour I spent it aloft. It simply reinforced the nagging ache to be back in the Navy, to be part of the organization I had missed so much.

At about this point I looked up through the windscreen and noticed to my satisfaction that the copilot was folding up his newspaper. Short-lived relief it turned out, as he proceeded to pull out a paperback and open up one more sandwich, the wax paper falling away from the sandwich so it covered up his compass and both our views of the control panel again.

Finally, about two hours later, the pilot and copilot folded up their reading materials, started fiddling with instruments on the control panel, and initiated a descent. Some conversation started on the radio, and I noticed that there was a cloud bank a few miles ahead of us that we gradually flew beneath. The perfectly bright sky that had been with us for about four hours now gave way to an overcast above us. The copilot reached back to tap me on the shoulder and said, "There's Mom."

"Mom" is the title pilots use for the ship. Probably a proper name, and a reflection of the way I felt about the ship at the moment, too, although it was hard for me to think about anything as my ears were killing me, and I could scarcely think about anything except getting the cranial off. Straining my eyes, I was able to see the ship way off, a small fleck, very nearly on the horizon, and even approaching at nearly 300 miles per hour it didn't get much closer very fast. A little bit of drizzle started to form on the windscreen, and just as quickly disappeared. The pilot indicated to the copilot that he was going to let him "take the landing." I noticed again how young the copilot looked. All naval pilots looked young to me at about this time. They were all scarcely teenagers. Even so, this copilot looked a little younger than most of them, and I considered he was probably about the age of my oldest daughter.

We approached the ship at about 5,000 to 3,000 feet and made one racetrack oval over the deck. The pilot said something about the amount of fuel we had on board. The only activity on the flight deck was a couple of guys running some yellow gear, but there were no other flight operations and all the other airplanes seemed to be folded up and parked. I had always read how small an aircraft carrier looks from the sky, especially for your first landing. I can't say I thought it was really minuscule. But then I remembered a runway in Marlboro, Massachusetts, that used to intimidate me because it was only 1,500 feet long, when I was trying to land on it at 50 knots. This one had landing area less than half that, with no grass around it, and we were approaching at 200 knots. Finally, we made our left turnaround loop to final, less than a mile out, much shorter than a civilian pattern.

I had waited for this for years. My first "trap." I set myself up. We locked our harness belts in place. Even with the pain in my cranial, I looked with anticipation to the landing. I wanted to savor every marvelous sensation in that experience. I knew it was going to be a sensory explosion. The first trap is something every pilot looks forward to, and it's shrouded in much mystique in all aviation lore.

Then finally there we were. In a blur that was so fast—a blink, a speeding bullet, or a bullet train in Japan can't quite describe it—we were coming over the fantail, and just as fast the entire superstructure of the ship whizzed by. I felt the sudden jolt of the tires on the deck, and the next thing I knew we were back over the water again. A "bolter." Wow, was this fun. On my first approach we were going to wind up getting to do a touch and go, and a bolter. It was great! We circled around again and began to set up for another approach. Although I enjoyed getting a second go-round, a bolter after all does mean a missed landing. Something was off. Either we were too low, wrong speed, failed to hit the three-wire, or some other wire, or we had been given a wave-off by the landing signal officer (LSO).

Regardless, it was twice coming around, and it was a marvelous thrill. The pilot said something about how much fuel we had on board and then told the copilot, "We'd better get down this time." We came around again on final. This time I decided I would watch the flight deck go by and watch the superstructure—the "island"—so I could always remember that particular experience. Once again our harness belts were locked in tight, and it blurred by so fast that all I could see was the flashing gray, one person standing over by the superstructure, and then we were airborne again!

Wow, this was great, even two of them. However, it did occur to me now, here we had flown five and one-half hours, my ears were killing me, we had a young pilot, possibly making his first approach to the ship, and we were getting low on fuel. In spite of all this fun, we had to get down now because there were no alternate airports. This time the pilot flew the downwind leg, and I could see we were a little bit lower as we came on to final.

They were speaking to one another a little bit more this time, and I was able to look out through the windscreen and see "Paddles"— the nickname given to the LSO. Years ago, before radios and fancy communication and before there were prisms that showed a light for landing, the LSO actually stood on the fantail holding paddles in his hands and would direct the plane to the proper glide path.

This time we hit the deck and jerked to a stop for my first trap. I will have more to say about the experiences of a trap and a catapult shot. The essence and the ultimate experience of each of them are the stunning suddenness. If I described in one spot all of the things that go on it would take so many words that it would blunt the smacking intensity and the suddenness—and it would be misleading. Think of a bungee jump from a height of about fifteen stories, but not being bounced, just being at the end of a perfectly rigid hemp rope. You reach 200 miles an hour at the end, and in less than part of a second you are snapped to a sudden, complete stop. Nothing springy or elastic about it.

Now, I think of myself as a fast thinker, and I'm an experienced pilot, but with all of that happening in such a flash I wasn't able to look at the flight deck, the superstructure, or to see anything except a sudden gray blur when the wire abruptly snapped us back. There's not an amusement ride anywhere in the United States or any training device extant in the U.S. Navy that gives an experience like it.

While I was indulging in this lusty sensation, I realized that throughout all of it the two pilots had remained busy with the aircraft, and a guy in a yellow shirt out in front of the aircraft was extending his left arm and beckoning with his right while the aircraft was being taxied over to starboard. Just at the same time, the two wings were being folded up by the copilot, and we were taxiing to a place to park. A forty-one-year-old man, I had waited all these years for my opportunity to land on a flight deck. Images of Van Johnson, Tom Cruise, John Wayne, and John Glenn all came bubbling up, but I didn't have time to enjoy them because as soon as we had turned that corner and traveled about four seconds, the door popped open and we all started unloading.

Since I was the most senior, I was ushered off first. You have to wear a cranial or a helmet at all times on the flight deck, so I wasn't allowed to get this thing off my throbbing ears. No sooner had I stepped out of the aircraft than a hand slapped down on my shoulder, pulling me by the survival vest toward the right side. It was a guy in a white shirt and with the letters "ATO" printed on the back of his survival jacket. We were all dragged into the island on the starboard side of the aircraft, and a large, watertight door closed behind us. We were then quickly shunted through a door into what I realized was the flight deck battle dressing station (BDS). Happily, I was able to take my cranial off. Oh, what a great relief! I knew my ears were red and about three times their usual size, but did it feel good to get that off.

So, that is how I came to arrive on the *Forrestal* by a US-3. Lieutenant Bunche, the air transport officer (ATO), having jerked me off the flight line into the flight deck BDS, was introducing me around to the corpsmen in the BDS, and also to the first medical officer I was to meet on the *Forrestal,* Lt. Brice Bostik. Bostik was one of two flight surgeons assigned to my carrier air wing. He was a muscular, hyperactive, enthusiastic mesomorph about five feet, seven inches tall. He pumped my hand a few times and said, "We were wondering if you were going to make it here, Sir," which I was to hear from a number of people as the day went on.

The First of the Supercarriers launching four airplanes: two F-14 Tomcats on the bow catapults, and a Tomcat and EA-6B Prowler on the two waist catapults over on the port side aft of the island. *U.S. Navy photo*

Bostik bounced around the BDS, telling me about the ship and his time there. I learned that we had arrived in the middle of a general quarters (GQ) drill. There hadn't been too many of these drills during the preceding two months because of the high operating tempo of the ship. Because GQ is an exercise every ship must practice periodically, and since there is a quota for how many times it has to be done during a cruise, we would have to do it many times for the remainder of the deployment to make up for the past two months. Because of GQ I couldn't be taken below to the medical department or to my stateroom yet. GQ was the reason there were no flight ops at the present, too. So we were stuck sitting around during GQ, practicing first aid drills, with the ventilation—and a lot of the passageways—closed.

It was probably a fitting time to arrive, though. Although, as a drill, GQ is the most boring thing you can do on a ship, it gave me time to catch my breath and prepare for taking on the role of shipmate.

Chapter 2

The First Two Weeks

■ It isn't the first thing you notice about the ship. In fact, you don't notice it until you're away from there. But from the very first, there's a constant, underlying hum always in the background. The hum is from the engines, from the electricity, from the activity, from passing through the water. It's just from the ship, and it's always there. It was there that day, although I didn't notice it then. It's like the smell of the turf on a football field. You never really notice it, until years after. But now you remember the smell of the turf most of all. I think of the hum now all the time. I miss it.

When GQ was over, we went down a series of ladders on our way to the second deck. The flight deck is four decks above the hangar deck, which is the equivalent of the main deck on surface ships. On the first aircraft carriers, a flight deck had simply been constructed on a trellis over the main deck, and that tradition is continued in the naming of the decks on current aircraft carriers. There are no true stairs on Navy ships, just steep, stairlike ladders. Some of them have actual handrails attached, but most have chains about waist high that run from the top of the of the ladder down to the deck.

Passing through the hangar bay, I was impressed, as everyone always is, by the size of the hangar deck and the number of huge aircraft it could hold. I had been on aircraft carriers before, but always in port, when there were no aircraft aboard. There is a constant melee of activity in the hangar bay. Squatty, short, but powerful diesel tractors are pulling and pushing aircraft and other heavy equipment all over. The tractors have to be short and squatty because they must pass underneath aircraft bellies and wings laden with drop tanks or electronic pods. Technicians wearing green and brown shirts climb all over aircraft twenty-four hours a day, cleaning them, taking them apart, working on engines, and so forth. It's loud with pneumatic and hydraulic equipment buzzing all the time, electrical machinery working, engines turning, hammers banging, and people walking every direction.

More than the activity or the noise, however, one had to be impressed by the attitude and expression of the young men in the hangar bay. Of course, they all looked young and healthy. Yet the vibrance, the attitude, the cheerfulness, the professionalism—these were the most striking. Here were young men, most of them barely past their teen years, working eighteen hours every day in a stressful industrial plant, in a dirty, grimy place, but they were all paying close attention to their jobs, laughing and joking, virtually all of them smiling. They also seemed to enjoy their work. A young sailor would find something small on the deck and reach down and pick it up. Whenever one worker thought he saw an area with oil dripping from under a wing or a tank, he quickly put a pan under it. When you passed someone on the hangar deck or in the passageways below, he smiled, asked "How are you, Sir?" or had some cheerful comment.

We eventually found our way into the medical department, virtually in the middle of the ship on the second deck. I was brought to an amidships passageway, where a door had a brass placard reading "Senior Medical Officer, Captain John Busby." We went into that office, which was to be mine for the next two years, and I met John Busby for the first time. He and I had spoken on the telephone back in the spring, when I knew I would be coming to the FID, but this was our first opportunity to meet in person.

John is a tall, lanky fellow with a scratchy voice and an innocent face. Regardless of the situation, he always looks to me to have an expression of bemusement. Although he looks all of his fifty-plus years, there is an adolescent quality about him as well. He reminds me of a young cowboy named Sugarfoot I had enjoyed on TV as a teenager. In fact, John had been in practice in Oklahoma once. His appearance was deceptive. John was an accomplished physician. He had come to the FID suddenly, after his predecessor was relieved abruptly under a cloud. In two years he had restored the medical department to a fine level.

"Well, I see you made it. We're glad to have you. I was afraid you weren't coming."

I learned that the captain and the executive officer (XO) had been teasing Busby about whether I would arrive during the deployment. After a little more than two years in the job, he was eagerly looking forward to his return to shore duty.

He introduced me first to Lt. Rick Cox, the medical administrative officer (MAO). During our turnover I'd need to sign for a huge inventory. This included all of the laboratory equipment and drugs (many of which were controlled substances) in the medical department, along with hundreds of litters, the materials in the four storerooms that belonged to the medical department, and all of the gear and equipment in the six BDSs, each of which could function as an independent medical department with OR in the event of emergency or ship's damage.

After the short initial tour, John said, "There's something you need to know about. I just found out about it today. One of the officers on the staff is an insulin-dependent diabetic. I already brought this up with the captain, but it looks like it's something you'll have to handle eventually." We both knew what that meant. There are a number of conditions that are considered disqualifying for sea duty. Diabetes is high on that list. The aircraft carrier has a large medical department, and of course has insulin as part of the regular formulary of the pharmacy—but for emergencies, not routine care of chronic conditions. Treating an emergency or an unpredictable new medical problem is one thing; a known, and therefore avoidable, chronic illness is something altogether different. There are so many potential complications or emergencies with chronic diseases such as diabetes that regulations prohibit diabetics from sea duty. So people often hide diabetes and other chronic conditions to protect their careers.

There are a number of things that can cause emergencies with diabetes, such as reactions to insulin and sudden worsening of the diabetes. Possible complications involve increased vulnerability to infections and a higher risk of heart attacks . . . even coma. These are situations all of us Navy doctors are trained to contend with, but preventing or avoiding a dangerous situation is always preferable.

That the involved officer was a member of the flag staff was a further complication. Aircraft carriers usually travel and function as part of a battle group, in company with two or more frigates or destroyers, and often a cruiser. Frequently, one or more submarines are somewhere in the area as well. Because the aircraft carrier is the largest and most capable vessel in the group, it is the flagship for the embarked task force commander and his staff.

The staff is a stable organization, a command in itself. People are assigned to it just as they'd be assigned to a squadron or a ship. Rear Adm. (lower half) Lawrence "Sniffles" Kohl was the battle group (or task force) commander of Carrier Group 6 (CCG-6). A gregarious, good-humored, energetic, and immensely likeable man, "Sniffles" Kohl was an A-7 pilot, highly decorated during Vietnam, well known to be a rising star in the Navy, and liked by most people in the ship's company. By contrast, everybody else on the staff was usually just tolerated. Perhaps we were just jealous, or perhaps suspicious. The most maligned were the poor flag secretary and the lonesome flag lieutenant. For some reason, most ship's companies accuse the flag lieutenant (or "Loop," so called because of the gold braid, or aiguillette, worn looped over the left shoulder) of being a bad guy. Rumor had it he was short on words like "please" and seldom made requests when commands could fit. Every sentence was alleged to begin with "The admiral wants . . ." or "The admiral told me to tell you . . ." Probably not exactly true, but the image is an occupational burden.

So all in all, the relationship between the ship's company and the staff was guarded, even antagonistic sometimes. As the admiral said once, "Staffs are an easy target."

The staff had their own mess, so they didn't have to join or participate in meals in the wardroom. The ship's company and wardroom (the officers) loved the admiral, but they kept a careful distance from the staff in general.

So this was the background of the reported individual with diabetes, a member of the staff. The situation might be tricky to handle, and would definitely require early attention.

Besides walking all over the ship with Rick Cox inventorying equipment and learning about the spaces on the ship, I spent a lot of time that week walking around with John Busby. John carried a hand-held Motorola radio everywhere he went. These walkie-talkies weighed about seven pounds and were eight inches long and three or four inches thick. There was a springy five-inch antenna at the top. They're the familiar radios you see police officers carrying everywhere in the United States. Such a radio is called a "brick" because of its size, shape, and weight. Busby had a holster for his that he wore on his hip, like Matt Dillon wore his .45 back in Dodge City. John would never leave his office without it, and he'd usually leave it on when he was in the office. He wanted to be reached at any time, at any hour. He showed me the brick and told me I would need to use it always.

At formal dining on my first night, John introduced me to the wardroom, where I was greeted with a round of applause (but less than John received for his imminent departure). The genuine warmth and welcoming from the wardroom were spontaneous, reassuring, and immediate. John passed the brick to me and said,

"Tonight I give him the brick, and over the next few days I intend to give him the entire medical department."

About two days later, John saw me one time without the brick and asked me where it was. I told him that if anybody needed me, I thought I could hear them over the 1-MC (the overhead announcing system), but John told me, "You never know when that could go out, especially in an emergency. You ought to have the brick with you at all times." So I put it back on and carried it until John left a few days later. After he was gone, I never put the brick on again except for special exercises, and through my entire two years I don't think anybody ever tried to call me on it. Afterward I did a study on the subject, and it appears that nobody ever tried to call John on it either.

The day after John introduced me to the wardroom, we had a meeting in the medical department early in the morning, and he introduced me to all of the medical staff. I had already met Rick Cox and several of the enlisted people, especially Hospitalmen First Class (HM1) Burt Rosen and Tom Dunbar, two first class petty officers, who, along with the chief petty officers (CPOs), were the mainstays of the medical department. The people on the aircraft carrier belonged to three main organizations: the ship's company, all those people who belonged directly to the ship; the staff, only about two hundred people; and the embarked air wing. The air wing consisted of the eight flying squadrons, their associated wing staff, and all the maintenance people belonging to the wing and squadrons. There were two flight surgeons with the eight squadrons in my carrier air wing, the senior being Lt. Brice Bostik, who would be leaving us in about three months, and the other Lt. Bill Kelly, a Yale and Georgetown graduate, who would be with us most of another year.

On a cruise, the flight surgeons and squadron corpsmen were assigned to the medical department. The flight surgeons, however, were expected to spend up to 50 percent of their time with their squadrons—giving instruction, looking after the health of the flight crew, and doing some flying themselves to maintain contact with their charges. Just as there is a traditional friction between the ship's company and the flag staff, there is often a milder friction between the ship's company and the carrier air wing, and this carries on even down to the medical department. Flight surgeons are often a little bit unpopular with other members of the medical department. For one thing, they're gone part of the time while they're off working with their squadrons or flying, and for another, they are only with the department under way. When the ship returns to port, they return to the home bases of their various squadrons in other towns. Also, flight surgeons wear wings and identify more with their squadrons than with the ship or the medical department. Some flight surgeons have been described as more aviation groupies than doctors.

In our department this friction was particularly palpable. On the *Forrestal* the medical department had three officers with very definite opinions about flight surgeons in general and our two wing flight surgeons in particular. First was the warrant officer physician assistant (WOPA), Art Corbett. ("WOPA" is pronounced to resemble the word "whopper." This is one of the things Art liked about his job.) Art was a former senior chief, an independent duty corpsman (IDC) on submarines, who had gone to physician assistant school. Art was reminiscent of Sergeant Bilko in the 1950s sitcom. He knew how to accomplish anything on the ship, seemed to know either everybody on the ship or everybody who could make anything happen, and was in very definite control of his lifestyle. The warrant officers had their own community on the *Forrestal,* their own bank of staterooms on the third deck, and their own ethic. Art enjoyed a particularly prestigious position among them. He had strong opinions about the way medicine used to be practiced on the submarines and how modern young doctors had sometimes gone astray. Art often considered flight surgeons a frivolous lot, although he hadn't had to contend with them back when he worked on submarines all those years.

Our general medical officer (GMO) was Don Kent, a classics scholar from Georgetown who had once very nearly decided to become a priest. Don was tall, spare, meticulous, and exceedingly hardheaded. Prussian in his outlook on life, demanding of himself and others, he was fiercely loyal to John Busby and to the ship. Don had no tolerance for frivolity, which he thought was suspiciously likely in anybody who would become a flight surgeon. That is, except for John Busby; John was a flight surgeon, but Don revered him.

Finally our surgeon. Young general surgeons usually hated to go to sea on aircraft carriers. They usually were aggressive young men, as surgeons always are, and were invariably sent at a time in their careers when they were preparing to take their specialty board examinations. They were plucked away from their surgical practices in Navy hospitals to go to sea in what they considered a situation worse than purgatory. Rock Tosser was our surgeon on the *Forrestal*. A bright but determined young man, he often mentioned his fundamentalist born-again faith. Quoting Scripture often, he found moral imperatives in almost every task of the day. Rock didn't seem to like having been taken away from the hospital, where his skills could be used to save lives daily. He reluctantly recognized that he owed the Navy a lot of money for his medical school scholarship, though, and if this was the wasteful way the Navy wanted to be paid back, he would comply, although not enthusiastically. I thought that what bothered Rock was that the department didn't make the best doctor on the ship the one in charge, namely the surgeon. Rock seemed to think that Don Kent was educable but that the rest of us were probably not. That any serious physician would waste time becoming a flight surgeon when he could be fighting the constant battle against death and disease in the operating room was no doubt unthinkable. Likewise, that anybody as old as John Busby or me would intentionally still be in the Navy when he could be out doing better for medicine and doing something more serious in life probably proved that we were at least lazy, and probably also incompetent.

When John introduced me to the members of the medical department, the most welcoming and effusive was either Art Corbett, who could charm the warts off a cucumber, or Brice Bostik, who was as friendly and genuine as Tigger in the *Winnie-the-Pooh* books. He bounced everywhere, had an exciting idea almost every day, and genuinely wanted to be everybody's friend. Don Kent was courteous in every respect, but it was perfectly obvious that he didn't like me, was not going to like me, and was not intending to change for anybody who was not John Busby. Rock Tosser shook my hand, said "Hi," and had a noncommittal, almost friendly chuckle. Until proven otherwise, I was a possibly nice guy, even if a little dumb.

John made a little speech about what a pleasure it had been working with all of them throughout the cruise. He pointed out that we were soon going to be in Naples and that he would be catching a flight back to the States from there. He told the department to welcome me as they had welcomed him, and he talked about how proud he was to have worked with them and how far they had all come together. Then he said, "It has been a good tour for all of us. We have had no loss of life. That, at least, is something we can all be proud of." No loss of life. That got my attention. Everybody knew there was at least one death on every cruise. John had been on the ship for two years without a single death. I knew the law of averages wouldn't permit that to go on. What a time to arrive! Anybody who was a good doctor on the *Forrestal* would not let people die. John Busby had set a high standard.

Several days later we arrived in Naples, the first port call for the ship after 108 days under way. Naples has a large U.S. Navy installation, including a naval hospital. As SMO, I'd have to make plans to visit the hospital, coordinate any patient or specialty transfers, and pay a courtesy call on the hospital's CO. Because we needed to free John Busby for his return to the States, because I was new and had to learn a lot about the medical department, and because everyone else on board had 108 days without stepping on land, I determined to have only a couple of days off the ship during our eight days in port.

Aircraft carriers are too big to tie up at the pier in most harbors. So it was in Naples. Inside the harbor proper there was a big breakwater setting off a smaller inner harbor, called a "molo." Although we were able to get a lot closer than we could in most ports, we were still about a quarter mile away from the fleet landing, perhaps a hundred yards from the breakwater. Beside us on either side were such decrepit and rusted-out old tankers, with no signs of life and absolutely no habitation, that you had to wonder how many years they'd been there. Much about Naples was like that. Amidst the flurry of activity and the frenzied pace that Neapolitans set were signs of fallen grandeur; pride in the artistry and history of Italy, and yet very little evidence of trying to restore any of that. Bob Harris, the air operations officer, told me he had once seen a dead horse floating in Naples harbor.

A Busy Shift

I missed all the excitement of pulling into port the first time, being stuck down in the medical department. From the moment the sea and anchor detail was called away, I began treating people for the accidents of haste and anticipation: lacerations on the scalp from people who tried to jump through the oval knee-knocker doors on the O-3 deck, corneal abrasions from those hurrying their various grinding jobs, and a couple of sprained ankles from the ones who fell while hurrying down ladders on their way to the hangar deck to line up for liberty call.

Since the ship couldn't tie up at the pier, sailors had to either take utility boats or rent ferryboats to get to the fleet landing. The ship only needed about a thousand people on board to man it, so nearly four thousand people wanted off the ship within a few hours. Even with ferryboats that could take 200 to 250 at a time, it took two or three hours to get everyone off the ship. A large ladder was put off at the fantail to a floating, flat, raftlike platform called a "camel." The ferryboats would pull alongside the camel, and the sailor would step from the camel up to the ferryboat—sometimes with a small ramp, sometimes negotiating an eighteen-inch jump. If the water was choppy, there were opportunities for falling, spraining an ankle, or getting stuck between objects, both where the ladder from the fantail came to the camel and where the camel abutted the ferryboat. The last of these was the most hazardous because both the camel and the ferryboat would have reciprocal movements. By going opposite directions, they doubled the height of the waves. The camel went down eighteen inches and the ferryboat went up eighteen inches, all in a split second, like a man-sized mousetrap. That was the cause of an occasional laceration, so I had some suturing to do on shins and wrists as the evening wore on and people came and went.

Beginning at about 2200, the medical department became a real growth industry. I was the only physician on duty that night, with a handful of corpsmen, notably HM1 Jackie Brant and X-ray tech Arden Womple. After 108 days at sea without parties or alcohol, the temptation was just too big for a lot of the young sailors. First came a nineteen-year-old with a broken nose who was only slightly drunk, bragging, "I'll fix that son of a bitch, Doc," but as soon as he said that he vomited all over my shirt and fell asleep in my arms.

Within minutes, three sailors came down with their younger buddy, who looked to be about fifteen years old. A fireman on his first cruise, he was kept awake only by his constant retching. After he vomited two or three times, I couldn't imagine a person as small as he was having enough food left in him to do it again, but it just kept coming, an orange and purple volcano. While I was explaining to his buddies that there wasn't much we could do for his emesis, the 1-MC called "Medical emergency. Medical emergency. On the fantail. Medical emergency on the fantail."

I sent away my two emergency response corpsmen, who went with a litter and their Unit 1, the corpsman emergency medical bag. The seas were getting choppy, and a sailor had fallen off the ferryboat between the edge of the camel and the boat. Just before the edges of the two slapped together and crushed his head, the CPO in charge of the receiving line plucked him out, but he still had a big gash on his shin and had fractured his ankle from the impact. He'd swallowed a lot of water and was coughing and sputtering.

No sooner had they arrived than we received another call, "Medical emergency. Medical emergency. On the fantail. Medical emergency." This time, a lieutenant from one of the squadrons had made it up on the camel and, although drunk and somewhat staggering, had begun to walk toward the ladder up to the fantail. A sudden lurch on the camel threw him down on the ladder, which he straddled, tearing his pants and cutting himself in the groin. He could not walk, began to vomit, and was bleeding a lot from the crotch area, frightening the people who brought him up. When he got to the medical department we noticed a large gash in the bottom of his scrotum and asked if he could void. He was so drunk that for twenty minutes he couldn't understand us, but it was clear that his bladder was growing larger. Finally, he was able to give us a urine sample, the color of grape juice, clearly indicating bleeding somewhere along his urinary tract, probably in the urethra (the tube leading from the bladder through the penis). We were unable to pass a catheter through his penis, suggesting that the laceration obstructed the passage of fluid, so we took a type of X ray called a urethrogram. This is a specialized technique that would usually not be done in a country doctor's office, but we had devised a technique of placing the catheter next to the opening of the penis, injecting a small amount of a contrast material (called renograffin), and taking a photograph. The X ray clearly showed disruption in what should be a smooth, columnar flow of fluid along the shaft of the penis. The fluid had a ragged, zigzag pathway, although it did pass through between the bladder and the outer wall of the urethra. This would almost certainly need care by a specialist, a urologist. Fortunately we were in Naples, and in the morning when the seas were calm we would be able to bring the young lieutenant to the hospital.

Although he was gradually waking up, he was still pretty drunk, reaching the boisterous, laughing, uninhibited stage. When we explained his injury to him, he said, "Just my luck, no score in town, and then I broke my dick on the way back to the ship."

HM1 Rosen, who was making the record of the case, asked me, "What should I write down for his diagnosis, Captain, 'Broke dick'?" This became a cause célèbre in the medical department over the next hour while people seemed to repeat for the fun of it the diagnosis of "broke dick." None of us had ever seen that particular injury before, but two hours later the identical injury happened to a young sailor, so we had two "broke dicks" in the same night.

Around midnight, Jim Bowersman was brought in by three of his buddies. Bowersman was a forty-year-old petty officer who had made rank three or four times and been busted back to seaman each time after some fight or other misadventure. Tonight he was tearful and morose, clinging to his buddies, scarcely able to stand.

"You're gonna have to help him, Doc. He keeps sayin' he's gonna do himself in. He was trying to cut himself on the edges of a bottle." In fact, there were some scratch marks on his chest, his shirt was torn, and there were some ragged, very unartistic scratch marks on the underside of his forearm. "It's no sense. This is the only thing I can do. Leave me alone." He occasionally would make some feeble effort to push people away, then he would swear or just slump down like he was trying to fall asleep. My job was to try to console him and to assess whether he was really suicidal or just impulsively drunk. We had to go off to my office so he and I could have some privacy and try to work through this problem. His buddies started to wander off like they were either going to go back to their racks or maybe back to the beach.

"Oh, no you don't, you guys sit down right out here." We needed to keep a few buddies nearby in the event he would have to be escorted off to the hospital or if we were able to send him back to his rack. A buddy would need to stay with him throughout the night. Bowersman and I went into my office, where he slumped down in my chair, looking at his feet in a surly manner, at this point having nothing to say. I sat quietly nearby, trying to give him time to talk, maintaining eye contact, but not trying to prod him. In medical school we had been taught to just nod knowingly or to say something soothing, like "Tell me more" or "Go on," at these times.

Bowersman and I sat in that position—him nodding off or muttering something about how life had been unfair, me wishing the night would hurry up—for what seemed like a couple of hours, although I guess it was only about fifteen or twenty minutes. We were interrupted by a loud noise in the passageway, what sounded like a wrestling or boxing match. When I looked outside, there was a tall, skinny sailor fighting with the four people trying to bring him into the ER. Three of them were shore patrol in their white uniforms, all stained with blood. The fourth was probably his buddy, also matted with sweat or beer, and with some bloodstains on his shirt. The protagonist, being pretty agitated and obviously also loaded, had a large zigzag cut on the right side of his face, from his eyebrow down to his chin, and a smaller one stretching across the left side of his forehead down to the middle of his cheek. About this time, Don Kent came back from liberty. Don, of course, was absolutely sober and, as usual, pretty cross. Although he was planning to become a psychiatrist, he prided himself on suturing—especially on the face—and offered to take care of the sailor, whose name we found to be Jimmy Fulford. The skin on his face was filleted and hanging over to the right side, flapping every time he moved. When momentarily he would hold still, it was obvious that he had a third cut running under his chin, penetrating most of the way through the mouth.

Don found a couple of corpsmen, plus the two shore patrol to help hold Fulford down. He couldn't be given a sedative because he was so drunk, but he'd fall asleep intermittently.

I did the best I could, patiently sitting and talking with Bowersman, who was gradually sobering up and becoming a little bit embarrassed about what he had done. Obviously all of his wounds were very superficial, and once we had ensured that they were clean with peroxide and adequate scrubbing, at about 0330 or 0400, he assured me he was safe. I had made his buddies stay nearby, and although they had fallen asleep on the bench in the passageway, they were with him now to go back to his rack and watch over him to make sure there were no further shenanigans that night.

Almost two hours had gone by now, and I stuck my head into the suturing room where Don was still working on Fulford. Deep sutures had been required to put together the soft tissues of the cheek and to close the floor of the mouth and the chin, and Don was now putting the finishing touches with tiny little silk sutures on the last closure on the left side of the face. Fulford was asleep most of the time, but periodically he'd twist his head or twitch in such a way that Don would throw his arms up, being careful not to put too much tension on any of the sutures. The suturing job was truly a work of art, and Don was justifiably proud. The fellow had obviously taken quite a beating. Besides the cuts, he had been pummeled by a far superior force, and his face was pretty purple. Finally, when Don was finished, he admitted Fulford to the ward so he could be properly restrained, because Don was afraid that he would have further troubles if he went out.

"Captain, I'd like to put this guy on liberty risk, because I don't want him to go and pull the damn sutures out first thing tomorrow." Liberty risk was a program prohibiting individuals with behavior disorders or some other problem from leaving the ship. We found out subsequently that Fulford had been in a fight with some civilians in town, done some local damage to a civilian bar, and insulted several Neapolitans. Before he had his clock cleaned, charges had been pressed against him by the local police, the *carabinieri*. The XO agreed to keep him confined to the ship on Class-A liberty risk, so at least we knew he wouldn't get into any further trouble in Naples.

The next morning, Sunday, the only day I would be able to go into town, I received a call from the officer of the day at Naval Hospital (NH) Naples. The CO, Capt. Bullis Butts, would like to come and visit the ship. Could I arrange for a tour and a visit between the CO of the hospital and the CO of the ship? He would be able to arrive at about 1100.

This was my first time ever to visit Italy. On my only day off during this port call I'd hoped to take a trip to see Mount Vesuvius and Pompeii. Now this character was going to come at about 1100. I took some smug pleasure knowing that the both the CO and XO were going to be off the ship. I said good-bye to John Busby and waited around until 1100. Then 1200. Then 1300. Finally, at 1500, I heard him announced with the bell and the 1-MC, "Bong. Bong. Naval Hospital Naples, arriving." COs from other commands were always "bonged" aboard, just like our own captain or admiral. On the small boys (cruisers, destroyers, and frigates) all captains or above got "bonged" on, but on the carrier there were too many captains. Ship's company captains other than the CO only got bonged off at their last departure.

I went up to meet Butts at the quarterdeck, and there he came, trying to imitate George Washington crossing the Potomac. A somewhat portly guy with an ill-fitting uniform and only three ribbons, the skipper of the Navy hospital was standing awkwardly in the bow of the small boat. He was wearing his own version of the famous MacArthur cap. His naval cover was flopping down on the edges, something naval officers never allow. Maybe in the movies people take pride in a "salty" uniform, but when visiting other ships naval officers try to have everything as spiffy as they can. The gold braid on the visor of his cap was tarnished and worn, looking more dusty tan than gold. This was "salty" all right.

When he came aboard, he confessed that he had never been on an aircraft carrier before. He had been CO of NH Naples for almost two years, during which time a number of carriers had come into port, but he had never come to visit them. He had never gone to sea personally, either.

I tried to show him all around the ship, from the fo'c'sle to the medical department to the flight deck, and offered him lunch in the wardroom. With studied nonchalance, he nodded knowingly about everything I had to tell him about the ship, as though he had seen it all many times before. But I thought that if I had called the fantail a goldfish or the fo'c'sle a fladderap, he probably wouldn't have known the difference. Finally, the boredom overtook both of us and it was time for him to leave. I noticed dusk was coming, guaranteeing that I would not have to worry about a day of liberty during my first and only time in Naples. I was happy to show him off the ship, not realizing that my most unpleasant encounters with Capt. Bullis Butts were yet to come.

That evening the seas were a little calmer and nobody fell down ladders or off the camel, although we had a few torn or bitten ears to sew up. The next day was busier, though. On that day, the ship's morale, welfare, and recreation (MWR) department put on a big picnic at Carney Park. It's a park utilized by armed forces of all the NATO countries in the Naples area, resident in a volcanic crater just outside town. Although a number of sailors drank too much beer, athletics were the main order of the day. These were not only people who hadn't been on dates or done any drinking for 108 days; they had also not engaged in any sports, except for calisthenics and running on the flight or hangar decks. No softball, no running or sliding in the dirt, and no soccer. It looked to me like they were trying to catch up all 108 days (on out-of-shape limbs) in one day. Four people had ankle or lower leg fractures, three had fractures of the wrist or forearm, and a number had black eyes or broken teeth, just from the sports.

Fractures of the lower extremity required casts, of course, and casts hampered mobility, so anyone with a fracture or cast on a lower extremity could not be permitted to go to sea. All of those people, even if treated on the ship, had to be sent off to NH Naples, later to be transferred back to the States, and had to be replaced in the ship's company. We referred to this day from then onward as the "Carney Park Massacre." Seven people had to be shipped off the FID that day, one of whom was in continual traction at the hospital. Finally, not having any liberty that day and having been awake most of the two previous nights taking care of drunks or people with facial lacerations, I crawled into my stateroom near midnight.

I was awakened the next morning with banging on my door. "Sorry, Captain, we have an emergency up in the flag spaces." It was Burt Rosen. "There's a guy passed out up in his cabin, Captain. It may be that guy with diabetes Captain Busby told you about."

I dressed as quickly as I could and followed Petty Officer Rosen up the four decks to the O-3 level, where three senior officers were huddled around a figure slumped over the edge of his bed. On the desk in the room were two bottles of insulin—one of them empty, the other half-empty and cloudy—and three insulin syringes. The patient, Cdr. Oliver Leen, was about forty and a very frail-looking individual. His pulse was 115 beats per minute, and he felt feverish. He was very sweaty, and he had the kind of fruity aroma suggestive of ketosis. The insulin was of two types—NPH U-100, labeled on the half-filled bottle, and another with the label mostly off.

"We haven't seen him for about three days, Doc. We thought he was out on liberty. Somebody was just looking for him today and found out he was in here."

"Commander, how long have you been sick?" I asked.

He was groggy, but he was clearly conscious and could understand the question.

"Been sick for about a week. I thought I was doin' okay until about three days ago. I'll be all right. Just let me rest, and leave me alone for a little while."

"Commander, I'm not going to try to hassle you, but your fever is hot as hell. Something is wrong. When you get an infection, you know, your insulin requirements change. I can tell by your pulse rate, and by the smell of your breath, that your diabetes is out of control. Do you know what ketosis is?"

"Yes, I know, I've had it before, but this isn't it."

"Look, Commander, you're sick, at least we all can agree on that. At least let us take you down to medical, check your blood sugar, and get you back into balance. You've got a high fever, so we have to make sure you don't have pneumonia or something a lot worse. Blood infections can happen to guys with diabetes, too, you know."

"It's probably a bladder infection. I get those sometimes."

Great! The guy knows that he's prone to bladder infections, he's had ketosis before, and yet he hides away with his insulin here on the ship. That's just great. This is the worst kind of nightmare we could imagine. For God's sake, the guy could have died if somebody hadn't just stumbled into the room.

He refused to be carried down to medical, walking mostly under his own power, although with support by his buddies, other senior officers on the flag staff. It turned out his blood sugar was 560 and he had ketones (breakdown products of fat) in his urine and blood. On what we call a "sliding scale" of insulin, we were able to get his blood sugar back in balance within fifteen hours, but, as usual, his level of alertness and concentration lagged behind the body chemistries by about a day. He had pyelonephritis, evidenced by tenderness over his kidneys and his back and abnormal urinalysis tests, as well as slightly elevated BUN and creatinine.

I told him he would need to be transferred to the Navy hospital, and that he really would have to be transferred off the ship.

"No, I don't think the admiral would agree to that."

"Don't worry, Commander, I'll go talk to the admiral about it."

I went ahead and arranged to transfer him to the hospital, which was, of course, the right thing to do, even though we were able take care of his ketosis on the ship and start him on proper antibiotics. The causes of pyelonephritis need to be found, though. Although diabetes predisposes, if there were some structural abnormality in the kidney or some other illness—for example, a foreign body or stone in the kidney—we sure needed to find it. Admiral Kohl recognized, of course, that medical necessity was the overriding concern, and he agreed immediately with transferring Commander Leen to the hospital. He said we could deal with the situation after Leen recovered.

I was at least relieved by the outcome of this. Diabetes is a controllable, although still dangerous, disease. The worst nightmare, though, was the possibility that somebody would try to manage it himself and not tell you about his condition. Worst of all, that somebody would confine himself to his own stateroom, quietly wasting away, either not taking his insulin at all or taking too much of it, and dying simply because he wouldn't communicate with the doctors. This was one paradox a Navy doctor feared more than any other. A patient who was more concerned about the bureaucratic ramifications of treatment for his illness than he was about the complications of the disease itself. A guy who would think like that might not only be responsible for his own demise but could bring the doctor down with him. It's not the way a doctor is supposed to think, but this was an entirely preventable disease, or possibly a preventable death. Besides worrying about the patient, a doctor couldn't help being a little angry, too.

We got under way uneventfully the next day. Under the careful view of Don Kent's daily evaluation, Jimmy Fulford's cuts were healing up well, and all the sailors on the ship were still joking about the two "broke dicks."

The Flight Deck and Other Decks

On the first day out of Naples, the ship was headed west toward Spain and I was about to get my first flight off the ship, this time on an H-3 helicopter, the aircraft flown by HS-15, the "Red Lions." Before the flight, I trundled up with all my flight gear and survival vest, up through the passageway in the forward port side of the ship just above the fo'c'sle, to HS-15's ready room. The passageway leading into their ready room was along the port side catapult, which is run by steam. The passageway was as hot as a sauna, and by the time I arrived at the ready room, which was well air-conditioned, my flight suit was soaked through.

Before every flight in a naval aircraft, there is a detailed brief for all flight crew members. Although as the flight surgeon I usually had very little to contribute, I was, after all, part of the flight crew, so I had to sit through the brief. In the brief, the mission and the weather conditions are reviewed, as are communications procedures—the use of all the various radio frequencies, how the call signs will be used, with whom the crew will speak, and how they will talk to the ship and to other aircraft. Emergency procedures—including how to egress underwater—are reviewed in the same picky detail for experienced flyers as for those on their first flight. Then the mission of the flight is discussed in some detail, along with how the exercises or training will be done.

The H-3's main mission is antisubmarine, although it has about five other auxiliary missions, including rescue. It has a large sonar dipper that is suspended or "dipped" from the belly of the aircraft into various depths under the ocean surface to emit sonar detection for submarines. In addition, sonobuoys can be propelled from the aircraft to float at pre-set depths in the ocean, trailing an antenna that floats to the surface. The sonobuoys send out and receive sonar images and then transmit the reception back to a receiving station on the helicopter. In this manner, one helicopter can have a number of sounding stations and can pinpoint a submarine. If two or three helicopters are functioning at once, they can look for submarines at some distance from the ship. Also, whenever fixed-wing aircraft—the jets—are taking off or landing from the aircraft carrier, there is a helicopter in the air at all times so that, in the event of an aircraft mishap, they can rescue any survivors.

Finally, after the long brief, my flight suit was partially dried and we began walking up to the flight deck. Once we got to the aircraft, I took my seat in the back of the helicopter because both the pilot and the copilot were necessary for controlling the aircraft on a takeoff. There is a wait before you can get clearance to take off, just like at an airport. Because the helos need to be in the air throughout all other flight operations, they are the first to take off and the last to land. I plugged into the ICS and listened as the pilot was speaking to the tower. They talked about this clearance and that clearance, the weight of the aircraft, the wind across the deck, and the amount of fuel in the aircraft. Then I heard something about "man overboard," then something about aborting the flight, and at first I thought there was going to be a man-over-board drill conducted below. As the talk went on, I realized it wasn't a drill. Oh no, man overboard! If they were to find him, of course, there would be first aid to be done, or a corpse to be taken care of.

I broke into the ICS, "Commander, this is the Doc here in the back. Is that a real man overboard?"

"Roger, Doc. Seems like a guy was either blown off the fantail or the starboard side."

"I'm gonna have to get off, Commander. Can I?"

No answer for a while. It looked like the pilot and copilot were speaking to each other, then they came up on the radio to the tower, "Boss, 602. The Doc says he has to go down to medical in case they pick up the man overboard."

I hurried off the helo and ran down to medical as fast as I could. About the time I got to the catwalk, another helicopter was just landing on the deck. It appeared that they picked up the man overboard about the time he hit the water. I got down to medical about the same time the victim did.

It turns out that Stan Mitchell, a nineteen-year-old plane captain from Plainsfield, Pennsylvania, had inadvertently stepped behind an A-7 and was blown off the fantail on the starboard side of the ship. It's a nine-story drop to the water. From that height, the mere impact with the water can cause injuries. All of the people on the flight deck go through a drill where they practice curling themselves up into a ball so they impact on their feet and buttocks when they hit the water. Airman (AN) Mitchell did everything perfectly. He calmly pulled the beads on his survival jacket and inflated his vest. He put out his dye marker immediately, was picked up within two minutes, and was back on the deck of the ship within seven minutes. His only complaint was soreness in his left wrist. When you hit the water from nine floors up it may break a wrist or an ankle, just the same as hitting the ground.

Down in medical, I examined him and found that all his parts were moving, his eyes were clear, his lungs were clear. He had full movement of his wrists, even the left one. We took an X ray, and it was clear.

I called the captain, who was relieved to learn there was no injury. He put out the notice on the 1-MC that the man overboard had been retrieved and was not injured. You could hear clapping and shouting throughout the ship. This was pretty satisfying to everybody, knowing that if somebody really was blown off the *Forrestal* we would recognize it and find him within seven minutes.

There was as mixed blessing in all this, in addition to the fact that I hadn't been able to take my flight. On the one hand, Rock Tosser had not been involved in the care of the patient, but on the other hand, it wasn't like Rock to stay out of the case. I began to ask around to find out where he was.

"I think he may be in the OR, Captain." I went up to the ER and to the door leading to the operating room. It was locked. "Where's Brant?"

"I think he's in there with Dr. Tosser," said HM1 Dunbar, clearly hoping he wouldn't have to get into the fray. "They have a guy with appendicitis."

You can't do an operation on the aircraft carrier without the permission of the captain. It's one thing if you're taking casualties and everyone knows that people are injured and dying. Under those circumstances you do what you need to, to save life and limb. An appendectomy may be an emergency, but it never has to happen within five or ten minutes. I have to approve all operations, and I have to get them cleared with the captain. However routine an operation like an appendectomy might be, induction of anesthesia and violating the human skin could always lead to an unexpected tragedy or complication. It was a hard-and-fast rule that the SMO had the prerogative to be involved in any decision to do an operation and had to clear it with the captain. I was irritated, but I figured this was also a chance for me to exert that leadership and persuasion I had been working on, so I thought I would try to rise above my anger. It wouldn't be easy.

I went back to my stateroom, got out of my flight suit, and showered so I'd be cool and calm when I had to talk to Rock about doing an operation without conferring with me. Knowing I had in fact been in an aircraft at the time made me feel a little bit cautious or defensive, I suppose.

About fifteen minutes later Rock came out of the OR. The individual did fine. I asked to see the appendix, which was not at all inflamed. Rock said you couldn't tell by just looking, and that it needed to come out.

"From now on, can you let me see the patient first?"

He said if I was where he could reach me that would be fine, but he had to do what he thought was right. There was only one surgeon on the ship, he said. Just then we were interrupted by the 1-MC.

"Medical emergency. Medical emergency. Seven-tack-seventy five-tack-six. Medical emergency. Seventh deck." Petty Officer Ramirez was our emergency response corpsman that day, and he came running into the medical department about the same time as the 1-MC announcement, "Man down on the seventh deck. Ryan Hart is giving him CPR right now!"

Tosser and I ran immediately to the scene, on the port side, through a watertight door in the passageway. We looked straight down to about the sixth deck, where we climbed immediately, diverting slightly to the left and then down one more ladder. Meantime, some of the other corpsmen were bringing the life paks and other emergency response bags.

Ryan Hart was giving CPR to a tall, skinny fellow in the corner, and two sailors were standing by in another corner.

I got up to where Hart was and looked down at the face stitched up like a baseball. It was Jimmy Fulford.

"What happened?!" Hart kept doing CPR.

No answer.

"What happened!"

One of his buddies said, "He just started shaking all over, like a convulsion, and then he fell down. He kept shaking on the ground, and then he just quit breathing."

At about this time, Ramirez arrived on the scene, too—breathless, just like the rest of us. He was carrying the emergency response bags and all of the contents for CPR and advanced cardiac life support. "He wasn't breathing when I got here. I was never able to feel a pulse."

On the deck near Fulford's feet were two empty cans of solvent spray.

About this time Bill Kelly arrived on the scene and picked up the cans, trying to determine their contents. He looked suspiciously at the other sailors standing in the corner.

CPR was continuing. "No pulse. No respirations." Hart was relieved by another corpsman.

By now I had the paddles set up for the defibrillator. This kind of life pak enables you to read a cardiac trace on a monitor from the paddles before you give a jolt.

"Here, let me take a reading," I said. Flat line.

"Everybody stand back." Two hundred joules. His body jerked. CPR continued. No pulse.

"Everybody stand back." Three hundred joules. His body jerked up again. Still no response in the ECG. No pulse.

"Everybody stand back." One more jolt. Again the body jerked quickly, but no pulse.

Rock was at his head. "OK. Intubate." Rock slipped the endotracheal tube in deftly. He put an ambu bag over the end of the endotracheal tube and began ventilating while I listened to Fulford's chest with a stethoscope. Full breath sounds bilaterally. "Good breath sounds, continue ventilating him." CPR continued on his chest. Bill Kelly was putting in an intravenous line in the antecubital fossa.

The code was proceeding just as smoothly as it would in any major hospital in the States. Still there was no pulse. We gave epinephrine intravenously, then we gave lidocaine, repeated lidocaine and epinephrine. We gave more shocks. Still no pulse.

It turned out Fulford and his buddies had been sniffing fluorocarbons from those solvent cans. Apparently, they had been using fluorocarbons down in this space throughout the cruise periodically. They would have a very good high from it, very much like sniffing glue. No chiefs or officers had known about it, but furtive glances among some of the sailors suggested it may have been more than a three-man secret.

While the code continued, Bill got out one of our toxicology books and read the complications of fluorocarbon inhalation. Ventricular fibrillation and cardiac arrest, or asystole, were known complications and were resistant to CPR, apparently. We continued with the code for about forty-five minutes, following everything just as it was in the book. Finally, Rock suggested, "We've done everything we're supposed to do. The only other possibility is cardiac tamponade. I know it seems unlikely, but we're not getting anyplace otherwise." I agreed. Rock used a cardiac needle to try to see if there was blood in the pericardial sac. There wasn't. Finally, after we had been going almost an hour, I had to call the code off.

"That's it. He's dead." So that was it. A twenty-year-old, slightly rebellious, but vigorous young man was dead. John Busby had said "No loss of life" in over two years while he was the SMO. I'd been the SMO for less than two weeks, and already one of our boys was dead.

The corpsmen stayed behind to clean up the mess. Someone called for a body bag. I climbed up the top of the ladder to the second deck, and there was Captain Guitar. I realized when I got there that my cheeks were wet, and I said, "We did everything we could, Captain." I think he patted my shoulder and said only, "I know you did, Doc, I know you did." As bad as we all felt about it, clearly the captain felt it at least that much. He walked back with me on his way to the bridge so he could send the message to Jimmy Fulford's parents.

After we finished up all the paperwork and I prepared the medical details for Captain Guitar to send off the ship, I walked back to be alone on the fantail. It had been a busy couple of weeks. I looked off at the wake in the night and remembered what Monty Aumin had told me. There were only fourteen people in the world who had my job.

Chapter 3

Benidorm

◼✚ It's important to deal with death. In a closed community like an
aircraft carrier, words, emotions, and attitudes all spread faster
than in any small town . . . which after all is what a ship is, anyway.
Death is just as hard for the medical folks as it is for anybody else, and
in a way worse. A lot of guilt goes along with losing a patient. This is a
painful and difficult thing for health care workers of any age to learn,
but as Busby had pointed out, this was something the *Forrestal* hadn't
seen for at least two years. It was the first encounter with death for
most of our thirty corpsmen, whose average age was less than twenty.

Once we had taken care of the scene and delivered the body to the
cooler, I made all members of the medical department who were not
asleep come to a meeting in Ward II. Only about a dozen people had
been directly involved in the resuscitation effort, but really everybody
was involved one way or another whenever somebody died. In a
department as small and tight as ours, a death is felt just as keenly as
it would be among a family. About thirty of us were there that night.
Even corpsmen who had been asleep when the code began came.
Some of them had been awakened when the medical emergency had
been announced on the 1-MC; others weren't awakened until somebody shook them to say a guy just died.

The buddies of the twelve or so who had been involved in the code
were particularly attentive now. They might have their arm around
the guy's shoulder, bring him a cup of coffee, or offer him their seat
or a place to sit on the rack. Except for these signs of deference,
though, facial expressions didn't indicate which members had been
involved in the code. There were a few wet cheeks in the crowd, but
everybody in the room was pretty sober.

"I wanted all you guys to come here right now so we could spend

42

a little time together working this out and for me to tell you a few things." I had been involved in dozens of codes over the last fifteen years, some at Bethesda, some at other hospitals. This was my first one on a ship. I had never seen it done more professionally, better, faster, or with more deliberate excellence than that night on the FID. The teamwork and love shown by those guys was as powerful a demonstration as I had ever seen in any hospital. Rick Cox was there, and although he was as shattered as the rest of us about the loss of a young man's life, I thought he was tearful, frankly, because he was so proud of what his boys had just done.

At this time we were steaming west in the Mediterranean, conducting air operations daily and exercising with members of the Southern NATO Fleet. Flights ops began shortly after dawn, of course. The morning routine started as usual. Just like every other morning, people were busily walking up and down the fore and aft passageways on the second deck, airplanes were moving in the hangar deck, hundreds of people were eating in the mess decks, and occasional joggers were running back and forth between airplanes in the hangar. Early that morning, the captain came on the 1-MC. "This is the captain speaking. We are 300 miles west of Sicily, steaming west, and we've just finished our morning cycle. We'll be heading on down to our next port call in Benidorm in a few days. The weather there is good. It's a beautiful Spanish coastal city.

"I want to talk to you guys about the tragedy that happened last night. A young sailor died on the *Forrestal* after inhaling fumes from an aerosol can. Most of all, I want to point out to you that his shipmates contributed to this. Two other guys were down there sniffing that stuff, too. Guys, this is not the way we stick together. A lot of you know that sailor. His name was Jimmy Fulford, and he worked in E Division. Tomorrow morning we're going to have a special service for him on the fo'c'sle. You're all invited."

The captain came on the 1-MC every day—usually in the afternoon—to give the guys news about what was happening, how well we'd done with prior exercises, children being born at home, and special events making the news. Captain Guitar was known to have a temper and to be a hard driver. The sailors loved him, though. He had a down-to-earth quality. He was said to have had a pretty wild adolescence, which was another thing the sailors generally liked about him. They liked being told what the ship was doing and why, but most of all they liked it that they mattered to the captain, that he knew how much it mattered to them to be informed. Every sailor on the ship knew about Fulford's death well before the captain's announcement. They didn't need the announcement to tell them what had happened; they just needed to hear the captain's voice, the way we all sometimes need a parent's presence.

The rest of the day, all the activities went on as scheduled. The crowds bustled up and down the passageways, we started sick call at the normal time. People went to the mess decks as usual, and all the ship's business and all the flight ops continued. It was different, though. Instead of the general buzzing level, people were a little quieter. There was less joking, people walked a little slower, not everybody spoke to everybody else.

There was plenty to do, so nobody on the ship really had time to sit around and stew about it, although it was on all of our minds as the day went on. Sick call started every morning at 0730. On a few ships it was held twice a day for the convenience of the crew, and even occasionally three times a day for people who worked at night. On the *Forrestal* we only had one sick call, with the understanding that anytime a person was sick he could come to the ER to be seen.

Sick call was basically the walk-in clinic. Ward II was used for sick call, muster meetings, special functions like immunizations, and sometimes for the guys to hang around after hours. I tried to curtail the hanging around, however. We wanted medical spaces used only for medical stuff, and nothing else, whether by us or others (like the XO). It was set up, like Ward I, with bays of the racks parallel, two or three in a stack. They could be folded and clamped back against the bulkhead so that a bay then could be made into a six-by-eight cubicle. Inside these little cubicles, we could pull the curtains closed (the curtains were used for privacy if you had patients) to make each cubicle into a small office/examining room, and this is where we did our clinic work during sick call.

These beds were like many other things that could be folded up and clamped in an upright position on a ship. They had to be clamped very carefully because they weighed a couple of hundred pounds apiece and could put an ugly gash in an arm, shoulder, or head if they came crashing down under rough seas or unexpected movement. Even so, these were the lightest of any of the things you could find bolted down on a ship. I'll talk about the hatches and scuttles later, but they were heavy, and if you ever looked at them and thought about how it would feel to have your finger crushed by one of those, it could keep you fretting for twenty or thirty minutes. I was always worried about how somebody might be injured by a door or hatch.*

Back out on the starboard passageway, on the inboard side of the passage, was the X-ray suite. As in any small hospital, this suite had a table that could tilt up and down and an X-ray machine that could take pictures while a person was standing up or could take a whole series of films while a person was lying down. Behind the patient room was the X-ray tech's working lab, a perfectly black little room with a small red bulb as needed and an automatic film processor. In the old days, ships didn't have automatic X-ray processors, and the corpsmen, if they ever took an X ray, would simply move it from one basin to another by hand, perhaps holding it with paper clips. We can process a film and have it out and dry nowadays in about one minute—probably faster than a Polaroid, but with a conventional X-ray picture.

There was more we had to worry about in our X-ray suite. SK3 Arden Womple was the moody technician who ran our X-ray department. He could take the finest X rays, with the angles just the way you'd need them, with such great efficiency and concern for your patients that you'd be impressed from day to day with his clinical function. As with every other person on the ship, though, the X-ray tech had to do more than just the apparent primary job. Arden also had to file all the X rays perfectly. He had to make sure that the requesting doctor put a summary report on paper so that it could be filed with the film as a record of the doctor's diagnostic impression of the X rays. The Navy had had a policy for the past few years that all X rays had to be read by a radiologist, too. Although doctors—especially those sent to isolated duty (as on a ship), where our ability to read films may be critical immediately—are well trained in reading X rays, there are specialists in radiology for very good reasons, and all of our X rays had to be read over by a radiologist as soon as the ship would return to port or arrive at a port where there was a qualified Navy radiologist. Womple was one of the guys who were supposed to see that all these films were kept in sequence and properly carried to the radiologist and that the reports were brought back to the ship.

Womple also was supposed to take care of the radiation badges. All X-ray techs and radiologists wear a little badge with a film that's a little bit like X-ray film, detecting whenever and how much they are exposed

---

*Hatches are the ones that open and close on decks, that is, the horizontal ones. The things that open in bulkheads, that is, the vertical ones, are just called doors. Even if they weigh several hundred pounds, are oval shaped, and have wheels for dogging them down to be watertight, if they are vertical, they're not properly called hatches, they're doors.

to radiation over time. It's an example of the myriad safety and health surveillance programs that the ship had. This one we customarily think of as primarily a medical issue.

There were other people on the ship who had to wear radiation badges, too; they were mostly in the weapons department. The Navy's policy was, and remains, to neither confirm nor deny the presence of nuclear weapons on any given ship. About two years after I left the FID, the United States decided to cease carrying nuclear weapons on any of its carriers. In my time on the ship, though, the Navy could neither confirm nor deny that there were any nuclear weapons on board, so we who lived there could neither "know nor not know" either. All we knew was that some people in the weapons department, who worked in an area in the ship heavily guarded by the Marine detachment, wore these radiation badges, and Arden Womple was responsible for them. You can understand that the Navy would want people in all weapons departments to wear the badges, whether needed or not. Otherwise, bad guys would be able to tell that ships where sailors did wear badges must have certain material, and ships where guys didn't wear badges didn't have that category of material. Womple was supposed to take readings on those badges periodically, save the badges, keep excellent records of them, and pass them on at the end of the cruise to the proper regulatory agency. Well, we were to find out later that Arden didn't pay attention to certain details, and this was one of them.

The next morning, we had the memorial service for Jimmy Fulford. The chief engineer (CHENG) and Jimmy's division officer (DivO) spoke about him. It seems he was something of a hellion. A number of people liked him, especially for his enthusiasm and sense of adventure. After the CHENG and DivO had spoken, the chaplain, Cdr. John Gunther, spoke. The fo'c'sle was packed. A few people sat on chairs we'd set up in the middle, but most of us packed in around the sides and around the capstans.

Gunther was in his mid-thirties, a well-scrubbed guy with good posture and wide-open sincerity. There was a captivating cleanness about John, a Midwestern intensity in his round, welcoming face that told me he had always known he would be a chaplain, somebody who could be both a minister and a scout leader full-time and all the time. He spoke some reassuring words and read a section from Scripture, but then his tone changed and he stopped being wistful and soft. The chaplain lashed out about shipmates not looking out for each other. He began to speak about how other shipmates had let the young man down by joining in the behavior, sniffing the fumes, how they had led him into trouble in port so that he had too much to drink, how they had failed to help him cope with the stresses of life at sea. Gunther's voice began to rise, he got angry, and he spoke about the "damnable" attitude that permitted one shipmate to let another shipmate get into trouble.

After John's talk, we sang the Navy hymn "Eternal Father." It's emotional anyway, but with several hundred people singing this special hymn about a lost shipmate, voices cracked and a lot of us were choking on tears. We filed out slowly. The ship did have a chapel, a very nice one, with a little altar in the front, nice paneling and wallpaper. The chapel, though, would be crowded with even thirty or so people. It was really not large enough for ordinary Sunday religious services or for a service like the one we just had. It was somehow more fitting, more proper, to have the funeral in the fo'c'sle anyway.

People went back to work that day pretty much choked up, but better off for the ceremony. We needed to speak to each other about the episode, air our emotions. Saying good-bye is not completely satisfied by a couple of hours of standing around talking, but it helps. It provides an open forum for dealing with the emotions. Certainly, one of our emotions was our collective outrage about how Jimmy had died, along with our regret of having lost a shipmate. Kind of unstated was the underlying, contagious sense of our vulnerability that was triggered by his death. Dealing with the situation in a funeral, ferreting out the causes—these help with the coping.

Preparations now had to go on for the second port call of the cruise. Naples is a dusty, grimy, busy place. In Naples there had been a lot of work to do. Some painting had to be done on the sides of the ship, stores had to be replenished, we had to meet with a bunch of folks. Benidorm was going to be different. Benidorm had been a sleepy little fishing village on the southern point of Spain up until about thirty years ago, when the emerging financial recovery and the rolling back of Franco repression permitted the evolution of a real bustling and forward-looking tourist economy. We were on our way up to an exercise called "Northern Wedding" around the Arctic Circle. That would be a little unusual for a six-month cruise. Usually a ship would be stationed in the Mediterranean or the Indian Ocean, occasionally both. To spend a few months in the north Arabian Sea and, on the same cruise, have a substantial commitment up in the Arctic Circle was a little wider than the usual cruise. It had also been unusual to spend 108 consecutive days under way without a port call. With sixteen-hour days and seven-day weeks, port calls usually came every forty or fifty days. Each day beyond that adds geometrically to the potential strain, and to accidents. This was an unusual ship and an unusual crew, who seemed to thrive on an operational pace that would wear others down. Even so, Captain Guitar wanted to give them a few days' reward, especially with the looming prospect of several more tough weeks of heavy operating up in the Arctic Circle.

Before coming into any port, all of the department heads and certain other key players have a conference up in the CV intelligence center (CVIC) to make sure that the procedures are all properly planned. Because of the kind of intel activities that go on in the CVIC, the fancy computers, the classified information, and so forth, there's a cipher lock on the door leading into the area, a security manager seated right inside the door, and then another locked grate door just beyond that. The security manager identifies the individual coming in, verifies all the proper security clearances, and then pushes a button to enable you to pass the grate door to get inside. Everybody was assembled inside, and then Captain Guitar entered. At this meeting in CVIC, all the nitty-gritty details about tides, how we would make the approach to the harbor, and procedures for dropping the hook would be discussed.

The person presiding at the conference was the 'gator, short for navigator. That was Bill Weber, a very tall, broad-shouldered guy, an A-7 attack pilot. He preferred to be called by his call sign, "Bohunk." Some aviators preferred to use their call signs all the time, others did not. For example, Captain Guitar's call sign was "Cajun," of which he was duly proud, but people always called him "Captain," at least in his presence.*

Bohunk showed us the route leading into the harbor at Benidorm, then the "weather guesser" told about weather and tides, and the assistant navigator discussed protocol observations, which American consulate we would visit, what colors we would fly, and so forth. The conference was long but bearable, and we all got very excited about the coming port call.

The next morning Benidorm was in view early. The approach to a harbor is an interesting and precise exercise. It takes a number of hours to slow down and stop a 75,000-ton floating vessel, which has

---

*You don't get to pick your own call sign. That is done for you by your shipmates in the rites of passage early in your aviation career. Ethnic identifiers like "Cajun" and "Bohunk" were unusual. Usually the call sign came from a personal flaw or a humiliating experience. One fighter pilot was named "Eagle," the kind of name you might expect a fighter jock to like, but I discovered he got that name because he wore a toupee, and he was called an eagle because of a physical trait other than eyesight.

to stay above five knots or so in order to simply maintain steerage (that is, the ability to guide and direct the ship by rudders). Then the quartermasters and 'gators have to decide how far they are from the point where they're going to drop the hook and time everything precisely. I decided I'd have plenty of opportunities to watch the precise approach from the bridge in the future, so I went down to the fo'c'sle instead. Coming into Benidorm, I wanted to see all of the excitement that accompanied dropping the hook.

The fo'c'sle is kind of a hangout for the deck department. The forecastle was a little box or castle in the front of old sailing ships from the Middle Ages. It was called the forecastle because it was the castle in the front part of the ship, from which galleons could fight others or keep lookouts and in which cannons could be kept. On surface ships, the fo'c'sle is a weather deck, that is, it's exposed to the sky and the weather. When aircraft carriers were first made, a flight deck was simply put on a trellis up above the main deck, and the fo'c'sle was still out in the open air with the forward part of the flight deck simply on top of it. Beginning with carriers in the 1930s and in World War II, the fo'c'sle tended to be enclosed, as it was on the *Forrestal*.

The fo'c'sle more or less belonged to the boatswain's mates, the rates in the deck department. They used it for their meeting place. They took pride in the cleanliness and the clean paint. A fo'c'sle is a place of chains, paint lockers, and grease. Like a big garage, a fo'c'sle tries organically to become grimy, littered, and dirty if allowed to. All of that boatswain mate stuff is in there—chains, ropes, capstans. Up in the very pointy end of the fo'c'sle was the ship's gym, the Nautilus equipment, rowing machines, stationary bicycles, and stair climbers. The fo'c'sle was also used as the main auditorium on the ship. You couldn't use the hangar bay because it was so full of airplanes all the time. We used the fo'c'sle for church services, assembly meetings, formal occasions, captain's mast—any event that needed a large space. Because the fo'c'sle could not permit other machinery or other "work stuff," it was always available as an open place.

Dominating the fo'c'sle were the anchor chains, of course. The chain lockers—the containers in which the chain was curled up when the anchor was stowed—were huge, cylindrical wells about 120 feet behind the pointy end of the ship. The chains stretched from those wells forward, coming at an angle toward the front where you could look down a hole and see the anchor clinging to the side of the ship. The anchors weighed many tons and were about one and one-half stories tall. About twenty or thirty links of the chain were exposed lying along the deck, each about four feet long and twelve inches thick. Each link weighed about three hundred pounds.

Gradually, as the ship slowed and slowed, the fo'c'sle became busier. Everybody was required to stand at certain positions way toward the back of the fo'c'sle. At one point the ship obviously was no longer moving, and the first lieutenant was standing there with his brick. He heard something on the brick and turned to the first class boatswain's mate standing by with a sledgehammer, who then smacked some metal thing back out of the way of the capstan, and all of a sudden you couldn't see the chain links anymore. The chain seemed to jump up and down and vibrate. All of the dust in the whole world obscured our view, and I felt like I was standing in a dust storm. Even wearing the Mickey Mouse ears hearing protectors, as well as internal earplugs, it was the most deafening, stupefying thunder I'd ever heard when those chains bounced along, kicking up dust and letting out anchor.

The chain itself gets heavier than the anchor once you let some of it out. The old legend goes that the anchor only holds the chain, and the chain holds the ship. The anchor hits the soft bottom and folds out so that two sharp prongs more or less dig into the bottom, but it's not those sharp prongs that hold the ship. They simply hold the first couple of links until the pile of anchor chain grows. My ears rang for probably over an hour, during which I couldn't hear ordinary conversation. Shortly after I could hear again, I heard on the 1-MC, "Shift colors." When the ship is at anchor or in port, the national ensign is shifted from its position up on the island and near the stack back to the fantail. You only keep the flag back there when the ship is stopped.

I guess it stays sunny and beautiful in Benidorm all the time. Certainly it was the whole time we were there. The first day there I was busy and couldn't leave the ship until late in the day, when I made a trip to the local hospital. I came armed with an bunch of *Forrestal* ball caps. There was no fund for paying for caps to give out, so I had to pay for them, but it was well worth the price of four or five ball caps to make friends with medical colleagues in another country and advertise for the ship. Someday, some Americans might see those docs wearing a *Forrestal* ball cap. Benidorm was the first Spanish hospital I ever saw, and it was to set the tone for an impression that kept getting reinforced. The Spanish hospitals were not merely professional and cleaner than most American hospitals. The people and the staff seemed familiar. In my first encounter with Spanish people I was impressed by how much their styles, mannerisms, and demeanor seemed more American to me than European. That wasn't a value judgment. At the hospital I met the head doctor, invited him to come for a tour of the *Forrestal,* and arranged for emergency care of any FID sailors if needed in town while we were there.

I wasn't able to go to the admin that night. An admin is a rendezvous, a lodging point, a base in a liberty port. The concept of the admin started as a squadron idea years ago. Whenever a ship would go to a liberty port, a few guys from a squadron would go out and rent a hotel room so officers wouldn't have to come back to the ship at night. This, of course, was done in the event that the seas were rough and boating couldn't be permitted, or if there was a late party. There was no question that a naval officer would be unable to return to ship for any reason of incapacity.

Aviators are frequently a little more flamboyant, a little more imaginative than the surface Navy (who are known as "blackshoes," or just "shoes," because surface guys wear black shoes with their khakis rather than brown, like aviators). Over the years, however, even the blackshoes on the aircraft carrier began to see the merit in having an admin. It takes at least twenty minutes to take a boat from the ship to the shore. For an officer who doesn't have duty, just spending a night off the ship can be a welcome diversion. So each department tended to have an admin, as well as each squadron. Also, the department heads, mostly being in their forties, liked to get together for a department head admin. It allowed them to let their hair down away from their men, talk about their current problems, and have some social time on liberty away from the ship. The department heads didn't have an admin in Naples because we'd been so busy and everybody had a lot of things to attend to there, but Bohunk had arranged for us to get an admin in Benidorm. Usually, captains didn't stand watches on the ship, but, being new on board, I wanted to become more familiar with my department, and since all the doctors who worked for me had gone those 108 days without liberty, I thought they needed liberty more than I did. So I stayed on board the first night. I was looking forward to getting to know the other department heads better, though, so I planned to go to the admin the next day.

An aircraft carrier may look big from the inside, and it looks even larger when you see one from the pier, but the two best views of an aircraft carrier are on final at a few hundred feet above the threshold or looking up at the great, gray expanse from the gunwales of a small boat. It is such a proud leviathan. Rising up so rigidly to the many stories above the water, the gray angularity exudes a confidence and a power that are both intimidating and assuring.

That evening as I came back to the ship, I had that view of the ship for the first time. You can look at it in photos a dozen times or read about it just as many, but that view is different—the hull wider, the deck higher—from the surface of the ocean in a small boat. No wonder we sailors are so arrogant.

Apparently, the first night in town the captain and the 'gator were obliged to meet with the dignitaries in town, as often was the case in foreign port calls. The next night, though, I was flattered when Bohunk told me that he and the captain wanted me to join them for the evening. We would first go to a hail and farewell party to say good-bye to the supply officer (SuppO), Joe Kinsey, and a couple of other guys, but then I was invited to join them when they went out to the local casino and then for a couple of drinks afterward.

First I had an opportunity to go to the admin, finally—a nice hotel room shared by the couple of dozen of us. The admin overlooked the main boulevard that ran along the beach, ribboned by a manicured park with palm trees, flowers, and benches. Even though I hadn't been deployed as long as the others, it had been several weeks since I had been able to run on dry land, so I ran for about an hour.

After dinner at a very patient restaurant in Benidorm, I was pleased to join the 'gator and the skipper in their car. This was heady stuff for me. I was still awed by this crowd, and here I was going out on the town with the two main guys in the ship's company. The 'gator was driving a rented Mercedes (in Europe, Mercedes appear to be as common as Ford Escorts in the States). I would have figured that the safest person to whom I could entrust myself in an auto ought to be somebody like Bohunk, a forty-year-old man whose profession was the control of complex, jet-powered vehicles and whose current job was the navigation of a 75,000-ton aircraft carrier. Wouldn't a reasonable person expect somebody like that to handle a small automobile as well as anybody? What a surprise! Bohunk had not been in an automobile for over four months, it was dark, and he probably hadn't slept more than four hours in the past four days. It was the most terrible ride I'd had in thirty years—since riding with drunk teenagers! Whoa—we zigged—we tailgated. "Hey, 'Gator! You OK?" I asked.

"Don't worry, Doc, I'll get the hang of it."

"'Gator, if you get us arrested in a foreign country because of your driving, I'll kill you," the captain said. "We don't need any international incidents here."

There must have been nearly a hundred guys from the FID in the casino. Everybody was having fun and was happy to bump into one another. Bohunk and I stood around and laughed at several guys pumping the slots one after another. Bohunk was tired. He and the skipper needed the port call. They spent hour after endless hour together on the bridge, and, this being only their second port call in over four months, they needed rest. We saw the captain chatting with some sailors over by the baccarat table, and we ambled over to the blackjack area. The 'gator lost fifteen to twenty dollars in short order. "That's it for me, Doc, I've had enough," he said. He went to sit on a bench near the door to nod off as he watched everybody else.

I was having better luck, and in fact was up forty to fifty dollars, when Josh Brant, the senior dental officer and my semi bunkmate on the ship, came by. He was accompanied, as I would learn he usually was, by an attractive young woman. "Hey, Red, say hello to Persepone. She's English."

I said something pleasant, but probably also sarcastic, about how Persepone shouldn't spend time with sailors, and it made both of them laugh. For the next two years, I would frequently be introduced to attractive young women who were just meeting Josh. I always told them something bad about him, but that just made them like him more! They would always laugh and squeeze his arm harder. "You should try the roulette table, Red, I made some money over there" (giggles from Persepone).

Bohunk was asleep on his bench over by the door at this point. I couldn't see the captain, but figured he was over in some other area with some of the crew. So, I edged cautiously over to a roulette table, my first time ever. Hedging first only small bets on two or three combinations, I won gradually up to several hundred pesetas—about two hundred dollars. Figuring that was good enough for a first time at a casino, I decided to stop, and besides, Bohunk was sound asleep and needed to go.

"Hey, 'Gator, wake up, it's time to go."

He woke up easily enough and said, in the requisite style of Spencer Tracy in *Captains Courageous,* "OK, Doc, we go bock sheep." We couldn't find the captain and decided he must already be back at the car.

Sure enough, when we got out to the car, the Cajun was sound asleep in the right front passenger seat, his head resting on the window ledge. Both the skipper and Bohunk were sleep-deprived. They spent more than the number of hours a day contains on the bridge, both of them. Coming into a port is especially demanding when the ship has never been there, and our operating schedule had been murderous for them. No wonder the 'gator had fallen asleep right in the casino and the captain had come out to the car to sleep. We couldn't wake him.

"Hey 'Gator, I've got an offer you can't refuse."

His eyelids at half mast, the 'gator asked what it was.

"Frankly you didn't distinguish yourself driving over here, 'Gator, and you can scarcely stay awake even now. Why don't you let me drive us back to the ship?"

"OK, Doc. Bock sheep." He gave me the keys.

While backing out of the parking spot, I immediately smacked into the Mercedes right behind us. Smashed its taillight right out with a loud, cracking sound that means the same thing in every language. Made an ugly contour in the two fenders, too, one vaguely recollects. I have to admit that it crossed my mind whether in this one itsy bitsy, never again, exceptional case, maybe I should just drive away. Two things decided me to do the right thing. My conscience, of course, was one. But what really convinced me was the Spanish cop standing right there.

Fortunately, none of us had been drinking at all. Imagine the embarrassment if we had been! Of course, the FID was about the biggest news in Benidorm that week, and here was a car with its CO sound asleep in the front seat. Could have a questionable appearance. So I got out and handed the policeman my identification. He didn't speak English, nor I Spanish. He saw the captain asleep. From the back seat, Bohunk was saying, "Yo, Doc, we go bock sheep now, buddy." He would sputter something now and then and fall back asleep. Lot of help. Impressed the policeman.

This was difficult for the policeman, too. He didn't want an international incident over a taillight, but he wasn't supposed to encourage this sort of thing either, especially with a car full of sleepy foreigners, one of them the reputed CO who was snoring audibly. The officer looked around furtively and then waved for me to get back in the car and drive away.

The captain was now snorting and sputtering little bit. I turned the car toward the admin, and somehow the captain woke just enough to mumble, "No, Doc, we've got to go down to that other place. I promised some of the guys I'd come and have a drink with them tonight."

"Captain, are you sure? You look pretty bushed to me."

"I'll be all right. We won't stay long."

It was late already, midnight or later, but the skipper insisted we go down to the club where most of the sailors were. The 'gator and I went to sit over by the bar, where he kept sleeping and I tried to stay awake.

But the captain wasn't sleepy anymore. It was like somebody had sneaked in a remarkable impersonator. The same guy who was sound asleep a minute ago was now the life of the party. FID sailors flocked around him, introducing their new friends and young Spanish,

English, and German tourists who wanted to meet the captain of the big American ship. A klatch of college-age women, like a sorority group, all asked him to dance. He thought he was just being an avuncular celebrity, but you could tell the sorority sisters thought differently. After about an hour, the 'gator's snoring was telling me we might never wake him up, and I was getting sleepy too. The captain, though, was more festive than ever. Finally, we somehow persuaded him to go bock sheep, and I drove us very gingerly back to the admin.

Chapter 4

Four Weeks of Variety

➕ The first several days after we left Benidorm the weather was beautiful, occasionally with small amounts of haze in the morning, and the routine on the ship wasn't too busy. We had flight ops going every day. The first day out I went up to pri-fly, which is equivalent to the tower at an airport. Pri-fly was a long, narrow compartment looking down on the flight deck from the island. It stuck out aft on the island, about half a deck higher than the captain's bridge. A little bubble at the after margin was where the air officer and assistant air officer sat in twin leather thrones. They were called the "air boss" (more often "boss") and the "miniboss" (more often "mini"). There were other kinds of bosses, especially the weapons officer, who was called the "gun boss," and the communications officer, sometimes called the "signals boss," but whenever somebody referred to "the boss" they meant the air officer.* The boss during my first year on the *Forrestal* was Ralph Eton, an S-3 naval flight officer (NFO). The mini, who was to become one of my best friends, was Larry Burns, an A-7 pilot. He sat in the right-hand chair, just like a copilot would. Both the boss and the mini had completed CO tours on squadrons assigned to the *Forrestal* air wing just before getting their current jobs, the boss to the VS-28 "Gamblers" and the mini to the VA-105 "Gun Slingers," one of the two light-attack squadrons in the air wing.

Behind the boss and the mini were airmen who marked on big Lucite graphs with grease pencil the names and numbers of airplanes, listing the weight of the aircraft, the name of the pilot, and the amount of fuel on board. In one column was the name of the tanker flying

---

*This "boss" talk was carried to extremes of cuteness. For example, the dental officer was sometimes called the "gum boss," or the chaplain the "God boss."

around to refuel airplanes as needed after taking off or just before landing. Over the mini's and the boss's heads, in the panel above the windows, were compasses and gauges that showed wind direction. The boss and the mini held microphones that they spoke into, but there were also two banks of communicator telephone squawkers. They spoke frequently to the captain and carried on a continuous dialogue with pilots in the pattern and with the LSOs down on the port side of the ship just past the three-wire. Periodically the boss or the mini would reach up and grab some other microphone so he could speak on the 5-MC (the loudspeaker system for the flight deck and selected other parts of the ship, such as the medical department).

On the 5-MC they'd give directions that were necessary for performance on the flight deck, or call to announce certain emergencies. The mini had a propensity for grabbing the microphone and shouting down to some yellow shirt who wasn't wearing his cranial, or reminding somebody else to put on his goggles. Whenever the ship would turn, the boss or the mini would speak into the 5-MC—not to tell the people on the flight deck that the ship was turning but to remind them that the flight deck would tilt one way or another.

One of the things that distinguishes a ship from a boat is that a ship tilts away from the direction of the turn. So when the ship would turn to the port side, the flight deck, especially on the after end, would heel over toward the starboard side. For flight ops the ship had to turn into the wind, so as the ship would begin turning, if it had to turn to port, the boss or the mini would warn people on the flight deck, "Heel to starboard, heel to starboard." This would warn anybody on the after end of the flight deck to watch out for what could be a rough, unexpected motion and a list, and maybe prevent somebody from falling overboard.

The mini was kind of a Renaissance man. There were a few of those among aviators, although they were more often to be found in the VAW or VAQ communities than among the single-seat attack guys. The mini was a scholar and a musician, but—of note in this job, where he held a microphone—he was also something of a vocalist and an orator. With a melodious baritone voice and a glib gift for the microphone, it was obvious that he enjoyed communicating with those who worked on the deck and in the cockpits. On the other hand, maybe that's not entirely it. Maybe he just enjoyed speaking into the microphone. Enjoy it he did, though, and I enjoyed hearing him enjoy it, too. Before each flight cycle, the mini had a paragraph of precise instructions. "On the flight deck! It is time for the cycle to begin. All unauthorized personnel must clear the flight deck at this time. Now all personnel don your equipment . . ." The patter went on to remind all the people to check their survival vests, cranials, and "Now put on your goggles, and make sure your sleeves are down." The words and their sequence were identical each time. I knew there must have been a required script in order to guarantee that every topic was covered. If it had been repeated in an obligatory mono-tone, as some clergy do with a litany, or as some minis do on other ships, the guys would also be bored with it and never pay attention. Our mini saw each iteration as a pleasure, though. His inflection was almost musical, so obviously did he enjoy it. He made the rote recita-tion of those instructions sound new and different each time because of a slightly different nuance or syllabic emphasis. Sincerity too; how he could make it sound as though he believed in buttoning up those life vests, and tightening those bootlaces!

Either in the morning before the launches began, or in the after-noon before all the aircraft returned to the flight deck, we had the foreign-object damage (FOD) walk down to clear the deck. Then would come the launch part. The last group of airplanes were still fly-ing around, and they hadn't yet returned overhead. In order to clear the deck for them, the current launch had to be sent out. The first aircraft to be launched would be the H-3 helos, which would fly around in the "starboard delta" pattern for the entire flight in the event a search-and-rescue mission were necessary.

The next aircraft to launch would be one of the tankers. Some of the A-6s were configured with a large extra fuel tank in the belly in addition to extra drop tanks on the wings. These would be up there to replenish anybody who needed more fuel, either at the beginning or end of the cycle.

Pri-fly was a busy place. On the *Forrestal* it had a special atmosphere because of the magical teamwork, starting with the symbiosis of the boss and the mini. For one thing, they made it all look so easy, so much fun, so under control. Also, they worked together as smoothly and cheerfully as a pair of disc jockeys on a morning radio show . . . where I suspected the mini longed to be at times anyway. Cheerful, light banter, witty repartee, they were obviously having fun. Yet their eyes never left the flight deck or airplanes in the pattern. The boss and the mini were always welcoming, and despite the high-pressure tempo of their jobs, they were always eager to show a visitor what was going on and the complexities of lining up the aircraft.

About the time half the airplanes had launched, other planes began to circle overhead and continued circling until the last one was in the air. Within moments, the conversation between the boss and the mini on their various speakers seemed unchanged, but their gaze now shifted away from the catapults to the after end of the ship. One or the other of them would pick up binoculars, and they'd look at airplanes coming in to land. Over the headphones at this point one could hear the LSO saying, "Power . . . power . . . come left . . . glide slope . . ." as they guided in the landing pilot. Periodically, the boss or the mini would snatch out at a microphone and curtly pronounce "Wave off." Usually thereafter you would hear the LSO's voice over the microphone saying "Wave off," and the airplane on final, just about to touch the threshold, would accelerate and begin to climb. For some reason he hadn't been set up correctly, and the boss or the mini didn't want him to land if he had a poor configuration.

Sometimes, eschewing the microphone, one of them would say something like "Dumb son of a bitch, I told him he had to stop that." Or they would make a comment that somebody had to go down and speak to the skipper of that guy's squadron. More often one of them would affectionately pass a cheerful joke or pun to a flight crew. Succinctly, though. Not much chatter on the radio. Sometimes just a terse, "Nice job, one-oh-three." After the last plane in the pack was landed, there was supposed to be a thirty- to sixty-minute lag before the next cycle started, but it always seemed like only ten or fifteen minutes because a lot of airplanes had to be readied, spotted, and moved in the interim.

"Vultures' Row" was sensually more exciting, though. Down on the O-5 level, one or two decks below pri-fly and only a deck below the captain's bridge, there was a catwalk on the port side (inside) of the island, right over the flight deck, where you could stand and watch the airplanes take off and land. It was louder than the inside of hell, though, and always had winds of at least twenty-five knots, even before the planes threw out their exhaust. You had to wear good ear protection, and it was best if you wore heavy Mickey Mouse ears in addition to earplugs. From there you could watch the jets—always blurred and angular at this speed, and real big—as they'd reach gradually up to the threshold of the ship and seem gently to stretch their wheels down to touch the flight deck, with the tail hook dragging. But then, as soon as those wheels touched the flight deck, they didn't seem to be floating anymore, but going faster than light. With the crashing thunder louder than anything you've ever heard, the airplane seemed to snap forward and jerk to a halt as the hook grabbed the wire. It all happened so fast. Nobody had time to catch a breath, because just as soon as the airplane stopped a yellow shirt was out there beckoning him on, bending a left arm to taxi the airplane off to the starboard side, as the cable (called a "wire") was slowly retracted back into place to catch the next airplane. In less than sixty seconds, and sometimes in as few as thirty seconds, another airplane would be stretching out its wheels to touch down on the flight deck and crash right into that same position, then another and another, each a little quicker than the last.

There are several reasons for the diagonal flight deck. The first is that if an airplane has to bolter (like on my own first approach), with the runway a little bit at an angle the plane can fly or skid off to the port side of the ship and not carom into all the airplanes that might be in front of it. A traffic pileup is bad enough on a freeway; it would be downright ugly on an aircraft carrier. The second reason for the slanted deck is that with air coming across the flight deck, the island sticking up on the starboard side of the ship causes a disruption of air flow over the flight deck. The resulting little "burble" distorts the wind coming across an airplane's nose at the most critical time and speed in flight. With a canted deck the ship can steam a little to the right of the oncoming wind, so a quartering port head wind comes down the angle of the deck. The landing head wind is unaffected by

An F-14 Tomcat just before launch. The steam is from the catapults.
U.S. Navy photo

the island and provides a direct head wind for the aircraft arriving at an angle to the ship's course, but directly into the wind.

By the time World War II broke out, our airplanes were all-metal monoplanes, and they were much heavier. All the bombs and bullets (which were supposed to be used up before you came home) made them even heavier at takeoff than at landing. Simple deck launching—just using the deck as a runway—didn't provide enough airspeed to get reliably airborne. This became even more critical when jets were developed in the 1950s. Every jet on the *Forrestal* was heavier than anything but the biggest bombers in World War II. They needed airspeeds near 200 knots to take off, so the catapults had to be enormously powerful. The acceleration is legendary among flyers. Movies can only hint of the feeling. It's something all real Americans want to experience before they die.

Flight in the Intruder

My first flight was in an A-6 Intruder, the two-seat, all-weather bomber belonging to the VA-176 "Thunderbolts." VA-176 was commissioned about thirty-five years ago, flying the A-1 Sky Raider. The Sky Raider, an enormous propeller-driven aircraft, was the last piston-powered aircraft sent into combat from Navy carriers. It was developed in the 1950s as an all-weather, medium-attack airplane and continued as a rescue airplane in Vietnam even after the A-6 stole away its bombing mission. When, in the early 1960s, VA-176 transitioned from the single-seat A-1 to the A-6, they kept their logo, squadron, and heritage but changed in the most fundamental way for a tactical squadron. They now had a second occupant, an NFO, the bombardier-navigator (BN), not only in the ready room but right there in the airplane. A cockpit for two is a team, not just an airplane with an observer. The BN didn't just "help" the pilot—he did other stuff, too, like working complicated computers and gadgets that put ordnance on target. The BNs delivered that which made the A-6 different from just an airplane.

At the appointed time, more than two hours before scheduled departure time, I came to the VA-176 ready room. I was going to go on a tanker mission. The pilot would be Lt. Cdr. Bob Sloh ("Slow Bob"). He was one of the few Academy graduates who would have to retire as a lieutenant commander. After being passed over a few times, he'd have to leave the Navy soon—in about a year. A remarkably easy-going guy, he obviously had thousands of hours in control of the aircraft. He also played the guitar and sang folk songs.

Before going on any flight, just as we had with the helo, we had to sit through the flight brief, the weather recording over the closed-circuit TV, and the operations brief, also over the TV. Since our mission this day was to be the tanker, it was OK to have a novice BN in the right seat. There had to be a lot of training in the airplane before I could go on any bombing runs. The A-6 in its bomber configuration is a very busy two-person aircraft. The right-seater in this airplane—and NFOs in *any* airplane—is not a copilot. NFOs wince if you call them that. To prove they're not helper pilots, there's not even a set of flight controls on the right side. The BN would tell you the flight controls over on the left side are just there for the chauffeur anyway; they'd get in the way of the important stuff if you tried to put them on the right side, too.

On our mission today, we'd be circling around not too far from the ship to help airplanes refuel right after takeoff and to be available toward the end of the mission. The big jets guzzle fuel ravenously. Some of the airplanes also have afterburners, and on our ship those were the F-14 Tomcats, the biggest airplanes we had. Afterburner on takeoff and climbing with a full airplane (all the bombs and bullets still aboard) burns up more fuel than just flying around, so some airplanes—especially the fighters—may need to top off their tanks right after takeoff and again while waiting their turn to land. Finally, if some pilot has some trouble getting down to the deck—because he bolters, because the deck is cluttered, or any other reason—that extra flight time forces him to ask "Texaco" for a drink.

"So this is your first cat shot?" Slow Bob was very understanding. I think he'd been stuck with flight surgeons on their first flights before. He knew I'd been checked out in oxygen masks and so forth. All flight surgeons have to be certified in ejection procedures and survival techniques, such as escaping from the shrouds of a parachute underwater, treading water with boots on, and crawling into the life raft. As part of the routine brief, though, he had to run through all of those things with me. We talked about the procedures we'd use if we lost communication. We wouldn't be able to hear one another in the cockpit if the ICS failed.

Every crew reviews ejection procedures before each flight. With a novice in the crew it gets special attention. You can eject by pulling a ring over your head, or one down between your legs. There are two different rings because if the aircraft is tumbling or under a high G force, or if one of your arms is blown off, you may not be able to reach one of the rings.

When crews work together, trust one another's judgment, and

have been through danger together, they usually use "crew eject." Most airplanes have two different ways to handle ejection. One is crew eject—if either guy pulls his ejection handle, both shoot right out immediately. With the other method, "manual," you only get out by pulling the handle yourself. If you're badly injured you might not be able to pull yourself out fast, or if something is happening too fast for you to see it coming, your buddy might. Crew eject lets him save both your lives. On the other hand, it's an unpleasant image to think of a fruity or skittish new guy in the right seat who pulls the loop too quickly or accidentally pulls it when he simply meant to reach down and untie his laces. If he just blows himself out when he shouldn't, it ruins a good canopy and that day's mission, but at least if the pilot didn't get ejected there's somebody inside who can bring the multi-million-dollar airplane home. Ejection can be dangerous and no pilot wants to eject unnecessarily, so with a new guy on board they seldom use the crew eject setting. These considerations are not completely reciprocal, though. The right-seater should prefer crew eject. If the pilot chooses to depart and leaves you behind, there's no good reason to stay in an airplane you can't fly. We would use manual eject on our flight that day. I was ambivalent; glad not to worry about accidentally shooting us both out of the airplane, yet not able to count on Slow Bob getting me out, either.

He laid out the procedure, "I will say eject three times: 'Eject, eject, eject.' When you hear me say it, you pull your ring on the second 'eject.' Because if you wait for the third time, I'll be gone." Now, I've heard that particular speech a number of times either in movies or in instructional briefs. Perhaps you've heard it too. Believe me, the first time you hear a real live guy in a flight suit looking you right in the eye as he says it before you get into an airplane, it comes across in a much more meaningful way.

We hurried down to the parachute loft to put on our G suits, torso harnesses, survival jackets, and the straps that automatically snap ankles back under the seat during ejection. In the rocket forces of ejection, the feet can flail out. If they do, they can be sliced off by the windscreen or get stuck on the control panel on the way out. The straps slap the heels back into the seat.

The ejection sequence blows the canopy off the airplane so you won't hit it. You may remember in the movie *Top Gun* that the guy in the backseat had his neck broken because he hit the canopy on his way out. That was because he hit the canopy frame, I presume. The fact is that many people eject right through the glass in the canopy.

Some airplanes are even designed that way. Just like a dancer popping out of a big birthday cake.

Later that year I would meet a fifty-year-old pediatrics professor from some research committee who came to the ship on a fact-finding tour. In a chat late one night, he told me that twenty years ago he had been a flight surgeon, and in his first flight off the flight deck in an A-6, there was engine failure right off the pointy end, and he and the pilot both ejected. On *his* first A-6 flight he wound up using every part of the brief. It's not just in movies. Flight surgeons have done it often. Of the experienced aviators on the ship, probably a third or more had been in a real ejection sometime in their career. I took all this stuff pretty seriously.

All the flight gear puts an awful lot of parts on you. The G suit is like leggings or chaps that fit tightly against the calf and thigh, but also well up into the abdomen. A big tube sticks out the side like a dangling appendage hanging obscenely off the left side of the body, then it plugs into the anti-G apparatus in the cockpit like a pneumatic umbilicus. The torso harness is a network of very heavy canvas that goes under your buttocks and thighs and locks you to both the seat and the parachute. The torso harness, which becomes the seat harness, has to fit tightly because if you ever eject, the ejection seat pulls you entirely out of the airplane, and the torso harness is what holds you into the seat and also into the parachute.

It's hot in the parachute loft, so by the time we left there, wearing all that gear, I was sweating pretty well. It was August just south of Spain to begin with. We walked up to the flight deck, which was a little smokier, a little hotter, and much more exciting than it had ever been to me.

The A-6 looks like a big airplane from the flight deck, but it looks much bigger when you start climbing up the ladder to get in. It has a big, bulbous nose sitting out in front, so to the uninitiated this large, round-fronted jet looks somewhat ungainly, less pointy, and to some people perhaps a little bit less sexy than the other jets. When you see the silhouette in the sky, though, it's transformed. The wings taper back from the broad shoulders of the intakes, and those bulbous eyeballs of the canopy are so ominous and menacing. It is a vicious-looking airplane. It may be big and ungainly on the deck, but it's sleek in flight.

After we climbed up into the cockpit and got strapped in, I nonchalantly tried to stick my G suit plug into the oxygen outlet. Twice, three times. Wrong plug. Not cool. I was glad it was Slow Bob with me. He patiently reached over to help me plug each tube into its proper receptacle. They all have different shapes, probably with the faint

hope of protecting flight surgeons from the kind of mistake I was trying to make. The shaded, bulbous visors on the helmets had to come
down. Then we got strapped in. Slow Bob showed me the things he
wanted me to do, when to push the lever to spread the wings out, the
things I was *not* supposed to touch, and the circuit breakers I was to
help him with during the rundown in the preflight inspection. Faster
than I could savor everything that was going on, there we were taxiing into position. The helos lifted off, so it was our turn. We taxied
up to the bow cats. There are four catapults on the *Forrestal,* two on
the bow and two others near midships, the "waist." The waist cats are
shorter, and since they have to reach the same speed in a shorter distance, they're rougher, so they aren't used as much. During a busy
launch sequence, having four launching positions in sequence
instead of two increases launch rates exponentially. There were four
jet blast deflectors, one behind each catapult, to protect workers on
the flight deck from the searing heat and tornado winds of the jet
exhaust as it spooled up to launch an airplane. Somehow, you didn't
see them all, but there were around a hundred guys working up there
during flight ops. It was only a couple of weeks ago that Airman
Mitchell had been blown overboard.

Suddenly we were very busy. Bob was doing the preflight checklist,
reading off items aloud, with me participating at the places where he
told me to, checking circuit breakers, looking around the flight deck
for the things he told me to look for. One of the flight deck crew
came up to the left-hand side of the airplane and held up a slate giving the airplane's weight and the number of pounds of fuel, and Slow
Bob gave him a thumbs-up sign. These weight calculations are critical for setting the catapult correctly for our aircraft. All of these things
happened in about five seconds.

Two guys rolled under the airplane to check the landing gear and
then just as quickly rolled off to the sides. The "shooter," an aviator himself, was standing in the middle of the flight deck waving his hand above
his head while pointing at Slow Bob. Bob looked at him. The shooter
saluted. Bob said, "Are you ready?" I told him I was, and Bob returned
the salute. The guy held up one finger, two fingers, three fingers, shook
his fingers, then he kneeled down suddenly, touched his fingers to the
flight deck, and pointed them straight ahead like a bird dog. Bob had
showed me how to bend my neck slightly forward so it wouldn't snap
back too suddenly into the seat. There was a little thud when the trellis
grabbed the front of the airplane, then . . . Oh! . . . mmmphhh . . . gone!

Ever since I first saw William Holden fly off the deck in *The Bridges at Toko-Ri,* I had looked forward to this, but as I already said, movies can't feel it. It sucks your teeth right back to your throat, and your eyeballs back to your elbows. The flight deck, all the guys, the antennas—everything—blurred by faster than you could see them. Then suddenly you're out in space, the catapult lets go, and it's like stepping gently off a cliff. Roaring under about four Gs through a keyhole into a quiet, weightless float. You're flying.

Too much sensation, too much experience, in less than one second to realize all of it the first time, maybe even the first dozen times. This all happens in the time it takes a tennis ball to fall from the hand to the floor. It is so fast and so rich, that you must notice one aspect or another each time in order to gradually see all of them. Just as quickly as we were thrown out into space, I looked over and noticed that Bob had been working that whole time. So much had just happened to me in the last part of a second that I wanted to revel in it. He spoke something into his oxygen mask that I couldn't hear, presumably to the boss. I looked down to watch the ocean as we flew by, remarking on how low we stayed as we went perhaps a half mile, two miles, some distance, and then started to climb. First we had to build up speed. Then our climb came rather rapidly. We were at our assigned altitude of 10,000 feet within just a couple of minutes.

We started a slow turn to the left, and Bob pointed toward that side, where there were a couple of F-14s. "There's our traffic," he said over the ICS. I hadn't heard them speak to us on the radio, nor him to them, so I asked how they knew where to find us. After all, these are warplanes, and one way the bad guys can find you in a conflict is to listen on their radios. So procedures were developed down through the years letting everybody know what to expect. On your way back at the end of a flight sequence, you knew where and when to meet the tanker. That was part of the reason for all the instructions and briefs we had in the ready room before taking off. Likewise, on the rendezvous up in the air, the two pilots didn't need to speak with each other. It was always the thirsty one who'd have to fly formation on the tanker.

Formation flying is a skill that all pilots learn in basic training. It's a lot harder than it looks on film. Both airplanes are flying at around 200 miles per hour. The tanker slowly dangles out a hose with a conical basket on the end, trailing it out fifty to one hundred feet behind the airplane. The other airplane sidles up from behind and gently sticks the refueling probe into the basket. Looks easy, but have you ever tried to ride up and take a handoff from one bicycle to another at just twenty-five or thirty miles per hour? When opened up in flight, the basket is probably about twenty-four inches in diameter, but while you're up there it looks like it's only about six inches across, and the airplane has to hit a certain spot right in the middle. All this is done without any radio communication and only hand signals between the pilots. A light goes on in the control panel, and a digital indicator near the light begins to click off numbers at a dazzling rate. After two or three minutes, the fueling aircraft pulls back just a bit, the basket lurches forward, and the two airplanes are simply flying in formation again, no longer attached by the long tether. The pilot of the F-14 that came alongside on the right to take the fuel touches his fingers and thumb together in a kissing gesture on his mouth and flips the hand, fingers open, toward us, the "kiss-off" sign. Just then, he banks steeply away and flies slightly downward in a graceful pirouette that no eagle could equal. His wingman then slides up underneath our aircraft to take his place, like the next calf to the cow, and within moments places the probe right in the basket and repeats the entire exercise. Minutes later, he, too, gives us the kiss-off sign and flies away.

Our first two customers were the only fighters from the prior sequence. Being the heaviest airplanes—and likely the most acrobatic of the flight—those two needed fuel just to sustain them in the pattern waiting for our launch sequence to clear the deck so they could land. Our next customers were airplanes from our own launch who needed to top off before getting on with their sortie. After that, we continued to circle over the flight deck at our present altitude while we watched the planes from the prior sequence come in to land.

The view was obviously a lot different from this high. The choreography of all the different airplanes following in their assigned sequence on the landing was fascinating up here where we could see all of them and watch the ballet from above. Radio silence was maintained for both security practice and safety. If all the pilots were chattering on the frequencies at the same time, it would be just like civilian airports where landing traffic sometimes has trouble getting through to the tower. There were well over a dozen high-performance jets, all buzzing around the ship like moths around a porch light. If each one had to have an individual conversation with the boss, they couldn't execute the tight landing sequence, bringing one plane after the other to the deck in less than a minute.

Each type of airplane had an assigned altitude coming in, based on fuel consumption and capacity, airspeed in the landing pattern, and where it would be parked when the sequence was over. The recovery cycle took fifteen or twenty minutes. The first airplanes would be coming back in about another twenty-five to thirty minutes, so we had about half an hour to fly around. Slow Bob couldn't show off in the airplane too much, since we were laden with loaded drop tanks on the wings. Besides, this airplane, like most of the A-6s on the FID, had first flown in Vietnam. She was too old for any athletics. There was a project under way to replace the wings on a lot of the A-6s, but it hadn't been done to many of our airplanes, certainly not this old KA-6, so we mostly just flew around looking at the scenery and the clouds.

The ship was close enough that we would pass through the Straits of Gibraltar the next day, so we flew over The Rock, which looked surprisingly small. Prudential Insurance had been fooling me for a long time. The straits looked just as narrow as I'd ever imagined. Morocco looked just as tan and barren compared to Spain's green as it did on my Rand McNally maps.

Shortly we had our first customer from the next recovery, an A-7 Corsair II. The refueling probe in the A-7, as in the F-14, fits into a groove along the side of the aircraft. In the A-6 it permanently sticks up in front of the canopy eyeballs, like a big, ugly stinger or a hooked nose. The A-7 has a big, gaping mouth of an intake right under the nose. It's a little ungainly and somewhat ugly on the ground because of this flat, gaping mouth, and it looks a little bit like the F-8 fighter of the fifties. Possibly because of that similarity, A-7s were often called fighters, which they were not—they didn't even have a gun when first designed. Like the Intruder, the A-7 became beautiful in flight. It had a beautiful planform with its short, swept wings and relatively slender fuselage, but this was recognized fully only when you could see it from above or below.

When the A-7 finished drinking, he slowly rolled over on his back and fell away descending, gradually rolling over in a maneuver called a split S. As he fell away, the wings arched out gracefully from the plane, and he looked like a diver gliding into a half gainer. One after another, airplanes came up to pump from "Texaco" to sustain them through the pattern. We watched our own recovery cycle to the deck just as we had the one before us, and finally there were no aircraft in the pattern except for us and the helos that were off the starboard side of the ship. Bob took us down to pattern level and described all the next steps gradually. We flew one racetrack pattern over the ship, flying in from behind at pattern altitude, directly over the flight deck. Then abruptly into the "break"—the point where the airplane breaks away sharply from over the flight deck and banks suddenly to the left into the downwind leg. In civilian airplanes we do this with a gentle, rolling, banking turn toward the left. As Ike and Tina used to say, Navy pilots like it rough. You abruptly yank the jet up on its left wing and curl around at a couple of Gs. The alleged reason for the high-G, tight pattern is to stay as close to the deck as possible when landing. If the engine stops, one prefers being close to the ship, since every hundred yards can be crucial in an ocean of ice water or sharks.

But the *real* reason pilots do it is because it *feels* so good.

Just before turning to final, the gear comes down, the airplane yanks again to the left and curls around toward the deck, wings level right at the threshold. Out on the ends of the A-6, the wedge-shaped air brakes pop up. All of this happens faster than it does in our civilian airplanes, but if you watch fast you can grasp it. The rest starts going too fast to follow, though.

Suddenly, the airplane is over the flight deck, that blur happens again, the wheels bang, and the tail hook grabs the wire. This is my first time sitting in the front. The blur is just too quick. One or two of the flight deck crew and some yellow gear are visible off to the right just before the wheels hit, but everything else whirls by in a tangled streak. The slam into the neck and chest surprises me as much as it did the first time, but it's even faster this time.

Faster than it started it was over.

Had it happened at all? Before I could be certain, it was over, the airplane was turning, and Bob was gesturing for me to put the ejection seat on safety and pull the wings up. The canopy was already rising. I pulled the right lever and looked out timidly, reassured that the wings were folding back as they were supposed to.

The helo was coming in to be spotted at the position on the waist just in front of where we had been. As the canopy came up, the blast of hot Mediterranean air reminded me it was August. I realized that the air conditioner on the A-6 must have been working pretty well. As calmly as turning off a Ford, Slow Bob shut down the engines, and it was time for us to climb out of the aircraft. I disconnected the G-suit tube better than I'd plugged it in, and checked my flight suit to make sure it wasn't wet anywhere it shouldn't be (it wasn't). Climbing out of the airplane, I noticed my legs were a little wobbly, and I had to be careful as I jumped down the three feet from the bottom rung of the ladder to the flight deck.

The Tomcat

A couple of days later, we were out of the Mediterranean and headed north. I went down to the ready room of the "World Famous Red

Rippers." VF-11 is the oldest surviving, continuously commissioned flying squadron in the U.S. Navy. On the bulkheads of the ready room,
paneled in simulated oak, were photographs of various generations of
airplanes over fifty years. There were open-cockpit biplanes, piloted
by toothy, leather-helmeted men with white silk scarves. The old
planes were adorned with the same emblem of a snarling red, heavily
fanged boar as on the F-14s that belonged to the Red Rippers now.
There were F-4Fs from World War II, and F-9s from the 1950s. The
Rippers had a grand old tradition, and they'd decorated their ready
room accordingly. All the ready rooms had closed-circuit TV, VCR for
watching movies late at night, and a nice stereo system. They all also
had those famous ready-room chairs.

I figure the first ready rooms on the *Langley* or the *Ranger,* back in
the 1920s, were furnished with surplus barber chairs or chairs from
an old Pullman railroad car. Thereafter, all other ready rooms felt
they had to use something similar. The pilots were given tall-backed,
cushioned chairs with funky metal arms, all of them having an ash-
tray mounted in them. I guess back in the old days pilots were expected to smoke, probably either Lucky Strikes or Camels. Almost no
pilots or NFOs smoked anymore, but all the chairs had those dys-
functional metal arm rails, with the semicomfortable Naugahyde
upholstery. The upholstery had probably been leather through

An F-14 Tomcat from the Red Rippers launching at dawn. *U.S. Navy photo*

World War II. The same yellow-tan pablum color was used in ready rooms throughout the fleet, and certainly in all the ready rooms on the *Forrestal*. The chairs were semicomfortable, but whether they were comfortable or not, they looked the way ready-room chairs are supposed to look. When my daughter Abigail first saw a ready room, she recognized the setting instantly. "Oh yeah, this is where the guy says, 'Gentlemen, you are the best.'"

They say every aviation community has a personality, and an hour or two in the ready rooms would surely bear that out. Aviators in general are more spontaneous, and a little bit more raucous, than the blackshoes. Within the aviation community, though, there are further distinctions. Fighter squadrons are a little more aggressive and have a little bit harsher edge on their sarcasm and in their taunting of one another. Fighters live to chase and kill the enemy, to interdict other airplanes. Air-to-air combat is still their main mission. Of course, a secondary mission might be ground support or bombing, but they are hired to look an enemy in the eye and kill him.

The attack aircraft, by contrast, are for attacking targets on the ground or ocean. It's their job to be deliberate and accurate in seeking out a target and hitting only that target, but hitting it accurately. Bombers aren't so much interested in killing a specific hated adversary one-on-one like the Red Baron. Their job is to fly out someplace, have a good time, and bomb the hell out of something. So attack pilots and attack A-6 crews maybe are a little bit more analytical, a little bit more deliberate. If aggressive, like all pilots, they are at least not quite as stinging among one another as are the fighters.

Helo pilots tend to be people who will do whatever it takes to get the job done. They stick together, yet might be somewhat more independent. In general, the helo pilots tend to be more flexible, more adaptable. Because the heritage of naval aviation has traditionally focused on the "go fasters" and the jets, helo pilots sometimes are just a little bit defensive. They quickly stop having fun if you forget that the H-3 is a very large aircraft. Helo pilots often say, "If you can't hover, you ain't shit."

The A-6 Intruder and the F-14 Tomcat are both two-seaters with one pilot and one NFO (and one set of flight controls). The role of the NFO in the two crews is different, though, and this difference is important. In the A-6, the BN sits side by side with the pilot (just a little lower and a little behind). In the F-14, the pilot is up front and the NFO radio intercept operator (RIO) is in the back (where, by the way, the pilot has his back to him). A-6 BNs, single-seat pilots, and F-14 pilots all enjoy speculating on what these seating arrangements mean. The F-14 NFO seldom enjoys this kind of conversation.

The brief for the flight with the F-14 had the same format as the brief for the A-6, but the mission was a lot different. We were going to go out and fly combat air patrol (CAP), then do some dogfighting—one-on-one air combat maneuvering (ACM). Then we'd come back and have some strafing practice before landing. I would ride with "Pistol" Robertson, the CO of the Red Rippers, one of the best pilots in the air wing. He was said to be a shoe-in for captain, and probably on the fast track for flag.

The F-14 was probably the prettiest airplane on the flight deck. It was certainly the biggest and the longest. Two great big cylindrical jet engines stuck out the back with nozzles that opened and closed depending on whether the afterburner was working. The wings didn't fold up like they did on the S-3 or the A-6, but instead had an adjustable sweep. For slow flight or landing, the wings would fold out (by a computer), and the airplane would look like a turkey in flight. The faster the airplane went, the more the wings were swept back, and the sleeker and faster it became. The slower it went, the more the wings would come

One of the Red Rippers launching on a bow catapult. Note the extended wings with flaps down, and the jet blast deflector behind it. The airplane parked over to starboard is an S-3 Viking from the Gamblers. *U.S. Navy photo*

out toward a nearly perpendicular position. This particular movement of the wings was similar to what the Air Force F-111 used, and one or two of the Russian Migs. When parked, the wings would be swept as far back as they would go to take up less space in the hangar or on the deck.

Sometimes in dogfighting, in order to turn tighter corners or to maneuver in a particular manner against an adversary, the airplane might slow down, so the computer would bring the wings forward. Fortunately, the pilot doesn't have to think about controlling the wings while he's busy doing other things. The computer takes care of that for him.

I tilted my head forward about forty-five degrees, as I had been instructed, and prepared for the shot. This time, my second cat shot, I vowed I was going to pay attention to the shooter and the flight deck crew while we shuttled down the catapult and not lose everything in a blur. I saw the shooter point toward the airplane, wiggling his hands overhead. Pistol saluted him to say we were ready. I held tight with my right hand, and then slam, the catapult drove us down the shuttle. Just as before, everything streaked and smeared; all I could see was one sailor over in the catwalk on the port side. Smushed tighter and tighter back into the seat, suddenly—like squirting my entire body through a keyhole and then dropping down into space—*Varrooom!* off the flight deck. Flying.

Imagine sitting on the hood of a car that's driving along at about 150 miles per hour and then suddenly going off a cliff. No more acceleration and yet not slowing either. Thunder to silence instantly.

In the movies, airplanes dip down below the flight deck after take-off before they pick up and climb. Modern jets have to gain speed to climb well, but they don't sink off the deck. Just as in the Intruder, we accelerated for a half mile or so before we began to climb—much faster in the F-14, though. First we formed up on our wing man, then up to meet the tanker.

Flying up on the right side of the tanker, our probe slipped out from the side of the aircraft and Pistol drove up as smoothly as parallel parking at a shopping mall. He slipped the snout of the refueling probe into the basket on the first try, and within three or four minutes our fuel tanks were full and we were gone.

The dogfighting was no different from dogfighting in a T-34 or small airplane, although distances were miles instead of hundreds of yards and we were much faster! We scrimmaged with another Tomcat from the squadron. Passing each other nose-on at a closure rate of nearly 800 knots, within seconds we were miles apart and craning our necks back and left to try to keep the sweeping adversary in sight. If you forget your airspeed, you'll find yourself spinning out inverted, or at the top of an arc without enough speed to angle back at the enemy. They call that conserving energy. It can mean life or death in a fight. Wearing the G suit, every time we pulled two or three Gs I was aware of the suit's bladder pushing in on my belly and thighs, but the being upside down and then suddenly closing at velocities of nearly 1,000 miles per hour was sensually more exciting than the movies had ever been able to convey.

Just before the end of the ride we went out for strafing practice. For a target we used the wake behind the ship. Pistol did a little jig maneuver, yanking to the left and the right, with a sudden dive, which would have been used to elude ground fire if this were a real mission. Then he shot off a bunch of rounds from the machine gun. I've forgotten how many rounds per second the gun fires, but the sound describes it better than a number would anyway. It doesn't make a "rat-a-tat" sound like you expect. The gun fires so fast that it makes more of a buzz, the "PPFFTHZZ" sound that you make when you stick your tongue between your lips and blow to imitate certain biological sounds. That's the way the machine gun sounded. I asked Pistol how many bullets we fired when we did that, and he said, "Oh, a few hundred."

Pistol had given me certain jobs to do on final, including reading off the altitudes. He left the ICS on so we could communicate in case there was anything he needed me to do or if he had to tell me to eject. This was an uncomplicated daylight landing, without any hazards. Even in this setting, with this experienced pilot, listening was educational. His breathing had been virtually inaudible throughout more than an hour of flight. As we came to the downwind leg, the 180, and then on final, his breathing got faster. I counted twenty and then twenty-two breaths per minute. The wings groped out sideways as we slowed, the nose came up, the wheels smacked down on the flight deck, the tail hook grabbed, and BOOM, the arrest. My head jerked forward, and the belts jerked my shoulders and abdomen back. This time I was able to look at the flight deck a little bit as we landed, and things blurred just a little bit less because I could note the stripes and the landing markers whisk by beneath us. If I hadn't been locked into my seat with the torso harness, my face surely would have tumbled into the control panel.

After we left Spain, we had almost a week sailing north up to the Arctic Circle, where we were going to begin participating in the NATO exercise "Northern Wedding." I had to take advantage of that time to satisfy some of my own qualifications in being a member of the ship's company. All members were required to fulfill certain qualifications in damage control (DC) and in materials maintenance management (3-M). The DC requirement was the same for just about everybody, regardless of rank or position, whereas 3-M depended on your job. If you had a job that involved using a lot of gear or supplies, or if people worked for you, the requirements were higher.

Damage control is obviously important on any ship, but especially a ship of war, and DC training is required at some level for everybody in the naval service, even those not likely to go to sea. Even those who think they're not going to go to sea may have to someday in the future, even reservists.

Fire fighting is an especially important part of DC—a world of its own, almost. The FID tradition, of course, knew that well. Everyone at sea needs to have a refresher trainer in shipboard fire fighting every four years, regardless of how many times he's done it before. Fire fighting is a two-day school, with several hours in the classroom and many hours practicing fighting fires, avoiding burn injury, and learning some first aid. The classroom sessions seem always to involve one more viewing of *Trial by Fire*. Some sailors have seen it so many times that they shout out some of the narrator's lines, just like groupies at *Rocky Horror Picture Show*. At the certified fire-fighting training centers, there are mock-ups of ship superstructures and spaces. Oil fires, wood fires, smoke inhalation, and the use of oxygen breathing apparatus (OBA) are all part of the training. In fact, the training can be pretty frightening when you're down in that enclosed metal space scarcely able to see your hand in front of your face. Knowing that the fire was artificially started doesn't make it any less scary. It's a real fire, and it's real smoke. You can't see where you're going, and if you put your hand out, the fire can sizzle your fingers like a hamburger.

A hundred years of evolution have produced some pretty clever gadgets and nozzles. The standardized, well-rehearsed lecture series and the obvious importance of the material make the fire-fighting classes pretty effective. They are physically demanding, though, and hot.

On the ship, there's a lot more to learn: where the individual fire mains are on that particular ship, how to do shoring, how to patch leaking pipes, what teams to belong to, what signals to listen for on the 1-MC, how to make good your escape from various places on the ship. One of the drills is to escape from the living quarters to an outside weather deck or a place to abandon ship in less than two minutes. It takes a little practice, but most people are able to escape from their berthing area even while blindfolded within this time. There are also two kinds of breathing apparatus everybody has to master. One is a little plastic hood kept right by the bedside and in every workspace. These emergency egress breathing devices (EEBDs) slip over the head and tighten around the neck, still permitting vision out the front. They carry a little oxygen cartridge in the back of the hood, because filtering out the smoke isn't all you need in a big fire. It's not just fumes and particulate matter that will kill you; fires also burn up all the oxygen. The EEBD provides a few minutes' worth, enough to make that blindfolded escape everybody had to practice.

Although there are more EEBDs than there are people in the crew, the other gadget—the OBA—is mostly for the use of DC teams or particular rescue individuals. The OBA is a peculiar-looking contraption, a cross between a SCUBA tank, an accordion, and a mask for the Creature from the Black Lagoon. A little green metal canister fits inside the black rubber compartment over your chest or tummy. Reminds one of the power pack that Commando Cody used when he flew around on Saturday morning serials during the Depression. This chemical canister, when activated, releases free oxygen. The reason for not using plain old oxygen tanks is that oxygen, of course, feeds fires. Heat and flame could either make compressed gas expand, and explode, or could leak oxygen to build up the fire. In fire-fighting school we all had to learn to use the OBA, but there were more practice drills on the ship.

One day I was attending my DC class when a corpsman had to come up to the lecture room way back in the after part of the ship over on the port side to tell me that Dr. Tosser had said I should be notified that he was starting an operation.

I ran down from the training room to the medical department as fast as I could—down about four decks and forward a little more than half the length of the ship. I was breathless when I got there after a few minutes. They had already started the operation. I put a mask over my face and cracked the door to the OR slightly. "How's everything going in there?"

Rock said everything was fine; they had just started an appendectomy. "When did he get sick?"

Rock said it was yesterday morning, and since then he'd had a high fever and had been getting worse. I asked Rock when he had first seen him, and he said it had been about an hour and a half ago. I closed the door to the OR and walked back to my office, hoping none of the people who worked for me would see how red my ears were.

We had gone over this several times since that day after we left

Naples. I had only left the department about forty minutes before to go to the lecture, and I felt that I should have been notified so that I could have examined the patient. I had no reason to question Rock's diagnostic skills, but I recognized that the surgeon and I had widely different opinions about when to operate and when not. I signed off on a few of the reports I had to finish that week and went to the ward to make rounds, feeling worried about how to avoid a dangerous confrontation. This would have to be watched, I knew.

We had only five people admitted to the ward that week. One was an individual with suppurative eczema on his feet and toes—in others words, infected athlete's foot. We saw a lot of that. Many of the young men had only one pair of boots, and they wore them every day. It's hot in the engineering spaces and on the flight deck, they sweat a lot, and if the boots never have a chance to air out they stay moist inside. If there's a fungus in there, it has a perfect home. We occasionally had to put a sailor with very bad athlete's foot on the ward. We kept him barefoot, usually kept his foot dry, sometimes with a lamp shining on it, and soaked it periodically with hexachlorophene or iodine. We usually treated it with a steroid cream, also.

Two other patients were post-op cases, one recovering from an appendectomy, another from a hernia repair. The fourth patient, Fireman (FN) Tommy Burns, had stomach cramps and diarrhea. Don Kent admitted him because he was afraid Burns might get dehydrated. When he'd become sick two or three days before, he stopped eating and drinking because, he said, "My mama told me once when you have the runs, if you don't put anything in your mouth, the runs will stop."

It may have seemed logical to FN Burns that if no fluid went in, none could come out. Wrong. Although the body in its healthy state has ways to conserve fluid, when it starts to get dry, once it gets out of balance, the adjustment mechanisms can't catch up. Even without exertion, most people exhale over a quart of water every day just breathing. A lot of our sailors could sweat out over a gallon a day—especially guys on the flight deck or down in the engine rooms, like Burns. Diarrhea would waste even more fluid and exceed the amount a sailor had been in the habit of replacing with normal eating and drinking habits. So a young man like Burns might be in precarious fluid balance already, but by not drinking for even a day he could find himself dangerously low in total fluid volume and some of the important electrolytes like potassium, chloride, and calcium. Burns's pulse was a little fast, but the rhythm was good. His skin turgor was diminished and his blood pressure low when he stood up—signs of relative dehydration—but he didn't seem to be in any danger at the present.

Even a single case of diarrhea could be the first sign of a foodborne epidemic, a warning that we had to take some drastic action on the mess decks to prevent further cases. Or a single case could even be the first case of a viral outbreak like the one they'd experienced a few months before I arrived. FN Burns had been crying all day. A big, muscular snipe, he had probably never been sick in his entire life, so this experience was especially difficult for him. When I came on the ward, Tommy had just been brought back to his rack by the corpsman after having been helped up to the head for about the twenty-fourth time that day. He really was not critically ill, but his pulse and blood pressure were still off, and he'd been receiving intravenous fluids, plus a fair amount of fluids by mouth. The corpsman, HN Bowker, was tired of getting up every five or ten minutes to help a whiney Tommy Burns get to the bathroom yet one more time.

"Doc . . ." Burns called out to me tentatively. "Doc, can I ask you a question?"

"Sure, Fireman, go ahead." I came over and took his right hand with my right hand and put my left hand on his elbow. When talking with the patients, I tried to sit down at their bedside rather than stand over them, and to hold their hand or put my hand on their shoulder whenever I could.

"Sir, do farts have lumps?"

"No," I told him, "just air."

"Oh, no. Then I think I just crapped in my pants." Sure enough, a very unpleasant aroma seemed to be spreading through the ward just then, and Tommy's diarrhea got the better of him.

After we cleaned him up we increased his diphenoxylate, the medicine for controlling diarrhea. I made sure to spend a little extra time with him that night, and we asked some of his buddies to come by and visit with him too.

Because of the operational tempo of the ship for the first 108 days, we were behind in the number of GQ drills. In order to reach the quota for the cruise, then, we were going to be doing a lot more of them for a while. We got in several during that week.

GQ is a training exercise. The objective isn't simply to see whether everyone wears the proper garments and closes the hatches the right way; those people who have battle functions during GQ have to exercise them. First aid was a requirement for everybody on the crew. Besides teaching basic first aid and first aid principles, there was a central core of the famous "five basic wounds" that everybody at sea had to be able to treat promptly and correctly: fractured jaw with facial injury, a sucking chest wound, an open abdominal wound with extruding viscera, an amputated hand, and a compound fracture of a lower extremity. During GQ, then, medical sent first aid trainers from station to station, giving refresher training on the five basic wounds and throwing down a flopper to test people on their proficiency. First aid lectures were part of the regular DC curriculum and included both commercially prepared films and live instruction over closed-circuit TV. We also had pamphlets we published right there on the ship about a number of first aid techniques, and we distributed those to all hands. But the most intense first aid training was done by the roving teams during GQ.

Those first aid sessions were the only break most of us had from the suffocating boredom during GQ! The engineers and DC teams had lots to do, checking water mains, watertight seals, and so forth. The rest of us just sat around for hours, manning our battle stations and staring at one another. My station was in the main BDS—the main medical department. Josh Brant, the gum boss, had the same station, so once we'd exhausted the training catechism with our corpsmen and dental techs and catatonic saturation had caught up with our collective boredom, we spent the time in front porch conversation. Josh was a fascinating guy. I always thought he looked like Clark Kent, but somebody had once told him he looked like Clark Gable, and he liked that comparison better. Sure enough, Josh was a big guy, a weightlifter and a fanatical bicyclist. His voice was a little graveled, although not truly Gable-esque. He used to call me "Red," which at first I figured was because of my hair, although it never really was red. Since then I've realized he was probably referring to my neck, an oblique implication of what he suspected to be my political beliefs. A Truman New Deal/Fair Deal liberal, I was usually way outnumbered in political discussions with the predominant conservative Republican population on the ship. Josh liked to imply I was only faking and must really be a rednecked reactionary Missourian.

We joked about a lot of things, including the shower stall and head between our staterooms that the two of us shared. The cold water knob worked correctly, but there was no handle for the hot water. By the way several layers of paint covered the faucet hub, it was clear there had been no handle on the hot water knob in that shower for years, perhaps even generations. To regulate the hot water, one had to reach up almost eight feet and turn the wheels on the hot water main coming into the whole room. Josh and John never told me about it, or how to make it work, but by tradition, nobody ever told them, either. You just had to figure it out for yourself. Josh had enjoyed a good relationship with John, whom he had clearly respected.

Something we maybe should have joked about a little less was flushing the commode. Old Clark too often forgot to flush. We joked about it, but truthfully I used to hope he'd figure that it was just my tactful and indirect way of asking him to do better. When he left the FID a year later, I had one of the flushometers—that's the shipboard name for the chrome flushing toggle switch—mounted on a nice mahogany plaque for him as a going away gift. I was hoping it would embarrass him, but he still thought it was part of our serial repartee.

After a few days the weather began to get colder, and the sky was overcast most days. We were up north of Scotland by this time and had been busy working on first aid drills and mass casualty scenarios a number of times. One morning I was making rounds in the ward and noticed a pale young man with an NG tube sticking out of his nose. Bill Kelly was making notes in his chart, so I asked Bill to tell me about him.

"He's been sick on and off for the last couple of weeks, with a lot of belching sometimes, and occasional stomach cramps. He's lost his appetite, has been pretty listless, and somewhat constipated. I've been treating him as an outpatient for a few days, but he's developed an ileus, so I put the tube down this morning, and I thought I'd watch him on the ward for a couple of days." His name was Sam MacDonald, a second class aviation electronics technician. Thirty-four years is a little bit old for a second class petty officer, but he'd entered the Navy late. It looked like the NG tube would take care of things, but it was a little unusual for acute gastroenteritis to cause an ileus in a person his age.

The next day Sam was still on the ward, and he still had an NG tube. I asked Bill about him again, and he said that Sam seemed to be doing fine, except that he still hadn't had a bowel movement and his abdominal films still showed a lot of gas in his bowel. We talked about the possibility of a bowel obstruction and asked Rock to see Sam, also. Rock thought his treatment was proper but shared our concern that the ileus continued even after the NG tube was in place.

On the third day the ileus was still not resolved, and Bill and Rock thought we needed to do an exploratory laparotomy. We debated all the various options. At this point we were outside the range of any of our aircraft to send him to a European hospital. I had to admit, he had normal blood counts, no laboratory abnormalities, his belly wasn't tender, and it was hard to explain why a man in this condition should have an ileus. For the first time since I'd arrived on the ship, I had an opportunity to discuss a case before the individual wound up in the OR, and, remarkably enough, this time I did agree with Rock (although a little reluctantly) that an operation was necessary. I went up to see the captain on the bridge and explained that we had to find out why gas was being trapped in the young sailor's bowel. I explained about how viruses or other forms of irritation of the organs could cut down on movement of the intestine, but that with an obstruction like this we had to look for some form of blockage—a place where the bowel could fold back upon itself—or even the possibility of a tumor, although that seemed pretty unlikely in a thirty-four-year-old man who had been healthy right up until this point. The captain asked if there were any alternative treatments we could recommend, and I told him that at this point, even if we were on the beach, if conventional treatment hadn't brought any relief, a laparotomy was necessary. Maybe if we had a CT scan or the opportunity to do a barium enema, we'd do that first, but ultimately, with a continued ileus and no explanation, he'd probably have to be decompressed. Out of everything we discussed, the possibility of a tumor was the most alarming to Captain Guitar. "If he has cancer, I want him off the ship."

"Yes, Sir." I took his direction to mean that if a cancer were found in the operation, which I knew wouldn't be the case, that somehow I was expected to get him off the ship. I didn't control the aircraft or the flight schedules, and there was nothing I could do for the present about our aircraft being out of range. Furthermore, we wouldn't want a guy with an abdominal incision to take the G forces of a catapult shot for several days. Helicopter evacuation might be acceptable because of the fewer G forces, but we were even further beyond the range of helicopter transport to land. In short, the captain wasn't interested in a two-way discussion on the subject, so there was no sense in opening a complicated matter right then. Besides, this was a young guy, and although we were forced to relieve the bowel obstruction, cancer was not a very realistic concern . . . even if the captain was sensitive on the subject.

Within minutes after making the incision, Rock discovered a mass in the colon. It was about the size of a plum and had all the characteristics of a malignant neoplasm. Cancer. Rock removed the tumor, leaving Sam with a colostomy. I found myself reluctantly trudging up the seven decks to the bridge to tell the captain that one of his patients had a probable malignant cancer of his colon.

The captain wasn't surprised. He should have been—it wasn't reasonable to have expected a cancer. I suspected the captain was one of those folks who has a semimystical fear of cancer or even the word cancer. He asked how the patient was doing, how he had tolerated the operation, when he would be able to have visitors, and if there anything else we needed to do at the present. I explained that the operation was very well tolerated, but that they were just at that point closing the wound, so he wasn't out of anesthesia yet. The captain said he'd be down to visit him that evening and reminded me what he had said earlier, "We've got to get him off the ship as soon as possible."

Sam did well after the operation. There was no evidence of metastasis at the time of the operation, but a lot of tests remained to be done to see if he had any spread of the tumor and to get started on whatever treatments he would need. Our first job was to be sure he healed well from the operation, that he was well stabilized. The next job was to deliver Sam as quickly as we could to good cancer treatment—although at this point it wasn't the kind of emergency that had to begin within one or two days—and get him to his family in New England.

We were arriving at the Arctic Circle now. Days were getting colder, and men had to wear jackets or double layers on the hangar decks and heavier garments up on the flight deck. Sam couldn't take anything by mouth for a few days after the operation, until his peristalsis would return and the colostomy work. His wound was healing cleanly, though. Aside from the captain's wishes, for purely medical reasons I wanted to send Sam to the Air Force Hospital in Lakenheath, or preferably back to the States as soon as we could safely. He was safe and well cared for here. A healing belly wound can be jostled a lot on a helicopter and can't tolerate the G forces of a catapult shot at all, so we wouldn't want to send him too soon. In addition, his attending physician was Rock Tosser, not me. The attending should have a central role in deciding when to transfer a patient. There should be a special relationship between the attending physician and the patient that any hospital, including this one, should always endeavor to protect.

About the second day after the operation, I raised the subject with Rock. The talk wasn't easy, because he had been cool toward me ever since our first discussion about the appendectomy after Naples. Always a diligent worker, he kept up his office hours and the training he had to do with the corpsmen, but he left the department immediately whenever his work was done. It was obvious we didn't get along.

And we didn't agree about Sam. I felt he should leave the ship and start getting treatment; Rock believed that he didn't need anything yet and could get his oncology at NH Jacksonville. I pointed out that Sam's family was in Newport and that in a week or so we'd be in England, from where he could walk off and fly back on a regular medevac flight to the States. Rock said he'd think about it.

Even though we disagreed, I didn't want to take away Rock's role as the attending physician. What Rock didn't know was that a couple of times a day, in addition to the morning and evening briefs that I presented regularly, the skipper would call me or step in my office to ask about Sam . . . and to ask when I was sending him off the ship. "Captain," I would say, "he's just not stable enough to take the vibration of a helo or the G forces in a COD cat shot."

"But you said he has cancer. He needs treatment, doesn't he?"

"Not necessarily, Captain. But you're right, he does need some testing and scans. Those can wait a little while, though. Certainly until he's stable."

"OK, but I want him off when we go to Portsmouth."

I felt like some of the camaraderie I'd built up with the captain in Benidorm might be slipping.

Up in the North Atlantic we exercised with the Brits, the Danes, and the Norwegians. The Norwegian pilots got especially high marks from our air wing. One day I got a chance to go flying with the Red Lions. They promised we could fly up around the fjords for some sightseeing and take Admiral Kohl over for a conference on the USS *Theodore Roosevelt*. We had to wear an extra piece of survival gear, a watertight suit covering toes to neck. Hypothermia, which can kill you in five minutes or less in the Arctic Ocean, is forestalled a little if you stay dry. Getting into the suits, which have to be personally fitted and swaged together, is an athletic feat, and they are insufferably uncomfortable. After a while I got used to it, though. It was never quite as bad as that cranial I had to wear from Diego Garcia.

The trip to the *Roosevelt* was great. We left the big barn door in the back of the helo open. Admiral Kohl showed me how to fasten the gunner's belt around my chest instead of my waist to enable me to walk around in flight and lean out the door to look around. The *Roosevelt* was the first of the *Nimitz*-class nuclear carriers that I'd been on. This new ship, just a couple of years old, was only 10 or 15 percent bigger than the FID, but it looked like more. I felt like a country boy who just came to the big city for the first time. Stepping into the island, I might not have known I was on a ship. They had a real

USS *Forrestal* (foreground) and USS *Theodore Roosevelt* operating together in the North Atlantic. *PH2 J. P. Buckner, U.S. Navy photo*

ceiling, not an overhead! The bulkheads didn't have pipes and rivets and cables—it looked like the walls in a fancy office building.

Stepping into the flight deck BDS, I felt a little more at home. Two corpsmen, aged and dressed just like my guys back on the FID, were surrounded by all the IV bags, bandages, lights, and sinks in a small emergency treatment room just like ours. As I stood there, though, something was very different. I couldn't tell just then what it was, but it gradually came to me later on. Not the bulkheads, or the overhead, or the size. Not just the more modern appearance. This ship didn't have the hum. It didn't have that smell, a kind of metallic steam and a distant memory of petroleum fuel. I guess it might be like playing football on artificial turf. It's still football, I guess, but if you don't have the smell of the turf to remember, how can you miss it?

For a couple of hours, while Sniffles was in the conference on the *Roosevelt*, we flew in and out of a bunch of the fjords. There were roads here and there along the mountainous coastline connecting the red, brown, and white cottages and villages, but I never saw a car or a truck on any of them. The craggy grey and wooden countryside was even more beautiful in three dimensions from 300 feet than in all the paintings and photos I had seen. The rustic simplicity of the fishing villages impressed me most in the apparent cleanliness and orderliness that one could recognize even from this altitude.

When we returned to the FID, I stopped in to see MacDonald. There was beginning to be some accumulation in his colostomy bag, showing that peristalsis was returning. Rock had let him have a little custard and some fluids by mouth. I thought once he could start eating, Rock would be more comfortable and we could think about sending him home when we got to England.

The "Northern Wedding" exercise was going well according to the ops department. We would be coming to Portsmouth, the largest British naval base, in just a couple of days. The closed-circuit TV was giving background information for the port call and telling the crew where to sign up for tours.

The captain sent word that he wanted me to come up to the bridge. It had to be that he was tired of waiting for me to send Sam off. Bracing for trouble, I hurriedly went by to examine the patient and check over his chart and current lab reports. Then I huffed up the ten decks to the bridge.

I always tried to catch my breath before going to see the captain. It wasn't just good manners, either. Of course, you shouldn't begin a conversation with anybody out of breath, so manners were part of it, but it was self-defense, too. Captain Guitar was a take-charge guy. He was going to dominate any discussions we had, of course—after all, he was the boss—but I didn't want to give him any more advantage than he needed. At least up here in the North Atlantic it was a little cooler than it had been a few weeks before, and my khakis weren't stained with sweat by the time I reached the bridge. After stopping for a little rest before asking the officer of the deck (OOD) for "permission to enter the bridge," I was still breathing deeper than I wanted to. The captain was all business that morning. Uh-oh, I thought, here it comes.

"Doc, have you seen this message?" The captain handed me a message that had arrived the day before. Relieved that I had read it already, and especially relieved that this discussion wasn't going to be about MacDonald, I found my breathing slowed a little. The message was from CINCLANTFLT. Apparently there had been some medical waste and plastics from the *Coral Sea* washed up on the shore in North Carolina. It had attracted some very unfavorable press coverage, and Admiral Kelso, who *was* CINCLANTFLT, was outraged. The message emphatically said we would no longer dump any plastics at sea, and especially medical waste. We were henceforth to store all medical waste and plastics until we were in port, where it would all be treated in accordance with standard practices from that locale. The message was dated 29 August. We had received it yesterday, the thirtieth, and Rick and I had begun grappling with what steps we would need to take to comply. It would be difficult. Virtually every container of any product on the ship was plastic. In medical, almost all the trash we had would either be plastic or have some biological fluid. Little of it could be incinerated, so we were going to have to find some place to store everything. We were on top of it, though, I reassured the captain. "Don't worry, Sir, we've got it under control."

"Good, Doc. This is going to be very important. Make sure we don't have any problem with this, OK?"

Of all the things the CO of this enormous vessel had to worry about, I thought it a little curious that he should be so interested in medical trash. Not a big problem in the big scope of things, I thought. Sure, it would take some work from all of us in the medical department, but it seemed funny that the captain would be so interested in this. Captain Guitar had a way of focusing on some topics that he thought were particularly important. One had to admit, though, that he did have an uncanny sense of what would become dangerous or important. Maybe it was a survival instinct. It made him react to hunches more than he should, though, I thought. This interest in the medical waste was an example of that, just like his agitation about Sam MacDonald.

A couple of days later we arrived at Portsmouth. It seems like it was overcast and drizzly the entire time we were there. It was my first visit to England, but for some reason the gray damp seemed right. The whole crew was in great spirits. Portsmouth was a popular port of call. The Brits and the Brit sailors welcomed Americans as enthusiastically as fond relatives. The local language was similar enough to our own that the guys were able to carry on conversations in which they understood entire passages.

The morning we arrived, Sam MacDonald had taken a full breakfast, and his NG tube had been out for over a day. Rock and I had a long talk about his plans, and he agreed that once the skin staples were removed the next afternoon, Sam would be out of any immediate post-op risks. Candidly, I told Rock that since the captain was so concerned about this case, it would be important to all of us to send Sam home as soon as it would be safe to do so. No cutting corners, but no delay, either.

"I think he wants to finish the cruise with his shipmates," Rock argued.

That's not what Sam had told me, but I didn't dispute the surgeon on that point. "Rock, we have to think about his family and the crew's apprehensions. They're all worried about him, the captain especially. And I know it's not an immediate emergency, but really we shouldn't wait an extra three weeks to get on with his oncology workup."

Finally, Rock reluctantly agreed. He expected to take the staples out the next day, and we could send Sam over to the Air Force Hospital in Lakenheath the day after for transport back to the States. "But only if he's ready. We can't just forget about the patients because the captain is superstitious." I let him have the last word. Guitar was far from superstitious, and I disliked Tosser's implication. . . . Yet I had to admit Rock was right on this point. We really wouldn't send Sam off unless it was clinically safe, but of course the captain wouldn't want that anyway. Rock's tone irritated me, but I didn't want to make him more argumentative, so I let it go. We had an agreement, and that was good enough for now.

Other than one sailor who somehow stole off with the logbook from the *Mary Rose,* the old ship that had been Henry VIII's flagship, we had no major problems or drinking incidents in Portsmouth. We were treated to VIP tours on the Isle of Wight, just across the bay, and several formal dinners with British naval officers. On our third and fourth days in port, I spent a day in London and an evening off the ship in the admin. Sam was up walking around, eating well, and Rock promised me he'd arrange for his evacuation trip back to the States. HM1 Rosen, who was every day proving to be a stalwart, promised me that he would assist Dr. Tosser to be sure it all happened.

After a whirlwind single day seeing the sights in London, I took the train back to Portsmouth and joined a bunch of *Forrestal* officers at a pub near the admin. One guy, named Ronnie Eggers, seemed to know a lot of rock 'n' roll trivia, a challenge I can never pass up. He and I battled back and forth, nearly neck and neck until I smashed him on a question about the Hollywood Argyles (the answer is, Glenn Campbell played lead guitar). Ronnie was from Kansas City, too, so we talked a little about our hometown. A former enlisted air traffic controller, Ronnie was a also a professional actor.

The next day the ship was scheduled to get under way at noon. Seas were so high that boating had to be suspended for several hours, so I couldn't get back to the ship until just before the sea and anchor detail was called away. As my boat pulled up to the camel behind the fantail, Rick Cox was waiting for me, hopping back and forth from one foot to the other like a little kid who has to potty. We started to greet each other when the 1-MC interrupted us, "Senior medical officer report to the captain's in-port cabin immediately." An unheard-of announcement. That kind of broadcast meant not only that the captain was mad, but that he didn't care that the whole ship knew it.

"That's what I came to warn you about," Rick told me, not that I hadn't already figured it out. Rock had decided the seas were too rough to let Sam leave in a boat. The British didn't permit flight ops at this anchorage, so we couldn't fly MacDonald off. The captain was angry that he was still on board.

When I arrived at his office, the captain didn't even look up from his papers. "Nice of you to grace us with your presence, Doctor, since we're getting under way."

I didn't know what to say, so I said nothing.

"I thought I told you to get him off the ship!"

"Yes, Sir, but since he's still recovering from the operation. Dr. Tosser and I didn't feel it was safe for him to be climbing in and out of boats, and the boat ride in these seas could be hazardous for him."

"Would have been nice for you to tell me that, don't you think!"

"I want you to get him off today, before we are out of helo range! Is that clear!"

It was clear all right. When I got down to the department, though, Sam was having a bad day. He had been nauseated all morning. None of us wanted to put him on a helo while he was sick, but if he didn't leave now he'd be stuck on the ship for the whole crossing. Tosser said he couldn't leave that day.

"It's a twenty-minute flight to Lakenheath. He can handle that," I insisted. "Rock, you just lost your vote."

Frankly, I wasn't enthusiastic about sending Sam off while he was sick, either. Yet it was a short flight to Lakenheath, and the man did need to get on home to his family and his workup. Burt Rosen told me that Sam had gone into town the night before and spoken with his wife by telephone. She seemed to accept the situation, Sam said, and since she had talked to him, she wasn't too anxious.

Wait a minute. If it was acceptable to Dr. Tosser for Sam to go in a boat to the phone, why didn't we just send him on to Lakenheath by driver? Rock said he didn't think Sam could be safely driven that far.

I contemplated telling the captain the whole story, but I decided not to. I didn't see the point. After all, I'm still the SMO. I'm the one responsible. Burdening the captain with the details wouldn't get Sam on that helo any faster.

When I went to see Rich Bricker, the XO of the Red Lions, about sending Sam off, my hopes were dashed. Only two aircraft were "up" for this afternoon, and both had just developed problems. We wouldn't be able to send one of our own helos for about ten hours. By then it would be dark, and NATOPS (flight rules) forbid flying anybody not aircrew rated over water after dark. By tomorrow, we'd be out of S-3 range.

Quickly I ran over to the ATO and air ops offices, both of which were on the O-3 level like the Red Lions' ready room. No, there were no deck-qualified American helos in the area that were not already involved in other ops. We called the British local air ops. They let me talk to a senior British flight surgeon. While they could send a helo for a true medical emergency, sending one for a guy who had been here all week and who didn't have an actual emergency at the moment wouldn't really qualify. Sorry, they couldn't send a helo either.

I went up to explain the situation to the captain. I told him that Sam had spoken with his wife, and she was OK. That made the captain feel just a little bit better, but not much. MacDonald would be with us for the crossing. The captain wasn't happy about it, but there was nothing else to do. Still, he had obviously given me some clear orders I hadn't carried out the way he wanted. Having developed respect and fondness for the captain, I regretted losing his confidence.

I went on back down to medical about the time I heard the 1-MC announcement, "Shift the colors." The deck shuddered and moved a little.

We were on the way home.

Chapter 5

Crossing the Atlantic

By the time we left England, I thought I was getting the hang of it. Day-to-day routines of the ship and the department were becoming familiar—to the degree that anything in this tempo and these eighteen-hour workdays could ever be routine. Now that I thought I had the job description in its most concrete terms under control, it was time to start working on the big picture. We needed to improve customer service, fix it so people didn't come and stand in long lines for sick call, for example. I wanted FID sailors to feel like the service in their medical department was as personal and attentive as what they'd receive in a private doctor's office. My other goal was to improve our preventive medicine and surveillance programs and do better with tracking patients. We wouldn't be able to do that without getting our records on a computerized data base, I was sure.

Putting our preventive medicine and surveillance programs on a regular, continuing schedule instead of mammoth, once-a-year marathons would improve quality and could reduce the size of lines sailors would stand in. Every member of the Navy has to have certain things every year, like HIV tests, TB skin tests, and flu shots. The tradition throughout the Navy in the past had been to line up everybody on the ship on a certain few days, draw blood from everybody, stick them with their TB test needle, and give them whatever shots they needed. Like a massive roundup to brand cattle. My, but it was ugly, though.

Massing everybody together created crowds and lines that spilled into spaces well beyond the medical department. Tables and equipment had to be set up in the hangar decks and mess decks to accommodate the masses. Every department on the ship was interrupted or involved. Operations dictated when space was available in the hangars, and adjustments in schedules and meal hours had to be made for the

90

mess decks. Worst of all was the indignity for the sailors. It hadn't changed since those photos from World War II, or for that matter World War I. Grim, expressionless young men were herded like beef on the hoof through impersonal lines of robotlike medical humanoids, also expressionless, holding some medical thing with a point on it, poised to puncture the beef in its arm. Huge, long lines. I hated lines!

Jamming hundreds of people together for all their shots and blood tests set up a grand opportunity for errors, too. If we could only get the whole system into a computer data base we could be more accurate and also schedule more rationally.

Somehow, besides getting the mass and preventive medicine programs straightened out, if I wanted to make the customer services better, I'd have to win over Don Kent. Don held forth on his own over in the ER. He saw patients more or less on referral from sick call and just kept the charts on his private patients in a drawer in the ER. He did have his own exam room over on the same side of the passageway as my office, but it was so filled with paraphernalia—his trunk, piles of amorphous stuff, neckties, old mail, and hideous stacks of unrecognizable clutter—that he really couldn't see patients in there. I always thought somehow I should tell him to clean up his office. If telling a teenager didn't work, though, I figured telling a grown-up doctor wouldn't work either. Besides, it didn't seem right somehow to tell a naval officer to clean his room. I once asked HM1 Brant, the leading petty officer (LPO) in the ER, if we couldn't just return Don's charts to the medical records file room with all the other records. "Oh, no, we can't do that. Dr. Kent wants them to stay here." Even though I was the head of the department, Don's authority over this private practice was a different matter. It didn't occur to Brant, or in fact to anybody but me, that I might have a vote in the matter. Dr. Kent wanted the records to stay there. That was that.

What if somebody needed treatment in the ER during Dr. Kent's treatment times?

Hmmm. Nobody ever thought of that . . . It doesn't happen. That's Dr. Kent's time in the ER.

Well, could it happen? What if somebody needed treatment?

That wasn't an easy one to answer. Maybe they'd have to come back later when Dr. Kent was finished.

Maybe Dr. Kent would let them use the other table, if they'd draw the curtain.

Don hadn't hesitated to speak his mind the first week I was on board. I could tell he wasn't comfortable with me yet. I wasn't sure he would ever become comfortable. He just didn't like me. I planned to talk with him about his "private practice" in the ER, but now wasn't the time. He was clearly the stalwart in the department, along with Art. I had a lot to learn from the two of them, and I needed to win their confidence and their friendship a lot more than I needed to sell my newcomer ideas. Don already saw me as an invader, I thought, and not a very smart one at that. Somehow I would have to win his trust.

The second morning after we left England, Lonnie Prinz came to sick call and said the captain wanted me to come up to his cabin when I was free. The skipper and I hadn't spoken since we left Portsmouth. He had clearly been angry that day, and I was afraid he still had more to say on the subject. I braced myself, but there was no escape, of course. About an hour later, when sick call was finished, I arrived. "You asked to see me, Sir?"

"C'mon in, Doc. Have a cup of coffee. How are things going?"

I mumbled a little about the flu shots, but nothing very coherent. The skipper was obviously busy this week, and I didn't expect him to have time to sit around and chat very long before he delivered the whatever it was I was expecting. He spoke about going home, asked if Ann would be able to come down to meet the ship. Told me he and Martha would like to meet her if she did. Shortly I was feeling more comfortable, but now I was a little perplexed about why the captain wanted to talk.

Gradually, I realized what this visit was about. He didn't invite me up here for idle coffee talk. What we were really talking about was our last meeting, the day we left England. John Guitar was not an apologizing guy. Neither of us would think he had anything to apologize about anyway. We finished our coffee and each had to return to work, but I understood. I had just been told, by my shipmate . . . Sorry I yelled at you, Doc. Maybe you were right. Let's drop it.

From Guitar it was more sincere than if he had said the words, and it was OK with me.

That's why he was the captain.

The crossing was a convenient time for people from the States to do all the inspections a ship had to be put through every year. They mostly had to be done while the ship was under way and the entire crew on board. Doing them at the end of a cruise hit the crew at their most experienced level, in a way, but people were also beginning to get tired then, and equipment problems were accumulating after six months of hard use and limited repair opportunities. Civilians would have a hard time comprehending all the inspections. The secretary of the Navy wanted inspection data, so did Congress, the DOD, and the Naval Occupational Safety and Health Agency (NOSHA). Even though the word "naval" might be in an organization's name, the inspectors were not on your side anytime they came for a visit.

One big inspection was the 3-M inspection, the materials maintenance management system. This inspection, which was one of the most taxing, had to be done every year and tied up every sailor on the ship at one time or another—sometimes for hours. The 3-M system covers every piece of hardware on the ship and every job that any member does, virtually down to the paper clips. For every piece of hardware or equipment there's a line in a master log prescribing the preventive maintenance cycle and a recipelike card outlining the steps in inspection and maintenance. A multimember team of real grouchy and finicky guys comes aboard the ship once a year to check the records in every department. They also nab four or five sailors in each division and test them on how well they do a maintenance job. When they do the test, how closely the sailor follows the card and how well he knows the 3-M rules counts more than whether the gear itself works or the sailor operates it correctly. The 3-M inspection is not just important because the score goes into some unfathomably obscure data base someplace in the Navy; the real reason seems to be that scores on the 3-M inspection are a big part of the competition for the Battle E. The Battle E counts.

The *Saratoga* had recently won the Battle E as the East Coast carrier, edging out the FID by just a few points. In the heartbreaking defeat, the FID had a low score on the 3-M inspection, so Captain Guitar, in his final year in command, wanted to win this time. He wanted very much to win. Captains never would say that they cared about things like Battle Es, though. Captains say things like, "Who cares about that? All we can do is strive to serve the United States in the best way we know how, and let others worry about awards." Captain Guitar believed it when he said things like that, but . . . he wanted to win, too. He liked winning.

This year we had scored 100 in nearly every Compex (competition exercise). We were reportedly a little ahead of the *America* on points, (*Saratoga* was in the yards in Norfolk for an overhaul), so the 3-M inspection was the only potential obstacle. As the inspection neared, we crammed for the test. Ed DeMaestri, a blackshoe who worked in the maintenance department, was put in charge of the 3-M training task force. Like every self-respecting blackshoe, Ed would have preferred to be on a cruiser or destroyer, doing shoe stuff. The exciting jobs on carriers go to aviators. Some things, though, are in the purview of basic shipdrivers, the shoes. Aviators like the XO (call sign "Ozark"), could work hard on 3-M business, but everybody knows that shoes are the best when it comes to this kind of grinding detail. Well, maybe bubbleheads (submariners) are really the best at mind-numbing arbitrary minutiae, but shoes are better at it than aviators. Ed made some really very entertaining film clips, with Ozark and others adding humor to entice the sailors to watch. He also assembled a tiger team of people who went department by department to give classes and coaching. When the 3-M team came, we'd be ready.

One afternoon, early in the translant, Cdr. Kit Hennesy, the CO of the Red Lions, came in for his annual flight physical. An Academy graduate, he had been an aviator for about fourteen years, and he ran a squadron with high morale and a great reputation. He was in fine physical condition, but for the first time, his visual acuity had been a little below 20/20. Looked like he'd need glasses. Glasses don't disqualify pilots anymore, if they already have their wings. Kind of like occasional impotence—needing glasses wasn't something they thought other people should be ashamed of, just a simple, natural, physical phenomenon, not a matter for either panic or shame. "Oh, no, I wouldn't mind wearing glasses if I had to," Kit said. However, he just didn't really think the test was accurate in his case. "You know, I was flying a lot the last couple of days . . . I've been tired. Never been below 20/20 before, Doc. Could you check it for me just to be sure?"

Sure enough, 20/25 both eyes, just a little myopic. Myopia often gets worse in the dark, right when marginal vision is especially critical, particularly in the big H-3 helicopter.

"Well, don't you think this can be just because I'm tired, Doc? Maybe I could check it again after we get back."

I just smiled. Vision is kind of symbolic to aviators. The heritage of that goes back to their first few hours in the culture, when some of their first comrades years ago couldn't cut it because of vision and had to become NFOs instead of entering the pilot pipeline.

"We can check it again after we get back to the States. You can get it done over at Jax, or it might be easier if you come back here to the ship, where we've done the rest of your exam. You know, though, that I have to give you a down chit until either you get glasses or your test is 20/20, right?"

"What about the fly-off? That'll be in daylight and we have two pilots in the cockpit."

"As the CO, you can decide to fly with a down chit, but you know I have to give you one."

Kit knew that, of course, and we didn't argue about it. I knew he'd never fly with a down chit. We agreed he'd come back to see me or a flight surgeon at HS-15's base in Jacksonville to check his eyes after the cruise.

I could have belabored the points that I didn't think fatigue was causing his myopia, or that even if it were, he would be flying fatigued often and we'd have to correct for it. I figured he'd be going to somebody else in the hope that a second opinion would reach a different conclusion.

That night I was invited to the captain's in-port cabin for a "seance" after eight o'clocks. A seance, I soon learned, was a euphemism for a card game. The admiral was there, too, and usually two other guys— at least one squadron CO and either another department head or another squadron CO. Sometimes a sixth player would come. Although we played poker, we of course never gambled real money, just poker chips. This was heady stuff for me, just a doctor, playing with the big guys. They were real good at this. One suspected aviators played a lot of cards in their younger days. Fortunately we didn't play for cash, or I may have lost some real money. It was a time for the admiral and the captain to relax. It had been a long deployment. The banter and needling was truly expert, and riotous. I knew these were smart people, but I was impressed with how funny they could be, too.

There were seances most nights at the end of the cruise, and I found myself invited to most of them, and to dinner beforehand a couple of times. One night, when I was really tired from a particularly long day, I was dealing a hand. The new SuppO, Brice Bennett, was playing that night, too. The captain and the admiral never seemed to be too tired to have fun and be fascinating in conversation. It was infectious, yet it was clear that although aviators could play cards all night, I'd never be able to match that energy. I also wasn't as experienced as the line officers at cards. They had games like high-low and baseball. I'm just a Kansas City boy and we aren't good at card games, so when I dealt we had to play something simple like straight poker. For some reason, a card came off the bottom of the deck once while I was dealing. How it happened I still don't know. My chubby little hands aren't dexterous enough to do that kind of thing on purpose, and the card was something dumb like a three anyway. The admiral quietly said, "No, I think you'll have to deal that one over, Doc. I don't want one from the bottom of the deck." Dealing off the bottom of the deck to an admiral! Who could believe something like that's a mistake? It's not like stumbling on a loose carpet tack. He didn't lose stride or show any rancor, and he kept telling jokes, never repeating any punch lines. Sniffles somehow knew it was just awkward clumsiness, I guess, because he let it pass. First, only quick eyes would have noticed the gaffe. But then, only a person with an abiding trust and patience in others would be able to just let it go and not wonder when it would happen again.

The next morning, the 3-M team flew aboard on the COD. Twelve or fifteen of them were in the team; some wore coveralls, the others khaki. Because of their squinty, gnarly expressions, I figured that either they had been sucking persimmons for the last week or they all had Tabasco sauce in their shorts. They gave us some speech about how they were here to help us, and then they dispersed to try to trip up as many FID sailors as they could. I went back to medical and asked Rick to assemble the corpsmen. Although I spoke to them most mornings at quarters, I wanted to give them one last pep talk about the 3-M inspection. I said I thought they were ready and told them not to feel any pressures from the inspection team. Halfway through my little talk, Chief Henderson interrupted me to say I was being called up in the combat information center (CIC). One of the small boys in the battle group had a medical problem they were calling about.

Speaking to other ships about sick people called for judgment and tact. The young doctors or the IDCs from the small boys only called because they needed help, not because they were looking for a lecture. Sometimes there was enough information, and a confident enough IDC, that we could handle the problem over the radio. More often, the very fact of their calling was evidence that they couldn't handle that patient on that ship. So I was developing the attitude that if the other ship wanted to transfer a patient that meant that they needed to, regardless of what it sounded like on the radio. The captain agreed with that approach. We insisted, however, on consultation first. We needed to warn them if we didn't think the patient could tolerate helo transfer, and we needed to prepare for some patients.

I greeted Steve West, the combat officer. West is a very intelligent guy with a clever wit and an uncrackable, stony expression. He and I had a running repartee, so we bantered for a few seconds as always, each of us sure we had outpointed the other (of course, impartial observers usually knew I had won). Ronnie Eggers was the tactical action officer (TAO) that day. "The *Roberts* has been calling, Doc. Their corpsman needs to talk to you." He handed me the headset from his chair so I could talk right across his desk.

All the ships communicating on the net could be heard, fragments of perhaps a dozen different discussions. The voices were all electronically scrambled so that other nations couldn't cipher the communication. American ships then unscrambled them, so the voices came out with an eerie metallic, machinelike timbre whose only human quality was kind of nasal—whiny and a little high pitched. You can't break in with "Breaker, breaker" like you can in a CB network on the highway. Only critical conversations are permitted on these overburdened nets, so presumably the ongoing discussions were all important. It would be unwise or at least bad manners to presume that one's own message is more important than the one on the air. I waited until there was a brief lull, then I broke in, "USS *Roberts*, USS *Roberts*. This is the *Forrestal* senior medical officer standing by. Over."

A lag for the *Roberts* to receive, unscramble, and respond to my call. "USS *Forrestal*, this is *Roberts*. We'll send for our Doc. Please stand by."

The doctor on the small boys was an IDC, usually a first class on a destroyer and a chief on a cruiser. The sick bay on their ship wouldn't be far from the CIC or the com center. Still, I thought, since he knew I'd be returning his call, he should have been standing by so I wouldn't have to wait around for him. However, it didn't bother me long because I enjoyed watching all the action in the CIC as the guys worked over all their various scopes and scanners and plotters. Because of all the sensitive equipment, the CIC is usually dark. Table or desk lamps are confined to small pools of light where paper has to be read or produced. Conversations are held in moderately low tones so everyone can keep an ear available to monitor background conversations on the several radio nets or hear directions from the combat officer or the TAO if he gives any. The nasal, robotlike voice was carrying on a discussion between two ships about some spare part, and between one other ship and some shore establishment regarding a port call. "Somebody wake the doctor up when the corpsman comes on in case he doesn't recognize where the medical conversation begins," West said.

"Good idea," I answered. "I wish you guys could let me know when Commander West wakes up, too, but I don't think you could tell."

Somebody suggested that neither of us should jump into full-time comedy work, and then the *Roberts* came in. "USS *Forrestal*, USS *Forrestal*. This is the SMDR [senior medical department representative] from *Roberts*. I have a twenty-three-year-old white male with acute abdominal pain. Over."

As usual, the corpsman began with the chief complaint and a little bit of the history of the present illness. In this situation, what we'd usually want to hear next was the physical exam findings, including the vital signs, and then the course of the disease from the first symptoms. We found that on the red phone the corpsmen and young doctors tended to focus on laboratory data and medications. This caller did that. He told me about the white blood cell count last night and again this morning, the urine analysis, the blood sugar, and the EKG. "What about the abdomen?" I had to ask. He answered that there had been no bowel movement. Finally, we determined that the patient's pain was very acute, but episodic. He had experienced some nausea and vomited once several hours ago. Perhaps the pain had radiated toward the scrotum once, but this was uncertain. The abdomen was tender, but not taut. Bowel sounds were either absent or not very active, but we weren't sure because we couldn't tell if the corpsman knew how to listen to the abdomen. There was no flatus. The urine was normal. They had no X ray on the *Roberts,* of course.

We had to suggest transferring the patient, and after he arrived we learned he was suffering from renal colic, symptomatic of a kidney stone.

That night I went up to the bridge to tell the captain that our transferred patient was doing well. I had already passed the word back to the *Roberts.* The captain invited me to a seance that night, but I told him I wouldn't be able to come. The next night was going to be the "Fo'c'sle Follies," so I wouldn't be able to work then, and I had a lot of work to catch up on. "OK, I'm sorry you won't be there, we may not be able to play again for a while." I didn't know yet that the captain was going to be busy with VIP visitors soon. "Look, I know you're going to be doing the flu shots soon. Don't forget what we discussed about medical waste and plastics. I don't want to go through what the *Coral Sea* did." He was really focused on that medical waste issue.

When I went back down to the medical department, we had a number of things to go over in meetings. I began by mentioning the captain's concern about plastics and medical waste. We doctors chuckled about how the aviators pick up on funny little isolated topics to dwell on. Here we just transferred a guy from another ship who could have had a dissecting aorta or some terrible thing, and the skipper was most interested in trash. Rick Cox was less amused. "I wouldn't brush off his concerns too quickly. The man has an uncanny instinct; that's how he got where he is." Rick also was plenty concerned about the medical waste and plastics. "Almost everything we have is plastic, Captain. We're not going to have room for all this stuff if we can't throw it over the side."

"You and I can go over that tomorrow, Rick. For now, it looks to me like we can fit everything in the preventive medicine office head."

Rick disputed that. He thought there would be too much for that one space, and suggested we first use the head from Ward II and spill over to the preventive medicine head, actually the former shower stall, only as a backup space. "And when do you think you're going to have time to walk around tomorrow? You said you want to be up on deck for the UnRep [underway replenishment], the shots are starting, and the 3-M inspection is going on." He was right. The next day was going to be very busy. I told him I'd make the time for a planning tour for the two of us in the stash of trash, but I wasn't very enthusiastic.

We had a number of things to talk about. Although I was beginning to convince the department that we needed to get mandatory surveillance and preventive programs on a continuous cycle, the facts remained: it was the season for flu shots, and while everybody was still trapped on board it would be easier to hit everybody now than after the cruise was over and they dispersed, took leave, and so on. Rick, along with HM1 Rosen and Senior Chief (HMCS) Myers, had worked out schedules for getting everybody done. Since flight ops were over by now except for an occasional COD, we'd be able to use the hangar bay, in three big lines. By taking two large departments, like aircraft intermediate maintenance (AIMD) and supply, in a day, and smaller ones four per day, we could get all the shots done before the preparations of the last couple of days. Those last couple of days, the entire crew would be busy getting the ship super-pretty for arrival, and people would be getting so crazy by then that concentration would be wasted.

For some reason, only about half of the supply of flu vaccine was the right formulation for the transdermal jetgun, so we'd have to use syringes and needles for the shots for half the crew. The gun isn't entirely painless, but it hurts a little less than a needle. Also, some people develop troublesome blisters or other reactions from the jetgun, so it can't cover everybody. With those exceptions, however, we in the department favored the jetgun. Sterilization is a lot simpler, and so are supplies: no needles to deal with, be pricked by, or throw away, and no plastic syringes. It's almost as easy as rubber-stamping correspondence. Step on the pedal. Next. Touch the gun to the arm. Step on the pedal. Next. The only time consumed is checking off the patient's shot record on the left-hand side of his health record. Too bad we could only use the jetgun on half of them. We decided to use it until we ran out of that form of vaccine and then shift over. We'd ask every sailor if he'd prefer to have the needle. Those who had trouble with the gun knew who they were. Everybody else would be amused by the question. What sane individual would prefer a needle? At any rate, we couldn't use the gun for more than half the flu shots.

That meant we'd be using an additional twenty-six hundred syringes and needles beyond the several thousand already needed for TB tests.

Finally the marathon was all set. We would start in the morning. Rick had called the DivOs together from all over the ship and explained the system. I had discussed it at eight o'clocks. Although I had an uneasy feeling about this big project, I told myself it was just because I hated the lines. After all, we did need to get caught up, and the crew did need the flu shots. We were going to do this right, and it was the right thing to do, so I resolved to quit worrying about it.

It was time to dismiss the meeting and let the medical officers and chiefs get back to work or, for those who could, to relax for the evening. "Not yet, Captain, did you forget we have to talk about Womple?" Yes, I'd forgotten. We had to talk about whether Womple could go home early on the COD. I had wrestled with whether just Rick, HMCS Myers, and I should discuss this, since it involved just one corpsman, or whether the other officers and chiefs should stay for the discussion. We wanted to keep discussions about individuals private, of course, which was an argument for the smallest group. On the other hand, sending one corpsman home early could have an impact on the thirty others who had to stay, and besides, I was new and all the khaki* in the department knew SK3 Womple and could advise me.

"OK, Senior Chief and Lieutenant Cox have to stay. We're going to talk about Petty Officer Womple. Everybody else is invited to stay, but you can leave if you want to." Nobody left.

The senior chief led off. "SK3 Womple's got neighborhood trouble again. We got a Red Cross message this afternoon. His neighbors are complaining about the chickens and pets in the yard, and the local health department may have the family evicted." One of the functions of the American Red Cross is communication with command about family emergencies. Arden Womple was a troubled guy. He and his family had a lot of problems because of all the animals in the house and the yard. Also, Womple was not a model sailor. He had trouble with alcohol for one thing, and he could never pass the semi-annual physical fitness test for another. Sometimes I wondered if the two problems were really just one. If he'd exercise now and then, he'd have less time to drink.

"Didn't he have to be flown back early at the end of our last deployment?" Don asked.

---

*Officers and chiefs wear khaki uniforms, and everybody else wears dungarees or some other work uniform, such as coveralls. So the term "khaki" is often used to refer collectively to CPOs and officers.

"That's right," Rick added, "and halfway through REFTRA too."

"Captain, I think this is just more of his manipulative BS," somebody added.

Well, given Womple's general attitude and surliness, his motives might be suspect, but it was a real Red Cross request. We didn't question the Red Cross. They were on the scene at home. I said we had to accept the Red Cross authority.

"There's no question about his going, guys. What we have to discuss is how to tell him, and how to deal with the rest of the department."

"No problem, Captain," said the senior chief. "I bet some of the other guys'll be glad to see him go, even though it'll leave more work."

It was true. Womple could act like a bully to the patients as well as the HNs and many of the other corpsmen. He was scrawny but he just looked mean. His streetwise diction and surly demeanor buffaloed even some of the corpsmen who outranked him. He was older and just seemed to have a lot of hard miles on him.

Womple had been counseled about his attitude, his appearance, and his demeanor toward patients many times. He usually would sulk about it, but he had a remarkable record of seeming sincere and winning reprieves just before the worst possible things, like captain's mast or administrative separation. Still, his promotions were slower than Congress, which was why he might face high year tenure expulsion. With almost sixteen years of service he should have been a chief—an E7—for a couple of years already, but instead he was still an E4 with no prospect of promotion. Also, Womple was an SK, a storekeeper, by training. Somehow he had migrated out of the supply department, so he was a little bit of a foreigner by working in medical anyway. He seemed to sulk around much of the time and generally spread gloom. About three times he'd been processed for separation because of alcohol, but it never quite went through.

The Navy had always required people to stay in shape, but an enforced fitness test wasn't widely applied until around 1980. With the gradual improvement in retention and pride in the 1980s, the Navy established a three-item battery: sit-ups, push-ups, and a mile-and-a-half run. You only had to do about thirty-five sit-ups and about twenty-five push-ups to pass, and the run could be done as slowly as fourteen and a half minutes at Womple's age. Arden usually failed the run, sometimes could barely pass the sit-ups, but never could do the push-ups. Two or three times, he had been in the process of separation after he failed the test. Once he worked out a lot for two months, and his prior command dropped the proceedings. A couple of years before, he was on his way out from the FID when the ship's legal officer found some procedural omission. Then Womple exercised for a couple of months and quit drinking, and the process had to start over.

However, I was worried that physical prowess might really just be a convenient scapegoat for dealing with a troublesome sailor. Was it honest to get him out just for a few calisthenics? The real reason was he should just flat-out be fired, but it's hard to fire people from the Navy, just like from any big company.

We talked about this for a half hour or so, everybody seeming to want to submit an unpleasant experience they'd had with Womple. Finally, though, everybody agreed with me that our frustration mustn't stand in the way of his family's needs. I resolved to discuss the matter with the chaplain, too, to make sure we gave Womple any support he needed. HMCS Meyers would make the arrangements with the ATO for Womple to leave on the COD as soon as possible.

The Follies

When the meeting was over I went up to the fo'c'sle for the "Fo'c'sle Follies," a tradition on all carriers. The Follies are put on by the air wing twice during the cruise. It's a long tradition for the "visitors" from the wing to satirize their experiences and alleged abuse at the hands of the ship, and to lambaste whoever from the ship's company has attracted the most ire from the wing. The first part of the program is for the wing to recognize the best performers in various aspects of airmanship and safety, with competition among the squadrons for the best landing scores, best aircraft availability scores, and best safety records. This competition is richly and ingeniously mixed with humor, but not gently. The pilot or squadrons with the lowest landing scores are hooted and squirted by waterguns. Catcalls interrupt the proceedings frequently.

After the formal part of the proceedings, each squadron in turn sings a song written for the occasion, usually bawdy, but always either boasting uproariously about themselves or cutting one of the other squadrons—or some unlucky target among the ship's company. This night, the "Bulls" of VA-37 had special T-shirts with the picture of NFO wings in a circle with a diagonal line through it, like a no smoking sign. The light-attack squadrons, VA-105 and VA-37, who flew the only single-seat airplanes left in the wing (and were proud of it), missed no opportunity to malign the NFOs, who were generally as numerous on the ship as the pilots. As the night wore on, a few of the

Bulls were struck by eggs or whipped cream from unseen assailants. The Bulls' song was accompanied by a trumpet and guitar duet and had some clever puns and insults about the miniboss.

The best song of the night was done by the VA-176 Thunderbolts. In a somewhat unusual departure, there was very little satire directed at specific individuals, except for an obligatory insult about how the miniboss slowed down flight ops by scolding pilots. Putting words about bombing missions to the music of "On the Street Where You Live," the Thunderbolts had the entire audience in laughter. It was certainly audience-specific humor, and would probably fall into the category of "politically incorrect" by now.

Then there were monologues by Pat "Martini" House, the air group commander (CAG), and by Admiral Kohl. Since the Follies are a production of the wing, the CO of the ship is an honored guest but not truly a participant. The CAG was OK, but Sniffles definitely stole the show. Somehow he squeezed in some inspiring words about the success of the cruise and the importance of teamwork, but his stage presence and stream of outrageous jokes were convulsive. Most of his jokes were about aviators and sailors, their families, and the stresses and apprehensions about coming home. Some had such crazy and baffling punch lines that any audience would have loved them, and yet even in that happy moment, more so later that night, everybody realized that the jokes were funny because they made fun of all the apprehensions and concerns that were gradually bubbling up as we were nearing home. It was sneaky. Every face was cracking and everyone was laughing, but Sniffles had slipped in a note about dealing with homecoming. He didn't dwell on it, but hid it in the merriment and let it linger there. Sniffles ended his conquering monologue and then the CAG introduced the skits.

For an introduction the CAG said, "The only rules are there are no rules." That was certainly an understatement. Hilarious as they were, the skits, one performed by each of the squadrons, were merciless. First was a brief one about a discussion between Captain Guitar and Admiral Kohl regarding alleged confusion on the bridge. Abruptly there were a couple of zingers about Captain Guitar's marital history—he had been married a couple of times—that were pretty disrespectful. I thought I saw the captain's ears redden, but he, being a dutiful aviator, would always just say "no rules."

The A-7 guys had a skit with faces stuck out of a sheet over boots, to look like short human puppets. These ridiculous-looking characters were funny enough, but they parodied confusion in a two-man

A-6 cockpit talking with confused air traffic controllers on the FID. Even the Thunderbolts who flew the A-6 laughed achingly, but in revenge they broke out their water pistols and shaving cream cans to pelt the other squadron.

Finally, near midnight, the Follies ended. The show was as hilarious as I'd always heard it would be, albeit even more caustic than its rough reputation. Some people may have seethed a little about the jokes, yet they knew the rules, and they had attacked senior officers back when they'd been junior officers themselves. It was a ritual for the end of the cruise, a permissible way to express some of the tensions from this dangerous and confining life. Come on, it said, let's open up those wounds, laugh and heal one another. We are all brothers here, and the cruise is over.

Still laughing as I filed out of the fo'c'sle with the crowd, I mulled over the ingenious value of the Follies. The culture of Naval Air depended on a complex blend of things. Dedicated loyalty and affection for the team. Imperative sharing and constant learning. Pervasive optimism, and conviction that ours is the winning team. Most of all, maybe, fun. Six months at sea with only three port calls can strain the fabric. The "Fo'c'sle Follies" wasn't just a hilarious show—it was, I realized, an example of why this team keeps winning.

Before I went to bed that night, I stopped down at the wardroom. In the lounge a number of guys were sitting around playing cards or chess, watching a movie on the big TV in the corner, unwinding before going to bed. The informal dining room had a popcorn maker like the kind you see at carnivals or movie theaters, and there was popcorn available most nights. It was near midnight too, so midrats (midnight rations) were available, usually just sandwiches and chips.

I saw Warner Hobs, the first lieutenant, who was getting to be a pretty good friend. "Hey, good show, huh?"

No response but a raised eyebrow. "Didn't you go down to the Follies?"

"Yeah, I was there for a while."

"Well, I'm still laughing. I guess you didn't think it was as funny as I did."

I expected Warner to make some blackshoe comment about adolescent aviator behavior, but he had liked the Follies fine. He just had other things on his mind. "Gonna be busy the next few days, Doc."

We in medical were going to be frenzied with catching up on all the TB and HIV tests and medical record reviews. We had agreed to do the annual body fat measurements at the same time, adding just one more notch to a hectic program. So I too had been thinking about how busy it was about to become. Thinking about SK3 Womple's problems, too, I had come down to the wardroom before bed to unwind. Warner had some other things on his mind.

"Yeah, I guess the 3-M inspection is going to be a hassle, eh?"

"Oh, hell, I forgot about that! That's even worse!"

"There's something worse?" I was getting interested now. The festive final week was beginning to sound threatened.

"Right in the middle of the 3-M inspection in a couple of days we have our last UnRep. I've got a broken pad eye we have to fix before that, and then you know all the VIPs are going to start arriving tomorrow and they'll all be hanging around while all the activities are going on."

I finished my popcorn in a hurry and went to bed. This was going to be a busier week than I'd expected.

Early the next morning, the corpsmen started getting set up for the flu shots, blood tests, and TB tests. We had special tables set up on both the aft mess decks and up in Hangar Bay I. Master Chief Morgan from the supply department had interceded on our behalf to use premium space on the mess decks. He said he owed us the favor because Doc Corbett had been so good to him. At the time I thought Master Chief Morgan seemed awfully solicitous. Was his speech a little slurred? I asked myself. Senior Chief Myers and Rick Cox had scheduled everything as carefully as they could. Right after morning sick call, we started the scheduled runs. People were to show up in their physical training (PT) gear to make it easier to take the waist and neck measurements the Navy required for body fat determination. Designated record keepers checked painstakingly assembled data bases to see what tests or immunizations the members needed. It worked remarkably well, but the whole department was involved. The usual medical department functions still had to go on, but we had pulled staff for the mass program. This meant the guys still in the department had to work a lot faster than usual, and everybody's work shift extended from twelve to fourteen or fifteen hours a day.

I have to admit I was kind of proud to see the process go so well. Hundreds of people filed into the lines and progressed as planned from one station to the next. Impressive and organized though it might have been, though, I vowed we'd never be in this position again. It was a part of military medicine we needed to get rid of. People should be able to sit in a private place and have private, quiet conversations and treatment when their health is involved. We were going to get to that point on the *Forrestal,* I determined. As a representative of the command, I had to feel that this wasted time. No matter how well we did it, making all these people queue and wait—even just fifteen minutes each—was very costly. Fifteen minutes times 5,300 would be over thirty-three workweeks tied up just by those standing in lines.

We were generating a huge mound of trash, too. Most of the squadrons in the wing had done their TB skin tests on a different cycle, but we were still going to use more than three thousand tuberculin syringes just for the TB tests and almost four thousand needle sets for the HIV tests.

Rick Cox went with me to check the storage of all the medical trash we were generating. The bags were stashed down in the head in Ward II—after they were sterilized in the autoclave. It didn't look as though we'd need more than the space in the Ward II head, but if we did we could use the former shower stall in the space we used as the preventive medicine office. Looked as though we had it under control. I didn't know why medical waste had caught the captain's attention so much. He sure had enough other things on his mind this week. Regardless of the reasons, Rick and I knew that proper disposal of medical waste and plastics was more important now than it had ever been, so we were determined not only to keep it under control, but especially to reassure the captain that it was.

Bostik Is a Book Lover

It was a busy day, like every day at sea. I had promised the doctors that we would review our medical library and order some new volumes. The department had a couple of journal subscriptions and about fifty books. All physicians are expected to own a few of their favorite texts, but the department really needed a few new reference works.

We went around the room, letting every member suggest books that the whole department needed. Rock suggested a current volume on basic orthopedics. Don wisely pointed out the large number of skin problems we saw and suggested a good picture atlas of dermatologic problems. Brice Bostik, in his Tiggerlike enthusiasm, jumped into the derm discussion.

"Have any of you seen this derm book?" he asked, pulling a small, spiral-bound pocket book out of a beat-up old canvas gym bag. "I used it in medical school, and I think it's just what we need here."

Rock asked if he was sure he didn't mean osteopathic school. Tigger didn't seem to take offense, even though some MDs are still a little contemptuous of DOs. In the military we've mostly outgrown that, but some still don't consider DOs their true equals. Didn't bother me; I didn't think Rock thought I was his equal, either.

"There doesn't seem to be much text and clinical guidance in that book, though," Bill Kelly said.

"It tells you just what you need to know," Brice answered. "Look, there's a picture of each lesion and right beside it the name and the dose of meds for treatment. Just what you need."

That would be fine, Don said, but we still needed a good derm reference. He suggested one in addition to Brice's pocket book. Then Don suggested we consider a good text on X rays of the extremities.

"This is just what we need," Tigger said, pulling another spiral-bound pocket book out of the old gym bag. "Great diagrams, easy to read, not a lot of useless text, you know?"

The group agreed his little pocket book was handy, but it didn't think it was quite as detailed a reference as we sometimes needed when there was a tough film to study. We went around, bringing up books on four or five topics. For every one, Brice had a little spiral-bound pocket book that he pulled out of that bag. "Brice, have you ever read an honest-to-god book? Do you know what a hardback *is?*" Don asked him. Don liked big, difficult books. "Hey, why bother," Brice answered, as proud as if he had just solved America's illiteracy problem. "This is the kind of book you really need. May not impress anybody sitting on your bookshelf, but these babies fit right in the pocket of your white coat. You've always got 'em right where you need 'em."

Art observed, however, that none of us wore white coats on the ship, and besides, since Brice had just shown us his entire medical library of nine spiral notebooks, a nine-pocket white coat was a critter he'd never seen. I'm still not sure, but I really believe those may be the only nine books Brice ever owned.

All that day, the lines kept coming and we moved people through. Fortunately, it wasn't a busy week for any illnesses or injuries, so we kept up with sick call and normal work.

On the day of the last UnRep, Warner apprenticed me to BMCS Jones, the archetypal bos'n's mate. Senior Chief Jones had a craggy Victor McLaglen face that matched his sawmill voice. He showed me what the guys up on the bridge had to be doing to steer us to our approach to the USS *Milwaukee,* from which we would take on fuel, mail, and supplies. Two ships can't just come alongside one another, shut down, and pass things back and forth. Dead in the water, they can't control their positions, so the waves would knock them into each other, and modern ships would flail one another to erector sets.

The solution was to maintain steerage by steaming side by side close enough to stretch cables between the two ships. The warship was to make formation on the replenishment ship, whose job it was to maintain a straight course and a steady speed.

Conning alongside required keen seamanship, because if you got too far away the cables and hoses stretched between the two ships would snap under high tension and could cut a bos'n's mate in half as they whipsawed back. If you got too close, the two ships would be sucked together (called the Bernoulli effect), perhaps so strongly that the rudder couldn't overcome it, or—just as bad—that such a keen turn was needed that the aftercoming fantail on the carrier would still dash into the hull of the replenishment ship. Years before I had seen in the news that two Navy ships, completely alone in the vast Indian Ocean, had collided. How could such a stupid thing happen? I had thought at the time. Big ocean; little ships. They had the whole Indian Ocean to themselves, why get in each other's way? Now I understood. It had to have been in an UnRep, and the Bernoulli effect sucked them together.

Down on the hangar bay, BMCS Jones talked one of the gunner's mates into letting me shoot the cat's paw over to the *Milwaukee*. "On the *Milwaukee*," our loudspeaker announced, "stand by for shot lines forward, midships, and aft!" With a shotgun, I fired the cat's paw, a ball of heavy cord, over to the other ship, trailing out line as it flew. Gunners forward and aft did the same. Bos'n's mates on the *Milwaukee* scurried to catch the line and then tied rope to the ends of it, after which we pulled the rope back over to the *Forrestal*. Finally, using those guide ropes, we were able to attach cables and refueling hoses between the two ships. Since it was near the end of the cruise, we didn't need much more than fuel from the *Milwaukee*, but we did take a couple of pallets of mail and some spare parts. It was dangerous work, with tons of equipment sliding over high-tension cables, arrested and guided by bos'n's mates pulling on ropes. Heavy leather gloves prevented most blisters, but careless movements could quickly sacrifice a finger. A number of the workers had to be tied to a capstan to be sure they wouldn't topple overboard if they slipped or fell.

The *Milwaukee* and most other replenishment ships carried a couple of CH-46 Sea Knight helicopters. These twin-rotor helos were used by the Marines to carry troops, but on these ships they were cargo haulers. They had a big capacity, and their superior maneuverability was important for the adroit transfer of cargo from one ship to the other. Replenishment done by air is called VertRep (vertical replenishment).

Most of the time UnRep and VertRep were done simultaneously. The whole UnRep and VertRep today was over in less than two hours, although the preparation and cleanup added another couple of hours. Art Hayes had once described the process as a ballet, and he was right.

However, normal work and UnReps weren't all the *Forrestal* did that week. The 3-M inspection team had been on board for several days, and they were like the commie spies in J. Edgar Hoover comic books in the fifties—they were everywhere. Anyplace a sailor was trying to work, there was a 3-M inspector asking him to demonstrate his preventive maintenance program. He had to faithfully go to the little instruction card kept in a special file place in the workspace and then pick up exactly the right tools for the job at hand and then go back and log it in the three separate books or charts. Ed DeMaestri or the XO—or their assistants—tried to go around and see how well we were doing. All FID sailors knew the 3-M inspection was important, but we all especially knew it was something you could put a score on, so it counted toward our winning the Battle E—the carrier championship, as it were.

The 3-M inspection wasn't all of it by any means. The Navy Occupational Safety and Health (NAVOSH) team was on board, too. Industrial hygienists, environmental health officers, technicians— they all came for the annual NAVOSH inspection. There are about two dozen screening and prevention programs on the ship, ranging from hearing conservation, heat stress prevention, asbestos surveillance, and mercury and lead monitoring, so the NAVOSH inspectors were in every workspace, too. Sometimes sailors were confused about whether the inspector at hand was from the 3-M team or NAVOSH. The NAVOSH guy would arrive with his air-sampling gadget, his chemical-testing set, or his questionnaire, and the poor sailor would dutifully head off to the cabinet to get his preventive maintenance cards, only to realize he was responding to the wrong inspection.

The food sanitation inspection team was on board from AIRLANT, too. Food sanitation was a target of stiflingly frequent inspections. For one thing, the preventive medicine techs in my own department inspected every gallery, scullery, bakery, and eating area on the ship several times weekly. The cooks and in fact the whole supply department hierarchy hated to see my guys coming. There is no acceptable level of mediocrity in dealing with cleanliness and sanitation. It just has to be done right, but that sometimes adds a level of frustration and tension for the cooks if the inspectors are not considerate or tactful. Indeed, I frequently had to warn HM2 Ryan Hart that it was our job to promote sanitation, to help the food service do better, not just to punish and expose them for shortcomings. So, when the food sanitation inspectors came on board, it was to add not merely one more in the endless parade of inspections, but even one more irritant to S-2 (the supply division that ran food services).

The ship was crawling with inspectors of several kinds, but just the number and range of all these inspections wasn't enough to explain what a nuisance they were. Ships get inspected to exhaustion by themselves and outsiders all the time. Although this was more than usual, and irksome at the end of a cruise, what made this klatch of inspections particularly irritating was that these were all especially picky inspections. The food guys crawl on their bellies to find the little nitty microscopic grease smudges that even my sleuths had perhaps missed the week before (you see, the food sanitation inspections would affect and reflect upon not just S-2, but also medical, the XO, and, of course, the CO). The NAVOSH guys come and interrupt a busy forklift operator to ask him about work and rest cycles, earplugs, and so forth. The 3-M inspectors more than once inadvertently asked one of the other inspectors to demonstrate some of their preventive maintenance procedures, provoking relieved pleasure from an onlooking crew member but surprisingly little amusement from the other inspector. The crew was beginning to get more and more restive about coming home. The hangar deck was full of lines of people getting their shots and TB skin tests; everybody had to get at least one needle, so this was a further aggravation in the hectic activities. With all these strangers and all this activity, nerves among mere mortals would have begun to fray.

One additional little feature for us in medical was that the food sanitation team and NAVOSH team were in fact composed in significant part of Medical Service Corps officers and some chief corpsmen, the environmental health and industrial hygiene specialists. They would come down to our spaces in any spare moments, letting us feel like targets of opportunity. Inspectors, you get the feeling, are like IRS auditors. Once they get in the door, anything they find they consider fair game. One member of the food service team was Lt. Cdr. John Poirot, a very intense, very precise fellow. Intense and precise are words that you like when you use them to describe a football coach or somebody who works for you. They're not happy words when they fit somebody who's inspecting you. Besides doing the food inspection, this prim, bookish fellow, who carried a thermometer in his pocket for measuring the temperature of cleaning water, had a personal interest in the new instructions about medical waste.

"I guess you got the CINCLANTFLT message about plastics and medical waste," he said, in what was disguised as a conversational tone, but which I was convinced was a ploy of some sort. I thought at the time that his lips were pursed as he asked.

"Yeah, we got it," Rick answered. "The captain is right on board, too. Do you want to see where we're stashing the stuff?"

"Oh, no, I'm not here for that, I was just curious. Just wanted to know if you needed any help."

This was my first contact with John Poirot. Brice Bennett had the same impression that I did, that Poirot was a snippy, inquisitive professional inspector. A couple of things didn't fit, though. Poirot was a former Marine, had a couple of tattoos on his forearms, and wore an impressive row of ribbons over his left pocket. These aren't things that often go with the kind of trouble-making inspector he seemed to be. Although I didn't think about it very much, I was troubled a little bit that I hadn't pegged John Poirot very clearly yet. Oh well, after these inspections I'd never deal with him again.

Too Much Company

In detail after detail, the inspections and all their derivative activities complicated the trip home. But there was still more complicated outside interference. The VIPs.

There had been what I thought were VIP guests coming on board in our three port calls—local dignitaries and people who commanded the special attention of the captain or the admiral when they came to tour the ship. No, those weren't real VIPs. Real VIPs came on board in small numbers when we got under way from England, or flew on board from the COD every day after we left. They all needed special tours of the ship—and staterooms, of course. The ones who attracted the most attention were Sen. Lawton Chiles and seven or eight of his staff. Senator Chiles, the senior senator from Florida—the ship's home state—had announced that he'd be retiring from the Senate at the end of this term, within just a few months. So clearly this fact-finding trip was not a ploy to garner attention. No press accompanied him.

Well, maybe the press hadn't come just to accompany Senator Chiles, but they definitely had come nonetheless. They seemed to leave the senator alone, I was told, but they wanted to see everything else. Human-interest stories from the end of a six-month cruise were maudlin, funny, provocative—a lot of things. The carrier is very photogenic, so the reporters, both TV and press, used their photographers a lot. A popular radio station sent along one of the most popular disc jockeys, who would record some shows from the ship to play on the air for a day or two before we arrived.

So, the cruise was coming to an end, and everybody was busy trying to maintain safety during the final few weeks. The XO and the first lieutenant were trying to get all possible cleaning and painting done before we got back to the States. The boss and miniboss were trying to clean the hangar and paint the hangar and flight deck surfaces for a good appearance for all of our families when we arrive in Mayport. The CAG and AIMD were trying to get all the airplanes in 100 percent ready condition for the fly-off so all the planes could leave the ship a few days before we landed. The 3-M inspection, a source of discontent from the year before and one of the most arduous and time-consuming inspections a ship must endure, was going on. A handful of other picky inspections were interrupting everybody's work. (We didn't have time to be grateful that INSURV and OPPE, the only two worse inspections for nonnuclear carriers, weren't happening.) We were using thousands of syringes we had to sterilize and store on board to give everybody skin tests and flu shots, for which everybody was standing in long lines—which I hated. Now, on top of all that, we have to put on the happy face and escort all these VIPs around.

Captain Guitar seemed to thrive on all this activity. His daily 1-MC talks to the crew made all the hassles sound like opportunities, and, in fact, the crew seemed to take it that way, too. Every time I stepped into the passageway, there was a tour going past with some of Senator Chiles's staff or a reporter, or an inspector was measuring and recording some gauge or quizzing some crew member. The hangar was busier than it had been for the past three months. Like Lilliputians buzzing over Gulliver's body, mechanics and technicians covered and protruded from every airplane and engine, getting them ready for the fly-off. Dozens of others from the supply and air departments were shifting loads back and forth to get ready for the end of the cruise and somehow touching up paint and the deck surfaces. All this extra turmoil was complicated by the passage of various visitor groups getting their tours (all greeted with smiles and welcoming grace) and lines of people over in the corners getting their shots. Ozark came around patting people on the back, and the captain got around a lot.

Sam MacDonald was recovering well from his operation, and he was up and around. We knew he'd require further specialist evaluation for his cancer when we arrived, and there were a couple of other guys who would require specialist consultations back in Jacksonville.

So Rick and HM1 Rosen arranged for an ambulance to meet us when we arrived in Mayport. The captain and the admiral faithfully came down to see all the sailors on the ward every day. Even on the busiest days, they never forgot to do this. Besides his genuine concern for the sailors, the captain still had a special discomfort with the specter of a cancer lurking on his ship.

On the day we finished off all the shots and TB tests, I was out in the port passageway supervising the storage of bags of syringes when the captain sprang out of the ward. "Well! Looks like the doctor is in today! Missed your nap time today, Doc? Seems like every time I come by here you're out." I enjoyed his repartee, but the corpsmen enjoyed it even more.

"Doc, got a minute? I'd like to talk to you about one of your patients." Rich Gilboy, the admin officer, was with him. We went into my office.

"How's MacDonald doing?"

"Very well, Sir. He's eating all right and doesn't have much pain."

"He's not in any danger now?"

"No, Sir."

The captain asked about flying him off the day before we arrived in order to get him to the hospital as quickly as we could. I discussed that with Rock, who was adamantly against a catapult shot. I had to agree with him, but his staunch inflexibility and angry arrogance were insidiously making me lean toward arguing the opposite position, even though I knew we shouldn't put Sam on the COD. Besides, we were now only about four days out. With each day that passed there was less difference between flight time and just waiting until we arrived.

Four days before we arrived, since it was the fall, the annual Combined Federal Campaign (CFC) was in season. Time for the annual FID TV marathon. The captain hosted the show late at night and people offered up various prized personal possessions or stunts in return for bids on lottery tickets for the CFC. Somebody offered up a Hank Aaron baseball, somebody else Jay Silverheels' autograph. I offered to swab and wax the decks in the medical department in return for a $300 donation, which my guys raised within twenty minutes. It took me over three hours to work it off, but for the whole three hours I was cheered on and jeered by no fewer than fifteen corpsmen.

Knowing we were going to be bringing Sam all the way with us, the skipper didn't want that to be the subject of press attention or of panic among other families. He said he wanted a tasteful but honest notification to be sent ahead to the ombudsmen, not for general release but so they could answer any questions if they were assaulted on the subject. I immediately went to the XO to see if he could talk the captain out of this. The ombudsmen weren't involved in this in any way, I told him. Can't you talk the captain out of notifying them? No, the message had to go. I went to Rich Gilboy. No, he said, he saw my point, but the captain was definite about it, and Rich himself agreed that the situation might be kept better under control if in a public panic the ombudsmen knew enough to help us keep calm in the community. I still thought nobody outside either the command or Sam's family needed to know anything, but I went along with Rich and helped draft the message.

I don't know how the captain thought we would send the message he wanted without the word cancer in it. But when the message was released, the captain was angry the other way. "Doc, of all people, you should know that cancer worries people! Why would you send a message like that!?" Rich and Ozark and I just looked at each other in befuddlement. He was our captain and we loved him, but we agreed he wasn't always easy to please.

The arrival was coming close. Three days out we were within range of the jets. All but one F-14 were "up." All the planes were cleaned and had paint and trim touched up. We all crowded up to Vultures' Row, pri-fly, and any places up on the roof where it was legal to stand while the squadrons launched their airplanes. Last to launch were the F-14s—flown by the Tomcatters of VF-31 and the Red Rippers of VF-11. After launch they circled back around and gave us a flyby. They are beautiful in flight. With their wings swept back, they look like they're alive. The Rippers had posted a guy in pri-fly who announced over the 5-MC, "And now, approaching from the east, gentlemen, the World Famous Red Rippers, Pistol Robertson commanding. The Red Rippers wish to thank you for the cruise. God bless America." The announcement was timed perfectly to be punctuated by the low pass of the squadron in a loud and tight formation.

The deck was clear now. The helos would leave the next day, then there would be no airplanes left. The hangar bay, cavernous without any customers, echoed in stark unemployment. The flight deck was empty. I'd been looking forward to the fly-off, but now that they were gone I wondered why.

The morning of 5 October was bright and sunny, about sixty degrees, perfect for Florida. We hit the St. Johns buoy right on time at a little after 0900. From the inlet you could see the crowds on the pier and a bunch of people standing all the way out on the breakwater. I went down to stand with John Gunther and a few other senior officers on

Sponson One, where the forward brow would go. There was a band playing and a bunch of TV cameras all around. We searched the crowd for our wives. The deployment had been a lot longer for them than for us. We knew that, but we were a lot happier to see them, we figured, than they were to see us.

I found Ann down in the crowd and got her attention. How would I be able to describe any of this to her? Whether I ever could or not, the *Forrestal* was home now.

Chapter 6

Bad News

✚ The bulkheads, decks, and colors may all seem just about the same, but it isn't at all the same ship once the "yard monkeys" come on board. The wear and tear on a ship from a six-month deployment is unequaled in almost any other industrial plant. Even commercial vessels that may operate just as often have only a few percent of the crew density that a warship does. Also, modern capital ships are constantly fine-tuned and upgraded to remain literally up-to-date in critical technology. During ship's restricted availability (SRA), an intermediate level of overhaul is done. Electronics, tactics, aviation, all of the modern science of warfare evolves just as rapidly as space travel in this electronic age. Five thousand people live, walk, run, and pout in that vessel for six months. The sheer pace and density of work takes a heavy toll, and periods of renovation and repair must be interspersed with operating times just to keep the ship functioning. A thirty-year-old ship such as the FID had undergone the cycle many times. Every year it would need more service to stay on the line.

While Mayport is not itself a shipyard, there is a genuine shipyard over in Jacksonville just ten miles away, with a couple of contractors. When one of the ships in Mayport needs an SRA-level overhaul, the contractors have branches out in Mayport, and they service our ships at our own pier. This is especially true for the aircraft carriers, which are simply too large to fit into the shipyard at Jacksonville Landing on the St. Johns River downtown.

Shipyard workers are a unique breed of people. Just being a welder, for example, doesn't qualify one for being a yard worker. There's a culture associated with doing welding, iron work, piping, sheet metal work, and all the other crafts on a ship. In fact, a high percentage of the shipyard workers are former sailors, largely hull techs and bos'n's mates. They sure don't look like sailors, though. Perhaps I saw two or three with hair no longer than their ears, but most of them had hair down at least to the neck, a few in pigtails. Stubble—not beards—was definitely de rigueur. The clothing selection kept consonant with hairstyle. If some of the garments had been newer or more expensive, they would have qualified for early Hell's Angels or the mode of the Baltimore homeless. It was a studied, and definitely purposeful, design. The work was incredibly dirty, with a lot of fumes, and there was a closeness among the yard workers. I figured the style was something of a work uniform. Perhaps they chose as diametrically contrasting a uniform as they could in order to stand out from the ship's crew. It worked. Nobody had any difficulty telling the sailors from the shipyard workers.

Easy identification actually had some dollar value because the contractor wanted to be absolutely certain that no jobs covered in his contract were done or shortened by naval labor. Whenever a sailor would be seen using a hacksaw, moving a pipe, or chipping any paint, the foreman was complaining to the maintenance officer within a nanosecond. This particular shipyard was a nonunion shop, so there was an interesting tension involved. The workers themselves had no complaints at all; they were always happy when a sailor would do some of the work or take over a task. No problem, I'll just sit here while you do it. It mattered to the foremen and company reps, though. They kept a close, protective watch on what work could be done (and billed) by them, and what could be done by sailors.

By the first evening in port, all the festivities had cleared out, families had completed the tours, and only the duty crew was left on the ship. Already the shipyard workers started invading the space. They had their big ventilation pipes, compressed-air hoses, ventilating fans, and heavy-duty electrical cables running everywhere. Most impressive were the ventilation pipes. These were compressible vinyl tubes, ten to twelve inches in diameter, that had to run down into any space where ordinary ventilation would be cut off or grinding would be done. There are spaces on a ship—called "voids"—that are purposefully designed to always be left empty. Voids needed to be painted, checked for rust, and inspected just the same as any other space. However, having been designed as voids, they had no intrinsic ventilation, so air needed to be piped in and circulated if a person was going to be in there.

Since the sides and bottoms of voids are made of steel just like the rest of the ship, they consume oxygen. Even though painting retards oxidation, paint can wear out or, furthermore, even under the paint, there is still iron, and over years it still loves to oxidize—otherwise known as rusting. In a closed space, the oxygen can come from only one place—the air in the room. Eventually the oxygen gets leached out, so when the void is entered it's not a vacuum (because all the other gases, the nitrogen, carbon dioxide, and so forth, are still there) but there's no oxygen. The worker cannot "feel" the absence of oxygen, but he needs to stay in the compartment just a few minutes before losing consciousness, and eventually dying. If the situation is intensified by physical activity in the space, like welding or other work, he and his equipment suck up the remaining oxygen even faster. That's why these big pipes travel everywhere throughout the ship, circulating air. They enter the ship mostly through the hangar bay, travel down through virtually every ladderwell, and pass along all the passageways.

The big air pipes usually were tied up along the overhead. A passageway barely high enough to permit a person to walk now became compromised if two or three of those pipes were tied up with brown twine along the overhead. Sometimes a fourth or fifth pipe would be lying along the deck or tied up along the bulkhead to allow room for feet. Then there were five or six small compressed-air hoses for blowing away dust, operating pneumatic tubes, or sandblasting. Skeins of thick, high-power electrical cable were mixed in there, too. There wasn't a normal passageway left on the ship. All of these various cylinders and cables ran through every passageway and obstructed anyplace you wanted to walk.

Further complicating travel around the ship were the canvas or Naugahyde barriers put up everywhere. To protect against welding torches or flying chips of metal, or to hide work that was classified, many spaces had to be barricaded from ordinary traffic. So, in addition to the passageways already compromised by the tubes and hoses, the fabric barricades completely closed down some that remained. Getting from one point to another during the SRA required relearning your way around the ship.

The simple construction fallout from all this work added a lot of litter and clutter to the ship, but it was only a minor element compared to the personal fallout from the shipyard workers. They weren't allowed to smoke on the ship, but cigarette butts lay every couple of feet throughout the deck. Also, tobacco juice streaks and polka dots were beginning to appear on the bulkheads and decks. The contract said that the workers would always come in and clean up behind themselves, but they did it only when forced. Not only were the shape and form of the ship changed by the shipyard workers, but a dirty, industrial ugliness was trying to squeeze out the sparkling crispness I had enjoyed so much.

The day after our arrival, I was alone in the medical department. I'd given Don some leave and sent Rock to work at the hospital, as surgeons always did when their ship came back to port. Sick call was relatively light. Most guys had other things to do that morning than pay attention to minor illness. Phone lines had been installed soon after we came back to port, so I called up my friend Cdr. Art Hayes, who was the SMO on the USS *Saratoga,* up in major overhaul in the shipyard at Norfolk, Virginia. Art went to the *Saratoga* at the same time I came to the *Forrestal,* but they'd been in the yard the entire time and were destined to stay for another six months. I told Art that I had a lot of sympathy for him, as I was just now beginning to understand what a ship was like in the yard. Since an SRA was much less intense than a complete overhaul, I knew I was only seeing a fraction of what was happening to the *Sara.* Having been on the ship only about three months, I knew that we SMOs all had a kind of bond, so Art was one of the first people I wanted to call. "Did you hear about the SMO on the *Coral Sea?*" Art asked.

No, of course I hadn't. We had kind of been out of the country for a while.

Well, the SMO on the *Coral Sea* had been fired the week before. It turns out some medical waste from the *Coral Sea*—not very much either, just a few syringes—had washed up on the beaches of North Carolina. I remembered Captain Guitar's pointed warning about medical waste, and that Admiral Kelso at CINCLANTFLT was real agitated about the subject.

"Was that all, Art? Surely he did something else. The doctor himself wasn't the guy to throw the syringes off, was he? C'mon, they didn't fire him just for that! What else was there?"

"No, that was it. Syringes on the beach, SMO's out of work. End of story."

Looked like the SMO on *Coral Sea* was going to pay the price. About one out of three SMOs get relieved. Art and I hoped this would be the only one for a while. Oh, the poor guy. He should have paid attention like we did. Now he'd be sent off to some isolated clinic.

"Well, Art, that could happen to any of us easily enough. We just did HIVs and PPDs on five thousand guys, you know. We've got a ton of medical waste, most of it plastic, that we're off-loading just today. I can tell you it really crowded our department." Art and I commiserated about that for a while on the phone, and while we did I formulated a plan to try to stay ahead of this problem and maybe impress Captain Guitar with my forward thinking. It wasn't very busy that day in the medical department. One fellow came by with a tiny foreign body in his left eye at around 1000, and another sailor had a burned left index finger from mess duty, but otherwise it was pretty quiet.

I took advantage of the time to concentrate on the problems of waste coming out of the department—especially plastic, which was the major part of our trash. I knew that CINCLANTFLT and AIR-LANT were both working on directives about medical waste, and we'd have to respond to their guidance. For the present, however, just plain common sense may not be sufficient. Sometimes you just need to paint lamb's blood on your door to show you understand. We were going to take an aggressive direction, not just to handle this right but to let it show that the FID had the message.

There were really two problems with plastic. First of all, it can float forever. Second, it lasts forever. Most other soft trash would gradually disintegrate in the ocean or be eaten by fish. Metal would sink to the bottom and either be buried in the silt or eventually oxidize and dissolve. Plastic would float forever and last forever. It would be around to pollute the oceans for eons, but especially it could wash up on the beach, like it did in North Carolina. The citizens, of course, had a right to be outraged. To me, though, that particular afternoon, the worst thing about medical waste on the beach was that SMOs could be fired.

I imagined for a moment, What if I were in the shoes of the SMO from the *Coral Sea?* I didn't have enough years of naval service to get a pension if I got kicked out. Having left private practice, I really didn't want to have to come back to a community and say, "I just got kicked out of the Navy. Can I open my office again?" I felt that my family would be dishonored. Maybe they could adjust to that, I don't know. But the being broke part . . . I knew that would be unpopular with my daughters.

As ugly as plastic or medical trash might look on the beach, it isn't really an infectious threat. Needles are ugly, of course, and people can be stuck or cut by them. Kids or bad guys might try to use beach needles for injections, I guess. Mostly they get too sandy or dirty even for that, though. The public outcry about medical hazards was obviously about AIDS. Medically that wasn't a realistic concern. The HIV virus is very fragile despite its public image. As infectious agents go, the HIV is actually not very hardy. The infections that are transmitted sexually are the ones from mostly fragile agents that can only survive in moist, warm, and *living* environments. Sex organs, for example. If they are out on a countertop, or in sunlight, they perish. They can be passed from one person to another only by means of moist, warm, "indoor" routes, like sex. That's why they are only sexual diseases and not respiratory or foodborne.

Ocean salt water is simply not a fertile place for germs. Neither the treponeme of syphilis, the cocci of gonorrhea, nor the HIV could survive in a syringe that floated in the ocean and then washed up on a beach. The problem wasn't biology. It was public anxiety and outrage. Irresponsible disposal of trash, pollution of public resources, and just the sheer ugliness of plastic medical stuff washing up on a public beach—all these were good reasons for public anger, sure enough. They shouldn't happen. Period. Still, what the public was mostly worked up about was AIDS, and that part was not a real issue.

Well, I knew this was important, and I was making a detailed plan to keep the FID out of trouble. We would account for every single syringe, from the day it came on board the ship until it was safely delivered to a responsible designated trash hauler. I refined our methods for storing plastics on the ship while we were under way. We would separate plain plastic trash from plastic trash with any biological contact, like saliva, stomach fluid, stool, or pus. There would be provisions for sealing and double bagging certain material. Anything that had biological fluids would be autoclaved after being bagged the first time and then would be bagged again so that sterilization was already guaranteed before we had to store it.

Of course, we'd been doing most of these things already ever since that CINCLANTFLT message came out on 29 August. All of the schemes I was working on this particular day were simply refinements of guidance given before, plus some new initiatives to make sure we stayed ahead of the parade. I was partly just dressing up the bureaucratic trace. I drew nice flow diagrams and designed a series of logbooks we'd use for the sharp object disposal canisters. We would handle and sign for disposed syringes and medical trash, just like it was gold or documents. In the future, not only would I be able to show that we had a good process for all of our syringes and plastics and medical waste, but I would also have a set of logbooks that could trace every piece of plastic or sharp object from when it came to our department to when it left.

I was smugly satisfied with all of the plans and SOPs I had just devised and neatly typed up. Next I designed a training program for the whole medical department. No university ever had a more clever curriculum for literature or science than the one I designed for our trash! Thorough and yet clear; sailor-proof, I told myself. And interwoven with such humor and cleverness in language that it even made me chuckle as I wrote it. We would make training mandatory, but we would make it fun. Finally, I typed out a clever memo that was to be distributed and initialed by all members of the medical department. Keeping up what by now I thought was a rollicking background humor for emphasis, my memo unabashedly noted the recent firing of the SMO from the *Coral Sea* and warned that we didn't want something like that to happen to the beloved SMO from the *Forrestal,* did we? I chuckled to myself as I read it.

I thought the guys in the department would kind of like the memo. It was one more example of the FID medical department being out in front. This had to be the most comprehensive plan ever for dealing with trash. After all, we were the Atlantic fleet carrier that had been under way when the new instruction came out. We were the ones who had gone through the exercise of giving PPDs, flu shots, and HIV tests to 5,300 people and had maintained all of those plastic products on the ship. Yet we had carefully avoided throwing anything overboard improperly. Of course, if we implemented my new plan about doing shots and lab tests on a continuous, weekly basis instead of just doing these mammoth catch-up exercises, there wouldn't have to be large amounts of plastic medical trash again.

I was interrupted from my thoughts when Petty Officer Davis said, "Captain, Commander Jones is on the phone for you, and he says it's pretty important."

"Commander Jones . . . who is Commander Jones?" Davis didn't know.

It was "Gus" Jones, the new deputy CAG. He had replaced Cdr. Terry Tower toward the end of the cruise, and I was just getting to know him. Since he was a member of the air wing and not ship's company, "Commander Jones" wasn't a name I recognized quickly. Still, he and I had hit it off well, and I could tell I was going to like him. I didn't know why he was calling me at 2000 on a Tuesday night, but I figured it might be to invite me to dinner or something.

"Did you hear about the syringes on the shore at Fernandina Beach?" What a coincidence. I had just spent the whole day on the subject of syringes on the beach.

"Where is Fernandina Beach?" I thought it must be something more about the *Coral Sea.* That poor SMO. There was a foreboding itch in the back of my mind about this discussion already, though.

"Fernandina Beach. It's just ten miles north of Mayport." This was my first time on the ship in Mayport. Since I had only joined them in the north Arabian Sea, I wasn't yet familiar with the Jacksonville and Mayport area. "The news says the syringes came from the *Forrestal.*"

"Don't worry, we didn't throw anything overboard, and we had real careful precautions to prevent it."

"Well, you'd better check into it, because the FID is being mentioned. I heard that CINCLANTFLT was interested in this, and I think they had some trouble about it on the *Coral Sea.*"

Trouble on the *Coral Sea,* indeed. "Thanks for calling, Gus, I'll look into it." I immediately went over to the ER. We have a TV in there up on a cabinet back in a kind of hole in the bulkhead. The ER is one of a handful of places on the ship where closed-circuit TV always covers flight operations under way. If there were an accident on the flight deck, obviously we'd need to know about it, so we keep a TV for video monitoring. In port it might be different. If the TV was running all the time, the corpsmen on duty might spend more time watching it than doing their work, so I had contemplated putting out some rules about when it could be on and when it couldn't. For the moment, though, I was glad it was there. "Have you guys seen anything on the news?" Petty Officers Fields and Womple (Arden had returned to duty once the ship returned to Mayport) were watching MTV.

"No, but somebody said they heard something on the radio about syringes on the beaches."

This day had promises of turning bad.

I immediately went down to the XO's office. It was evening, and he was gone. I called the command duty officer (CDO), who acted as the CO's representative when the CO and XO were off the ship, to tell him what I had heard. He said he'd heard some rumors along the same lines. Rumors are only rumors, but the more of them you begin to hear, you either suspect they may be true or at least recognize they can be repeated enough to become self-sustaining, like crabgrass. In any case, I was beginning to get worried. The CDO told me that both the captain and the XO were out of town for a few days. The captain had gone to an annual convention of naval aviators called the Tail Hook Association. Ozark, the XO, was on leave visiting family in Arkansas. Captain Box, the CHENG, was the acting CO.

I went back to my office and called Rick Cox at his house. He, too, had heard some of the rumors. I asked him to stay on top of the news and to come in early the next morning. Then I called the CHENG at home. He hadn't heard about the rumors, so I told him that I'd heard them from several sources.

"Doc, I thought you told me that we didn't throw anything overboard."

"Well, we didn't. There's no way those could be *Forrestal* syringes. We made damned sure that all of the corpsmen knew what we were supposed to do with the plastics and the syringes. There's got to be a mistake here. But I assure you we're looking into it."

"I'll be in early in the morning, Doc. We'd better try and stay on top of this."

The next morning at quarters, Rick and I got all the corpsmen together, and I told them about the rumors I'd heard about syringes washing up on Fernandina Beach. I asked if any of the corpsmen had heard any of the rumors. They had not. "How many of you guys remember when we talked to you about disposing of medical waste and plastics at sea back in September?" About half our corpsmen were on leave at this point, and some had duty the night before. Of the fifteen or so who were there now, only five or six raised their hands. "But I stood right here in front of you guys in September and mentioned this to you. Petty Officer Womple, don't you remember my mentioning this?"

"No, Captain, I really don't. Petty Officer Dunbar did tell us that we had to be careful about plastics, though. I don't think we threw anything over the side after something like the first of September."

Two or three others remembered that I had come to talk to the corpsmen at quarters, and a few more than that remembered that Lieutenant Cox had discussed it with them. More than half of the guys assembled there realized that we had been stacking up bag after bag of medical waste back in a couple of our heads, but to my amazement four or five of the guys didn't even know that we had changed anything about trash disposal! Happily, none of those four or five guys had been involved in trash details over the last part of the cruise.

It was one of those lessons in communication. If only half of my department was present, and among them there were four or five who had no idea that we had a change in policy about throwing plastic trash over the side, that meant that if the entire department were there, as many as ten wouldn't know about it. This, despite my coming to lecture the guys during quarters, passing it on to all the petty officers, and the conspicuous stacking up of plastic and trash in two of our heads where guys couldn't use toilets anymore! I was beginning to get uncomfortable again.

"Did anybody here throw any syringes or plastic over the side after the first of September, when we said not to do it anymore?"

"No."

"Nobody on the ship could have done it?"

"Well, it could have been some of the air wing corpsmen who aren't here anymore. Some of those guys seemed not to listen to instructions."

"Wait a minute. I felt we made it perfectly clear that the air wing corpsmen are integral members of this department when we're under way. Lieutenant Cox and I talked to you at quarters, too. We are all supposed to be one department. What do you mean, 'Some of those guys'?"

Stifled expressions, shuffling feet. Another one of those gaps in communication. I thought we'd solved the air wing/ship's company gap in the medical department. Maybe we hadn't.

I asked Rick to call over to Bill Kelly at Cecil Field, where some of the squadrons were. I called Gus Jones to fill him in and asked if he and Kelly would try to check with the corpsmen from the air wing. Gus hadn't heard any more since the night before. We scoured the newspapers, and there were no comments.

I went down to see the CHENG, but since he was the acting CO, he was hanging out up in the captain's office on the O-3 deck. When I finally tracked him down, he was busy with all the other ship's activities. "Good morning, Doc. I hope your day started better than it ended last night." He was in a chipper mood and had no further bad information. I told him about my disturbing information at quarters.

"Welcome to the Navy, Doc. No message is sailor-proof. You never tell them anything just four times when you can tell them six or seven, and tell it in six or seven different ways, too."

Besides, it looked as though it might have been a false alarm. There was no substantiation about the reports that morning. We had been back in port three days, so if anything was going to come of it we would've heard it by now. None of the guys in the department had thrown any medical stuff over the side. Besides, I'd seen all the plastics and all the trash being stored in the preventive medicine room and in the head on Ward II, so I had firsthand knowledge that we hadn't thrown anything overboard, and we had a pretty good system in place. There was the nagging concern that some guys seemed not to have gotten the message, and I realized that we needed to work on documentation of disposal—something I had only thought about yesterday, not while we were at sea. The attention to those new procedures was obviously necessary. We clearly needed to do some training so this wouldn't come up again.

Meet Billy

Back in the medical department, there was a guy just checked in who had been beat up the night before. His name was Billy Dorsey, and he looked about fourteen years old. A short fellow, around five feet, six inches tall, he had what would have been a cherubic face if it hadn't been all pummeled, cut, and spattered with crusted blood. One front tooth had a diagonal chunk taken out, and his right eye was nearly closed. The left ear had a cut halfway down from the top. He had that mélange of stale fruit and vinegar that is characteristic of last night's drunk. For some reason, only cheap whiskey or cheap wine leaves just that exact smell. Beer can come close, but it isn't quite sweet enough. And particularly among people who have been vomiting and haven't rinsed out their mouths or had anything to eat, the combined smell is not only characteristic, it's just downright repulsive. The smell is so bad you're inclined to feel sorry for anybody else who has to be in it with you, even the guy it came from, so I already had sympathy for poor Billy Dorsey because he had to put up with that smell, and longer than me. Dorsey didn't have much to say. He was obviously very tired, and he looked like he still might be a little bit drunk.

Apparently, he and his buddies had been to some of the local bars last night. They started at Big Jim's and then went over to Cap'n Odie's. Dorsey started being belligerent with a couple of sailors from another ship and had taken a punch at one guy, who made quick work of him but only left him with a black eye. According to his buddies, Dorsey just kept drinking, although they told him he needed to get back to the ship, and he fought with one guy after another. Not only is he little, but apparently Billy wasn't a very accomplished pugilist either. Finally, his buddies couldn't stand it anymore, but they couldn't get him to come back to the ship, so they returned without him. Somehow he must have caught a cab and made it back himself.

Looking at him, you'd never figure how anybody could want to punch such a cute little guy, this angelic-looking creature about the size of a leprechaun. He had a way of tilting his head to one side and slanting his shoulders a little bit the opposite direction that called to mind either the Pillsbury Dough Boy or Winnie-the-Pooh. If he didn't smell so bad, I would have wanted to take him on my knee and ask him, "What would you like for Christmas, little boy?" But he just smelled so bad.

We looked him over, and none of the cuts looked as though they needed sutures; besides, it had been too long since his fights. We usually didn't like to close cuts with sutures after several hours because of the risk of infection. I arranged for him to be seen in dental that morning because of the broken tooth, and to see if there were any others broken. I phoned his DivO, as we usually did for these young fellows who got too tanked up the night before. Alcohol was a major concern for us. Considering we had five thousand young guys, most of them away from home for the first time, we really didn't have as much trouble with alcohol as most groups of men that age. However, any were too many, and we took those we had seriously. These young fellows needed some supervision and guidance.

Besides talking to his DivO about his drinking and his injuries, Petty Officer Parker called his LPO to make sure he had some senior enlisted supervision. Finally, whenever there was an alcohol-related incident, we made a referral to the command alcohol-abuse counselor (CAAC). Even a single, isolated event related to alcohol had to be referred to the counselor. It's my opinion that even a single incident means a problem with alcohol. The individual doesn't have to be an obvious drunk already. A driving accident or injury shows that the person has failed to control alcohol and could get worse in the future. What appears to be an isolated event may be the first act of a new habit, and the command owes it to him to begin tracking it, get him directed to treatment if necessary, and mobilize the resources that the Navy has. We have a long way to go on this problem, but at most commands we take it seriously, and we did on the *Forrestal*.

I tried to get Dorsey to talk about what happened, but I just didn't seem to be able to engage him in any conversation. I asked him about his drinking habits, what he had done the night before, and so on. He shrugged at me in a very engaging manner but didn't want to talk.

That afternoon I went over to meet with the officer in charge (OIC) of the clinic at Mayport. The clinic was supposed to back us up medically, and since we were in business just a few hundred yards apart, I wanted to make sure that we had met each other and taken every opportunity to work together. The clinic was a branch of NH Jacksonville, which was more than an hour away. Mayport is about twenty miles east of Jacksonville, and Naval Air Station (NAS) Jacksonville is ten to twelve miles southwest of the city. Jacksonville traffic is almost as bad as Boston's, so it was approximately an hour drive between Mayport and NH Jacksonville, longer at rush hour.

The Mayport Clinic wasn't open after 1800 and didn't have a staffed ER. They did have a night watch, however, for emergencies. I thought this was a little bit incongruous. Since all emergencies had to be sent elsewhere, what was the staff for? A bona fide emergency such as a heart attack wouldn't be sent all the way to NH Jacksonville, but over to the Dunes Hospital in Atlantic Beach, which had a marginal local reputation. Somebody with chest pain who seemed stable enough to last would be sent to either Mercy or Baptist Hospital. Those two were a little further than Dunes, but at least twenty minutes closer than NH Jacksonville. The unstable ones, those who couldn't travel, would stay at Dunes. Too bad, maybe, because that might be the worst place for somebody who was very sick. Nonemergency, hospital-requiring problems would be sent by ambulance to NH Jacksonville. With all this, although there were four ambulances parked outside the clinic, none of them were licensed as advanced cardiac life-support (ACLS) ambulances.

"You know you and your doctors have to stand watch over here at the clinic, don't you?"

"Well," I said, "with the air wing gone, our flight surgeons go back to the naval air stations that the squadrons come from, and our surgeon has gone back to the hospital, so the only medical officers left on the ship are myself, Lt. Don Kent, and CWO3 [Chief Warrant Officer Third Class] Art Corbett. We stand the watch on the ship twenty-four hours a day, and we see patients twenty-four hours a day, which is more than the clinic." Also, it looked as though the clinic had six or seven doctors on their staff, so they had a six- or seven-section watch, whereas we had only a three-section watch on the ship. I told him I thought we would choose not to be in their watch rotation. "Well, there's a SOPA [senior officer present ashore] instruction that says you will," the OIC said.

"If you want, I can ask Captain Guitar or Admiral Kohl to call SOPA to work it out." Since we planned to see all the *Forrestal* people right on the ship, though, it seemed best for the clinic to drop the subject. In the past, some of the carriers had closed down their medical departments at the end of the workday while they were port, so it made sense for their physicians to join in over at the clinic. I intended for the FID to keep up its medical services around the clock right on the ship. We did have better capability on the ship than the clinic did. We were our own hospital—a self-contained medical department—for six months out of the year, so there was no reason in my mind that we should close down when we were in port. The OIC liked that approach, although he told me that his doctors probably wouldn't. I suggested they all come on over and get a tour of the ship. It turns out none of his doctors had ever been to sea, although their clinic was in a home port that took care of about fifteen ships, including two carriers, the FID and the *Saratoga*.

I had been over to visit the OIC at about 1440 that afternoon. He and I finished speaking somewhere around 1530, and he gave me a tour of the clinic. I asked if I could meet some of his doctors, but none of them were in the building. "They secure a little early if there's nothing going on." Well, there it was about 1530, and none of the doctors were in the clinic.

I went back to the ship that day without as much comfort as I would have liked about our relationship with the clinic.

Formal dining in port was a real pleasure, but different from under way. For one thing, there were far fewer people who came to dinner. Not many officers or CPOs lived on the ship in port. You could live on the ship without paying rent, of course. Some of us older people with families in other cities stayed on the ship, rather than pay for an apartment in town while supporting a household elsewhere. Single, young enlisted guys had better things to do with the small amount they earned than pay for an apartment, but almost everybody else lived in town. So the only people who came to formal dining were the duty crew and the handful of us who lived on the ship. That meant only about fifteen officers in the wardroom. At least one officer would have his family visit for dinner most nights on the ship.

The president of the mess was, of course, the XO. In his absence, the senior officer present would usually preside at formal dining. Being a captain, I was always the senior officer. Yet, as a staff officer, I could never really be in charge of the ship, and since the CDO was the captain's representative in the absence of the skipper and XO, he would usually preside at dinner and sit in the XO's chair. In fact, with rare exceptions, at formal dining in port the head table usually seated everybody. We usually ate by candlelight, although by the time the meal was over the lights would come on for coffee.

On the third night back in port, Merv Schultz, the ordnance handling officer (OHO), was the CDO. Merv was a limited duty officer (LDO), the official term for what had been called a "Mustang" in the old days. Reported to be the most knowledgeable man in the fleet about aviation ordnance, Merv was responsible for ensuring that all the magazines were fully stocked, maintaining an inventory of all the weapons on the ship, keeping all the weapons and their fusing in good condition, and overseeing the management of the day-to-day activities of the weapons department. He was basically the primary assistant to the gun boss. It was rumored that the OHO and the gun boss were not close.

Merv was a loud, outspoken fellow with a raspy voice and a ready laugh. A gregarious man with a bountiful inventory of anecdotes and jokes, his vocality and expressiveness put some people off. Nobody was indifferent about Merv Schultz. He also had a tendency to be a little bit of a needler, but he was willing to take a good joke, as well as dish one out.

Merv had an interesting characteristic. Many of us discover when we pass forty that hair starts growing on our ears or our eyebrows get bushy. Every couple of days the hair on the ears has to be cut off, or embarrassing tufts start to grow out on earlobes or the tops. The OHO was similar but different. Merv was the only guy I knew who had a tuft of hair growing out on the tip of his nose. He wasn't only different by having hair on his nose, but somehow by not noticing it either. He quite conspicuously didn't shave it off. I figured he had to see himself in a mirror most days when he would shave. He did shave his cheeks and his chin, I know, because he never had any unsightly stubble on those parts. Yet the hair on his nose seemed to grow out close to an inch long. It was hard to look at Merv without looking at the tuft of hair on his nose. He didn't give any sign that he saw you looking at it, and never made any comments like, "I see you're looking at my nose. Does the hair bother you?" To the contrary, almost everybody who would talk to Merv just simply had to see that hair and had to be curious, as I was, about why he didn't cut it off.

It wasn't just a single hair like the hair that might grow out of the middle of a wart. It was a rich, full little tuffet. I had a little fantasy sometimes that maybe he was planning to braid it, or that he would comb it to one side when he got particularly dressed up. In fact, the OHO was one of the few people I knew who still wore hair tonic. He had dark hair, and when he combed it swept back somewhat, he used the exact style of Robert McNamara, the former secretary of defense, or the characters from F. Scott Fitzgerald novels. Sometimes I wondered if he was hoping the hair on his nose would get long enough so that he could put pomade in it.

Everybody enjoyed formal dining when Merv was the CDO. Not everybody got a chance to speak because he rambled on so, but that didn't matter because Merv had good stories and good jokes, and we all secretly enjoyed looking at the hair on his nose and wondering about it. Interesting, though, nobody ever seemed to talk about it. I think we all probably wanted to, and we all knew that if we said anything to Merv about his nose hair, he wouldn't mind. We just never asked. Maybe we thought it was bad manners. A lot of people seem to have hair that grows out from the inside of their nose, which was something you definitely would not talk about, but this was right out there on the tip.

Leaving the wardroom that evening, I ran into Master Chief Morgan, one of the most senior chiefs in the supply department, the guy who had helped us get our tables set up on the mess decks for the shots. He was always a kind of crusty fellow, but he seemed especially brusque tonight. When he returned my greeting, I thought his speech seemed a little slurred, something I'd noticed a couple of times in the past few weeks. I reminded myself to speak with the SuppO about it. Master Chief Morgan might have a little drinking problem.

I went to bed that night generally content. I was adjusting to life in port, the routine was working out well, and, other than all the pipes and disruption on the ship from the SRA and all the noise, dust, and racket from the shipyard workers, things were going well. Admittedly, I'd been jarred by the needle and syringe rumors, but they seemed to have died out by now.

Next morning during sick call, the lines were a little longer than they'd been the prior few days. More people were returning from short leave or liberty periods, and one of their first stops was back in sick call. It was getting to be winter, so we had minor illnesses and a string of colds. Some of the guys had sprained their ankles or had other athletic injuries from their short time at home. Athletic injuries would start to be a bigger part of what we saw in sick call now that we were in port and guys could play basketball, softball, and other sports every day. Also, the automobile was back in our lives. Sore necks and facial injuries from automobile accidents were beginning to take some of our attention. When I finished in sick call that morning, there was a note on my desk to go see the acting CO up in his office.

"Doc, we got a call from the PAO [public affairs officer] over at NAS Jax. They've started to have some syringes wash up on the beach down at Daytona. There was some stuff mixed in with the syringes that had the *Forrestal* name on it."

"But this is five days after we got into port. Besides, we didn't throw anything overboard."

"Here is the guy's number. Can you give him a call? He seems pretty sure that the name of the ship was on some of the stuff."

The PAO from Jacksonville was not very cordial. "You guys are in some kind of trouble, and it's really causing us a problem here. You better go on down to Daytona and get a crew to clean up their beaches."

"Now wait a minute. We haven't even determined for sure that *Forrestal* was involved with this in the first place, and in the second place, I'm the senior medical officer, not the trash detail."

"Instead of arguin' with me about this, you better get on down to Daytona and see what they're talkin' about. Whether you stay the senior medical officer on that ship, or anyplace else in the Navy, might be an open question pretty soon."

I just hung up on him. I didn't like the direction that conversation was taking. He had given me the phone number of the beach patrol in Daytona Beach, so I asked Petty Officer Parker if he'd give me a ride down there. It was a couple of hours' drive, and when we got to the beach patrol office, sure enough, they had a red plastic bag—just like the ones we used on the FID—that had washed up on the beach. Inside the bags were some papers that clearly had the *Forrestal* name, and a handful of syringes. Fortunately, all the needles had been clipped off, but there it was, living proof of syringes and a plastic bag, with the name of the ship right on the bag. Oh, my God. The beach patrol officer was a little bit sympathetic, but insistent. "There have been a bunch of syringes washing up on the beach, too. Every hundred or feet or so, we find a syringe or two washed up along here." I spoke to him for another twenty or thirty minutes while we worked out a plan for me to get a bunch of FID sailors to walk the beaches and pick up any refuse we could find. My head was reeling. How could this happen? We had been so careful not to throw anything over the side. But there was the evidence, right in my hand.

HM3 Parker and I drove back to the ship as fast as we could. I went up to the see the CHENG to tell him what we had found and to make sure we started dealing with it immediately. We had to get down there and pick up any possible scrap from the *Forrestal*—or any plastic that could in any way be attributed to the *Forrestal*—but most especially medical waste. During the drive, Petty Officer Parker and I talked about how we'd get the teams together and get volunteers to deal with the pickup, spicules of fear about my own career poked into my mind periodically, interrupting my train of thought. The SMO from the *Coral Sea* hadn't been kicked out of the Navy, apparently, but he'd been transferred to an assignment in a small clinic somewhere at the end of the earth. At my court-martial I could just see the judge or the admiral saying, "And Captain Riley, *your* crime was all the worse because you had been warned by the *Coral Sea*."

Back at the ship, I immediately went to see Chuck Box, still the acting CO. Before I could give him my report, he showed me the morning newspaper. There it was right on page three, reports of medical waste washing up over along a twelve-mile stretch from Daytona Beach northward.

At quarters that morning we put out word about what had happened and called for volunteers. Chuck rented a bus for the next three days to take all the volunteers who would come with us down to the beaches to pick up syringes and any other medical waste. Only two volunteers from outside the medical department came. When we called the squadrons at Cecil Field and NAS Jacksonville, none of the corpsmen volunteered to come with us. More than a dozen of the corpsmen from the ship were willing to come. We spent most of the next three days walking up and down about fifteen miles of beach, looking for anything that could be from any naval ship, and anything medical. Over that three-day period we picked up probably a thousand syringes and five or six prescription bottles, two of them marked "USS *Forrestal*." Two other prescription bottles, however, were clearly marked "USS *America*." My heart leapt up. Could some of the syringes be from the *America*? She had just been operating off the Florida coast during workups.

A couple of the guys who helped us the most during this pickup were HM1 Dunbar and HM1 Hugh Beaumont, our new orthopedic therapist. Beaumont, like Dunbar, was older than most of the corpsmen. He was in his late thirties, a very intelligent guy with a pleasant personality. He was either a college graduate or had several years of college, and like myself was a Beach Boys fan. He had grown up in the Daytona area and was very familiar with this neighborhood. He obviously felt bad about the syringes, and, along with Dunbar, was one of the few corpsmen to realize that I was going to be fired because of this. That troubled him, and he tried to cheer me up the entire time. He made jokes, bantered with me about rock 'n' roll trivia, and generally tried to make this into a fun exercise. After all, it was an opportunity for guys from the department to get together and spend a little time on the beach. If it had been under other circumstances, we maybe even would have enjoyed it.

When we got back to the ship at the end of the third day, Captain Guitar was there, back from the Tail Hook convention. I learned that the inspector general (IG) from AIRLANT had been making some calls down to our area. Oh, no, AIRLANT knew about it! Well, that wasn't the end of it. Not just AIRLANT, but also CINCLANTFLT and even the IG for the Department of the Navy up in Washington had heard about this.

I remembered how angry the captain had been with me about the Sam MacDonald case a month ago. I immediately went up to give him a full report. Might as well face the tempest head-on. To my surprise, he not only didn't yell at me, but his face wasn't even red. He asked me a few questions. He said, "You told me that you had this situation under control. Remember, you and I spoke about this back in August."

"Yes, Sir. Remember, I told you that we were saving all the medical material in the department, and nothing was being thrown overboard. I can't explain how this happened, Sir. I thought we had it under control."

"Sometimes things happen just beyond your control, Doc." The captain pointed out that with this level of public and Navy attention, we had to do an investigation to try to account for it. What he didn't say, and what I knew, was that somebody was going to be punished. The Navy always had to have retribution. For one thing, the public insisted on it. But it was an old Navy tradition. This was very definitely in the medical department, so we all knew who would have to be held responsible. The SMO.

There are two books that govern investigations and justice in the Navy. One is the *Judge Advocate General Manual*, or JAGMAN. The JAG-MAN describes how investigations shall be done and sets standards for evidence, interviews, and documentation. Following an official JAG-MAN investigation, the findings may lead to such proceedings as a board of inquiry, captain's mast, or, finally, court-martial. The other important book is the *Manual of Courts-Martial*. It seemed to me that we were going to wind up using both of those manuals before this was over.

The JAGMAN investigation was convened. The investigating officer was given the CINCLANTFLT message of 29 August, with the explicit directions about handling medical waste and plastics at sea. I submitted a written report, not only accepting responsibility for the medical department but clearly stating that Captain Guitar had instructed me regarding his concern about medical waste and plastics. If there needed to be such a thing as a noose for me, it was that the captain had gone out of his way to warn me about medical waste. He had even told me that it was one of his priorities. It was a John Dean–quality smoking gun. The investigating officer spoke to Rick Cox, and also interviewed Don Kent after Don returned from his leave. Every corpsman on the ship was interviewed, and some were called back from their leave early.

When the JAGMAN investigation was in its third day, the IG from AIRLANT, along with John Poirot, the environmental health officer I'd met during inspections and already considered a sourpuss, flew down to Mayport to do an independent investigation. Although we had scoured all the beaches and cleaned up every piece of trash we could find (including non-naval trash such as plastic milk cartons), people who lived down there had found more. When the IG and Poirot came back from Daytona, they carried with them two boxes with some more syringes and a bunch of other plastic trash, most of which wasn't even Navy. Since the FID was on the hook, though, nobody thought we should argue with the people who lived there. Any medical stuff found for months would be blamed on us, no matter what.

During one of their visits, John and the IG were accosted by news crews from two local TV stations and a protest group from one of the towns. John told me he suspected that the community group had been alerted by the news camera crews. When a camera was stuck in front of their faces, a reporter asked, "When is the Navy finally going to take some action on this custom of polluting public beaches?" In the background, protesters were carrying signs about Navy pollution and the Navy being a poor neighbor. When the sound bite was played on local TV that night, the two naval officers were obviously caught off guard and could only say things like, "The investigation is still ongoing." But the chanting and bobbing signs of the protesters showed up well and looked like a multitude on a TV screen.

One editorial in the main Jacksonville newspaper the next morning argued that the Navy should be a more responsible neighbor. It mentioned the risk of AIDS and other terrible diseases that could be spread by medical waste on the beaches, and the danger this posed to children. The writer hoped the Navy wouldn't just have another cover-up.

Two days later, I was called up to the captain's cabin to go over the findings of the investigations. Lt. Cdr. Mike Kunin was the investigating officer.

Here were the facts: By the rules that had applied up until 29 August, trash—including medical trash—could be thrown over the side as long as the ship was fifty miles or more offshore. Judging by the currents and where our plastic had washed up, it had to have been thrown out three days before we landed. Had it been thrown out in the last couple of days, the trash would have gone to an entirely different area. So by the former rules, although what had happened was bad, it would not have been illegal. The investigating officers found that the SMO and the DivO, Lieutenant Cox, had set up proper procedures for handling the medical waste, and we had notified our department not to throw medical waste or plastic over the side any longer. Yet it appeared some corpsmen did not understand. Although the investigating officers were convinced that everyone in the department had been told, there were some corpsmen who didn't fully understand or didn't remember. Therefore, it was the fault of leadership in the department for failing to guarantee that everyone understood.

Despite that failure, the investigation found that there was only a single incident of a corpsman from one of the squadrons who threw a single bag containing syringes and some other plastic medical containers over the side three days before we came into port. The individual had to be one of three corpsmen from the air wing, but it was impossible to determine for certain who it was. Judging from the amount of refuse picked up on the beach, a single bag probably accounted for all that was found. When it came apart more than a hundred miles offshore, it scattered the little floating devils like seeds from a dandelion.

So there it was: the syringes and plastic were from the *Forrestal*. CIN-CLANTFLT was furious about the matter, and the public was clearly outraged. The CO of the ship had been mindful of the potential for medical waste being thrown over the side, and he had specifically directed the head of the medical department to ensure that such a thing could never happen. While the SMO and his principal assistant had taken steps to follow up on the captain's guidance, a failure of leadership allowed a handful of corpsmen to not get the entire message, and on one occasion a bag of medical waste was thrown over the side in violation of directives. Since a handful of the corpsmen had not understood the directions, the corpsman who threw the bag over-board—whoever he was—could not be the one who was blamed. Of course, the officer responsible could and should be blamed, namely me.

Too many things had come together at the wrong time. The time of the year for flu shots, the end of the cruise, a new SMO who wanted to catch up on preventive medicine—all of this at the worst time there had ever been to have medical stuff wash up on a beach. Just after CIN-CLANTFLT announced this as incongruously one of the Navy's highest priorities, *Forrestal* got into the production of medical waste bigger than ever, raising the opportunity for this kind of misfortune and giving us a real good load of stuff to put into the hopper. Uncanny timing.

I didn't like the part where they included Rick Cox in the leadership problem. He worked for me, and I was worried that his reputation would be tarnished by the incident. He was only carrying out my directions at any point. Since I knew I was about to be fired anyway, I told Captain Guitar the responsibility was mine, not Rick's, and I apologized to him for the embarrassment to the *Forrestal*, and to the IG for embarrassing the Navy.

The captain said, "Thank you for a thorough investigation, Mike. You couldn't have reached any other conclusions. I'll make a full report about this to CINCLANTFLT and to Admiral Kohl. Doc, I think your new instruction on this matter would prevent this from happening anymore. There isn't anything else you can do now. The Navy just has to stop throwing plastics over the side, and we all know that, but this policy was new. We wish it hadn't happened, but fortunately nobody was hurt, and really it was a kind of freak accident." The captain asked me to stay while he dismissed the others.

I thought that he was going to privately tell me that he was going to send the case to a board of inquiry. I also expected him to express some anger or maybe hit me hard over the head with some heavy metal object. After all, something like this is an embarrassment to the whole ship (the whole Navy). It was going to cost the *Forrestal* the Battle E, and would probably hurt the skipper unless he was vigorous enough in my punishment before I was dismissed. I at least appreci-ated his doing what had to happen next in private.

It didn't happen that way.

The captain told me he had confidence in me and the medical department. He told me had no choice but to issue a "letter of caution," a stern, official letter that serves notice that the recipient had better watch out and not mess up anymore. While no officer wants to have something like that on his record, it's the sort of thing that needn't ruin a career if your performance is OK thereafter. It's like probation. Under the circumstances, it was about the least punishment the captain could have given me. By doing that, he left himself in further jeopardy, though. If he had me court-martialed or sent the case to a board of inquiry, that would have been the pound of flesh that tradition or the news media would have wanted. Somebody's career would have paid for the syringes, and the captain himself would have been cleared by striking the swift blow for justice. By issuing me only a letter of caution, he could potentially be blamed for a cover-up or for going easy on the culprit. These were days when the public suspected cover-ups.

The captain never said another word to me about that event, ever. He didn't raise his voice, he patted me on the back on the way out of the room, and he told me that he was also sorry that he had to give a letter of caution to Rick Cox, too. Apparently, since there were two officers involved, each one had to get a letter. Once again I told him it was my fault, not Rick's, and that I didn't want Rick's reputation to get tarnished by this. He told me not to worry, that if Rick's performance continued to be the way it always had been, the letter of caution would be forgotten by the time he left the ship.

Most commanding officers would have fired the SMO at that point, and both Captain Guitar and I knew it. Knowing how discouraged I was, he invited me over to dinner at his house that night. He never mentioned the syringes to me again, and never, never showed any lack of confidence.

The next week, Hugh Beaumont came to see me, somewhat sheepishly. He told me that he and a number of other corpsmen knew who had thrown the syringes over the side, and that the person did it intentionally because he was angry at the LPO in the department. It wasn't an accident, but was vengeful purposefully. Apparently, that was why Beaumont had been so solicitous the days we went down to pick up syringes, since he knew I was going to take the rap for somebody's angry stunt. He said it had been bothering him a lot the past few days—not only that it had happened but that he and his shipmates hadn't come to tell me about it. He said that he'd been worried that I might be fired, and that nobody had taken steps to try to protect me. He wouldn't tell me who the corpsman was who did it, though.

What good would it do for me to pass that on? It was over now.

Chapter 7

SRA and in Port

The SRA was going to continue for another three or four months. We wouldn't start our workups for the next cruise until late February. It was all mapped out. The exact dates for the first exercises and first movements of the ship were scheduled almost down to the minute. Usually, the carriers operate on an eighteen-month cycle. After a six-month cruise—like the one we'd just finished—there would be an SRA to make any repairs or updates, and then workups stretched out over most of the next year. In our case, the cycle was being compressed from eighteen months down to a year. We had arrived in Mayport in the first week of October, and we were going to go out one year from then, so we had to squeeze in all of our workups and any other things we were tasked with. It also meant that once we started steaming in late February, we'd be at sea or deployed at least half the time during the next six months, and then deployed for the next six. For the present, though, we were going to stay tied up, so I had to get used to operating my department with all those pipes and wires running through the passageways.

Doing business was going to be a lot different tied up in Mayport than it had been under way. For one thing, my department no longer had a monopoly on the medical business for FID sailors. They had options now, and several of them. A sailor could go to the Mayport Clinic. Even if he lived on the ship, he could simply walk off the bow, go a mile and a half over to the clinic, and be seen in military sick call there in the morning instead of by one of us on the ship. It was two hours to NH Jacksonville, but some of the sailors lived over on that side of town anyway, where they may have been stationed before. For one reason or another, they or their families might prefer to be seen over at the hospital. It was common knowledge that the doctors at the hospital and the

138

clinic were more apt to write a recommendation for "no duty" than the doctors on the ship. Although everybody is taught in boot camp that a "no-duty" chit signed by a doctor is merely a recommendation to the command, many people in the Navy manage to forget. Only the CO and his delegated agents in the chain of command can excuse a person from work. To be sure, a chief or officer disregards the advice of a doctor only at some risk. Still, the member given a no-duty chit is supposed to either call his boss to let him know he won't be at work, and then turn in the chit when he returns, or bring the chit to the boss on the way home. Apparently, a number of the medical staff at the Mayport Clinic didn't realize this advisory relationship between physicians and command. Some of our sailors didn't recognize it, either, and some of them found it convenient to not recognize it. In the first few weeks, a much higher percentage than usual of our sailors were turning in no-duty or light-duty chits signed by doctors at the clinic and the hospital. A number of those chits recommended seven to ten days in bed and then a mandatory follow-up with that particular doctor back at the clinic or the hospital, not with the ship's doctor.

I had spent a lot of time with the corpsmen telling them that I intended our department to be the primary medical contact for all FID sailors, that I wanted us to be the "family doctor," not only for the sailors but for their families as well. This would entail a helpful attitude and an eagerness to assume responsibility for their care, though. Several times I walked by the ER on the way to my office and overheard a corpsman telling a patient, "You'll have to come by tomorrow morning in sick call for that." That was exactly the kind of comment I'd tried to fight the entire time we were under way. It always amazed me how the guys expected the rules to change as soon as we came into port. Whenever I heard it I would intervene, find out what was bothering the sailor, walk right into the ER with him, and make the corpsman help me with the treatment.

After the patient left, usually with some minor problem, I'd ask the corpsman why he hadn't gone ahead and treated the patient at that time. "Well, I thought that's what sick call was for."

"But you weren't doing anything. It would be different if you were busy. You're just sitting there reading a book."

"Well, we always just tell them to come back the next morning."

No, we did not tell them to come back the next morning! If you're treating somebody else or if we're in the middle of an emergency, that's one thing. Sure, we schedule sick call so people can bring in their routine problems in the morning, but if he's here right with you now and alive, why not treat him right then if you have time. That way he won't have to come back in the morning. It's another way to cut down on lines in sick call. I tried to impress on the corpsmen that there was a reason why the guy came in when he did. Maybe an injury was hurting him, maybe he was worried, maybe he didn't have time the next morning. Trying to get across the service aspect of medical care was a constant effort. So often, people who work in a medical setting think that people should have to conform to the system. No wonder, if sailors got turned away on the ship, that they'd go to a clinic. Our corpsmen all understood this, and they, too, believed in giving service. Sometimes, though, when people are accustomed to a routine, it's hard to break out of it.

One day I was writing out some charts and realized I hadn't spoken to the SuppO about my concern that Master Chief Morgan might have a drinking problem. It's only about fifty feet down to the supply department office, so I went down to discuss it with Brice.

"I appreciate your calling it to my attention, Doc. We'll look out for it. Did you actually smell alcohol on him?"

"No, just the speech. Now that I think of it, he's been kind of grouchy lately, too, and don't you think he's been looking real tired?"

"Yeah, but we're busy as hell. He's a pretty good chief, Doc, but I know you can't always tell. He doesn't have any past history of alcohol trouble."

Just then I felt a little embarrassed and a little guilty. As a neurologist, there should have been a lot of things I'd think of in a guy with slurred speech. Was I starting to confine my diagnostic thinking to automatic lines? I'd have to talk to Art Corbett about this. I knew he'd been seeing Master Chief Morgan for something.

Back in the office, I returned to the paperwork and left the door open. I heard a sailor come in and complain about a cough and a sore throat. SK3 Womple was on duty, and in cynical tone he said, "Well, there's nothing I can do about it now. You can either wait until sick call tomorrow, or, if I were you, I'd go on over to the clinic over on the base." That kind of comment tripped my fuse. I immediately jumped over to the ER.

As usual, Womple hadn't even left his chair when the sailor came into the ER. He had a magazine opened up on the desk and hadn't taken the sailor's pulse, temperature, or blood pressure.

"What's the problem, sailor?" I asked.

The guy had been feeling ill for a couple of days and had a fever. He'd been coughing and had a headache. I spent about half an hour taking his history and treating him. We gave him something for his cough, and I called up his DivO to ask for him to have the rest of the day in the rack and to stop by to see me tomorrow morning to see whether he could go back to work then. Then I closed the door. Womple looked surly. I reiterated for him my desire to treat people on the ship rather than send them over to the clinic.

"Yeah, but what are we supposed to do if somebody comes in sick in the afternoon? We can't treat them here."

"Who says we can't treat them here? I'm a doctor, and there are twenty corpsmen around here at work. We've been treating them here for the last six months."

Womple just shrugged and began reading his magazine again.

"Did you just decide this conversation is over?"

"I thought you were through."

"Look, Petty Officer Womple, we are here to provide a service, and we are *going* to function just like a real clinic around here. If you don't give me some sign that you understand that, I'll try to get you assigned somewhere that you do understand the boss."

"Yes, Sir." He sort of stood up, but when I left there I didn't feel any better about what he was going to do.

A couple of days later, still worried about that interaction, I met with HMCS Myers and Rick Cox to see if Womple was having more personal problems, as he had during the deployment. Myers checked with Womple, who told him to bug off, and with Family Services, where the counselor said the family problems weren't too severe. In fact, the center was surprised that Womple had been allowed to come home early from the deployment.

When we had been back in Mayport about a week, Cdr. Kit Hennesy, the skipper from the Red Lions, called to follow up on the eyeglasses matter we had discussed at the end of the cruise. He wanted to repeat his visual testing when he wasn't tired. I knew it was still going to show that he needed eyeglasses, but if it would make him feel better about it, why not? When we repeated his refraction, he still needed a little correction for astigmatism and about a -1.25 correction for myopia. When we dialed that up on the phoroptor, he recognized that his vision was much better.

Since we had first raised the subject during the cruise, he'd thought it over and was willing to go ahead with the glasses. Frankly, I think the reason he'd wanted to wait was simply that when the cruise was over he'd be living at home, not among his fellow aviators, so wearing glasses wouldn't be quite as visible. He would, of course, wear his glasses when he was flying. No aviators wanted to wear glasses or to admit that they needed them, but modern aviators also wouldn't expose themselves or others to hazard by leaving them off. With their visors down, other people couldn't see them wearing the glasses most of the time, anyway. Still, aviators are aviators. They'd wear them if they had to, but just as soon not talk about it.

Although he was the first, Kit wasn't the last of my patients from the cruise that I heard from that week. In the mail I received a summary of Oliver Leen's treatment at NH Naples. The course of his pyelonephritis was detailed. Intravenous ampicillin had been able to cure the infection. Once that was under control, a small adjustment in his insulin dosing got the diabetes under control, also.

After his pyelonephritis had been repaired and the insulin dose adjusted, Leen was back to appearing pretty healthy. He convinced the internist at the hospital that he felt well and that the staff needed him. The internist knew we had a robust medical department on the ship, and saw that with just two and a half weeks of hospitalization the patient's blood sugar was back in normal range. Leen showed the doctor that he knew how to take his insulin, and they agreed that he should be able to return to the ship. Of course, the young internist had never been to sea, so he didn't realize limitations in our medical department. Most especially, he didn't realize that Leen had hidden his illness at a time when he was very sick and alone in his stateroom. If he had become comatose, and if his fellow officers had not gone to look for him, he might have died.

The regulations—and, in my opinion, just plain common sense—called for a "medical board," a process that establishes and documents an individual's diagnosis and limits his duties and assignments. In this case, dependence on insulin would prohibit Leen from going to sea. With Leen's prodding, however, the internist simply wrote a discharge summary that allowed Leen to return to the United States, and at the bottom of the summary he recommended that Leen return to sea duty. I was frustrated by the results and angry at what I considered manipulation of the system. Probably I took it too much as a personal affront when I should have confined the focus to the matters of Leen's health and effects on the command. His health was important to me, though, especially on the ship. I was afraid that the next time, particularly if he hid his illness again, the outcome might be worse.

I telephoned Leen and told him I thought there had been a misunderstanding. "No, there was no misunderstanding. The doctor at Naples thought I could return to full duty without any problem." I told him I had no choice but to discuss it with the admiral and to refer the case back to another internal medicine consultation at NH Jacksonville. Leen obviously didn't like that information.

When I went to see Admiral Kohl, he had already spoken to

Commander Leen. Always loyal and concerned about his officers, the admiral wanted to be sure that Leen's career wasn't damaged. As long as Leen took his insulin, wouldn't he be the same as anybody else?

The last thing I wanted to be was the adversary of a naval officer. I was supposed to help guys like Leen fill out their careers and stay healthy, not punish them. I told the admiral that and assured him that it was Oliver's safety I was most concerned about. None of us wanted to find Leen dead in his rack some morning. I had carried this discussion as far as it needed to go. Sniffles Kohl didn't need my elementary sermons on things he understood very well. Furthermore, I knew he was every bit as concerned about Oliver's health as I was. He just wanted to protect the man's career if he could.

I recommended that the admiral let me refer the case to the chief of internal medicine over at NH Jacksonville, Capt. John Seibel, and that we have him review the matter.

The commander reluctantly went to see Dr. Seibel. As I expected, John agreed that with the amount of insulin Leen took he should not be on sea duty, and that was what he recommended in the medical board. Finally, it was settled. Cdr. Oliver Leen was officially not fit for sea duty. I felt somewhat guilty, like I did when I had to tell an aviator he couldn't fly anymore, but I was relieved that Oliver Leen wouldn't be in that dangerous position at sea again.

Mayport

The first three to four weeks I worked just as many hours as I had while under way. Don and Art took some leave, so I was the only doctor on the ship. I was still learning about the ship and the crew, so by the time I finished seeing patients and writing up my notes it was usually pretty late in the day. Gradually, however, I was able to get a little spare time. When Don and Art returned from leave, I didn't have to see all the patients myself. I was getting a little faster working with the ship's bureaucracy and records systems, so I began to have time for jogging again and seeing a little bit of the town.

The Mayport and Jacksonville area is way up at the northern part of Florida, so it's not entirely unscathed by winter. It never got really cold, though. Most days the temperature stayed up in the fifties or better, and only very rarely dipped down to the thirties. We had a lot of bright days—maybe because of the coastal winds. I jogged from Charlie pier down to the main road on the base, which was called Maine Road. There was a large lagoon in the middle of the base, right across from the exchange area, with a sign that said "No swimming. Beware of alligators." These were earnest signs in northern Florida. The kids who hung around the pond saw the alligator occasionally. He apparently was only about six feet long, but we all took him pretty seriously. More of a hazard than the alligator, however, was the flock of geese who hung out at the northern edge of the lagoon, right by the day-care center. Geese are not only confident animals, they're also pretty aggressive. A sensible jogger would be hesitant whenever going by them—even more than with a pack of barking dogs—because they would run up and nip at your ankles. Sometimes I imagined being in the headlines the next morning listed as "Navy Doctor Mauled to Death by Pack of Wild Geese."

Just a quarter mile past the geese was the beach. The beaches in this part of Florida were flat, had very find sand, and stretched for miles and miles uninterrupted. To be sure, there was a big chain-link fence all the way around the base, extending right down to the beach, halfway between the high-tide and low-tide lines. A guard was stationed there to make certain that unauthorized strangers wouldn't just walk onto the base.

On the very north end of the beach at the naval station, right at the inlet, was a complex of buildings called the Fleet Training Center (FTC). Here a conglomeration of training activities were carried on, both for people who were assigned to ships and would come for refresher training, and for people en route to assignments at sea. For example, the fire-fighting school was here. It was just like the schools at San Diego and Norfolk. Some of the people who had come to the *Forrestal* would have intermediate orders to the FTC for a couple of weeks for fire fighting if they hadn't had that training elsewhere first. Every Tuesday and Wednesday around midday, a big black cloud would rise up from the FTC while people suffered through the exercises for fighting an oil fire on the simulated deck.

There was also an eighteen-hole golf course, always busy, winding through the base. It ran from over near the housing area on the beach all the way back to Maine Road, and then crossed the road over toward the naval air station, just inland and along the southeast side of the main naval station.

The air station was primarily there for the LAMPS helicopters on the small boys. The H-2 helo, now almost thirty years old, had been developed for the antisubmarine mission primarily off the backs of destroyers and cruisers. It fulfilled a number of other functions for the small ships, of course, but its main mission was to hunt submarines, just like the H-3 on the carrier. A small but very capable aircraft, the H-2 had a crew of three, two pilots in front and the sonar operator/crewman in the back. All Navy helos had two pilots.

One of the places I liked to run the most was out the back gate from the naval station to a perimeter road around the runway. The perimeter road ran out to the right and bordered up against the old fishing village of Mayport, a rustic little settlement along the St. Johns inlet. There were no openings in the chain-link fence around the air station, but of course you could see through to the old village. Some of the people had chicken coops, with very funny looking chickens. They were both scrawny and sinewy-looking, with high, red topknots and real long, pointy spurs. They were kept in different cages from the kind you usually saw for egglayers or roasters, so we figured they were fighting cocks. The houses were an eclectic collection of shacks and old Gulf-style southern homes. The road turned down along the main runway and ran past a mile or more of marshes mixed between long expanses of green, lawnlike grass. After going all the way around the runway, I'd double back and run north again on the other side. Turning right would divert the run back to the golf course, a circuit of around five and a half miles. If instead I went all the way around the main road and back up to the beach, the trip was a little over eight miles.

Only one road—appropriately enough named Mayport Avenue— led into the naval station and naval air station. Stretching three and a half miles without a bend, curve, or even flicker, it seemed a lot longer than it was. There were only a few kinds of businesses on that route: honky-tonk bars, tire stores, used car lots, and pawnshops. Well, that's not exactly true. There was one small shopping center, the first Food Lion store I ever saw, and a couple of tattoo parlors. Mayport Avenue had two very different identities. During the day, especially at rush hour, it was a three-and-a-half-mile parking lot for the unfortunate souls who were squeezed into the home of two dozen ships and a dozen helicopter squadrons on a single road. By night it was North Florida's Times Square.

Among the nightspots on the Great Honky-Tonk Way were the Flamingo Lounge, Cap'n Odie's, and Big Jim's Gold Coast (just "Big Jim's" to the insiders). Also, down at the corner where Atlantic Boulevard, the main east-west road, intersected Mayport Avenue, there was a fake-adobe liquor store and bar combo that had a semi-pseudo-Western motif and a big brown horseshoe painted on one wall. It didn't have a name, at least not where you could see it. I never went into Cap'n Odie's, the Flamingo Lounge, or Big Jim's, but of those three, Big Jim's scared me the most. I'd fancied myself a pretty rough hombre in my younger years (no doubt a laughable self-delusion), but I freely confess that there was no time in my life when I would have been brave enough to go into Big Jim's. It had the kind of look on the outside—and the intimidating impression in the parking lot—that anybody who hadn't killed five or six men with his bare hands didn't have a chance.

However, the toughest looking of them all was that semi-pseudo-Western place down at the corner of Mayport and Atlantic. I called it "The Corral" because that just kind of seemed like what it should be named. Occasionally, somebody would roll one of those illuminated trailer signs out front to advertise country music or something. There was always at least one misspelled word or missing letter. The sign might say, "L_dies nite Wesday nite." The place looked rough. I was told that the reason they had a Western motif wasn't so much that the people there were especially devoted to country music, or any other music for that matter. It was just that they hoped the music would drive black guys away. It was so rough looking I sometimes felt nervous just driving past. I don't remember ever seeing any cars in front of the place, but it never went broke in all the months I was there.

The sailors mostly stayed away from Big Jim's. Even sailors as young and feisty as they can be, especially with a snootful of booze, recognized that Big Jim's was a good place to avoid. The worst beatings I had to take care of in the ER seemed to come from Big Jim's. One night, a sailor had a deep knife cut almost from ear to ear from an attempted throat-slitting. Somehow the attacker had just not pushed hard enough. I admit this particular sailor had a fleshy double chin, but the attacker seemed to miss all the major vessels and never even cut into the windpipe. Most guys who got beat up at Big Jim's had at least two inches bitten out of one ear or the other—it seems like the right ear a little more often than the left. Their noses were almost always broken.

Another interesting thing about Big Jim's was that no *Forrestal* sailors seemed to lose a fair fight in there. From what my patients told me, there was some mystical dirty fighter who always seemed to sneak up from behind and hit my guys. For any of the sailors who were sober enough to talk, it was always "He sucker-punched me." This mystery puncher wouldn't have touched my guys in a fair fight. They never saw the guy who hit them. He always seemed to jump out from behind them and punch them for no good reason. The *Forrestal* sailors were "just standing there, minding my own business," or "talking to this girl," when they were attacked without provocation. How he was able to keep punching them for so long and so accurately, and also to bite out a piece of their ear, was always a mystery to me.

By contrast, the beatings from Cap'n Odie's weren't nearly as bad. To be sure, the guys from Cap'n Odie's had a lot of black eyes, an occasional broken tooth, and less often a cut from a knife, but the sailor always reassured me that he had eventually finished off the other guy. About a third of the time, the beaten sailor had a buddy standing behind him who would silently shake his head, smile, and look down at the floor. The buddy would discreetly signal me that the FID sailor had lost. However, I prefer to believe that all the guys at Cap'n Odie's won their fights and that at Big Jim's they were all sucker-punched.

One tragicomic irony from Cap'n Odie's never seemed to register with the FID sailors. The main reasons for going to Cap'n Odie's were that the music was good and there were a lot of very friendly women. Now, no FID sailor in history ever had to pay for a date, so I know these women danced and spent time with our sailors just because they liked them and wanted to spend time with young men. It was said, though, that some of the good-looking and friendly young women at Cap'n Odie's were married to sailors from other ships. Indeed, when we returned from our deployment, a few FID sailors found that their wives had taken up with other men, some from Mayport. How many of those had met their new loves in Cap'n Odie's I don't know.

Petty Officer Ryan Hart was very fond of Cap'n Odie's. He was also fond of falling in love. It seems like the first night we got back into Mayport, Ryan had to make it over there. By the time we'd been there about a week, he brought his new girlfriend in to show her around the department. It was around 1900, and he brought her by my office to meet me. (The corpsmen liked to bring their girlfriends to meet me, as teenagers would bring them by to meet their parents.) As usual, I was finishing up my paperwork for the day. "Captain Riley, this is my girlfriend, Linda." She was a very clean-cut, outgoing, charming young woman. She stuck out her hand with a lot of confidence and didn't have the kind of shy frivolity that a lot of the young women who came around the medical department had. Ryan was around twenty-two, and I guessed that this young woman was somewhere between twenty-six and twenty-eight.

"Where are you two off to tonight?" I asked.

"We don't know yet," Linda said. "We both like to go dancing." I guessed they were probably going to Cap'n Odie's. About a week later I learned that Ryan was planning to get married. This was the modern age, so I guess they weren't in a big hurry to get married, but Ryan seemed to spend a lot of time at her house. I tried not to get into the private lives of my corpsmen or to give out too much advice. I knew advice was usually not welcome even with your own children, so you had to be very careful how you used it with others. I told Ryan, however, that moving into somebody's house wasn't like in the movies. It carried more commitments than he might realize, and probably a young man in his position should be just as careful about that as he would be about getting married. You could tell my advice amused him by its old-fashionedness. It was as though he thought it was cute for me to be concerned, but found it quaint and outdated just the same.

Art Corbett popped into my office one afternoon. "Skipper, I need your help with a patient, or I guess with his boss." Art and I both knew I was no skipper, but he called me that, I suspect because he knew I liked it. What a craftsman. He had won me over, though. Art worked harder than I had realized at first, and despite his deceptively spicy exterior he never stopped thinking about his patients. "It's Master Chief Morgan, Skipper. He refuses to take his damn blood pressure medicine and he keeps smokin'. He knows he's supposed to be in here to let me check his pressure every week until we get it under control, but I just can't get him in here. He keeps givin' me excuses. Can you talk to the SuppO?"

"Sure I can. What's his pressure been running, Art?"

"Last few times its been around 105 to 115."

"What about the systolic?"

"That's been as high as 180 to 190. But that's been almost a month ago. I can't get him in here. When I go down to his spaces, he always seems to be someplace else."

As bad as those pressures were, considering the fact that they were in a guy in his forties who was on treatment, they might be worse than the numerical values suggested. I called the SuppO immediately. Guiltily it again crossed my mind that the speech problem I'd noticed might not have a thing to do with alcohol. High blood pressure causes disease in the small arteries in the brain: that can affect speech. Medications can slur speech. Hypertension can damage the heart, and diminished cardiac output can affect the brain. His blood pressure was out of control.

"He's on leave, Doc," Bruce told me.

We called Master Chief Morgan's leave phone number. Disconnected. He would be back in less than a week. Art would bring him in so I could go over the case with them.

"One last thing, Art. Does the master chief have a drinking problem?"

"Used to. Don't think he does anymore . . . but you know, I've wondered whether that has anything to do with the pressure getting out of control. Seems like it got worse about the time the cruise ended." Art and I worried about the master chief the rest of that week.

One day around that time, my morning started off bad. The OOD called me from the quarterdeck to tell me my bicycle had been crushed. There was a bike rack tied to the brow on the pier. I have to admit I sometimes thought it a little strange that nobody but me used that rack. It seems that overnight, the tides had been a lot worse than usual and the metal frame from the brow shifted quite a bit, in the process smashing the bike rack and my ten-speed into an eight-foot paper clip. I was still stewing about that when HM1 Dunbar came to my office to tell me that Petty Officer Beaumont was on the phone.

"Hey, where is he, by the way? I didn't see him this morning. Did I forget he was on leave or something?"

"No, Captain, that's why he's on the phone," Tom explained. "He didn't come in this morning, and he's calling in now."

Beaumont impressed me as being a little older, a little more mature than the others. Even though he was a first class petty officer, he seemed to belong higher, like a chief. We had a trusting approach with our guys as much as we could, so we wanted to work with someone like Hugh if he had a problem that kept him away from the ship for a day.

"Sorry, Captain, having a little personal problem at home. Can I get leave for today?"

I told him we'd try to help. What was the problem?

"Well, my parents and I are having some problems, you know, after the cruise and all." Beaumont was a bachelor who lived with his parents when we were in home port. "Guess we just need to get the trust thing back, you know?"

Ah, the famous "trust thing." It means so many different things to different people. Certainly I knew that my simply coming back to the Navy and being so far away from my family was a strain on trust in our home. Sure, I worried about it, too, but maybe it meant something different to Hugh. "What about trust, Hugh?"

"Oh, you know, what they're thinking, what other people are thinking. You know it can all run together when people think or talk about you."

I didn't get it. "When people talk about you, Petty Officer Beaumont?"

"You probably can understand what I mean. I know it's been hard for you, too, Captain. I mean, I know there are people who would like to see you hurt around here. And I think that's too bad. It's that same trust thing. Loyalty. You know that's what's wrong in this country, trust and loyalty. It's like back with McCarthy, you know? . . . Oh, I'm so tired, I'm not making any sense," he realized.

"Not really, Petty Officer Beaumont. I don't follow you. Have you been up all night?" He had. "Have you been drinking or taking medications?"

"No!" he said quite angrily. "I told you once that I don't have any substance problems anymore." As a teenager he drank too much for a few years. "Substances are part of the problem in this country."

I told him to get some sleep and come to see me in the morning. Immediately I asked HM1 Dunbar and Chief Henderson to come into my office. "You guys been seeing anything funny about HM1 Beaumont?"

No.

"If I wanted to check with some of his buddies, who would I ask?"

"He's kind of a loner, actually, Dr. Riley," said the chief. A man his age who still lived with his parents was not common, but not real alarming either. Neither of them had noticed any wandering speech or anything else strange. I asked them to pay attention and resolved to be sure to check up on Hugh the next morning.

We were interrupted just then when Billy Dorsey was brought in by his DivO. Once again, he had a big cut over his eyebrow, and his mouth and cheeks were swollen. He had some scrapes on his hands and elbows. He'd obviously been beat up again the night before. He was walking a little crooked, bent over slightly to the right. As I examined him, I pressed over the midaxillary line on his right rib cage, and he jumped about eighteen inches instantly. I was a little afraid he might have a broken rib.

"What happened last night, Billy?"

"Nothin'." Funny, while it was nothing that happened to him, he still had that coquettish little grin. It kind of made you want him to be your little boy. On the one hand, I wanted to scold him, but on the other hand, I thought I should find a rocking chair someplace and sit down and cuddle with him a little bit. His tousled red hair had the character you used to see in the Buster Brown ads, like somebody purposefully laid it at those angles. Only if you got within two feet and had the smell of that stale, semirotten alcohol from the night before pierce the cuteness were you reminded that poor Billy's life was beginning to be a mess.

"Billy, we asked you to see the alcohol counselor the last time. What did he say?" I knew what he said. The note back from the CAAC had said that AN Dorsey was an immature fellow who had been introduced to his first alcohol contacts and would need a lot of watching. The counselor had recommended that Billy be directed to attend AA meetings for several weeks. We had an AA group on the ship that was very vigorous and met every day, twice a day while we were under way. His DivO hadn't followed through on that, however. I had phoned his DivO twice in the interim, but had found only indifference. "Boys will be boys." Now here Billy was again, beat up for the second time in a short period. I filled out another CAAC report and resolved that I had to talk to the air boss about him directly.

To check out the possibility of a rib fracture, I requested a chest X ray. The HN who was on duty shuffled his feet, mumbled something that might have been a little bit like "Yes, Sir," and then left the room. AN Dorsey and I were alone then, and he looked at me sheepishly, like a little boy whose daddy might not take him fishing that day because he'd been naughty. In a few minutes, HM1 Dunbar, who was supervising that day, came in to take Dorsey for his X ray. I figured SK3 Womple was back warming up the X-ray unit or putting film in the cassette.

While they went off to get the X ray, I looked after a patient who had a fishhook in his finger. Just outside the Charlie pier where we were tied up, there was a long, rock breakwater that stretched out beside the St. Johns inlet. When guys were off duty, they'd frequently fish off that rock pier. Anglers know it's common for people to get fishhooks stuck in their earlobes and fingers, but only people who work in emergency rooms know just *how* common it is. There are little barbs at the end of a fishhook, so it can't be just pulled out the way it went in. The hook needs to be pushed all the way through if it isn't already, and the eyelet has to be cut off so the hook can be curled right back out, by the pointy end. This is usually pretty easy to do on fingers and earlobes, but sometimes it's a little tougher on cheeks or chins. The thing we were most concerned about was the possibility of an infection. Fish, fishhooks, and worms can bring a perplexing panoply of bacteria and cause serious cellulitis. I didn't like to give prophylactic antibiotics, but after I removed the fishhook I usually required the individual to soak the affected hand in a disinfecting soap solution for thirty minutes or so. That's what we were doing with this patient when a very sheepish HN Rodney walked in.

Corpsmen Too

Rodney was a new corpsman, a very quiet fellow, always eager to help. He walked into the ER, sidled over in front of the desk where I was writing a few notes, and just stood there with his hands behind his back, looking down at the deck. He could see that there wasn't anything more to be done with the patient, who was just sitting down and soaking his hand, and obviously I didn't need any help writing the note. Still, he stood there shifting his weight from first the left, then the right foot, then back again, staring at the deck, saying nothing. Now and then his foot would kick at the corner of one of the tiles.

I finished writing the note about the fishhook patient and was still waiting for Billy Dorsey to come back from his X ray. I looked up at Rodney, who still had nothing to say, just shifting back and forth from one foot to the other.

"What's up, HN Rodney? Do you need me for something?"

"Yes, Sir. Well, Sir. I guess I need to talk to you. Senior Chief said I should ask to see you in your office." He said all that without making real good eye contact, still mostly concentrating on the deck tiles. I didn't need all my powers of marvelous insight to recognize this was a bad sign. "Well, it looks like you've got some kind of trouble. It will be a little while before they get back with those X rays. Why don't we go into my office and find out what's wrong."

Getting HN Rodney to tell me about his problem was harder than opening a box of cornflakes. Every time I thought I could get him to come to the point, he figured out some other way not to open up. It seems that he had just bought a new pickup a couple of days after finishing the cruise. The vehicle had needed some new tires, but he couldn't get the kind he wanted in Mayport. To get the right kind of tires, he'd gone down to Neptune Beach, then over to the outskirts of Jacksonville. Nobody had what he wanted. So he decided to get them someplace else, and he finally did. Then last night he'd gone out to eat with some buddies, and one of the friends needed to be dropped off at the post office. Then he had to call his mother, then it was getting too late. Then his buddy had to go over to somebody else's house. Then there was . . .

"Enough! Will you please tell me what the problem was?! Did it have something to do with the car?"

"Well, Sir, I'm not sure they could really make it stick."

"Make *what* stick?" It turns out that HN Rodney and some buddies had gone to Cap'n Odie's for a few drinks. When he came back on the base in his new pickup (Why did a single, nineteen-year-old kid who lived on ship need a pickup truck?), he'd been stopped for driving while intoxicated.

"Why did they stop you if you weren't doing anything wrong? How did they know you'd been drinking?"

The answer to that is the old standby familiar to all doctors. "I just don't know. I only had two beers." Any drunk person you ever see in an emergency room, especially if they've just been stopped while driving, or if they just got beat up, always consumed "just two beers."

Rodney hadn't really sought me out because he wanted my advice or because of his conscience. DWI is a major offense in the Navy, and a major offense to Captain Guitar. Being stopped for DWI on a military base causes an entire cascade of unpleasant things to happen. There is an official notification to the command, which Rod knew was already in the works. Unless there were some remarkably unusual extenuating circumstances, and there never were, the member's driver's license would be suspended on all military bases for at least one year.

Captain Guitar, like most COs, took DWI seriously and insisted that being caught for DWI was a ticket to captain's mast. It was a way for him to personally keep track of guys who had alcohol trouble and to demonstrate his concern. Although my one experience at captain's mast had shown that Captain Guitar's reputation for harshness at NJP ("nonjudicial punishment," the legal term for captain's mast) was grossly exaggerated, the sailors didn't know that. Most of them would much prefer to stand in front of any hanging judge, or perhaps to be flogged or keelhauled, rather than stand before Captain Guitar at captain's mast for anything, much less DWI. So, Rodney hadn't come to me as a conscience-troubled supplicant. He knew very well that he was in a whole bunch of trouble, and that I was going to find out before too long anyway.

I had spent so much time talking with the corpsmen about drinking and driving that HN Rodney knew very well where I stood on the subject. We had talked about recreation and sports the guys could participate in when off duty. We worked on departmental group activities without alcohol. We had buddy systems. And on top of all that, we'd given warnings about consequences. Furthermore, I was tied up with Billy Dorsey, and one other patient was now waiting out in the passageway. I was beginning to wonder why it was taking so long to get Dorsey's X ray. Truthfully, my frustration with Dorsey's drinking had already tightened my spring about young guys' alcohol problems. HN Rodney was nineteen, just like Dorsey. There was a more than additive effect having both of them there with me at once.

"HN Rodney, I'm so mad at you I can't talk about this right now. If you expect me to give you some sympathy under these circumstances, you can forget about it. Do you remember the four or five times at quarters before the end of the cruise when I stood in front of you and all the other corpsmen and asked you to be very careful about drinking and driving when we returned?"

His response to that was the same as his circumlocution a few minutes before. He threw his arms up and started to talk, babbling on about how he really didn't think he'd had too much to drink. Teenage excuses. I knew the security force on the base was experienced. They knew all the signs. If they said a nineteen-year-old guy was driving under the influence, it was probably because he had been zigzagging, had avoided apprehension, or had run a red light. If they said a guy had been drinking, he had been.

"Never mind. I think you'd better see Senior Chief Myers, then make sure you get hooked up with the CAAC, and then you'd better go down to see Master Chief Shapiro to see if there's anything we can do to save your career. I want to talk to you this afternoon. I hate it when any of my guys have to go to captain's mast. I swore that nobody in this department was going to go to captain's mast. You let me and the whole department down, now get out of here!" Master Chief Shapiro was the command master chief (CMC). He was the senior enlisted on the ship, and he maintained a kind of paternal oversight on the enlisted guys, keeping all the chiefs and master chiefs organized and bestowing the right attitude as much as possible among the troops. He also was available if a sailor needed an advocate with his own department head or the skipper.

I liked Rodney, so why was I getting this upset, I asked myself. Isn't this one of those predictable leadership situations? Slowly it came to me. It was, I realized, more of a parenting situation. One of the reasons I felt so close to Rod and a couple of the others was that they were exactly the age of my own children. I was feeling guilty these weeks about not being with my daughters, and when I saw guys like Rod needing a parent it struck me that this day, my daughters were missing a father because I was down here. The situation was real enough by itself—I was worried about the kid! In my guts, though, I was mad at myself, as though I were somehow letting something like this happen to my Mary or Abby by not being with them (Deirdre at that time was way too young to drive).

Already worked up by all these thoughts, I was starting to fester about why I didn't have Dorsey's X ray back yet. When I stepped across the passageway to the view box, I saw that Petty Officer Laflame had brought three chest X rays back. One of them was so overpenetrated that it was just a black shadow with the faintest evidence that there was a heart someplace in the middle. Another one had pretty good black/white contrast, but it completely cut off the top of the lung. A third one was an attempt at a rib view. To look at ribs specifically requires angling the chest in a certain manner so that the profile of the ribs at a certain level is up against the film in a way that gives the best resolution of detail. Rib detail was not entirely clear here, but good enough that I could see that there didn't seem to be a fracture in the tender point.

The fact that HM3 Laflame had to bring the films, and especially the fact that the films were so poor, told me that SK3 Womple hadn't done them. Arden Womple was often sullen, not an inspired genius, and usually pretty listless, but he took excellent X rays. These were not his work. "How come Womple didn't take these films?"

"Well, Sir, maybe you should talk to HM1 Rosen." HM3 Donovan Laflame was real difficult to understand. He was born in the United States but raised by his Haitian parents and married to a Haitian woman, and he spoke exclusively Creole except when he was on the ship. He was nearing completion of his baccalaureate degree, and he was probably one of our brightest corpsmen. It was just hard to understand him. He could sense my frustration about this situation, and it was quite apparent that he was quite discouraged about his own difficulty with the films.

One of Laflame's traits was that he never liked to be the bearer of bad news. It was becoming clear that had something to do with Arden Womple. There I was already angry, so out I went looking for Rosen. Burt wasn't in the administrative office, and he wasn't over in medical supply. Finally, I found him in medical records. I didn't even have to ask him the question. "Arden is UA, Cap'n." UA (unexcused absence) is the Navy term for AWOL.

"Where is he?"

"Don't know, Sir, but I think we can guess. This has happened once or twice before. In port, Arden sometimes takes a room over at the Quality Inn and drinks all night. He usually gets up OK the next morning, but once last year he overslept, and he probably did it this time, too." We sent one of the corpsmen out to find him, and sure enough, he was hibernating in a drunken funk on the second deck of the Quality Inn a half mile outside the gate.

By the time they brought Arden back to the ship, Petty Officers Laflame and Brant had worked together to finally get a good set of chest and rib X rays on Billy Dorsey. Nothing broken and no pulmonary contusion evident. He apparently just had a bad bruise. I had spoken to his DivO, as well as the CAAC. We couldn't legally confine him to the ship without captain's mast, but his DivO told him he couldn't leave the ship for the next two days, and we were going to check up on his attendance at AA meetings. After a thorough evaluation with the counselor, we'd decide whether he had to be in Level II treatment or whether just putting him on buddy care and making him go to AA for a while would be adequate.

Two and a half hours later, Arden Womple came into the medical department. He had bags under his eyes, which looked a little bloodshot, but he had a clean set of dungarees on and was cleanly shaven. Oh my, he looked so ashamed, so dejected, and so contrite. His demeanor contrasted starkly with HN Rodney's. For one thing, Arden was older. Whereas Rodney was full of excuses and wanted to tell me all about how the situation wasn't as bad as it looked, Womple was so sorry, and so embarrassed. Here was my third major alcohol flap of the day, a guy who had been UA—a pretty serious offense—and had jeopardized adequate medical care. All that made me pretty angry. And Womple's laundry bag was already full!

There was more, though. I was frustrated because of the alcohol in those two younger guys, but in retrospect I think I was angriest because of my frustration with the medical department. Although only one fully trained X-ray tech is assigned to the department, there is supposed to be adequate cross training so that good X rays can be taken by several, if not most, corpsmen even if the X-ray tech is away for some reason. In Arden's absence, it had been a classic goat rope to try to provide a simple chest X ray and rib films. It wasn't just Womple's fault that he hadn't been there so that we had to call on the other corpsmen. It was also his fault (but especially my fault) that the others weren't adequately trained to take good films. Training the other corpsmen in X-ray techniques was one of the main functions of the full-time X-ray tech. Obviously that had been woefully neglected in the crew we had on duty that morning.

Given all that, I was surprised to find that instead of being angry, I was worried about Arden.

"Petty Officer Womple, I need to know if there is something wrong."

No answer from him. He just sat there looking at the deck. I decided to give him some time to talk. Maybe if he wasn't pressured he'd tell me more. It seemed like we waited there for most of the day, although I guess it was probably only five minutes or so.

He shuffled in his chair a little bit, looked up at me as though about to speak, but then it dropped out. He put his hands together and looked back at the deck again, and we started another long, silent interval.

Finally I couldn't stand it anymore and was about to talk when Arden decided to say something. "I'm sorry. I know that doesn't help, but I've just had a lot on my mind." Again, I let him be in control as much as he wanted to be, so I didn't say anything. A few more minutes went by. "Sorry I was late this morning. I didn't do it on purpose." We waited silently again.

"Petty Officer Womple, do we need to talk about what's wrong?"

"No, Sir, I can handle it myself." Another one of those painful, long silences. I was beginning to wonder if this was going to make me miss my next couple of meals. Finally, when he still didn't say anything, I had to. "Petty Officer Womple, I'm not going to put you on report. You know I prefer that we handle problems within our department. However, you are a petty officer. The more junior guys look up to you. Try to help me out here. They know that UA is a fairly serious offense, and a petty officer would usually lose a stripe for that. We didn't turn you in, and you're back on the ship now, so UA is out of the question. I'm not interested in giving you a hard time about this, because it's clear there's something bothering you. But I can't help you if you don't tell me about it."

Still more silence, still looking at the deck.

"Well, you sure have a right to not want to talk just to me. I really think it looks like you need to talk to somebody, though. Maybe you should think about talking to Petty Officer Brant or one of the chiefs. In the meantime, you know I have to turn you over to the CAAC."

Arden had been to Level II treatment before. He had been recommended for Level III—the inpatient program—twice at prior commands, but he always transferred right around the time he was supposed to go in. That shouldn't happen. A sailor who needs Level III or has unresolved alcohol difficulties isn't really eligible for transfer. A command can't just ignore a fellow's problem and dump it on the unsuspecting next command. It's a safeguard that works most of the time, but a few guys slip through the pages occasionally . . . and the sailor himself sometimes participates in the slipup.

It was hard to imagine that with his attitude and performance Womple had any chance of promotion or even retention. Art Corbett and Senior Chief Myers determined to spend more time with him, encourage him, see what other help he needed, and be sure we got him back with the CAAC.

It turns out that Arden had been an active participant in the AA meetings for a while, but had only been going sporadically, if at all, for the past several months. I also asked the CAAC to help us decide whether SK3 Womple should get into Level III treatment. "We need to have a course of Level II first, Captain."

I pointed out that Arden had already been to Level II. "Well, not here on the FID, and he never really finished it." Level II was a kind of intense daytime treatment program that involved classroom, group meetings, and a little individual counseling. It had a good track record in some cases, but generally with people who were on a brink more or less, not really hooked. The Level III inpatient program was reserved mostly for Level II failures.

"How about Antabuse, Dr. Riley?" the CAAC suggested. Antabuse, or disulfiram, is a drug often used in alcohol treatment programs. There's some controversy about its role, and even about whether it helps at all. The patient takes the pill once a day, usually in the morning when well motivated. If a person taking Antabuse consumes any alcohol, he gets violently sick. Knowing that, presumably he won't take or won't tolerate alcohol in a moment of weakness later. Antabuse is surely not for everybody. Whatever merits it may or may not have, I always felt it had no role at all if the subject wasn't the one who wanted it. So the CAAC and I decided we might talk it over with Petty Officer Womple, depending on how things went during Level II and his AA meetings.

The next day I went to see the XO about HN Rodney. "I know you got the report chit about Rodney's DWI. He's a great corpsman, though, and I really gave him hell yesterday. He's got the max number of hours of EMI I could assign, and the base security took away his driver's license, so he won't be driving his new pickup for at least six months. XO, is there any way you could just keep this down at XOI [XO investigation] and not make him go to mast? Honestly, he's had plenty of punishment about this, and I'm sure we've got it under control."

"Doc, you know how strongly the captain feels about DWI."

"Yeah, but if he knew how hard I've already come down on this guy . . ."

He said he'd do what he could. I even called up Lonnie Prinz, the ship's secretary. I told him what I'd told the XO and asked if he could look out for the chit and maybe avoid mast on this one case. If at all possible, I wanted to keep our problems inside the department; I never wanted one of my guys to go to mast.

It didn't work.

Three days later, HN Rodney had to stand before the commanding officer at captain's mast. Under way, mast was usually held in auxiliary control so the captain could stay near the bridge. In port, mast was held on the fo'c'sle.

The captain stood behind a lectern. The offender, in dress uniform, marched smartly to attention in front of the lectern, then respectfully removed his cover. The CMC and the chief master at arms (MAA) stood on either side of the CO, and the witnesses—in this case Rick Cox, HMCS Myers, and me—stood to the captain's left of HN Rodney. Although conducted a little bit like a trial, captain's mast is not a procedure to determine innocence or guilt. If you weren't guilty, you wouldn't be there. (That's why it's called nonjudicial punishment.)

Captain Guitar started off easy and reassured me that his frightening reputation at mast was exaggerated. I had come this morning to stand by my sailor. Usually only the DivO, Cox, and the CPO would accompany the offender. I was concerned about Rod, though, and wanted both him and the captain to know that. I guess I hoped my being there would make it easier on him. The captain said in a normal voice, "You are accused of operating a vehicle while under the influence of alcohol, and furthermore of doing that on a military reservation. That is violation of the UCMJ code, isn't that true?"

Oh no. Rod lifted his arms in that way he used with me and started to ramble on with an explanation. He was supposed to stay at attention. Captain Guitar didn't like BSers.

Senior Chief Shapiro, the CMC, intervened. "Just say 'Yes, Sir' or 'No, Sir' and stay at attention."

"Yes, Sir."

Fortunately, the captain didn't show any irritation. "Captain Riley, do you have anything to say?"

"Sir, HN Rodney is an excellent corpsman, and until this matter a squared-away sailor. We've given him a very stern punishment in the department, he's going to AA meetings, and I really think we can trust him to go back to the standards he knows we expect. With the captain's permission, I think he has learned his lesson." I hoped that would be persuasive.

"Son," he said to Rod, being I thought paternalistic, rather than intimidating, "How long have you been in the Navy?"

"Two years, Sir," Rodney said, remembering to stay at attention—and obviously being even more relieved than I was that the captain was going to counsel him rather than devour him.

Continuing on just as quietly, the captain asked, "How long have you been a bum?"

Rod was puzzled. He angled his head to the left like a confused puppy.

"Stay at attention when I'm talking to you!"

Rodney started to gesture again as though to speak. Master Chief Shapiro didn't bother to step in this time. It was too late. The captain was roaring as he cut him off.

"I'm tired of writing letters to mothers about dead sons! I'm tired of answering the police about innocent people killed by drunken bums who are too dumb to stop drinking or too damned unconcerned not to drive! Which one of those are you?!"

"I—" Rod started, unwisely, to answer.

"Don't interrupt me when I'm talking! What are you staring at me for!"

This was the captain's mast I'd heard so much about. Captain

Guitar's neck and temple veins bulged out. His head tipped to the right and to the left as he excoriated Rodney. Standing at least ten or twelve feet away, even I was a little frightened. Finally, Rod was fined about $500, restricted to the ship for about a month, and given a suspended loss of one pay grade. That meant he wasn't busted one rank yet, but he would be with any slipups at all. Most emphatic of all, though, was that Rod and the rest of us were trembling.

Bad News Just Won't Go Away

The syringe matter wasn't quite over yet. One day, Captain Guitar was interviewed on the evening news in Jacksonville. Fortunately, he had a lot of poise. It looked like he'd probably been on TV before. A very young reporter, somewhere between her first assignment in a very small town and her hoped-for next assignment in a bigger market, was conducting the interview up on the flight deck. It was kind of a cloudy day, so the picturesque opportunities of the shipyard were suppressed by the gray background. In fact, the gray sky, the gray day, and all the gray hulls around the basin behind us set a tone that was far from upbeat.

The interview began with the reporter saying something about the Navy being a longtime, well-known neighbor in Jacksonville (she didn't say "good" neighbor, though). Then she described the aircraft carrier as a floating city and spoke about the remarkable responsibility of the captain "for any tragedies or crimes" on the ship.

Obviously the captain had some experience with the press, because he took charge of the interview with his personality and open answers. It was a sparring match, though, with the reporter trying to stay on the offensive, but the captain answered all her questions like a friendly neighbor.

Then her eyebrows rose ominously and she said, "But the only medical waste on Florida beaches this year was from the *Forrestal.*"

"That's not really true, you know. There were a number of items of trash from a British vessel down in the Key West area, and a number of containers of various medical supplies down in the Canaveral area that had the names of some of the commercial vessels, too. But that's not the point, Gloria. What happened a couple of weeks ago was inexcusable. We on the *Forrestal,* and in the Navy, feel very bad about it, and we're going to redouble our efforts to prevent this sort of thing happening again."

She then asked if anybody would be made to pay for the mistake, a question that I, of course, took rather personally. I was kind of afraid the captain was going to mention my name. He said, "Remember, I am the captain, so I am ultimately responsible for this kind of thing. If anybody should be punished, I guess it should be me. However, to answer your question, yes, there was disciplinary action taken against the department head involved."

The reporter asked, "Do you mean the medical department?" but the captain just said he thought that was as far as he should go, and with that the televised portion of the interview ended.

That same night, the captain had me over to his house for dinner again. He had done that the night after the first investigation, too. We didn't even talk about the syringes or the investigation.

Your captain is your captain, whether you're playing racquetball with him or having dinner at his house. Away from the ship, he didn't think of himself as the skipper, just as John, and he invited a friendly cordiality. He and Martha were good hosts. He was a friend, but of course he would have to be The Captain to me. They had a lot of books in their house and enjoyed history, Stephen King, and long, probing discussions about human nature, so I enjoyed visits at their house and conversation with both of them.

Captain Guitar had begun his career as a navigator on transport aircraft, I believe. During the Vietnam War, there was a great need for A-6 BNs because so many A-6s were being shot down. Captain Guitar loved the go-fast side of aviation, so the A-6 appealed to him. A lot of people, especially A-6 BNs, will tell you that the person who is really in charge of the A-6 is the BN, not the pilot. (Of course, A-6 pilots, of whom Tim Louis—the next captain of the *Forrestal*—was an example, had a somewhat different view.) Well, Guitar apparently became one of the most decorated aviators in Vietnam, and he had thousands of hours in the A-6. He had a very successful military career after that, too.

Nobody seemed indifferent about John Guitar. Some people in the A-6 community just didn't like him at all. They'd say he was pushy and aggressive. The others, about equal in number to the first group, either had worked for him and said they'd follow him anytime, anyplace, and under any circumstances, or they hadn't worked for him but admired the way he fought for his squadron and to get good things for his squadron.

While he was a squadron commanding officer, and maybe a few years before that, there was a reservist named John Lehman, who was also an A-6 BN. Lehman apparently had never been on sustained active duty; he'd served all of his Navy time exclusively in the reserves. His full-time job was in and out of government, with various jobs in the Department of Defense. At a certain time, though, in his very early forties, he became the secretary of the Navy. While in that position, he continued his reserve obligations, including his annual two weeks of active duty. John Guitar was known to have been a friend, and Lehman spent at least one of his active duty times serving in the squadron Guitar commanded. In those days, when asked what it was like having the secretary of the Navy as a lieutenant in his squadron, Guitar used the standard answer, "It's no problem. I treat him just like I'd treat any secretary of the Navy."

The competition is keen to become a squadron commanding officer. The competition for ship commands is even tighter, with choices made only from among the very top-rated squadron COs. So at each cutoff point, there are plenty of opportunities for jealous also-rans to complain about those who win the jobs. There were rumors that Captain Guitar won command of the replacement air group (RAG, an advanced tactical training squadron) because of his connection with Secretary Lehman. The same rumors would suggest that's how he was selected for command of a carrier, too. Captain Guitar knew those rumors. He didn't ever comment on them in my presence, and I'm sure he didn't to anybody else either. Being friends with the secretary of the Navy wouldn't explain why his first squadron and the RAG were both fabulously successful, nor would it explain why he got the Battle E as CO of the *Savannah*, his requisite "deep draft" command before taking over a carrier.

Therefore, it seemed to me that if there were any advantages to being a friend of the secretary of the Navy, they were indirect. Also, Guitar was no yes-man, so I was convinced that his success was deserved. His time on the *Forrestal* was drawing short, and he'd be up for admiral in about a year. Years earlier, he had decided that if he didn't make admiral he wasn't going to hang around. Being a Navy captain is something a lot of people aspire to, not what I would call "hanging around." He'd been on the fast track his entire career, though. I knew what he meant. Although we didn't discuss it, I was more than a little worried about whether this flap with the syringes would spoil his shot. We'd find out in a couple of months, when the Battle E would be announced. If *Forrestal* could get the Battle E, I figured it wouldn't leave any lasting scars on the captain.

As the autumn wore on, Art and the SuppO forced Master Chief Morgan to let us monitor his blood pressure. Sure enough, the medicine Art had been giving him worked . . . when he took it. No particular side-effects that bothered him, he just didn't like to take medicine. Also, the master chief's wife, the SuppO, and Art all told me he didn't have slurred speech at all. That's the way he'd always talked. Must have been my imagination. I did worry now, though, whether the blood pressure could have done it. As a neurologist, I knew that a lot of people have subtle cerebral or pontine effects from their hypertension that unsuspecting observers don't easily recognize. While we couldn't convince him to give up the cigarettes, he did take the medicine, and his pressure stayed around 135–145/95–100.

These were the last days that our beloved XO, Ozark, would be with us, so I spent as much time as I could hanging around his office. That wasn't much with the schedule we were keeping, but in our short friendship he'd been good to me, and he was a fountain of much-needed wit and humor. On his office bulkhead there was a painting of a squinty-eyed, gnarled-up cowboy with his tobacco-stained teeth gritted and his stubbled chin in a sneer. A caption at the bottom of the painting read, "There was a helluva lot of things they didn't tell me when I signed on with this outfit." I used to like to come and sit in his office and bask in the wisdom of the painting.

The New XO

One day I flounced in looking for his reassuring optimism and humor, but I was suddenly struck dumb. There was a strange commander sitting with him, wearing a leather flight jacket without a *Forrestal* patch.

"Hey, Doc, I'd like you to meet my relief, Mitchell Vaughan!" Vaughan had just come by to begin an orientation. He wouldn't be checking in until later. A year or two younger than I was, he had a friendly handshake, an open smile, and a great reputation. With a quick excuse about needing to go save lives or something, I ducked out of the office. The nerve of that guy, taking Ozark's place! We would get acquainted later, I knew.

One late October evening we were finishing coffee after dinner when Lt. Steve Tabor, the junior officer of the deck (JOOD), got a call on his brick. A young sailor from the air department who was UA from work that morning was reportedly holding his wife at gunpoint in their mobile home and refusing to let her out or anyone else in. Steve excused himself to uncover the details, but the story pretty much took the pleasure out of after-dinner conversation, so the crowd dispersed. I followed Steve out to the phone in the lounge and sat around while he got the story.

"Well, I guess there's no firearm. That part was incorrect. Domestic dispute, apparently no violence, just a lot of shouting. He refuses to come out. Apparently his wife is still there, but he's not forcing her to stay."

"You going to call him?"

"They don't have a phone. They just use the phone booth at the trailer park."

There were several mobile home parks out on Mayport Avenue, ranging from pretty nice to OK. None of them were really awful, although a couple adjoined auto salvage dealers or honky-tonks.

"I think I'll have to go out there and investigate," Steve said.

"Lieutenant, I don't think that's a very good idea. First of all, investigating is the police's job. Secondly, there was a report of a firearm."

"We know that was incorrect, though."

"How? You only have the same quality of information refuting it that you had reporting it! Domestic disputes are some of the most dangerous things that even professional, experienced officers deal with. People get blown away by husbands with guns. Why don't you ask the base police to go check it out first?"

Lieutenant Tabor was willing to try that, so he called the base police. They had no jurisdiction in town, they told him.

"Well, you'll have to call the local police."

That was a less popular idea.

"Doc, we don't even know that there's anything illegal yet. If we get the local police involved, it really escalates everything a lot further than we want it to go. I'll have to go out there and check it out."

There was no talking him out of it, so I went along.

We drove out the gate down Mayport Avenue, and I noticed the trailer parks more than I had before. The first couple of parks closest to the gate looked pretty rough. One on the left side was out behind an auto parts and salvage lot. In fact, it wasn't so much behind as it was merged with the gravel-surfaced lanes of the park. The aluminum and powdery, faded paint of the frayed, small trailers blended imperceptibly with the car carcasses and hubcaps scattered around. One expected chickens to run out from under the scattered machinery parts. A little further down, there was a park with the big seventy footers, many of them with siderooms sticking out. None of these were frayed. The lanes were paved, and there were small, well-kept yards around each trailer.

Finally, we came to the one we were looking for. This one had only rental mobile homes. It was out behind a laundromat and a small, half-occupied shopping row. It was a hot evening, and all the hinged windows on the trailers were open—which meant these weren't air-conditioned. Here and there folks sat on the little steps up to their front doors, sipping from an RC or beer bottle.

Two naval officers in uniform, one carrying a brick, are pretty obvious in a trailer park, even in Mayport. "That's the one you're looking for. Over there," shouted one of the porch-sitters, a guy in bib overalls and no shirt. The brown trailer he pointed to was one of the few with all the windows closed, but at least the door was open.

I insisted we call to the trailer from behind a tree. Tabor was embarrassed by this, but went along anyway. "Jones," he called, "This is Lieutenant Tabor from the ship! Dr. Riley is here with me. Can we talk to you?"

No answer.

He called a couple more times, but still no answer. I was getting a little nervous. Could this be the behavior of a dangerous young man? Or could he have killed himself and his wife?

The neighbors had been watching this for a while, but the guy in the overalls spoke up again. "Ain't nobody in there anymore. They been gone a half hour or so."

Timidly, we walked up to the trailer and peeked in. No bodies. There was a .45 automatic pistol on a table in the living room. So much for the "It's safe, there's no weapon" philosophy. Back at the door, a little boy on a bicycle said "They're down at the phone" and pointed over to the laundromat. Over there was a young couple, one of them just hanging up the phone, the other staring toward us. When they saw us looking at them, they started walking in our direction.

The young woman didn't look disturbed at all, but the sailor was obviously very tired. His eyes were boggy and dark, and his clothes were all rumpled. "He's OK," the woman said. "He's calmed down now."

"You ready to go back to the ship, Airman Jones?" the lieutenant asked.

The sailor said he'd go, but he wanted to get some things out of the trailer. I talked him out of that because of the gun. Lieutenant Tabor took him back to the ship when one of the chaplains arrived.

It seems that AN Jones was eighteen and Mrs. Jones sixteen. They'd been married only shortly before the deployment, and neither of them had been out of Tennessee before. They couldn't afford a car. She hadn't been able to get a job. The only way they could afford the rent of this trailer was to take in a couple of subletters to rent bedrooms. When Mrs. Jones and one of the renters told Jones the day before that they were having a child, AN Jones expressed his great disapproval of that plan. The other guy left in a hurry, but Jones kept his wife in the trailer all day fretting about the gun. They'd just been on the phone with her parents, trying to get enough money for her to return to Tennessee.

We brought Jones back to the ship. A skinny, morose fellow who looked a little older than his eighteen years, he didn't want to talk much. Later that night we arranged to admit him to the psychiatry unit at NH Jacksonville because I was worried about him injuring himself. The chaplains and ombudsmen tried to help Mrs. Jones get back to Tennessee, but she needed a couple of days to get her things together.

I sat down late that night trying to figure how to write up the report for the captain.

Chapter 8

Change of Command

Gradually, autumn gave way to winter, as much as it can in Florida. The SRA remained intense. With the needle guns clanging away all night to resurface the hangar bay above my stateroom, I had to shift up to the 'gator's cabin on the O-3 level for a few weeks. My admiration for Don and Art grew weekly. Their workdays began before 0700 every morning and often ended late in the evening. On rare occasions they were able to finish up and go home by 1600. Years ago when I worked at Bethesda, I scorned medical folks who went home that early. I used to think it was more evidence that the guys on the ships didn't work as hard as us hospital doctors. I knew better now. Their average workday, even in port, was more than ten hours, sometimes stretching well past sixteen. Even that tally overlooked the fact that sometimes they'd go to work in October and not get home until April. Whenever they could find an eight- or even a six-hour workday, they were welcome to it. Despite Art's crusty attitude and Don's stern Prussian personality, they were both very good clinicians, the kind of people I'd like to have for a family doctor.

Turnover in the ship's company was high at this time. The ship's personnel department, along with the Bureau of Personnel (BUPERS) in Washington, tried to limit the turnover to home-port periods, so we were probably seeing more than two hundred new people every month. Also, the Reagan buildup years were conspicuously drawing to a close. Not everybody who left the ship was going to be replaced. All the parts of the ship still had to function, but we'd be operating with fewer people. The fact was that the services were shrinking. Little did we recognize how much they'd be shrinking in the next five to ten years.

One of the new people was the XO, Mitchell Vaughan. Shortly after he relieved Ozark, he summoned me down to his office to brief him on the medical department and the health of the ship. Vaughan had a reputation as one of the hardest-working and brightest people in the HS community (the people who fly the H-3). In the first few minutes with him, it was obvious that he deserved the reputation. After showing him a few tables and lists of our personnel and our inventories, I started a prepared brief to describe the department. "Our main functions can be described as preventive medicine, occupational health, medical treatment—"

"In preventive medicine, do you distribute condoms?" he interrupted.

Caught off guard a little, I said, "Well, yes and no." The issue of condoms was really more complicated than it seemed on first blush. Yes, we did have condoms in the department, and whenever a sailor came to ask for one, we gave him at least two—sometimes opportunities to use them came up more than once a night. Condoms were also for sale in the ship's store, where sailors could easily get them. Furthermore, by tradition and regulation, certain self-care hygienic items like sunburn lotion, insect repellent, and condoms are Class VI items—self-care supplies, not medical. It had been demonstrated over the years that a sailor who had enough foresight to come down to medical for a condom would be just as likely go to the ship's store and buy one. It wasn't the price of condoms that kept sailors from using them, it was failing to think about them in advance. The fortunes of youth sometimes place young people in opportunities they haven't foreseen.

"Do you make them available when guys leave the ship on liberty?"

We were getting into details here, when I thought we were going to be going over the department in general. Only thirty minutes were scheduled, then the SuppO was coming to brief him. Were we going to spend the whole time on condoms, I wondered?

"Not on the quarterdeck—"

"Why not?" the new XO interrupted, "I think we ought to be proactive on this, don't you? I mean, you're the doctor."

I tried to explain that the use of condoms wasn't related solely to ease of acquisition. He didn't agree with that. Then I reminded him of the complications of wives' opinions and PR considerations in giving out condoms as sailors depart the ship, and he said, "We'll do it smart, though, we won't just do it without thinking."

The XO conducted the rest of the brief by asking questions. He was well informed and knew the most important areas pertaining to health on the ship. I didn't always get a chance to fully answer his question before he brought up a new one, but I was impressed by his depth of information and his energy level. Beyond the information we exchanged, though, this interview brought home something that was already clear for me. Without being told, I knew who was in charge. But if I'd had any doubts, today's talk demonstrated who was the XO and who was the Doc.

The drudgery of the SRA was wearing on everybody. Although the yard workers had been cheerful at first, the incidence of minor skirmishes between the yard workers and crew members was increasing. Cigarette butts lay here and there on the deck. Workers usually didn't clean up at the end of a shift unless they were forced to. That caused friction because the crew—even the youngest and newest members—thought of the ship as something more than just home. The ship, kind of like Jonah's whale, was alive to us, part of our family. To the yard workers, it was just a dirty place where they had to come to work. That difference in attitude, taken together with the crew's restlessness, set a little bit more distance between the yard workers and us. We never had any major outward problems with them, but the everyday friction built up gradually. The yard workers—with their black, grimy Harley Davidson T-shirts, their scraggly hair poking out from under their hard hats, and their cigarette butts accumulating on the deck—shared the tight passageways and workspaces with well-scrubbed young men in dungarees or khakis, who were proud of doing well on inspections and looked on the environment as a kind of parent.

The yard workers, nonunion mostly in this shop, periodically complained about the "great deal" the military people had with various benefits packages. For their part, all the military realized that their ragged-looking counterparts had incomes double or triple a Navy salary.

The SRA just seemed to go on and on. We'd reached a point where the big, round pipes and myriad cables seemed to be just regular parts of the ship. The nuisance was so ingrained we almost forgot to wish for it to go away. We saw shipmates moving on and had to adjust to new coworkers and new bosses, but somewhere in the back of our minds we knew we had to get ready for the deployment with a long series of workups yet to come.

As January wore on, we began to think about Captain Guitar's relief. The captain had been in a command a little bit more than a year and a half, and his time had to be coming to an end. The Battle E wouldn't be announced until sometime in late March. We all wanted to win it, as much for the captain as for ourselves, and we wanted him to be there when we got it. The crew would miss him.

In the department head meetings, we were already missing the old XO. Things were different. Where Ozark used to ask for advice and invite interchange, Mitchell said how he wanted things done. He was a bright officer and had a lot of experience, which gave him lots of confidence. He didn't seem to need our advice or experience as much as his predecessor had. The new AIMD officer, Cdr. Kevin Millet, a feisty shortstop of a guy, joined me and "Clark" in trying to needle the XO whenever we could. It didn't make much difference, though. The new proliferation of memos and instructions kept growing, and the XO never let up on his constant attention to detail.

Captain Guitar had inherited a good ship's crew from his predecessor, Tom Black. The ship had just completed a major renovation before Guitar took over. Despite his version of "tough love"—occasional detonations at captain's mast—his affection for the crew was obvious, and he would be missed.

Since the SRA began, there had been about a 15 percent turnover in the ship's company. Of the 85 percent who had been there a while, none were indifferent about Captain Guitar. About 10 percent were deadly afraid of him. They had either seen him at captain's mast or observed him reprimanding somebody, or they'd heard the legends. Another 5 or 10 percent disliked him, or worse. These might include officers and chiefs he'd chewed out. I still considered myself a little bruised from the episode after Portsmouth, for example. Some didn't like his cowboy reputation, his old-fashioned hell-bent-for-leather aviator attitude. Some people—mostly aviators—were simply jealous of his success, I suppose. Everybody else thought he was one of the best leaders in the Navy and was devoted to him.

I was among this last group. I admired the way both he and Sniffles came down to the ward every day on the cruise to see our patients, each of them coming alone and not drawing attention to himself when he did it. The positive attitude among the young sailors on the ship, the exuberance of everybody who was a member of the team—all these were the responsibility of the captain. Most of all, though, I was impressed by the way he had stood behind me after the incident with the syringes. I would always wonder whether that event and the notoriety around it were what kept him from making admiral. He must have wondered about it, too. He never showed me any rancor or resentment. On my lowest days, he just invited me over to play racquetball. Of course, I was one of the few guys he could always beat, but I think he might have invited me even if I could beat him.

The new CO had been identified, an A-6 pilot named Timothy Louis. We began hearing one thing or another about him in January. He had mostly been a West Coast sailor. The OHO, Merv Schultz, had worked with him when Captain Louis was the CAG on the *Midway*. Merv liked him and said he had a particularly good touch with the crew. The XO warned that he was known as a religious zealot and implied there would be a puritanical change in the way things were done on the *Forrestal.*

Captain Louis was apparently a chief of staff in a surface group up in Norfolk. During the first week in February, he came to visit the ship for a few hours. We heard him bonged aboard, but nobody saw him. He and Captain Guitar visited for a couple of hours, then we heard him bonged off again. That kind of surprised me, because if it took seven days for John Busby and me to turn over just in the medical department, I figured it would take at least ten days for the COs to go over everything about this behemoth.

The SRA continued. The passageways were dingy and dusty, and the noise continued to be awful. However, the week after Captain Louis came to visit, we had a going-away party for Captain Guitar and Martha. It was held down at the fancy Saw Grass Hotel in Ponta Vedra, south of Mayport. We had some roasting speeches and an opportunity to give him some gifts as mementos. The medical department gave him a fishhook that Don Kent had been saving for over a year, and I recounted—with a few embellishments—the story behind it. During the last workup cycle before the deployment, the FID was operating in the Caribbean. In the middle of one critical tactical operation, the radio beamed up an emergency call from a fishing trawler. Someone on the trawler had reportedly traumatically amputated his arm and was bleeding to death. Captain Guitar turned the ship around and traveled about twenty miles to come within helicopter range.

They'd launched an H-3 from the Red Lions to save the fisherman's life. It turns out that instead of an amputation of his forearm, he had a fishhook through one of his fingers. When brought to the ship, he was crying out and thrashing about, but Don Kent simply removed the fishhook and soaked the finger, and the man returned to his trawler with only a minor puncture wound. In order to "save" this life, the supercarrier had terminated an entire day of tactical operation, hundreds of flights, and an awful lot of fuel. Captain Guitar was pleased to have the fishhook as a memento. Then at the end of my speech I said, "I'm sorry that's all we have to give you, Captain. We in the medical department also bought you a very expensive gift, but in a moment of carelessness I just threw it over the side." Everybody in the audience knew what throwing things over the side meant to us that year, so the remark brought the house down.

The week after the dinner, all of the trailers and wagons were finally removed from Hangar Bay I and the doors between Bay I and Bay II were closed. The deck up in Bay I was painted nicely, and all the pad eyes were painted white. Banners and flags were hung from the overheads, and a dais was up in the forward end of the hangar. Clearly, preparations were being made for the change-of-command ceremony. It was announced that Captain Louis would relieve Captain Guitar on 25 February.

Preparations for the change of command told us a little more about the new XO. Meetings with him were not exchanges or dialogues, but soliloquies. These often involved his pointing out that some department or another hadn't taken some action he wanted. "But how was I to know you wanted that?" the department head might ask.

"Didn't you read the 5050?" That's the serial number for administrative notices about conferences or meetings. The XO and his new admin officer, Max Small, liked to put things in writing. There was a proliferation of 5050s on a bewildering variety of subjects. They had become so numerous that they sometimes got all clogged up in the memo production line—a memo logjam. Like too much paper in the commode, their bulk hampered their own flow. The 5050s sometimes didn't arrive until the deadline listed in a memo had passed, so at some meetings the XO found himself berating somebody for not complying with a memo that hadn't been received yet.

For the change of command, Rear Admiral Dunhaven, commander of Naval Air Forces Atlantic Fleet (COMNAVAIRLANT, or just AIRLANT), would be the guest speaker. Admiral Dunhaven was about the first NFO to reach flag rank, and probably the first NFO who had commanded an aircraft carrier. He was an A-6 BN, just like Captain Guitar, and the only flag officer I ever saw who had a Boston accent. According to rumor, Admiral Dunhaven and Captain Guitar didn't get along, and apparently it went back a number of years. Some speculated that it was because of Captain Guitar's close relationship with John Lehman, while others said it was because Guitar's squadron had shown up Dunhaven's some years before. Still others noticed a difference in their personalities and suggested Admiral Dunhaven may have disliked or envied Captain Guitar's flamboyant style.

Since Admiral Dunhaven had the main vote in awarding the Battle E, many doubted that we'd have a shot at it as long as Captain Guitar was in command. I, of course, fretted that the ship's otherwise flawless record would be blemished by our syringes. They had, after all, received a lot of press at the end of the deployment.

The week before the change of command, Captain Louis came to the *Forrestal* for two days of meetings with all of his department heads. The XO lined us all up and requested that we rehearse our briefs with him before we spoke to the new boss. He suggested I change a number of the things I was going to say and gave me some guidance on words and sentence structure in my brief. From the grumbling that afternoon in the wardroom, I suspected the XO had given other department heads similar explicit guidance in how to brief the new skipper.

When the time came for my brief, Josh Brant and I discovered that the XO had scheduled us in a combined brief, as though medical and dental were part of the same department. Walking down the passageway to the office being used for interviews, we encountered a tall, thin man with frosty grey-white hair and recruiting-poster posture. He was wearing his leather flight jacket with a squadron patch on one side and a *Midway* patch on the other. Josh whispered to me, "He looks like he's been sent from Central Casting." I knew what he meant. The new skipper had a bearing a little bit like Jeff Chandler's. His squared-back shoulders and crest of white hair reminded me of what I'd been told about his being a religious zealot, and I braced myself for a strict introduction.

As soon as he spoke, though, my apprehensions disappeared. A very cordial and friendly person, Tim Louis had a folksy manner about him and actually a kind of country accent. He was from western Pennsylvania, but his manner of speech was Midwestern, almost Missourian. Before he heard anything about our departments, he wanted to learn about us personally. He told us a little bit about his own background and his family, and he said, "Look, I can't learn everything about your department in two weeks, much less a half an hour. I just wanted to meet you guys now and see if there's anything you need me to work on immediately. We'll get into detail gradually as we get to know each other." Neither of us had emergent problems. We were both so fond of Captain Guitar that we were anxious about whoever would take his place, and we probably expected some kind of ogre that day. We were so relieved by how pleasant he was that we were almost speechless.

There were a number of interesting contrasts between Captain Guitar and Captain Louis. By his own description, Captain Guitar had been a borderline juvenile delinquent, and he used to say that he spent a major part of his teenage years on probation. He had one of those handmade tattoos with the word "John" on his left shoulder. He'd like you to infer it was put there by a rebellious teenager on his first night in jail. If you suspected there was still just a touch of the outlaw lurking under the skin, Captain Guitar wouldn't intentionally dissuade you. Captain Louis was a scholar-athlete who went to the Naval Academy. After the Academy, he was married to his high school sweetheart for over twenty-five years. Guitar's second wife, Martha, was almost twenty years his junior. He drove a bright burgundy Porsche, Louis a small, tan pickup. Except in his flashes of fire, Guitar had an urbane, smooth way about him. Captain Louis, by contrast, had an open, almost "aw shucks" ingenuousness. While they both came from A-6s, Louis was a pilot, Guitar a BN.

Yet they had much in common, too. After all, they were both from Intruders. A camaraderie exists among people who have flown thousands of hours in that airplane. There is an attitude about counting on the other guy, about sharing, about an entire philosophy of flight that extends into your general being. Both of them operated at a very personal level. Their styles were to give trust and to be trusted. They demanded a lot from their people, but gave instant and permanent loyalty to those who lived up. They were both very accomplished officers—after all, they had both achieved command of an aircraft carrier. Ambition is the driving force among a lot of naval officers. These were two men who cared more about their crew and about accomplishing the mission than they did about their own careers. That was one of the most striking features about each of them, and something that became evident within the first day of knowing them.

There were a number of changes of command that winter. Just a week or two before, I'd been to one for the VA-37 Bulls in which "Shaky" Jacobson took over from "Jet" O'Hara. The bigger the organization, the better the ceremony. Change of command on an aircraft carrier is a rousing experience! At a time of year with a better weather guarantee, a ceremony could be held up on the flight deck, but in winter we had to settle for the hangar bay as a reasonable second. It's as tall and wide as a big city auditorium, and much longer. Over in one corner the band plays a medley of marches, mostly Marine and Navy songs. The ship's divisions stand at parade rest in formation in their sparkling uniforms. Then the music stops, and, over in another corner, the XO reads off the names of the dignitaries. By naval custom, a bos'n's mate rings the ship's bell to introduce flag officers or other commanding officers.

Just like watching a Shakespearian play or a familiar opera, knowing what's coming next only intensifies the pageantry.

Bong, bong . . . "Commander Carrier Air Wing 6 arriving." Pat "Martini" House, the CAG, entered. Bong, bong . . . "Captain Timothy E. Louis, U.S. Navy, arriving." The bell again, and then "*Forrestal,* arriving," to introduce Captain Guitar. The CO is never introduced by name, just by the name of his command.

Then came the flag officers. Navy and Marine Corps bands always try to do outdo one another in the jaunty, snappy, almost jazzy quality of Ruffles and Flourishes. It has such a spunky, sassy swagger that it announces to any audience, "We may be admirals here, but don't forget we're sailors." Admirals get more bongs than captains. First came the flag officer who would soon become our new battle group commander, Rear Adm. (lower half) William T. Barnes. His call sign was "Sweetcakes." It was going to take a while for me to figure out why they called him that. The first few times I saw him, he had such a stern, almost frowning, appearance that I expected him to be a grouch. I wouldn't get to know Admiral Barnes as well as I did Admiral Kohl or my captains, but I came to realize he was a man with a good sense of humor and a warm personality. Finally came the star of the day, Rear Admiral (two stars) Dunhaven.

For true believers, these ceremonies are almost intoxicating. The music, the choreography, and the celebration of pride and dedication convey an overpowering and pervasive sense of community, of family, of belonging.

The chaplain said a brief prayer in the ecumenical, all-encompassing style that Navy chaplains use. Then Admiral Dunhaven gave his speech.

There was a rumbling of anticipation as to whether he would announce the winner of the Battle E, but we knew the announcement wasn't due for another month or so. It just would've been a nice touch if he could tell us that day. Dunhaven had a way of pacing semi-informally on the platform when he spoke. It would have been a distracting habit in some speakers, but it just seemed natural with him; it conveyed his sense of comfort and conversation with the audience. He spoke of these being uncertain times, years of change, and that the only thing certain about our future was uncertainty. He said that the face of national defense would have to change, but that America would always need the kind of people we had on *Forrestal* to represent American values. Familiar ideas shared sincerely among friends are not mere platitudes. Besides, he told us things we liked hearing, so we were all pretty well pumped up.

Then at the end of his speech he said, "I know you're all wanting to hear about the Battle E. It's not due for another six weeks. . . . But the *Forrestal is* the E! Here, John [speaking to Guitar], you know you won it, or rather your crew won it in spite of you. Congratulations, men of *Forrestal*." We were all on our feet cheering one another and the captain, and not a few of us were choked up. Then the admiral turned to give Captain Guitar the Legion of Merit.

On the starboard side of the hangar, a gray-and-white blur flickered in my peripheral vision and I heard a tublike "thunk." Four sailors in the formation suddenly slouched down on their knees to look at something on the deck, and an arm waved in my direction. I ran over and saw a six-foot-tall bos'n's mate facedown on the deck. There was a little blood over by his left shoulder. He slammed over like a tree right in formation, staying at attention all the way down to the deck. Military formations not uncommonly have somebody black out, a little bit more often in a hot environment. It was a little warm on the hangar bay that day, but not hot. Nonetheless, standing at attention, immobile for about forty-five minutes, the blood pools in a young man's lower extremities, and he can faint. Usually his buddies will grab his elbows to prop him up. They may think they're helping by doing this, but they're actually depriving him of the horizontal position that would allow blood to go back to his head. In this case he fell straight forward, just like there were hinges on his toes and he was a straight oaken door.

Well, that was the end of the change-of-command ceremony for me. Seaman Crowell had a through-and-through laceration on his chin, an abrasion on his nose, and one broken tooth. Fainting was what made him fall, but he hit the deck so hard that he sustained a concussion also. We had to take him down by litter to the medical department to scrub up his abrasions and sew his chin back together. About the time I finished sewing him back up, I heard on the 1-MC that the dignitaries were departing the ship to go over to the officers club for their formal luncheon. After the admirals were bonged off, I heard Captain Guitar being piped over the side by name for the first (and last) time, "Captain John A. Guitar, U.S. Navy, departing." And then, almost incongruously, bong, bong, *Forrestal,* departing." That, of course, was Louis. The change of command was complete. We had a new skipper.

It was quiet most of the rest of that day. It occurred to me a few times that the quiet could be a harbinger of how things would go with our new, easygoing captain. The SRA was drawing to a close, and we knew workups would begin pretty soon.

Late that night, after finishing up some paperwork in the office, I trudged out toward my stateroom and bumped into HM1 Beaumont in the passageway. He'd had duty the night before, I thought. Why was he here tonight?

"Tell you the truth, Captain, my parents and I are having some problems, so I'm staying on the ship for a while."

"Sorry to hear that, HM1. Seemed like things had been going better for you." When he'd come to see me after our last talk, a couple of nights' sleep had made him a lot better. The rambling, peculiar talk had disappeared, and I dismissed it as due to fatigue. Beaumont's work and records had been slipping a little lately, though. The chiefs and I had discussed it just the day before.

"Anything I can do, Hugh? Want to talk for a while?"

"No, they're just tired of me, that's all. I'm just not enough anymore. They're mad and they want to get even, that's all." And he walked away downcast. My Dad always warned me not to get involved in people's families or romances.

I went to bed that night around 2000 and started reading the Larry McMurtry book *Texasville,* which I enjoyed until I fell asleep about an hour later. At 2300 one of the corpsmen came down and banged on my door. "Captain, we need you down in the ER." It was Master Chief Morgan, the guy with the blood pressure problem. He was having trouble breathing. His wife was there, too, and she was pretty anxious. Although they lived only ten minutes from the NH Jacksonville—an hour's drive from us—they never liked it much there, so they came all the way here to the ship, where, despite Art's scolding, the master chief trusted the medical care. Probably not the best choice that particular night. He was plenty sick.

"He can't breathe," his wife said. "He says he can't get a deep breath. We just got home today, and he's been like this the whole time. I had to talk him into coming in."

"You having any pain, Master Chief?"

He didn't want to talk much, like he had to spare his breath. "No . . ." quick inhale, "just hard to breathe."

I listened to his lungs while one of the corpsmen took his blood pressure. His pulse was over 100. His lungs had the wet rales throughout, which meant pulmonary edema . . . severe congestive failure. His blood pressure was around 220/150. He was restless, couldn't sit still, also characteristic of pulmonary edema.

"Let's get some oxygen started right now. Master Chief, have you been taking your medicine?"

He nodded yes.

"No he hasn't!" his wife interjected. "Yesterday I noticed most of the pills were still in the bottle, so I got on him about it."

I gave him some furosemide, a diuretic, intravenously, and we took an EKG. It showed what we call a strain pattern, but the rhythm, except for being fast, was normal.

On my way to the phone to call the Mayport Clinic for an ambulance,

I told the guys to take a chest X ray right away while we waited for the ambulance.

"You'll have to wait while we call the ACLS ambulance from town. We can't send a cardiac patient in our ambulances," the corpsman from the clinic told me.

"OK, but this guy isn't having an MI or an arrest. He's got malignant hypertension and pulmonary edema. What he needs isn't ACLS. It's to get to the hospital in a hurry."

The chest X ray confirmed the pulmonary edema, and the master chief was doing a little better after the diuretic and on the oxygen. Ten minutes had gone by and no word about the ambulance. I called the clinic back.

"One of Liberty's ACLS ambulances is down and the other one is on a call. We had to call another one from town. They should be over there in about half an hour."

"No way! This guy needs to go to the hospital. You people have four ambulances over there, why don't you send one over here like I asked?"

"Sir, I told you we can't send a BLS [basic life-support] ambulance for a cardiac patient."

"But what this guy needs is rapid transport, not defibrillators. Do you have a physician on duty?"

"Yes, Sir. I'll have Dr. White call you."

We gave the master chief some nifedipine, and that got his pressure down a little.

Two or three minutes later, Dr. White called. "Hello, Dr. White speaking. I'm a family physician."

I explained the case again and asked for help in transporting the patient as soon as we could over to the hospital.

"Well, what if something happened en route?" he asked.

"What if something happens by *not* sending him? He's not having an arrest, he needs to get to the hospital for treatment. What are those ambulances for?"

"All right, but you'll have to take responsibility—"

Take responsibility! "You son of a bitch, that's what I *do* for a living. Just send us the ambulance, please."

I called the ER over at the hospital—where I was wishing Mrs. Morgan would have brought the master chief in the first place—to pass on all the details and to tell them the patient was coming.

Our ER was busy that night, and I sent along one of our best corpsmen in the ambulance.

About an hour later I was finishing up with a fellow who had sprained an ankle when a doctor from the ER at NH Jacksonville called.

"Is this *Captain* Riley?" When they want to show contempt for you, they call you by rank rather than "Doctor."

"Yes. Are you calling about Master Chief Morgan? Thanks for getting back to us so soon."

"Yes. Well. Did you know that Mr. Morgan is in pulmonary edema?" Funny what goes through your mind sometimes. A master chief petty officer hates to be called "Mr." His name is "Master Chief."

"Of course, that's why we sent him to you."

"Well, for a life-threatening disease, don't you think you should tell us before transporting someone like this? I mean I'm going to go ahead and take care of your patient, but we don't have to accept a patient in transfer without prior consultation."

In fact, it had been a different doctor I'd spoken to forty minutes ago. "But I did. Didn't Dr. Holt tell you the patient was coming?"

"No. The first we knew of the patient was when he arrived at our door."

I explained that I had discussed the entire case with Dr. Holt, including past history, EKG findings, course and treatment here, the whole works. Dr. Holt's shift ended after our conversation, and he hadn't passed the information along to this angry doctor.

"I find that hard to believe," the new doctor told me. "That doesn't sound like Dr. Holt. We have the patient here now. They can sort out the rest of the problem in the morning."

Master Chief Morgan was admitted to the ICU that night, and his breathing improved a little as the night went on.

Early the next morning I called to find out about his progress, and, as usual, the nurse in the unit said, "I'm sorry, we can't discuss patients on the telephone."

"May I speak to the master chief's doctor, please?"

The staff doctor was too busy to talk to me all day, but I was at last able to talk to one of the interns on his case, who explained that it was hard to get his blood pressure down still, but "I guess you know Mr. Morgan was pretty sick. They really botched up his care over on the ship. He's lucky to be alive. They didn't call to say he was coming over or anything. Just sent him over in a BLS ambulance. Lucky he didn't have an arrest on the way over here."

Yeah, lucky.

About an hour after that I got a call from the CO of the hospital, who had been called by Dr. White from the clinic. "What the hell's going on over there!"

I yelled back a little and he backed off. Later, though, I found out that Dr. White and the second ER doctor had filed a quality-assurance complaint about me at the hospital.

The most important thing was that the master chief got the treatment he needed for his blood pressure. A couple of months later, we learned that he was transferred to one of the universities for further treatment and finally had to leave the Navy on disability.

That was a busy week in the department. Besides looking after the paperwork that seemed to be growing as we filled out more and more reports in the advancing workup cycle, we had a lot of patients. We were still readjusting the department for the new XO and skipper, too. This week the XO wanted to talk about "no-shave" chits. He decided that we'd been too lax in issuing no-shave chits, and he wanted to tighten up the system.

Navy uniform regulations require a clean-shaven face. Sailors can wear moustaches, but beards haven't been allowed for a decade or more.* Whiskery stubble, however, has never been allowed. Well . . . except for the no-shave chit. With a medical excuse, a sailor would usually be permitted to not shave. Sounds simple, doesn't it? It is simple for the individual healing from a transient problem, like eczema or a cut. He grows a little stubble for a few days until the lesion heals, and then resumes shaving. The chit from the doctor shows the boss that he's under treatment.

The problem is something called pseudofolliculitis barbi (PFB). The term refers to a condition of the beard (barbi) that imitates folliculitis, which is infection of the hair follicles. It brings tears to all ship's doctors in the U.S. Navy. A saga of our time, there is pain in the PFB story for everybody. It is a legalistic, bureaucratic mire, a recalcitrant medical problem, a military principle, a turf battle, and in the bargain a racial symbol, too.

Curly or kinky hair is shaped the way it is because it grows out of its follicles real flat and loops around the way package ribbon would if you pushed it out from a slit. A long, curly hair with a naturally rounded tip merely circles itself around and around making loops. When a flat hair is cut, though, its own tip turns into a sharp little flat edge. As it grows, each sharp little hair kinks back around and likes to dig back into skin or an adjacent follicle. For white guys, this may cause an occasional

---

*Beards were permitted briefly during the 1970s as one of the Zumwalt initiatives. The novelty probably irritated more people than it pleased, though, and I don't think we'll ever see them again.

ingrown hair, a form of bothersome pimple. Black men, though, have more curly, kinky hairs than straight hairs. They can have dozens, hundreds, of these backbending little stabbers, which can create lots of bumps on the skin, some of them developing abscesses or cysts—PFB. We aren't real good at treating this. The best way is just to not shave.

What about regulations?

Uniform and personnel regulations say that if a person has a condition that makes it impossible for him to comply with the uniform, he's unfit for naval service and must be administratively separated. BUPERS Instruction 1910.2. Can't shave, can't be in the Navy. While most commands consider it a medical problem (it's a skin rash, isn't it?), most medical guys say it's only a medical condition if you shave skin that shouldn't be shaved.

To black sailors, shaving rules and no-shave chits are a form of racial harassment. PFB is not only something confined to black men, it's very common among them. It's not a disease, but a trait of being black. If they have it, they have to show their no-shave chit to go on liberty if they have stubble.

When I arrived at the *Forrestal,* Don was handling most skin problems, and he usually gave out six-month no-shave chits. By promoting a half-year interval, Don had cut the PFB visits quite a bit. Recently, though, we'd had this new influx of CPOs and officers, all of whom had accumulated years of their own expectations about how long no-shave chits should last—none of those expectations addressing the reality of the situation. Foremost among this group was the XO.

"Doc, I saw a guy with an actual beard last week. He had a six-month no-shave chit. I thought these chits had to be renewed every two weeks," he told me.

Showing him one of Don's chits, I emphasized that the note said it was a "medical recommendation" to the sailor's supervisor. The note recommended that the sailor should be allowed to trim his stubble down to an eighth of an inch or less because of his condition. "Doesn't sound like a beard to me, XO."

"Doc, I want you to change our policy about this. I want all no-shave chits to be renewed every two weeks, and no beards."

If every one of the hundreds of FID sailors with occasional PFB would need a doctor's note, that would increase our attendance at sick call significantly. We'd have to deal with this later.

Later that week, Petty Officer Rosario brought in a health record and a special-request chit to release the health record to the clinic. The sailor involved had a follow-up appointment over at the clinic.

"What's the problem? Why can't we see him?"

Del just shrugged, so I asked him to bring me the patient. The twenty-year-old seaman looked tired, but not terribly sick. He'd seen Dr. Darrow over in sick call at the Mayport Clinic a few days before. She filled out a "bed-rest" chit, told him not to work for a few days, and asked him to come back to her with his health record for follow-up.

He lived on the ship, I noticed. "Was there a problem getting into our sick call?"

"No, Sir," he didn't make eye contact, "it's just . . ."

"Have we offended you somehow here?"

"No, sir, it's just I really have been feeling bad, and I thought if you were really sick you should go to a real clinic. When I went over to the clinic, that's what they said, too."

Who knows who "they" were—maybe the receptionist, maybe Dr. White. Going through the history, the seaman had been sick for a little over a week. Mostly fatigue, headache, sore throat. Dr. Darrow, who seemed to be one of the better doctors over at the clinic, thought he might have mononucleosis, and she took some blood tests that she was going to follow up on that morning. I examined him myself, felt some big lymph nodes and the tip of an enlarged spleen, and found myself agreeing with her diagnosis.

We sent him over for his follow-up with Dr. Darrow. I called to talk with her about his case, compliment her on her management, and ask her to send the FID sailors who found their way over to the clinic back to our sick call so we could look after them. She agreed to "release him as soon as he's stable." Dr. Darrow was the nicest doctor over there. I thanked her and bit my tongue.

No sooner did we hang up than the XO was on the phone. "Doc, can you come down here right now?"

Chuck Johnston, CO of the Marine detachment (MARDET), and his first sergeant were already down at the XO's office when I got there. One of our Marines, a twenty-year-old private, had shot himself in the head with a .44 Magnum in his garage. His roommate had found him when he came home from work around noon.

There had been no clues. He was a good Marine, no recent problems, no drinking or drug history. No suicide note. No signs of background mental illness or recent crises.

Despite our efforts, the threat and specter of suicide would prove to be a growing menace in the Navy.

Chapter 9

Springtime and Workups

Finally, we were about to do what ships were supposed to do. Our long SRA period was over. It took only about a day to get all the fladderap out of the passageways, all of the tubes and hoses and pipes. Workers had been gradually moving one or another of them out over a couple of weeks. Once we got them out, we had to have a pretty busy field day to get the entire place cleaned up, but the crew was so glad to get rid of the SRA stuff that it wasn't hard to get all hands to turn to.

We were entering the cycle of workups, underway periods that would grow progressively longer and more difficult while we prepared for the next deployment. During the year between the recent deployment and the beginning of the next one, almost half the crew would change, so a lot of people had to learn their jobs, learn about flight operations—all the complicated things an aircraft carrier does. They had to absorb all the subtleties of dealing with one another, and all the traditions. Classes and reading could teach us all a lot, but the only training that really counted was under way: "You fight like you train."

There would be a sequence to the workups. First, the ship's company would begin by moving the ship, driving it, just making it work. No airplanes. Then we and the air wing would practice together, landing airplanes and shooting them off the pointy end. Next we'd get into fancier driving of the ship and flying of airplanes. We'd even let some other squadrons come in to practice landing on our flight deck and do their carrier quals (qualifications). At a certain level in its readiness cycle, every carrier had to take its turn doing the carrier quals for the East Coast. Later, once the ship and the air wing were trained in all their fundamental movements, the captain and his war fighters had to practice all the complex interactions of battle techniques and tactics. There would be some exercises of tactical maneuvering, and during these times we'd test out the new equipment the operators had put on board during the SRA.

Inspections! Throughout the entire process, various oversight agencies would come by to test and inspect us. Every department on the ship would have progressively more difficult things to do. This included the medical department, right along with air operations, engineering, weapons, and everybody else.

Finally, we would go through a rite of passage called REFTRA (for "refresher training"), a legendary "hell week" experience that all ships of the line had to go through at a near-graduation point in their workup cycle. The term "training" in REFTRA had been a ludicrous misnomer for perhaps more than a generation. It wasn't training, it was harassment and (to whatever degree there was anything legitimate about it all) it was testing, a kind of certification that the Navy used to let you move on to the advanced phases of workups.

On the East Coast, the organization responsible for REFTRA was down in Guantánamo Bay, Cuba, also known as GITMO, so a synonym for REFTRA was "GITMO training." The small boys would actually go down to GITMO for ten or fourteen days, pull into the pier, do some of their testing while they were tied up, and then do their operating in the Caribbean. Aircraft carriers had to do the whole exercise under way down in the Caribbean.

There would be five or six underway periods before REFTRA, which is something you could pass or fail. Well, you couldn't really fail it, because you just kept doing it over and over until you passed, even if the ship had to stay another two or three weeks. REFTRA was more about safety and basic shipboard stuff than it was about being able to fight or do tactics. Surely, the war-fighting stuff was included, but the ship would have to go through that during the advanced phase and then, finally, during battle group phase. Those two cycles carried progressively more difficult tactical and strategic work and more coordination with other ships. Especially in the battle group phase, the important goal was effective coordination with other ships in the battle group. This included coming alongside for UnRep with the auxiliary ships, coordinating antisubmarine warfare (ASW) with the destroyers and our helo squadrons, and coordinating antiair warfare (AAW) between Aegis cruisers, our E-2 aircraft, and our fighters.

The first step in workups was called "fast cruise." It's an oxymoron. Nothing fast about it. Nothing cruise about it, either. You don't even sail. Fast cruise is a one-day dress rehearsal for getting under way. All the cables and connections to the pier are shut down, each department goes through its particular procedures for putting the ship in action. A sea and anchor detail is assembled on the fo'c'sle, and the entire team, including the quartermasters on the bridge, practices getting under way. Communications go down to DC Central and the entire engineering department. We exercise moving the deck-edge elevators up and down. Internal communications is tested. The ship makes its own electricity, meals are prepared. In other words, we practice as though we were under way, but with the safety of really not going anywhere. The ship stays tied up.

For all of the not going anyplace, fast cruise can still be a very trying experience. With all the new people on board, it isn't just the sailors who are new, but department heads and DivOs, too. In the past few weeks only one major department head had changed. Ed DeMaestri, who had been the assistant maintenance officer and the rescuer of our 3-M program, was now the first lieutenant. Warner Hobs had gone on to the staff of a reserve center in New York.

Bob Morris, the ops officer, would soon be relieved by Steve West, who had been his assistant as the combat officer. Roper Byrd, who had been the skipper of the Thunderbolts, would become the new combat officer and, like West, would fleet up to ops officer in a year. Larry Burns, after almost two years as the miniboss, finally fleeted up to boss when Ralph Eton left.

Roper, Steve, and the new boss invited me to join their bridge group. When all our work was done at night—usually around 2300 or midnight—we'd play bridge for a couple of hours and unwind. We were all about the same age and all had teenagers, and we chatted and joked while we played. Roper and I were stuck with one another as partners, though, because both the boss and West got cranky, especially at these late hours, if you lost count or opened a bid wrong.

It was becoming evident to everyone that over the next six to nine months the pace was going to accelerate and we'd be getting under way more and more. Those prospects mean different things to different sailors—adventure to some, unspeakable apprehension to others, but stress in one form or another to everybody. Even if you didn't know the ship's schedule and all the extra time the chiefs and DivOs were spending with their guys, you could review the logs of the chaplain's visits or the roster of cases at captain's mast and know that something was stirring in the crew. Romantic problems with girlfriends, drinking and brawling in town, disciplinary problems in departments—all were showing up in those two places.

Hugh Beaumont had been looking rumpled and worn out, so I

asked him to sit with me late one afternoon. "I think we have to talk. Things aren't going well for you these days, Petty Officer Beaumont."

He stretched his elbows out on the desk, bent his head forward. I was glad he felt he could open up. "Can I just tell you a few things, Captain?" I nodded. "Well, you know I told you a while ago they wanted to get even with me. Well, now they're really serious about it. They may be satisfied to just humiliate me, but Captain, they don't know how these things can get out of hand. Somebody could get hurt real bad, and I think a man with your experience knows what I'm talking about."

"You're giving me too much credit here, Petty Officer Beaumont. I don't know what you're talking about."

"Let's just say they've called the credit bureau, OK?"

"Why would they do that?"

"They'd say debts. And me their own flesh and blood. Tell you the truth, I wonder about that too sometimes. It just doesn't add up."

"How about if I called to talk to them?" He agreed to that reluctantly. He knew they would refuse, he told me.

When I called Mrs. Beaumont the next morning, she was very guarded—even cold. "I won't talk to you now, not without my husband. Are you on the ship?" Of course. "Then we'll call you back."

Immediately she rang back. "Oh, good, it *is* you, Dr. Riley. He's been so strange, we weren't sure who he might get involved to call us up." Hugh's father was there too, on an extension phone. He said, "You know, Doc, he sneaks around the neighborhood at night and watches us from the neighbors' shrubs. He's not really good at it. We and all the neighbors hear him and see him out there peekin' out from behind somebody's rose bushes. It would be kinda comical if it weren't so heartbreaking."

"Has he hurt either of you, bought a gun, anything like that?"

"Oh, no, Hugh is not violent at all. It just frightens us," his mother said.

I notified the XO, and we had to give Hugh official orders to stay away from the family and the neighborhood for a while. Most important, I arranged for him to see the psychologist over at the Mayport Clinic the next day.

Besides the family and romance stresses, which reflected what was happening in the lives of the crew, the case mix in sick call was different, too. Bob Dylan might be right about not needing a weatherman; we could tell the wind was changing (or that there was some bizarre new virus in the air) just by the sign-in list. We were beginning to see people with a new cluster of maladies. For example, sleepwalking, bedwetting, and flat feet—things doctors usually see a lot less than sore joints, coughs, and headaches—had become actual outbreaks.

These three conditions are old standbys for medical attention before a ship starts getting under way, but the mix varies from one crew to another, perhaps with the local grapevine. Homer Moore, the SMO on the USS *Enterprise,* told me that they didn't have too many flat feet but a lot of sleepwalkers on his ship. Now, sleepwalking and bedwetting are well-known signs of anxiety and should reasonably be anticipated among young people about to go to sea. Proper medical evaluation, reassurance, and sympathetic attention are generally warranted for such transient sleep disturbances. And yet the form these conditions take just before ship's movements tends to be distinct. The sleepwalking always occurs where a crowd is gathered and several witnesses are wide awake. Miraculously, these patients never seem to fall down any of the ladders or trip on hatch covers. Their hands are always stretched out horizontally, like in the movie images of ghosts. Bedwetting, which most people would like to hide, gets quickly reported—announced, in fact—by the patients to everyone in the berthing compartment. In the confined spaces of those compartments, the prospect of a recurring urine smell throughout a deployment agitates the shipmates, so they become vigorous witnesses.

This year though, the most common new condition in sick call was flat feet. Whether or not these sailors' feet had ever hurt them before, it wasn't until now, in late winter, just before we were going to get under way, that they needed to see a doctor. Years ago, it seemed intuitively obvious to physicians, as well as the lay public, that if God gave most of us arches in our feet, those who didn't have such arches must have some kind of disorder. I guess we've thought that way about a lot of physical things. In the last twenty to thirty years, though, evidence began to suggest that biological variety is not the same as disease.[*] Even among soldiers who do a lot of marching, it turns out that if God put less of an arch in your foot than he did in somebody else's, that's not a disease. Although doing a lot of marching or working on your feet on a steel deck may make your feet sore, it happens to people *with* arches just the same—no less and no more—as it does to people with flat feet.

Some guys didn't come for treatment or for our examination at all, but just to bring us a letter from the private physician or the family doctor

---

[*]There are a couple of diseases that cause laxity in ligaments and tendons and cause foot pain and other symptoms. Conditions that do this only to the feet and no other part of the body are exceedingly rare. When real diseases of the muscles or joints cause flat feet, other parts of the body are invariably affected, too.

from back home, saying that the flat feet disqualified them from sea duty. "Doc, my family doctor said that I'm going to have to leave the Navy because of these flat feet. He said to give you this letter."

All of these complaints had to be considered and examined. A number of things have to be considered in each history, and sometimes X rays or lab tests have to be done. So sick call was growing busier and taking longer every day.

"Seaman Jones, I'm glad to tell you that you don't have a major problem here," we might start up our summary after all the testing—carefully avoiding a comment that would imply "nothing is wrong," because experience proved that would anger them. We tried to be reassuring and lay out a plan for helping with, say, the flat feet. It never worked, though. A veil came down over the face, the eyes kind of glazed over. When a sailor wanted off the ship and considered himself ill, no medical explanation would work.

"I want to see a specialist!" was usually expressed in the tone generally reserved for "I'm not talking until I see my lawyer!" In fact, two sailors on different occasions presented me with letters from their lawyers on the subject of flat feet.

Setting up a consultation to see the specialist was problematic. When we could fully handle the problem on the ship, we didn't want to overburden the specialty clinics. There was already a three-week wait in the orthopedics clinic, so adding unnecessary consultations only stressed out the oversubscribed doctors further. I also thought we should let the crew know we were confident of our diagnoses. If we always needed a specialist to back us up, how reliable could we be? During the three to five weeks a sailor might be tied up with visits to the specialty clinic, he could be lost to his department, and with our sailing soon, that was a concern. Such an absence was sometimes necessary to take proper care of our sailors, but for an unnecessary consultation it would be wasteful. On the other hand, we in the medical department wanted to be as certain as we could be; some days we would have liked to have a specialist go over every case.

There were other causes for more business, too. It wasn't only the new outbreaks. The number of minor accidents—corneal abrasions, lacerated scalp, cuts on fingers—was also accelerating. The number of sprained ankles and other athletic injuries didn't increase, but now they were a little more trouble and healed slower. More guys were observing when they came to sick call, "You know, Doc, I don't think I can work with this," or, "Can I have a no-duty chit?"

There was another kind of chit besides the no-duty ones that was causing us problems again: the no-shave chits. The XO had insisted that the fuzzy stubble and every-third-day distant shave that we advised for PFB would be acceptable, but only if the sailor got a renewed note from the doctor every two weeks. Not a note from a corpsman, not a form letter. There were a couple of hundred guys on the ship who had this problem. If they all had to come in every two weeks, that just added a whole flock of people who didn't need real treatment.

"Doc, this is the way it's done everywhere in the Navy. Why do you have to be different?"

"XO, for one thing, it's done differently at just about every command. For another, for some of these guys, most of them, once we've tried antibiotics, or retin-A, or hydrocortisone. If they still get it, they're always going to be vulnerable!"

Mitchell wasn't so much a hardheaded man, it was just that I usually couldn't persuade him to listen to me. That day I just got lucky, I guess. I showed him the parts of the personnel manual about suitability for service. "Look XO, it's not really a medical problem at all. It's a personnel or uniform issue. You can either separate these guys from the Navy because of their condition, or you can let them adapt to these shaving practices . . . but it's permanent. They aren't going to quit being black just because of my medicine."

"OK, Doc, I've got work to do, for heaven's sake! You win." Finally! The XO agreed. We in medical would first try to treat a guy for a transient condition. We had a three-step, several-week protocol for that. If he still had shave bumps, we could send a note to his boss. Then his boss would either separate him from the Navy according to BUPERS Instruction 1910.2 (which we knew would never happen) or permit modified shaving. Either way, the medical department would no longer be involved. So from now on our only shave chits would be for the few guys with transient or first-time problems.

Finally Getting Under Way

The week finally came for our first independent steaming exercise (ISE). It was only going to be about two days under way. We would leave about midday, giving ourselves time to take everything very slowly in the departure, avoid the mistakes of hurry, and have as few accidents as possible. All the other departments, just like mine, welcomed the chance to spend the morning tying up the inevitable loose ends before the first underway period. Indeed, we had plenty of loose ends, and some of them smelled a lot like alcohol.

We had to have sick call just like we did every other day, of course. Not surprisingly, about twice the usual number showed up. By now we'd made sick call more efficient and diminished the lines quite a bit. Sick people and people who said they were sick went to the front of the line. Sailors who were just finishing the night shift were next. Everybody else was asked to return thirty minutes later, at 0800. The longest anybody waited before seeing a doctor or corpsman was ten minutes.

By now I'd been able to enforce the rule that our corpsmen didn't turn people away. If a person felt he needed to be seen at 0630, he didn't have to wait around for sick call to open at 0730. He came to the ER and he was seen. There were minor exceptions, such as with SK3 Womple, who still would turn people away even if they were vomiting or bleeding on the deck. We tried not to assign Womple to ER duty. For the most part, the corpsmen knew that whenever somebody showed up he'd be treated.

Well, on this morning the line started forming around 0630 in spite of our new system, and there had been a steady stream of people outside the ER from about midnight onward. Since we were going to be getting under way, Big Jim's and Cap'n Odie's had had a lot more business than usual that night.

When sick call hours were over at 0930—a little later than usual—I had a handful of sailors I needed to call the hospital about. Two guys had fractures. One had a "boxer's fracture" of his right fifth metacarpal, a typical fracture from punching something hard. Occasionally it can happen from punching a particularly rigid jaw, but among sailors nowadays this fracture is usually the result of angrily punching something even more rigid than somebody's face, such as a concrete wall. That's what it was in this case. A young bos'n's mate punched a wall. They do that for different reasons: taking dares, showing off, temper tantrums. Another crewman had a fractured forearm from falling off his bicycle.

We couldn't keep guys with casts on the ship. Of course, if we were deployed, days away from any port, then we could put casts on people, but we didn't like sailors with casts to stay on the ship. A fracture, with or without a cast, limits a person's mobility. Imagine what would happen if the ship ever went down or the individual were blown over the side into the water. Either a fracture or a plaster cast would compromise swimming and water survival. Admittedly, this was a pretty small possibility, and to people who didn't have to think about it a lot, it could seem like a silly concern. It was peacetime; why should you expect an aircraft carrier to sink? Well, in the short time I'd been on the ship, we'd already had one guy blown over the side. What if his survival at sea had been compromised by a cast on his arm? It would be worse yet on the leg. Even getting up and down the ladders on the ship became hazardous if you had a cast on an extremity.

The orthopedists at the hospital were usually pretty unsympathetic about this, and even their surgical director was at times, also. When I'd call about these problems they'd say, "What's wrong with the cast?" I would explain the problem, and they'd say something like, "Well that's not my problem. If you're going to worry about things like that [implying anybody who would ask such a stupid question must not have enough important things to think about], you'll have to take it up with somebody else." Finally I'd wind up calling the XO of the hospital, who would speak to the orthopedist, and eventually the patient would go over to the hospital.

There should have been a way for us to make arrangements to berth a sailor with a cast someplace on the shore while we were at sea. As it was, we were forced to get an orthopedic surgeon to take responsibility for the patient from that point forward. Surely the orthopedists were right—a minor fracture that was adequately casted shouldn't have to tie up an orthopedic appointment when people were already waiting too long for orthopedic appointments. Regardless, I couldn't take them with us to sea, and our only choice at the time was the hospital.

I wish it had just stopped at ankles and wrists. We had another guy with a broken face. He'd been punched a number of times at Big Jim's, had a broken nose, and by our sinus films looked as though he had a fracture with a fluid level in his maxillary sinus. I had to call the ENT doctor about him, a phone call I always dreaded. When I phoned the otolaryngology department I was put on hold, where I lingered for five or ten minutes. Finally a corpsman came. Suddenly there was a dial tone. Somebody at the hospital must have pushed a button accidentally. Surely they wouldn't hang up on me on purpose.

I called again, was put on hold again for five minutes, and once again the same corpsman came to the telephone. "Good morning, this is Dr. Riley again. I was waiting for Dr. Eilers."

"Oh, he's tied up in the OR and won't be able to come to the phone for a couple of hours."

"Well, we're about to get under way here. Can I talk to one of the other ENT doctors?"

"No. Dr. Simons is on leave, so it's only Dr. Eilers."

"Well, what can we do? We're about to get under way, and I need to ask Dr. Eilers about a patient."

"I don't think there's anything you can do. Maybe you can write out a consultation, and Dr. Eilers will call you back."

"But I won't be here in a few hours."

The corpsman didn't say good-bye, jump off a bridge, or anything. He just put me on hold. I waited about another five minutes.

"This is Dr. Eilers. What do you need?"

Dr. Eilers and I had spoken together in the past. I had tried at various times being normal, submissive, aggressive, angry, or supplicant, and it never seemed to work, so I just described the patient, leaving any emotion out of my description.

"Well, that's no problem, just bandage him up and put him on an antibiotic. I'd recommend Keflex, or ampicillin. Then just make a routine appointment and I'll see him in a couple of weeks."

"Well, we're going to be under way here, and this guy works in the engine spaces where it's pretty hot. He looks pretty bad, and I'm a little concerned about his going up and down the ladders in all that heat. Do you think you could help us by putting him in medical hold so he can stay behind?" We couldn't do a medical hold in Mayport at that time. Since it was technically a status of hospitalization, only one of the hospital doctors could arrange it.

"No, he really doesn't need that, you can just put him on light duty there on the ship, and I'll get to him in a couple of weeks."

"But I don't have the option of just putting him on light duty here on the ship. He needs to stay behind while we're under way."

"Well, what would you do if you were on a deployment?"

I tried to explain to him that we were not on a deployment. It just isn't the right thing to take a guy to sea on a two-day exercise when you don't really need to.

"Well, just assign him to the beach detachment." The beach detachment is a small group of the ship's company, mostly from the supply, administration, and security departments, that stays behind looking after certain ship's business while the ship is under way.

"That's not what the beach detachment is for. I'm not allowed to put patients there. This is what the medical hold is for, though, isn't it?"

Finally, we got to the bottom line, "Well, putting a guy on medical hold requires a lot of paperwork. I just don't have the time for that. I'm a lot busier than you are. You'll have to figure something else out." Dial tone. He had hung up.

This was already taking a lot of time, and I had a few other patients I had to deal with. We were going to be getting under way in a little over an hour.

After all these months, I had looked forward to getting under way with some kind of romantic anticipation. I don't know what I'd

expected—perhaps a magical voice singing whaling songs throughout the ship. We were just so busy.

The First Drill

In addition to all the paperwork and the minor injuries we were seeing in the medical department that morning, about thirty minutes
after we passed the St. Johns buoy we heard the call for a man-overboard drill. "This is a drill, this is a drill. Man overboard. Man overboard. All hands muster at your battle stations immediately. Up and
forward on the starboard side, down and aft on the port side. Man
overboard. Man overboard. This is a drill."

Whenever somebody hit the water, a number of things had to happen immediately if there was any hope of saving him. At speeds like
ours, we could quickly be out of sight of a shipmate who fell overboard.
Sometimes, especially in the dark or during rapid operational tempo,
somebody might just see a splash or see something appear to leave the
deck. So you might not be certain that a shipmate had gone over.
Turning the ship rapidly to come back and get a guy or launching three
or four helos or boats to search is dangerous in itself. Every time you
have to dangle a wire down over the water or put a boat over the side,
there's a chance for somebody else to drown or break a leg. Not to
mention the literally thousands of dollars it costs to turn a behemoth
like an aircraft carrier around. So we don't take it lightly.

The first thing that has to happen when there is a possibility of
somebody falling overboard is to verify absolutely that somebody is
gone and, if so, who that person is. That's why one of the main things
in a man-overboard drill is for everybody to muster at a designated
spot within five minutes. This is harder than it sounds with 5,300 people.
An accurate count is critical. Yet, the announcement "This is a drill"
lets some people take it less seriously. The members of the air wing
are famous for this. Some guys just stay in their racks; others never
hear the announcement. Some don't know what the drill is about or
think it involves somebody else and never come to the muster. Until
we can prove that the ship's man-overboard drill works correctly,
though, we can never be comfortable that we're ready to go to sea, so
the drill is something we take very seriously.

While all that body counting is going on, other people are launching
boats and helicopters, doing all the things you need to do to find the
person. The medical department has a couple of crews of corpsmen
who go on boats or helos if they have to rescue the fallen sailor. They

get mustered as they pick up their medical rescue bags on their way out.

The drill this day was not going well. At the end of the last deployment, we were able to get everybody mustered in well under five minutes. Since every work center has a list of all members, those who don't muster within five minutes are easily identified. Of course, that's how you know who's really overboard in a true emergency. It's also how the XO catches the laggards in the drill.

At about the seven- or eight-minute mark, the XO came on the 1-MC. "Good morning. This is the XO. The man-overboard drill is not going well. Anybody knowing the whereabouts of the following people lend a hand." He then read the names of the people who hadn't been mustered yet. In a real man overboard, reading those names would be important. Perhaps a shipmate would need to go into those sailors' racks—or anywhere else they might be—to verify who was actually lost. Everybody had to be involved. About four or five minutes later, now eleven to thirteen minutes total, the XO's voice came over the 1-MC again. He had a way of being a little whiney when he was irritated. "This is the XO." No "good morning" this time. "This drill is not going well *at all.* We have spoken about it before, most of you guys have been to sea before. This is inexcusable. I want the following individuals to report to XOI." Then he read the list of names—about a dozen guys.

Finally, at what was almost twenty minutes out, the XO came on again, "This is the XO again. We are calling this drill off, but at almost twenty minutes there are a bunch of guys who still didn't check in. We're going to keep doing man-overboard drills until we get it right." So we'd been under way only a couple of hours, and we already got scolded.

In the melee to get 5,300 people checked fast enough, the inevitable hyperenergy of youth finds an opportunity to express itself. Sound a starting gun and the boys want a race. That morning we had seven guys with scalp lacerations (from bumping their heads at the top of knee-knocker doors), two with bruises, and one with a facial laceration from falling down a ladder. Some are careless, some are inexperienced, but most are just exuberant adolescents with an excuse to run. Maybe they haven't been under way before. Sometimes they forget where metal hangs down from the overhead. This was our first man-overboard drill, and we had seven scalp lacerations; by the end of the cruise, we'd only get one or two with each drill.

After we took care of the injured, I stopped down to the XO's office to fill him in on the day's epidemiology. He was flushed, irritated not only by the drill but by our general difficulty getting under way. I noticed he'd gained a little weight since he came to the ship. He was also smoking a lot more and had bags under his eyes. The extra pounds weren't so surprising, with his working overtime and munching on doughnuts or sandwiches late at night. His khaki shirt was beginning to blouse just a little bit over his belly, so there was a little rippling around the buttonholes. In fact, the same thing was happening to me, I noticed just then. Funny I noticed it first on him.

It was getting into late afternoon when I got back to the medical department, but I could tell when I saw Father Hix, the Catholic chaplain, pacing back and forth in front of my office with a morose young guy in dungarees slumped on the bench, that there was still more to be done that afternoon. The padre told me that this young man had been in to see him a couple of times in the prior week. The sailor had begun by telling him that he had discovered that the Navy life was not for him. He just couldn't handle the hassle he was getting from his boss, and he realized that the kind of structured life in the Navy was bad enough, but nobody ever told him what shipboard life was like. He told the priest that he had enlisted to try to please his parents, but he just couldn't handle it anymore. Father Hix had been pretty supportive, apparently. Navy chaplains are trained in counseling techniques and psychotherapy. Of course, they remain ministers above all, but on the ship their role is just as much social worker, guidance counselor, psychologist, and community maintenance.

Finally, this morning, the young sailor seemed more morose than he'd been before, and he told John, "I just can't be responsible for what I might do if I have to stay here." That hits the trip wire. At that point, the chaplain always brings the member down to see the medical department. The chaplain and I sat alone with the young sailor for a little while. He was clearly well oriented, not psychotic. His vital signs and physical examination were normal. He wasn't physically sick. After we spoke for a while, he seemed a little bit less sad with each minute, but I asked him, "You know, Chaplain Hix is concerned about your safety. Have you been thinking about hurting yourself?"

"Not really, Doctor, but I'll do anything I have to get off this ship."

"Now, does that mean injure or maybe even try to kill yourself? Is that what you're telling me?"

"I really don't want to die, Doctor, but you can't keep me here if you think I will."

Neither the medical department nor any other place on the ship really has a truly suicide-proof room. With all the potential hanging places, myriad electrical sources, sharp objects, and so on, it's hopeless to try to find a such a place on the ship. Our safest places are in the brig, but strict rules forbid keeping a patient in there, even for safety reasons. The only thing we can do is keep somebody on guard with the sailor constantly.

Father Hix and I called his DivO and arranged for him to stay in his berthing space with two people with him all the time. I reassured the sailor that we would get him to psychological counseling the next day when we got back into port.

"What about today?"

"We don't have any planes on board today. There's no COD, and no way to fly you off."

"Can't we just bring the ship back?"

It may be a kinder and gentler Navy, but we haven't reached the point of being able to turn a dreadnought around for an unhappy sailor.

When his buddies came for him and his DivO left my office, I saw that HM3 Laflame was waiting restlessly to talk to me. It seems that Rock was planning to take a guy into the OR to undo a testicular torsion. Somehow the testicle twists around inside the scrotum in some young men. The vas deferens and the blood vessels attached to the testicle get tied up in a knot, and because of that torsion the testicle is strangled. A true emergency, it almost always has to be treated by an operation, even when diagnosed promptly. Tosser had already sent a corpsman down to tell the XO that he had to operate immediately and was preparing the patient for the OR. I knew it was going to be another one of those scenes, but nonetheless I had to confront Rock about it. I stuck my head into the ER and asked, "Commander Tosser, can we talk for a few minutes?"

He said he had an operation to do.

"Really, Commander, this won't take very long."

He stormed over across the passageway into my office. I asked if he would let me try to manually reduce the torsion. Sometimes, with proper angulation, you can untangle the mass. You can tell it's effective if the pain disappears. Usually the patient will need an operation eventually, because a torsion will occur again if the underlying tendency isn't corrected. My thought, however, has always been that, whenever possible, elective operations should be done at a real hospital. If we can relieve the problem, the operation can be done under calmer circumstances "on the beach."

Rock didn't feel an exam by me was necessary, but I didn't bother with a "who's in charge" debate.

The guy had already been shaved and prepared for the OR. He was twisting in pain on the exam table, sometimes would sit up, then lie down, then stand up and take a couple of paces. The severe pain with testicular torsion is typically grabbing, gnawing, undulant. Victims say it's worse than any ground ball in baseball or knee in football. I asked him to lie down on his back on the exam table with his knees up and apart. Gently pulling the testicles first straight down, then rotating them both upward and outward, on the right side there was a little give, like clicking a styrofoam bubble, and his facial expression changed. I asked him to stand up, which he did, and he took a few steps around, saying that his pain had disappeared. Rock said nothing.

The sailor said, "Gee thanks, Doc. That was a lot easier operation than I thought. Did you already put the stitches in?" HM3 Laflame choked back a giggle, but Petty Officer Casad, who was standing in the background, couldn't help himself and chuckled aloud. I knew I had to keep Rock happy at this point, too, and it was true that the individual would still need an orchiopexy (the operation to fix the strands inside the scrotum). I told him he would still need the operation, but I would rather he go see the genitourinary specialist as soon as we could send him there. Today's operation was canceled.

I went back to my office to finish up the day's paperwork. In a few minutes I heard the captain on the 1-MC. I think at CO school, the captains must get a heavy dose of 1-MC technique. Of course, officers like Louis and Guitar were the type who would talk to their sailors without somebody telling them to. Still, one had to notice how much Captain Louis liked the 1-MC. "Good evening, this is the captain. We're a little over a hundred miles off the coast of Florida, on our first underway period. People are working very hard today. We have a few glitches, but we'll work 'em out fine. This crew has a fine reputation, and I have to tell you I'm proud to be under way with you.

"I need to speak to you, though, about the man-overboard drill. The XO is right, that's something we need to improve." The captain spoke a little about the drill and the need for concentration, but in a more upbeat tone than we'd heard earlier. He was obviously letting the crew know that he would be a communicator, so I thought it was fine that he gave a rather long announcement. Most people have to stop or at least slow down their work while the captain is speaking, so a few skeptics grow restless if the announcement lasts more than a minute or two. Louis chatted on as though having a casual Sunday-afternoon phone call, nothing else going on. There were a few customary routine announcements: babies born that day back at home (of course, the first the fathers had heard of it), the daily news, major sport scores.

Now the announcement was going a little longer than usual, but the skipper went on. He was interesting to listen to, and with his congenial accent he was the kind of person who could be likable as he chatted. He announced a new program, "Letters to the Captain." He invited the crewmen to submit comments and questions in any of the suggestion boxes around the ship and promised that he would respond to them every day on the 1-MC.

People were starting to chuckle about the length of the announcement. Oh well, first day out. Getting acquainted, maybe there was a lot to pass on.

The captain finally ended with a pep talk about how good it was to be back at sea again. The 1-MC is really for brief announcements. The bos'n's mates and quartermasters are warned to always "keep it brief." The captain seemed to warm up the longer he talked, and he was obviously enjoying holding that microphone. Amused by the lengthy fireside chat, the crew liked it, and they liked the new skipper. When he closed with "and above all, have a fine Navy day," the crew knew he meant it.

It stayed pretty busy the next day and a half, but the first underway period finished uneventfully. The shakedown had shown us a lot of things we had to work on, like our man-overboard response and a number of issues in each department, but we made it home safely. No big pieces of equipment were damaged, and nobody was injured. If we weren't exuberant, we weren't dissatisfied either.

Chapter 10

More Workups

The despondent young sailor was sent over to the psychiatry department, and a couple of days later he came back with the diagnosis of a personality disorder. He knew the difference between right and wrong and had a firm comprehension of reality. He wasn't psychotic or sick in diagnostic terms. Although the sailor didn't have a treatable psychiatric disease, his personality would remain an obstacle to functioning in the military, so the psychiatrist recommended separation at the convenience of the government, in accordance with BUPERS Instruction 1910.2.

"Why did they send him back to us if he's medically disqualified?" the XO asked me. It's just as confusing for most doctors as it is for everybody else. There really is a sound logic to the problem, but it's difficult to make it clear.

I tried to give my usual explanation, but I knew from years of experience that it wasn't very convincing. "The personality is a personal trait, like being tall or being left-handed. It's not a disease that we can treat, like pneumonia or even schizophrenia. People tend to have certain behavior patterns that they either prefer or just use habitually. If a person is very dependent or rebels against authority, that's a behavior pattern, not a disease."

"What are we supposed to do with him now? What if he tries to kill himself?"

"XO, he's rational, and the psychiatrist feels he knows right from wrong. You either have to hold him responsible . . . or with identification of a personality disorder you can just administratively separate him. In other words, it's a leadership problem, not a medical condition."

"Doc, that's a cop-out, and you know it!"

I had the same discussion later that same day with the captain.

199

"Well, then, if it's a leadership problem, we'll deal with it that way." Naval officers take leadership very seriously, and personally. They can accept being unable to cure a disorder, but not failing a leadership challenge.

"Captain, maybe I didn't make myself clear in the right kind of way. It's not *just* a leadership problem. Once you reach the age of these guys, personality isn't that adaptable. This guy is going to continue to be a problem for the command, and eventually he's going to cause us more trouble by being here than if we let him go."

"People can change, Doc, you know that. If he needs guidance and discipline, that's my job."

"Yes, Sir, but a guy with an antisocial personality is not likely to respond."

"Then it's a medical disability," he insisted.

That discussion never got any easier.

The suicide potential added a whole tangled dimension to the problem. Suicide had become one of the leading causes of death among young Americans. It's frequency was about the same in the Navy as in the general population—a fraction lower, actually—but it was something we were very concerned about. The medical department was generally held responsible for the suicide prevention programs, but the chaplains and the chain of command were also critical. Medical needed to be involved in case there was a treatable illness, such as encephalopathy or schizophrenia. Also, some people may be injured in an attempt, and the injuries would have to be treated.

The captain pointed out that if a guy with a personality disorder did kill himself, it would surely be medical at that point. I tried to be respectful but pointed out that once he was dead it was most especially not a medical problem . . . just like murder wasn't a medical problem. That kind of explanation is not usually taken well by the boss, but Captain Louis understood. "Now you're accusing me of murder?" he chided.

We couldn't predict every sailor's behavior, but some of them were more prone to act out until they got what they wanted. Maybe they wouldn't intentionally kill themselves, but in acting out they could be very disruptive and might well die in the process.

Two weeks later, the sailor got in a fight with a CPO and hit him with a wrench. When he was hauled off to the brig, he sat and cried in his cell until he was taken to see first a chaplain and then another psychiatrist. The chaplain thought he was depressed. The psychiatrist, a new one this time, concluded again that he had a personality disorder. When the sailor came back to the brig after seeing the psychiatrist, he made slash marks on his left wrist with a fingernail clipper. There were a total of eight scratch marks, but no bleeding. He was transferred to NH Jacksonville, where he was admitted for suicide prevention and further reevaluation.

After our first ISE, two weeks went by before we went to sea again. Those were two hard weeks for me because that's when Donny Feldman left and our new lab officer, WO George Lucy, reported on board. We had been back in port just a couple of days when Lucy reported, and he and Donny had a seven-day turnover period. George was about twenty-five years old, had six or seven years of prior enlisted time in the Coast Guard, and had been in the Navy about four years, although he'd been a physical therapist most of his career.

A remarkably good-looking guy, he obviously was a weight lifter. Muscles like his didn't come simply by genetics or even just by ordinary athletics. He was only about five feet, eight inches tall, and wasn't so deformed by all of his muscles that he had to wear abnormal-sized garments. However, the muscles were such a prominent part of his being that neither an observer nor George himself could ever quite be unaware of them. He had a habit of shrugging his shoulders or slowly flexing an extremity when he spoke with you. To look at his wristwatch, he would elevate his left arm, maintain a ninety-degree angle between the forearm and upper arm, and slowly twist his fist toward one side in order to look at the watch. Kind of reminded me of ancient Egyptian paintings. Sometimes his chin or an extremity would flex slowly and move to one side—not quite writhing, and not quite in a twitch, but like he practiced it—in a way that would make one muscle here or there stand out. It was as though his body, poised ever to unfurl like a great eagle, couldn't quite be contained.

He had another disarming quality, and that was his continual countenance of surprise. He often looked startled. An expression of shock, with his eyes particularly wide open, came over him sometimes when he was asked a question. I first saw it the day we met when I asked him if his check-in was going all right. His jaw dropped, and his eyes opened wide—the way a deer looks when it's caught in your headlights on the highway. If you put that stare together with a twitching movement of one muscle in the thigh or arm, it was sometimes hard to concentrate on what you were trying to say or what he was saying to you.

I learned that George had worked part-time as a professional wrestler for the last several years. He wrestled under the nom de tussle of the Red Pharaoh. This was something I decided I didn't need to learn more about for the time being. Meantime, another new officer reported the same month, our new nurse anesthetist, Lt. Rob Emerson. Most of the time, the anesthetists, like the surgeons, prefer to be sent to hospital when a ship is in port and work on board only while under way. Understandably, they're concerned about keeping up their skills in the OR, and most of them far prefer the hospital to the ship's environment. Rob had been an anesthetist for over fifteen years. "I've done that long enough that being out of the OR for a few weeks won't make me forget it all. We're going to be steaming soon. I want to be as much part of the crew as I can." He really did talk like that. With Rick leaving, Rob would prove to be our salvation.

Rob and George weren't our only new members. Senior Chief Myers had left us about the beginning of the year, and we'd been without a leading chief for a few months. HMC Abercrombe joined us when George Lucy did. From his appearance, I figured Chief Abercrombe was a nearly perfect CPO. He had a good military appearance but a classical CPO's pot belly. This will be the chief who'll help us with our enlisted guys, I thought. Rick Cox didn't share my enthusiasm, though. "I don't know, Captain," Rick told me one evening. "Something about that new chief. Think you better keep an eye on him." Rick was prone to be skeptical—heck, downright cynical—about strangers, so I chided him about giving the new chief a fair chance. Still, I never took anything Rick told me too lightly.

Brice Bostik had moved on, too. Although the air wing docs and corpsmen weren't part of our ship's company, I always considered them members of the department, even when they weren't aboard. After all, they would be living and working with us during the deployment—the real life of the carrier. George McDonough, a new flight surgeon, relieved Brice. Bill Kelly would be staying on for another year. The night before George's first underway period with us, I took him out to dinner in Mayport. He was a lot different from Bostik! Curly headed and serious, George wore John Lennon spectacles, the kind we called "social concern eyeglasses" in the late sixties. We found we had something in common almost immediately when I learned that George was planning to become a neurologist. Even though he'd never read any of my published articles, we had a pleasant evening. I was impressed by how intelligent George was. He certainly was serious, though, and there was something else about him, that old Gaelic thing from either Brian Boru or Robert Emmet; Forrestal had it too, something between being intense and very dedicated . . . no, maybe just: stubborn. Yes, that's it. He was a stubborn cuss.

Womple Back on the Program

One day shortly after our first ISE, we needed an X ray on somebody because of a shoulder injury. Arden Womple was off the ship on an errand, so one of the other corpsmen had to take the films. It was taking a long time, so Burt Rosen went back into the X-ray suite to help. Shortly we had the films. They weren't technically very good, but the shoulder could be seen well enough. We gave the patient a sling and sent him on his way. "HM1, those films aren't very good. I thought we were going to do some cross training on X ray."

"We did for a while, Sir, but lately it's hard to get Arden to do the training. He's getting down again."

After our talks a couple of months earlier, Womple had been going to the AA meetings and his work had really improved. While he hadn't turned into a glittering personality, he had been congenial, and until the past few weeks he'd been coming to work on time. Lately, though, he had turned more surly again and was making careless errors at his work. Now HM1 Rosen told me Arden had let the training slide, too. In fact, Burt looked like he had more to say. "I think I should get Lieutenant Cox and Lieutenant Emerson," he said. Rick hadn't detached yet, and since it was after 1600, Lucy was already gone for the day. To my relief, Rob was spending a lot of time with Rick. It looked like he'd be doing a lot of the administrative things, besides the nursing and anesthesia duties.

Obviously Burt thought something was bad wrong if he wanted somebody else to have to tell me about it. "We got us a problem, Captain," Rick said. When he used those words, I knew it was an understatement. When the three of them went back to the X-ray suite, they discovered that nine months' worth of X rays had never been sent over to the hospital for reading by a radiologist. Back in October, when we returned home, all the X rays from the deployment, six months' worth, were to have been brought to the clinic immediately. We'd had very specific discussions about it, and Arden assured me it was done. Every week, he was supposed to have sent that week's films over to the clinic on the base at Mayport. Workups were starting now, and we were nine months behind. Furthermore, the radiologist ought to be furious about having nine months of films dumped on his lap late and all at once!

We went back into the X-ray file room to check it out. There they were. Hundreds of them. Rob inadvertently bumped a locker door open with his shoulder, and a brown paper bag fell to the deck. A couple of little white, clipped badges with photographic film tumbled out. The radiation badges. As the X-ray tech, Arden was responsible for handling and recording data about the radiation badges worn by selected people in the crew. Himself, of course, but also a group of people in the weapons department and the MARDET. Because of the sensitivity of those badges and the potential health concerns, letting them lag was a much bigger problem than the delinquent X rays. Arden was back in trouble, and this time it was serious.

Art was our radiation safety officer. He had to come in from home that night, and he called a number of official people all over Jacksonville to tell them about our predicament. I went down to the XO's office to tell him about it. He was on the phone and gestured for me to have a seat while he continued to talk. Ten minutes later he was still on the phone, so I left. Miraculously, Art had been able to contain the bureaucratic damage. He arranged to have the badges read that evening, and since none of them had any significant exposures, he was able to get us out of an obligatory late report. We spent about two hours carefully wording the accompanying report, and I brought it down to the XO, who was working late as always. In green ink, the color the XO uses, he changed a couple of my verbs, so we had to rewrite the entire report. I would discover that the XO always changed a few words. Why he preferred Navy-speak jargon to real English I could never figure out. Nonetheless, the radiation badge fiasco was repaired with much less hassle than we had deserved.

Womple and I would have to speak soon.

The next morning I asked Petty Officer Womple, who was wearing a particularly long face, to come and talk with me. He shambled into the office without looking at me and slunked into the chair next to my desk. Just like at our last meeting, he sat square in his seat and yet looked slumped somehow. Saying nothing, he stared at the deck.

"Petty Officer Womple, I don't have time right now to go over things the way we should. The fact is, things have gone bad again. Do you want to talk about it? Have you been having trouble with drinking again?"

As though pinched, he started at the second question. He was alert now, and even angry. "No, I haven't had a drop!"

I thought for a minute he was going to be more animated, maybe open up a little. No, his irritation subsided and he lapsed back into deck-staring and hand-wringing.

"Look, this business about the radiation badges could be big trouble. And what about those damned X rays you promised you'd take care of? I backed you up before, but if you don't help me out here, we're going to have to send you to mast this time for sure."

"Everybody keeps looking for me to mess up. I never see any *white* corpsmen in here."

"Wait a minute. You think you've been treated differently because you're black?"

No answer. Just a shrug. Momentarily stymied because I was both astounded at and resentful of the allegation, I said nothing and waited for more. Finally he said, "No, not directly, not from the department, I guess, but it's always there. I got personal problems, too."

"We offered to help you with that once before."

"I can handle it myself."

"Not so far!" I told him. Finally, Womple told me how badly he felt about these lapses. He vowed he hadn't returned to drinking. He knew he was late with the badges and the X rays, but as he'd grown more and more delinquent he was more afraid I'd get a notice when he turned the late work in. In fear, he just got further and further behind.

I made him promise to hook up with one of the chiefs, preferably one from our department, but elsewhere would be all right if he didn't feel he could relate to one of the HMCs. Later, the CAAC told me that Arden's attendance at the AA meetings had become irregular the last few weeks, but he still came periodically and didn't seem to be drinking.

Sick call was dragging that morning. After securing the XO's permission to get rid of those frequent no-shave chits, we also had begun to schedule guys with shaving rashes only on Thursdays and Fridays, our otherwise slowest days. This was a Tuesday, and one of my patients was a young black guy with a neatly trimmed beard. I tilted my head and stared. Beards had not been legal in the Navy for six or seven years. This one wasn't baggy; it was short and had a clear margin, right at the angle where the jaw and underside of the chin and mouth meet the neck. "Dr. Sergeant over at the Mayport Clinic said I was not to shave. Said I should give my chief this chit and tell him I could wear a beard 'cause of my PFB. Then this morning the chief said I had to come down here to get a new chit."

The place where shave bumps erupt most is right at bends in facial structures or places where the grain shifts . . . exactly where this sailor was still shaving. The places that Dr. Sergeant had told him not to shave were ones most guys didn't usually get the bumps anyway. That's one of the reasons why just wearing a neatly trimmed beard is not a solution. The beard is illegal, and if you trim it where beards usually get trimmed, you still get bumps in the usual place, namely the neckline! Lately, though, a bunch of our sailors had been going over to the clinic on the base to get no-shave chits because the doctors over there gave them what they wanted—a chit that said "may wear a neatly trimmed beard." Despite our efforts to spread the word and educate all the chiefs and DivOs, most supervisors were in the habit of simply accepting anything from a doctor, so the sailors usually got away with it.

I phoned Dr. Sergeant over at the clinic to talk it over.

"Look, Dr. Riley, I understand you see your job as enforcing the Navy's regulations regardless of the effects on the patient. I have to put the patient first, though. I'm not like you. I didn't check my diploma at the door when I came in. The chit stands. He doesn't have to shave."

"I'm not trying to talk you out of your own approach to things, but you know a doctor's chit is merely a recommendation to the command. Over here on the ship, I have to make sure I take care of the sailors and at the same time help them get along with the rules. Just wanted to explain for you what the command is looking for so we can work this together as well as possible—"

"Look, *Captain,* we know all about you over here. I'm not selling out my standards just to give in to some archaic rules." Notice, he's calling me by my rank; that means he doesn't like me.

"Hey, I'm not asking you to sell out anything. I was just trying to explain about—"

Dial tone. Dr. Sergeant had hung up.

I tried to explain about the PFB to the patient and gave him our guidelines about shaving every third day with clippers instead of a razor. "The doc over at the clinic said you'd make me shave," he grumped. Grabbing the packet of information from me, he stormed out of sick call.

When sick call finally ended that morning, all the khaki in the department met to talk about what to do with Womple. Lucy took up the chair next to my desk, his multisectioned notebook/organizer open on his lap. Moving his chin in such a way that his sternocleido-mastoid muscle flexed photogenically, he poised his pen over the page as though to show me he was ready to record my every syllable.

The whole team agreed it was time to deal with Womple. Every officer, chief, and petty officer in the department had had trouble with him one time or another. His evaluations were terrible. He had just failed the physical fitness test (PFT) again. We all agreed we shouldn't just use the PFT as an easy scapegoat excuse; his whole performance was so bad, after all. Yet he had more than a year left on his current enlistment. It's hard to get a guy out for poor performance in the middle of an enlistment. We'd push the administrative separation, but if that didn't work we'd be sure not to recommend him for reenlistment when this tour was up.

"Warrant Officer Lucy, when you take over for Donny as the lab officer, you have to stay in constant contact with the command master chief and admin officer about this. Besides doing it right, we must be sure we're fair with this guy at all times."

Lucy spread the fingers of both hands and looked surprised.

"The captain means follow all the right procedures," Rick said.

"That's not all," I continued. "We have to make sure that Petty Officer Womple gets all the support and treatment he needs. Dr. Kent, since you and he don't get along, you shouldn't be his doctor. As his boss, I shouldn't be either. Art, you should be his primary doc here on the ship, but when the flight surgeons are here, be sure you get one of them or the surgeon to go over everything with him."

Then I told the group that Arden had implied we had racial problems in the department. Chief Wilson, the only black man among our khaki, said that just wasn't so. Still, I planned to talk about it with the corpsmen at quarters the next day. Later that week, we met with the chaplains and the equal opportunity reps in the command to ask them to visit our department. I was convinced our guys were too close for racial problems, but I was well aware that as a white guy twenty years older than most of them, my conclusions could be challenged.

As for Womple himself, Rick said, "Captain, I think he's got you buffaloed. I know Womple. He's drinking again sure as hell. We caught him red-handed letting those films and badges go. If you think we got in trouble about those syringes, that was nothing compared to what hell could break loose for letting the radiation-surveillance program slide. Send him to mast!"

Lucy's eyes widened. His left biceps flexed along with his right shoulder. He began to realize what he'd have to deal with every day as the DivO in the department.

"I think Rick means it," I said. "See, Womple just doesn't accept his own responsibility."

More Help from the Mayport Clinic

New people were still coming to the ship every week. We had to capitalize on every opportunity to use days in Mayport for any training or repairs. An example was fire fighting over at the FTC on the base. Everybody on the ship had to have fire-fighting training, so we had to make sure all newcomers and those needing refresher training went over to the FTC. Always a demanding program, fire fighting was even tougher in the heat, but at least the instructors paid close attention to heat and smoke hazards. They were careful, even anxious, about both of those. To a fault, some said. It was springtime now, and the days were getting hot. Wearing the long sleeves and the heavy rubber OBAs made it worse. On an already hot Florida day, wearing all that gear inside a metal box, surrounded by flames and smoke, was hard work.

The teacher-student ratio in fire fighting is high so that each student has somebody looking after him, helping him avoid burns, watching for unsafe movements, protecting him. A flustered student might be inclined now and then to pull a mask off so he can wipe his brow, so the instructors guard against that most of all. Smoke inhalation is a constant focus of instruction and a great worry to the people who run the school.

Teachers have to learn, too. In some sessions instructors are trained how to instruct, and those classes have lots of pupils of both kinds. That week there was a crew of new instructors along with our couple of dozen FID students. It was well over ninety degrees, and everybody in Mayport was uncomfortable. Even down in the medical department it was warm despite the air conditioner. I remember wiping sweat off my forehead when I got the phone call from the quarterdeck.

"Doc, we just got word that a bunch of guys were injured over at the FTC, fire fighting. They activated the base mass casualty plan." A mass casualty plan means about the same thing for a base that it does for a ship at sea: too many or too badly injured for the resources at hand. Triage was necessary to prioritize treatment, and help would be sought from others.

With the controlled setting at the FTC, there must have been an explosion to injure that many. How many must it have been, I wondered. With five or six doctors on duty at the clinic, and four ambulances, to overwhelm them, it must be severe injuries and many of them. With Don on leave and Art over at the hospital with a patient, I was the only doctor on the ship that day, and there were a couple of people in the ER, so I couldn't leave right then. Phoning the clinic, I was told "The clinic is in emergency status, please call back later." The hospitalman hung up without even letting me talk.

We gathered all the corpsmen we could spare that day and sent them over to help at the clinic. I tried to concentrate, taking care of the minor injuries in our ER, while I worried about the burns—and maybe life-threatening injuries—to the *Forrestal* sailors at the fire-fighting school. After about an hour, Burt Rosen brought in a new corpsman who was reporting this week.

"Captain, this is HN Clay. You should let him tell you about the mass casualty."

Clay's story was interesting. There had been six students in the tower when one of them complained to the instructor that he was feeling faint. The instructor asked two others if they were feeling OK, and they both said they were "hot."

"Wait a minute," I asked Clay. "Just hot? Nothing else? Not weak, having trouble breathing?"

"Oh, no, Sir, nobody had any trouble breathing!"

"What about this smoke inhalation? Did you guys take off your OBAs? Did some of them malfunction?"

"No. Mine worked all right. I think they all did. Oh, no, Sir, we weren't allowed to take them off. You get in trouble if you do that!"

"Did somebody pass out?" I asked.

"No, everybody was walking around and doing all right after they left the tower."

"How about burns, or coughing, or shortness of breath?"

"No, none of that."

"Well, where did the idea of smoke inhalation come into it, if everybody was wearing their OBAs and nobody had any trouble breathing?"

"Dr. Sergeant over at the clinic, he's an emergency physician, and he said you never can tell with smoke inhalation. He said that the FTC was very dangerous, so he wasn't taking any chances. He sent four guys over to Dunes Hospital for admission."

Still nobody had called our medical department. I tried once again to call the clinic. Dr. Sergeant was too busy to talk to me. About that time, Art came back from NH Jacksonville, so I could go over to the clinic myself. By this time, none of our sailors were at the clinic. Except for the four sent to Beaches, they'd all been discharged. Every one of their medical records had the diagnoses of heat exhaustion and smoke inhalation. They were all told to return the next day to the clinic—not to the medical department on the ship—for follow-up. Every one of them had undergone an arterial puncture to measure blood gases— all normal—and they all had complete blood counts done. Most of them had blood electrolytes and urinalysis, all also normal. It was 1430 in the afternoon. Dr. Sergeant had gone home for the day.

I went down to Dunes to check in on our sailors. The doctor in their ER greeted me warmly. "Dr. Sergeant," he said, "Nice to meet you!"

"No, Terry Riley," I corrected him.

"Well, nice to meet you, Terry. Dr. Sergeant was very helpful. I guess it's a good thing they got all those guys over to the clinic. He says the doctor on the *Forrestal* is a real bozo. Who knows what would've happened to those poor sailors if he'd been treating them."

"Yeah, who knows?" I went along. "What about the patients you've got over here?"

"Well, we got gases, X rays, 'lytes, and urinalysis on all of them. They were all normal. We released all but two of them."

"What's wrong with those two?"

"One's a 'rule out cerebral hemorrhage' and the other's a 'rule out hypoglycemia.'"

"Cerebral hemorrhage?"

"Yeah, he had a headache, and Dr. Sergeant sent him over for a 'rule out,' so we did a CT scan. It was normal."

The term "rule out" had always struck me as a buzzword, and this afternoon's experience was giving me no reason to rethink my opinion.

"But," I asked, "was he groggy? Was his neurologic exam abnormal?"

"I don't know, really. But with the history of the fire and the headache . . ." So far, there was nothing that sounded to me like a hemorrhage or something that would require a scan.

The patient with "rule out hypoglycemia" had a blood sugar of 55 milligrams per 100 milliliters. Who knows why they checked it, but the time was around noon on a hot day. He'd worked all morning in the heat and hadn't eaten lunch yet.

I went to visit our sailors. The young man with the headache said he'd had it since the night before. He got headaches a couple of times a month. This was just an average one for him. The other guy was feeling fine, but he was in the middle of a five-hour glucose-tolerance test (on the same day as the admission!). "Either one of you guys breathe in any smoke?" I asked.

"Oh, no!" They hadn't dared take off their OBAs.

"Can you release these guys tonight?" I asked the doctor on duty.

"Well, in the morning, if they're stable. I'm kind of afraid for them to go back to that ship. From what they tell me over at the clinic, I'm worried about the medical care on the ship. Sounds shoddy. Dr. Sergeant wants to make sure he takes care of the follow-up himself to keep them away from that doctor . . . What's that guy's name, anyhow?"

"Riley," I told him, and left. Since my back was turned, maybe I didn't hear him, but I don't think he said good-bye.

All of our sailors were back the next day. They were all fine. About a month later, we got the bills from Dunes. For the CT scan and all the labs, it totaled over $3,000. I tried a few times to phone or visit Dr. Sergeant, but he was never in when I called or stopped in. He hadn't been to the fire-fighting site. I called Jim Gentry, the XO over at NH Jacksonville, and suggested maybe the doctors at the clinic should visit the place. Seeing an OBA might be interesting for them too, I said.

Getting Under Way Again

About a week later, we were preparing to get under way again for our second ISE. Except that the new combat officer, Roper Byrd, had to suddenly fly off because of a potential emergency in his wife's pregnancy, this departure went much more smoothly than the first. We had a couple of man-overboard drills that didn't go very well, but they were a lot better than last time. During this exercise, we had a number of observers and advisors from AIRLANT. They were there to check out whether we were ready to take on airplanes up on the flight deck and whether we'd mastered things like GQ and DC, which would be important for upcoming exercises. In the medical department, we had conferences about the mass casualty drills we were planning to practice that week.

The second day under way, while we were still within H-3 range of the beach, a member of the AIRLANT team came down to the ER with tight pains in his chest. He was a chief, in his forties. Stocky guy. A smoker. He was having a general dull, pressurelike ache in the sternum region and was sweating. Of course, since he was an engineer type, it was hot where he was working, so the sweating didn't necessarily mean much. From his EKG and exam, we decided he had angina pectoris, a sign of coronary artery disease, but not a myocardial infarction (a "heart attack")—at least not yet. Although we were able to alleviate his pain rapidly and he was stable, he needed to go back to the beach where he could have a complete cardiac evaluation and definitive treatment. We could take care of a patient with an acute myocardial infarction, but in peacetime, a little over an hour from a full-service cardiology department, we were really obliged to send him to a hospital if he was stable enough to travel safely.

In the department we discussed whether we needed to give him tissue plasminogen activator (TPA), a new drug that seemed to help dissolve clots in acute heart attacks. If it's ever to be effective, it needs to be given in the first minutes during which clots are forming in coronary arteries. After consulting and going over a few papers we had reviewed as a group within the past few weeks, we decided not to use TPA since this wasn't an infarction. However, we all agreed that the chief needed to fly off to the cardiac department at NH Jacksonville, where we could have him within a couple of hours. I went up to talk it over with the skipper. This would be my first encounter with the new boss about a medevac from sea.

I quickly grabbed my ball cap (you're always supposed to wear a hat when you enter the bridge). There are ten decks between medical and the bridge, so I was always breathless by the time I got to the captain's chair. Flight ops were going on. Captain Louis, I would learn, was very attentive to the flight deck during every flight cycle. This, however, was in the very earliest phases of workups, so he was especially focused that morning.

"Permission to enter the bridge," I panted out to the JOOD, and saluted. Entering the bridge requires a protocol not unlike coming aboard the ship. Granted admission, I struggled to slow my breathing, to seem as in control as I could. Trying to hold my breath still only made me feel more breathless. With the panting and the dark sweat stains streaking my khakis, I felt pretty rumpled when I came up to the captain's chair.

"How bad is he, Doc?" the captain asked me.

"He's stable now, Captain. In fact, I don't think he's actually had a heart attack. It's too early to be certain, though. He definitely has coronary disease, though. With your permission, Sir, I think we need to send him back to the hospital."

"How soon can you get him up on the flight deck?"

I should have worked that out before now. Quickly, I calculated the time to unhook all his wires, hook him back up to the portable monitor, get the elevator . . .

Uh-oh, the captain wanted an answer. You could see he was impatient that I hadn't anticipated his question. "Twenty minutes," I blurted out, having finished my calculations.

"OK, Doc. Twenty minutes. Thanks."

Down I went to get the patient ready. I asked George Lucy to arrange for the elevators up to the flight deck. Startled expression; wrist and shoulder pose. Long period of silence. Petty Officer Rosario said he'd take care of it. I examined the patient again, then was called back to my office. Somebody called to ask if I could write a refill on an antihistamine prescription, and somebody else had a skin rash. I told them to call back. Rob Emerson was running around getting oxygen and setting up monitors.

"Hey, why isn't the chief going!" I shouted to nobody in particular, but everybody who could hear.

"Captain, we've got to get his records together," Burt Rosen said. Rosen was the only guy who kept us within bounds on all bureaucratic stuff, but sometimes it seemed to slow us down.

"Captain, phone for you. It's the miniboss."

"Hey Doc, where's your patient? We're holding flight ops up."

"I told the captain twenty minutes, Mini. I've got seven minutes left."

"All I know is we're holding things up. Can't you move it along?"

I didn't have time to argue. Had to go check the patient again. No pain. Lungs clear. Finally, they had him on the gurney rolling out into the passageway. Bill Kelly would accompany him on the flight.

The elevator wasn't ready! The twenty minutes were just about up now. I called the gun boss because the weapons elevators that we'd need to get to the roof belonged to his department. He said he'd take care of it.

Finally, more than six minutes later, Bill and the patient were on their way up to the roof.

The captain called again. "Hey, Doc, we're holding up these flights."

"He's on the way up right now, Captain."

"Look, I counted on what you told me. Next time I'd appreciate it if you wouldn't just pull a number out of your rear end."

Oh well, the patient was stable and on his way. "Yes, Sir." Excuses wouldn't help. Taking care of the patient was the most important thing, but all the same, you'd just as soon not irritate the captain in the process.

The rest of that week was uneventful. We got home without any more injuries and tied up in Mayport without a hitch.

The Elusive Billy Dorsey

Our second night back in town, I was busy in the ER with a sprained ankle and a sailor who thought he'd swallowed his high school ring. HM1 Grant, our lab tech, was the LPO that night. When I sent the bos'n's mate with the swollen ankle over for his X ray, Petty Officer Grant came to tell me about a phone call. "He won't say who it is, Sir, but you're the only one he'll talk to."

We were too busy for me to enjoy a prank, but I was afraid to not take the call. It took a few minutes to reassure the caller that nobody else was listening, but by then I thought I could tell who it was. "Dr. Riley, this is Airman Dorsey."

"Airman Dorsey. Are you all right? Why are you calling?"

"I've been drinking."

"Sorry to hear that. I thought you'd stopped. Are you drunk?"

"You could say that."

"Where are you?" I asked him, fearing he might be UA, run off somewhere.

"Afraid I can't tell you that," he said, his words a little slurred, but still with that childish charm. You could almost smell the stench through the phone. There was a lot of activity and laughter in the background. Probably a bar or pool hall, I thought.

I asked him to tell me where he was so we could send somebody to bring him back to the ship. "Oh, I don't think that would be in my best interest," he said in remarkably grown-up syntax. We talked for a while, and I was able to determine that he hadn't been fighting and wasn't threatening to hurt himself. Gradually I recognized some of the noise in the background.

"Now, Airman Dorsey, I can tell you're at a bowling alley. Are you at the one here on the base?" I took the long pause for a yes. "Now listen, Billy, you stay right where you are. I'm going to send somebody to get you and bring you back to the ship so you can get in bed tonight without any trouble."

"I'll be in trouble with my division, though. I don't think I should come back right now while I'm drunk."

"But you don't have overnight liberty right now. You'll be in *more* trouble if you don't come back."

All right, he agreed. I hung up and called base security. It was easy to persuade them that giving this young man a ride back to the ship while he was just a little drunk would be better than what we'd deal with later if he got worse.

Half an hour later, they called back. He wasn't at the bowling alley. He had been there, witnesses said, but nobody could find him now. I started to worry. Billy didn't have any close friends. If he was feeling helpless and was drunk, I worried what he might do in a desolate mood.

Never should have worried. Ten minutes later, he was back on the phone.

"Billy, where *are* you?!"

"Right here. Bowling alley." He was perplexed. Why hadn't I sent somebody like I said I would. Well, yes, he'd been in the head for a while. He thought he might have fallen asleep in the stall. Maybe that's why the MAAs couldn't find him.

"OK now Airman Dorsey, listen very carefully. Do you hear me?" I made him promise to stand right there at the main counter, fall asleep if he had to, wet himself if necessary, but to *not* move a single foot from that point. The base police refused to go after him again. "Sorry, we're not a cab service. You'll have to send somebody else."

The JOOD got one of the ship's vehicles and sent a couple of watch-standers from Dorsey's division to go after him. They were back in forty minutes. Empty-handed. No Billy. "Just refused to come, Doc. He said you ordered him to stand right there and not budge for any reason until you got there. He said he promised you he wouldn't move."

Finally, after three or four more phone calls and another couple of hours, Dorsey was back on the ship. He was more sleepy than drunk by then, I thought. He was cleaner than usual under these circumstances. His red hair wasn't even too badly tousled, and he hadn't been in a fight. We had somebody tuck him in for the night, like a little cub scout who fell asleep during the bedtime story.

Besides Level II, I thought Billy Dorsey might need Antabuse.

Chapter 11

Getting Ready

✚ It was late spring, but it felt like midsummer in Mayport. A surly young fireman had just slammed angrily into the chair in my office and dared me with his frown to take a history. Don Kent opened the door just enough to show his face. "Captain, when you're free, can I talk to you?" I wondered what Don wanted to talk about. Summer was coming, and he would be transferring in July.

I glanced at the patient, FN Tyrone Hill, I guess to check his permission to even answer, since he seemed so angry. He must have read my mind, because he shrugged just a tiny, grudging permission. When Don closed the door, I asked, "OK, Fireman Hill, what seems to be the problem today?"

"My feet. I have flat feet. They hurt all the time. My mama says I'll have to leave the Navy."

"Well, let's see . . . You've been on the ship for about seven months now, been in the Navy a little over two years. When did your feet start to bother you?"

"Always have. Just worse now on these steel decks all the time."

I looked at his feet. Sure enough, almost no arch. The soles of his boots had a normal wear pattern, though. Mobility and bulk in his feet were normal, too. "Your feet look OK to me, Fireman. Why don't we get you a set of arch supports, try those a week or so, and look at it next week?"

"Knew I'd get a runaround down here! I want to see a specialist!"

"Well, let's see how it goes for a week with the arches and then we'll decide, OK?"

"You can't make me deploy if my feet hurt. I can ask to see the captain." I realized it wasn't just his feet that made FN Hill angry, but it never worked to argue with the young sailors while they were agitated. So I sent him out with the arch supports we both suspected he wouldn't like and made an appointment for the next week.

Don had become more friendly during the workups. While I could never take John Busby's place, Don knew how much I counted on him, and his devotion to the ship spilled over to me a little bit. When he wanted to chat, as he did this morning, I learned to be glad for the opportunity. He came in now, after Hill left, and took the same chair. Often with Don you had the feeling that your English teacher or pastor was about to explain something about basic manners or deportment to you. His posture was straight, but not rigid. His gestures weren't cold, but they were deliberate. He had an air a little bit like being proper, or maybe it was correct. It was natural in Don, though, not at all pretentious. He was just a correct kind of guy.

"You know Lieutenant Pompadour, the new nurse?"

He waited for me to nod. We had a copy of orders on Lt. (jg) Gary Pompadour, who was being assigned as our first nurse.

"I think you'd better watch out. My friends up in Baltimore say he's bragging that he'll get out of the assignment. You might want to think about getting somebody else."

I told Don that Pompadour's visit to the ship a couple of weeks before had gone well enough. However, I never told anybody that I was troubled about why the young officer avoided eye contact. Pompadour also spoke about coming to the ship in the subjunctive mood. That seemed curious to me too, but I didn't share that with anybody either.

"Also, I might as well tell you I called him last night," Don continued. "He wouldn't tell me when he was going to report, and that bothered me." Of course it did. Don doesn't tolerate uncertainty. "I tried to tell him about uniforms and things he would need, and he acted like he didn't care. So I told him, 'Look, if you think *I'm* tough, you better watch your step, because Captain Riley will kick your ass!'" Don's face widened in a proud smile when he told the story. He thought he had flattered me. He also figured he'd given the new young nurse fresh motivation.

I winced. If Pompadour had any doubts at all, I suspected Don had resolved them. What irony. Should I celebrate that Don had become so fond and loyal to me, or should I wonder what I had done to let him think "kicking ass" was a virtue. Regardless, Don was so proud of their little talk that I decided not to question it right then.

When Don left, I remembered I had to call Van Hardy, too. Tosser would be leaving, and Hardy, the new surgeon, wouldn't give me a firm answer about when he would report, either. Van was nice enough on the phone, but I just couldn't pin him down. "Hey, we've got underway periods in August, and I have to know when you're going to get here." Why wouldn't he ever give me a simple, straight answer?

This afternoon, his wife answered the phone. She was a lot less reticent than Van had ever been. "I'm not crazy about the idea of a deployment, I can tell you that!" she said. "Why did the Navy send us here to Newport if they expected him to go to a carrier in Florida?" (Not a bad question, I admitted to myself.)

"Uh, I don't know, Mrs. Hardy, I'm just the doctor on the ship."

"Well, Van's out now. I don't know when he'll be back."

Happily, Art interrupted me to see a patient. We were about to get under way the next day for a little over a week, so the department was starting to get busy with all the pre-steaming maladies. Art's patient was Tommy Cage, the first class photographer's mate (PH1) I'd met during my orientation to the ship the year before. Cage was old for an enlisted sailor, in his late forties. Like me, he'd returned to active duty after years as a reservist. He had run his own insurance business for years, put some money aside, and was happy to be back at sea. He was having attacks of "tightness" and "trouble breathing."

"At first I thought it was asthma or cardiac, Skipper, but it just doesn't fit," Art told me.

Cage looked fine, except a little anxious, maybe depressed. "Dr. Riley, these attacks come on me suddenly, like I'm tight all over. It's hard to breathe, and my ankles swell up real bad, see?" Cage looked well groomed even in his dungarees, the work uniform. His wavy, pomaded hair reminded me of Tommy Edwards, a singer from the fifties. He insisted his ankles were swollen, but they weren't. His work boots were slit up the sides.

"What happened to your boots?"

"Have to cut 'em like that so there's room for my ankles when they swell up this way." The ankles were not swollen. No edema.

His lungs were clear. Heart sounds, pulse, ECG, chest X ray—all were normal. As we spent more time on the history, the sudden panic quality impressed me. For a man in his late forties, we needed to be sure we checked his heart and his metabolism, but I was thinking about panic attacks, maybe a panic disorder. We arranged for Petty Officer Cage to be examined by an internist at NH Jacksonville, and I scheduled some blood tests, including one for his thyroid, before he would see the specialist. On my note to the internist I suggested considering a stress test as part of the evaluation.

Later that week, we were preparing for advanced-phase training, a ten-day cruise with the air wing and the whole battle group. It was late the night before an early morning departure. A gunner's mate had pain in a very tender testicle. He could scarcely stand, and his testicle was so tender that he was jumpy when I tried to examine him. It wasn't red or swollen. The pain seemed to have begun early that morning, but it wasn't too bad at first, so he'd stayed at the beach with friends. However, it had grown so severe a few hours ago that he couldn't bear it anymore. Rock was off the ship until morning.

I called NH Jacksonville to speak to the duty urologist for the night. It was Dr Savorini. Good. Of the two at the hospital, he was the cooperative one. He returned my page in about thirty minutes, at a little after 2300. "Dr. Savorini, thanks for calling. We're getting under way in about seven hours, and I have a sailor with a very tender testicle. It could be epididymitis, but I'm concerned about a torsion, and regardless we can't take him with us in the morning."

"What did his urinalysis show?"

"He hasn't been able to void, yet, but—"

"You mean to say that you called your urological consultant without even checking the basic laboratory tests on the urological system!" Indignant outrage. I think I was supposed to be embarrassed. I had been about to say that in his condition I'd have to send him to the hospital regardless of the urinalysis, but Savorini interrupted me. He went on to lecture me about the logic of medicine and about how real doctors consider the thoughtful, ethical use of consultants' time.

And here I'd thought Savorini and I would get along.

"Well, Dr. Savorini, it's almost midnight. This guy is in a lot of pain and your hospital is almost an hour from here. What would you like me to do?"

"That's the kind of question I expect from a medical student, not a practicing doctor. As I said, you should do a urinalysis, and then, if you still feel you need a consultation, call for one at that time."

Almost thirty minutes later, the urinalysis was done. It was virtually normal. We gave the patient some pain medicine and transported him to the hospital in the morning before casting off. From that day forward, anytime Dr. Savorini and I spoke, he addressed me as though I were an idiot.

We were now late in the workup cycle and becoming a very proficient crew again. Our man-overboard drills were going much better, for example; that is, they were going better in the XO way. Sailors still loved to run down those passageways, so we still had scalp lacerations and falls, even if fewer than before. On this first morning at sea, a messman came to the ER after the drill with a cut on his knee.

"You shoulda seen it, Doc," his buddy said. "That fork was sticking right out there. Just like a dart in a dartboard." Running down the chow line during the drill, he had somehow jammed a fork into his knee. It left a three-centimeter cut and seemed to go deep.

I irrigated the wound profusely and contemplated suturing it closed. We're usually reluctant to suture closed puncture wounds, especially if they may go into a joint. We don't like to "close in" any bacteria. This guy worked in a dirty place, though. Rock and Don were doing a procedure in the OR, so I couldn't get Rock to look at it before deciding. I went ahead and sutured the wound, and the guy felt fine. Just then the DivO and leading chief from engineering brought Douglas Williams in for an exam, and I forgot about the guy with the knee.

"He won't talk, Doc. At first I thought he was just being stubborn," the chief said.

"That's what we both thought," the DivO added, "but this isn't like him. He's usually one of our best guys."

Williams and another sailor had got into a fight, and when they were disciplined later Williams just stopped talking. "Could this be a shock or something, Doc?"

I asked them to leave us alone. First I examined the sailor. Except for not speaking, his neurological exam was normal. He could understand very well. He just sat quietly, fingering a notebook that he looked at longingly. Williams was a handsome man. He had fine features, like a model. Every strand of his uniform lined up perfectly. Even in a uniform, only somebody who really cared, who really thought about his appearance, would be that neat. He also had a shiny silver cap on one of his front teeth, with a stylish cutaway heart design in it.

In a few minutes I could tell he wanted his book to be noticed. "What's in the book, Seaman Williams?"

He shrugged.

"Can I see it?"

He let me take it easily, although he didn't quite hand it to me. The book was full of rhymes, mostly one or two pages long. The margins were trimmed with drawings of roses, trees, and women's faces. A lot of the words were misspelled, but the handwriting was flawless and beautiful. The meter was forcibly iambic in every line. Either all lines or pairs of lines rhymed. There were three subjects: his mother, love, and violent fighting against oppressors.

"It looks like you spend a lot of time with your writing."

Another shrug. He liked that.

"Do you think you would be able to speak if you read some of your poems?"

He took the notebook and was able to read a short rhyme about his mother. "You can call me Douglas," he said. He didn't like Doug. Douglas.

Douglas and I decided he was mostly just hurt from being lumped in with that other guy in the discipline. His DivO and chief were relieved he wasn't sick. We agreed Douglas would come by to see me for a couple of days and we'd see if he could get a little better. He decided he could go back to work.

VIP Aviators

The Florida weather was beautiful this time of year, and the beautiful days, together with the short trips and nice flying, guaranteed a steady stream of VIPs. Not as many as at the end of a deployment, like last year, but still quite a few. Congressmen and important people in the Department of Defense always have some important information gathering that they can only do at sea for a few days at a time. We were always proud to show off our ship, and they were invariably charming people (how do you think they *get* those jobs?), so we enjoyed show- ing them around and answering their questions.

One of the people we had to show around was a young surgeon who was a friend of Rock Tosser's. Rock said his friend was thinking about joining the Navy, so Rock wanted to show him around. I was a little skeptical at first, because I didn't suspect Rock would be trying to recruit anybody he liked into the Navy. The visitor, young Dr. Simmons from New York, was never seen outside of Rock's company. I would bump into them here and there that week, and their quiet con- versations ceased abruptly whenever I walked into a room where they were. They both seemed to become suddenly interested in some kind of mark on the deck just at those moments, because they both would look down at the tiles and make little scraping movements with the edges of their soles.

One day I determined to engage Dr. Simmons in conversation and try to answer any questions he might have about the Navy. "So," I began, big smile announcing my aggressively friendly intentions, "have you been thinking about joining the Navy?"

Seemed like a fair question to me, but it seemed to surprise Dr. Simmons.

"Uh. Umm. Well . . ." That seemed to be all he could think of, so he looked over at Tosser. I'm not sure, but I think they smiled at each other. "I think I'm like Dr. Tosser." They spoke of each other not only in the third person when around others, but also only by their pro- fessional titles. They didn't refer to one another by first names when talking to the rest of us, although when they spoke directly to one another they did use first names. "This setting is not . . . well, I just wouldn't be . . . I mean . . ." Then he just looked over at Rock again, and our conversation kind of trailed off.

"Yeah, I think I understand," I told him. "Let me know if there's anything I can do for you."

During this at-sea period, a tall, dignified man in his fifties was on his first carrier trip. He was something along the lines of an assistant secretary of the Navy or a deputy assistant for something or other, and he seemed fascinated by everything, especially the flying. After dinner one night, I was shining my shoes and watching closed-circuit TV in my stateroom when Kevin Millet, the AIMD officer, knocked. "Hey, Doc, do you have a jet helmet?"

Yes, I told him, I did.

"Oh great! Nobody else seems to have a big enough head size for Mr. Bigwig. Can we try yours?"

"What's this about, Kevin?" I asked suspiciously, but I already knew the answer.

"Oh, no problem, Mr. Bigwig wants to go for a ride in an F-14."

"Jesus, it's night, Kevin!" Nobody but essential crew flies over the water at night!

"Well, he's leaving early in the morning, so they can't do it tomorrow."

"What about his NATOPS? Water survival? Does he even have an up chit?!"

Kevin was obviously a trapped middleman. "Hey, Doc, I don't know! He says he got all his clearances before he came out here. He's in great shape. Runs five miles a day."

I gave Kevin the helmet, but I frowned. I called the XO to complain.

"Don't worry, Doc, Mr. Bigwig says he got clearance before he left D.C."

"Has anybody seen his NATOPS sheet or up chit?"

Who was going to ask an assistant or deputy assistant secretary of the Navy for his up chit? Half an hour later Kevin called to thank me for the helmet, which was the only one on the ship big enough for our visitor.

I watched on the flight deck monitor as the Tomcat with Mr. Bigwig took off.

On the climbout and ascending left turn, Mr. Bigwig told the pilot he had some pain in his abdomen and that they ought to land. Turns out he'd had an inguinal hernia repaired two weeks ago and didn't tell any of us that. Seems he forgot about it.

Naturally, they brought him right to the ER. I was there to examine him. The hernia had not recurred; the operation was well healed. Just the ordinary G forces of the flight caused local pain in the region of the recent operation. I reassured Mr. Bigwig that he was all right, and he left the medical department with no apparent embarrassment.

Thirty minutes later the XO called me. "Hey, Doc, Mr. Bigwig asked if we could have the surgeon examine him. No offense, but he's heard there's a civilian surgeon on board and he feels that might be even better. OK?"

Drs. Tosser and Simmons arrived together. I never realized until then that two people could seem like a parade. They had found two starched white coats somewhere, and despite their ages they looked like two professors on Grand Rounds.

When the assistant secretary/deputy assistant lowered his trousers, Dr. Simmons knelt down like Lord Essex or Sir Walter Raleigh in front of Queen Elizabeth. He closed his eyes and bowed his head to keep out any distractions, and as he prodded and examined—about four times longer than I'd ever seen anybody take sticking their finger in an inguinal canal—he nodded his head, yes, yes, as though responding to a message only he could hear.

Dr. Simmons looked first to his surgical colleague, smiled, and then turned to Mr. Bigwig. "Who did your hernia operation, Mr. Bigwig?"

"Hal Famous at Upscale University."

"Yes, I know him," young Dr. Simmons said with a knowing but patiently forgiving smile. The two surgeons made eye contact and nodded. "He's very good," Simmons said of Dr. Famous in such a way that we all knew he didn't quite mean it, but wanted somehow to comfort the patient in front of him.

I thought to myself, this politician will be so glad to know that our visiting thirty-year-old surgeon approves of the renowned Dr. Famous.

"But I don't think he got the hernia absolutely closed. Only an experienced surgeon would be able to notice that. I'm not surprised Dr. Riley couldn't tell. Nothing wrong with that. He's just not a surgeon, that's all. I don't think it came loose in the flight, though. You'll be fine, but I think you should call Dr. Famous this week. He probably won't need to do the operation over again. This isn't a major problem. Some surgeons would consider it good enough."

"Well, I am certainly glad there was a civilian surgeon aboard to examine me."

"My pleasure," Dr. Simmons said. "So often other doctors are reluctant to ask for help when they really need it."

That ended a generally pleasant evening for me. A politician went for a jet ride he shouldn't have, concealed his medical history without being embarrassed by it, and a young surgeon was able to come to his rescue. The good part was that nobody got hurt.

*   *   *

A couple of days later we were steaming up to New York for a port call, and the young man with the puncture wound to his knee came to the ER. The whole knee was swollen and red. I'd been afraid of that. I shouldn't have closed that wound. Probably should have left in a drain or a packing. He didn't have a fever or much pain, happily.

I removed the sutures, and a small amount of clear, thin fluid came out. No pus. As much as I hated it, I called Rock immediately to see the patient. I thought then, and I still do, that irrigating the wound, leaving in a drain, and giving antibiotics was what the wound needed at that point. However, since it was my treatment that caused this complication, it was my responsibility to follow the consultant's advice now. We needed the surgeon.

Rock said that he had to go to the OR right away. "If we're going to save that knee, we have to open it up immediately." I wasn't surprised at what he said, but I was glad that, once in the OR, Rock didn't open the joint space. He irrigated the wound, put in a drain, and started antibiotics. The guy was healed fine in a few days. After that he always asked for somebody other than me whenever he came to the medical department, though.

We steamed into New York the next day in a cloudy drizzle. I stood up on Sponson One when we slipped into what seemed like a shoebox berth on the West River. By this time Tommy Linker, former CO of the VS-28 "Gamblers," had taken over from Bohunk as the 'gator. Bohunk wanted to stay assigned to the *Forrestal* as long as he could, though, so he'd arranged to fly ahead to New York to help with our port call there. He was waiting for us on the pier, holding a brick in his hand.

At that moment I began to despair about Bohunk's steering skills. Recalling his driving in Benidorm, I began to panic when I saw him waving to the bridge and to the tugs and speaking rapidly into the brick while he scurried back and forth on the pier. Was this guy who couldn't keep a Mercedes in the traffic lane going to direct us into this slip? The 75,000 tons turned, but not enough, and began to push the big, flat starboard side of the ship into a big, sharp, stabbing edge of a granite-and-concrete pier. It was right below me. Like in slow motion on a tragic movie, and yet too fast for me to cry out, I saw us sliding right into certain puncture. Twelve feet, six feet. Here it comes!

I closed my eyes and crunched down.

We didn't collide. I'll never know why. We slipped in just like Cinderella's foot into that glass slipper.

The *Forrestal* minutes before I thought we were going to crash into the pier in New York. *PHCM Dittmar, U.S. Navy photo*

New York City welcomed *Forrestal*. Liberty call set the hangar bay and quarter deck abuzz with departing sailors and visiting New Yorkers.

On the first full day in port, when it was time for Rock to leave the ship for good, he didn't come to say good-bye to me. HM1 Rosen said, "I think he's on his way up to the brow now, Captain," so I hurriedly ran up to shake his hand. We didn't agree much of the time, but after all we had been shipmates. I got there just before he stepped out to the quarterdeck. Rock looked right at my hand, but not at my face. He turned to ask the OOD for permission to leave the ship, saluted the ensign, and left. I never saw him again.

Several thousand visitors had guided tours of the ship that day. First they passed a greeting board with photos of the captain, the XO, and the ten department heads. Then they toured the hangar bay, flight deck, and mess decks. The only excitement that day was when the XO stormed into the wardroom and asked, "OK, who did it?" He had just discovered that the seven thousand visitors that day all wondered why there were ten pictures of the XO (with moustaches drawn in ball-point pen) on that greeting board and no other officers' faces. I don't know if the visitors ever figured it was because the department heads thought the XO was a micromanager, but I think he did. I don't know who did it myself. Really I don't.

About a week later, back in Mayport, we were busier than ever trying to balance everybody's final leave before the last time at sea, and treating all the sailors who didn't think they were well enough to deploy. FN Tyrone Hill came back to see me one morning in sick call. "These things don't do me any good." He threw the arch supports at my desk.

"Now, you're going a little too far, Fireman! You stand up now and get control of yourself."

"I'd like to know if you'd talk that way to me if we weren't on the ship!" he said.

"What do you mean?"

"Just what I said. I wonder if you'd have the guts to talk to me this way if we weren't here where there are other people to protect you."

"If you mean am I afraid to fight you, of course I am! You think I'm nuts? I'm forty-three years old, man! On the other hand, it's kind of bad judgment on your part to ask me that." I reminded him how much trouble he could get into for threatening an officer. Once again I explained to him about flat feet, and this time I arranged for him to be seen by a podiatrist. Hill left satisfied. He knew as well as I did that if he wanted to get out of the deployment, he would eventually find a way.

Just then George Lucy came to the door with Gary Pompadour. Lucy flexed both shoulders, the left a little higher than the right, and looked speechless momentarily. Pompadour, though, was as smooth as ever. He tipped his head back a little, raised his left eyebrow in a friendly gesture, and stuck out his hand. "Lieutenant Pompadour reporting, Sir." Was he smiling or smirking? I'm still not sure.

Only as an automatic platitude, I said "How are you?" Didn't really mean to ask a question. It's just an expression.

"Well, my eye's a problem, you know. They wanted me to have an operation, but I'm putting it off as long as I can." About then his right eye twitched and the lid sagged slightly.

"I thought it was your back." In fact, I had called the clinical director and an orthopedist at NH Baltimore, Pompadour's last duty station, and I'd been told that the guy complained about his shoulder but didn't have a real orthopedic problem.

"Well, they're both problems, but I'll get by." Gary had come by to get permission to move some things the following day, which was going to be our family-day cruise.

"I'm really going to need some help. I'll be the only doctor with all those civilians, some of them children and old people."

"Hey, I'm really sorry, but I just can't make it. I'm not officially on board yet anyway."

A quick couple of phone calls to the detailer revealed that Pompadour had put in a letter requesting exemption from sea duty because of his back and his eye. The waiver had been turned down because he couldn't get medical verification. Also, I learned he hadn't closed out his apartment up in Baltimore. That kind of worried me.

Stewing about Pompadour's future was interrupted by new problems with our X-ray tech, Womple. I'd been worrying about him for a few weeks. After our last set of problems, Master Chief Shapiro, the CMC, had been counseling Arden like a union steward would. Arden had been through complete Level II now, and although Master Chief Shapiro was serving as his sea lawyer to assure that we wouldn't hassle him, he also insisted Arden stay sober. Lately, although his work was still acceptable, he had been avoiding me. I found out he'd been avoiding all khaki in the department. When I stepped into the X-ray room that afternoon to check on a patient with a sprained ankle, I smelled liquor.

"Petty Officer Womple, do you have something you want to tell me?" No. He knew what I was asking, though.

"I just had a couple of drinks last night, that's all."

I grimaced for him. A doctor for seventeen years, I knew that smell was more than a two-drinks-last-night smell. "You're in AA, Petty Officer Womple. They agree with *any* drinks?"

"Uh . . . sometimes," he lied, even knowing that I knew it.

He went up to see the CAAC, who suggested Arden start Antabuse. There are a lot of limitations to Antabuse, and serious side effects for some people, so I never prescribe it unless the patient is willing. Arden wasn't. And even though I didn't need to be told, Master Chief Shapiro phoned down to my office to inform me that Arden could not be forced to take Antabuse.

"Looks like Level III, Petty Officer Womple." He pouted about that for a week, but we put in the application.

Two days after we sent in the application for rehab, Master Chief Shapiro was knocking on my office door.

"Captain Riley, Petty Officer Womple came down to tell me you've been harassing him."

"He's been drinking again, Master Chief."

"He says he hasn't been."

"I smelled it on him this week. His job performance is slipping again."

"Captain, did you do a fitness for duty on him? Get an alcohol level? Notify the command?" Master Chief Shapiro called me "Captain" whenever he was stern or wanted to lecture me.

"Hey, Master Chief, I notified the CAAC! What is this? If you care about this guy you'll help us get him treated."

"He still hasn't had a full Level II, Captain. If you just force him like this, it's discrimination, and I think he can make a case for harassment."

That week, Master Chief Shapiro, the CAAC, and I met about four times, with Womple present at three of the meetings. Finally, at the master chief's insistence, the ship's lawyer got involved, and we had to drop Arden's Level III application.

Two weeks later, during sick call, a beaming FN Tyrone Hill was waiting for me. He had refused to be seen by any of the corpsmen or by the WOPA, Bob Willmore. "No, I got a note here just for Dr. Riley from the specialist."

The note from the podiatrist said that the fireman had constitutionally flat feet due to lax plantar tendons, and that he could be administratively separated from the Navy according to our old friend BUPERS Instruction 1910.2. I called the phone number on the consultation form.

"Captain," the podiatrist explained, "there's nothing we can really do for this, and really FN Hill's feet shouldn't be causing him pain, but if he keeps pushing this, he'll eventually get out. You can't stop it. It's not worth fighting."

The podiatrist was right, of course. Experience had shown that eventually there would be enough angry letters—from lawyers, relatives, and congressmen—that the sailor would get out. The myth of the flat feet is a powerful one. It hurt the ship, though, because administrative separations, whether for physical reasons of unsuitability or for personality disorders, don't entitle the ship to a replacement. The ship's company would remain short until the separated person's tour was supposed to end. It was inevitable, though, so I took a deep breath and sent the fireman back to his departmental office with the initial paperwork.

About 0900, as sick call was winding down, HM1 Dunbar came to tell me Arden Womple had failed to report aboard that morning. We had to go bring him back from the Quality Inn where he had passed out the night before.

"I guess you were right, Doc," the CMC admitted with no contrition at all. He seemed to call me "Doc" when he wanted me to feel that he liked me or wanted me to agree with him.

Family-Day Cruise

I had dreaded the family-day cruise for months, even before it turned out I'd be the only doctor on board. We had a screening questionnaire to exclude very sick or immobile people and those with unstable conditions. We discovered, though, that sometimes people falsified the questionnaire or the XO overruled me. So we had a menagerie of several thousand innocent and not-so-innocent family members climbing all over the ship while we steamed from eight in the morning to three in the afternoon.

An F-14 was going to fly by and break the sound barrier alongside at 1300. That was the only thing I insisted that I must see. I was resigned to be busy, but I underestimated the load dramatically.

Forget it. It was all such a blur that I can't even recall all the day's events clearly. A woman had a hysterical seizure on the flight deck, and a middle-aged man with angina fell down a ladder on the hangar deck. Lots of people smashed fingers in doors, and a dozen or so felt overcome by heat up on the flight deck. A few got sunburned, even though we warned everybody about sunburn and provided free sunscreen. The only two things I remember clearly are Chief Abercrombe being missing all day and the lady who broke her knee on the flight deck.

Amid the melee of getting everybody signed up and counted while getting under way, Lieutenant Lucy came to me agitated. Striking an anxious pose with an extended left arm and flexed left quads, he began, "Uh, umm, I mean . . ." Momentary shrug. "Captain, we can't find Chief Abercrombe."

"Did you check his rack?" Of course. "Chief's mess?" Yes.

"Well, what about the head down by his rack?"

"Sir, we've checked all the heads in chiefs' country! He's not on board." That can't be. Chiefs just don't go UA. Couldn't find him all day. We had to report it in case he was injured somewhere in town. As the day went on and we looked everywhere, including his rack and the heads over and over, it became clear. He was gone.

About noon there was a 1-MC call, "Medical emergency. Medical emergency. On the flight deck. Medical emergency. This is not a drill."

A very large woman about seventy years old had tripped on the arresting cable and fallen on her knee. Her family was huddled over her. "Are you the doctor?" asked one daughter, about forty years old, before I could introduce myself. Yes, I told her. "Are there any civilian doctors on the ship?" No, that's why we took histories before signing people up for the trip.

The rest of the family—about seven of them—buzzed in the background while the boss daughter kept asking me questions. Please, I said, let me examine her first to make sure she doesn't have anything else wrong. "You mean like . . . ?" and she silently pointed to her heart. Well, yes. That and other things. "Oh well, you don't have to worry about that. She doesn't have any heart trouble. But I'm worried about that leg. At her age, you know you have to worry about the hip, too, and I think she broke the knee anyway, don't you?"

We took the lady, who was very nice, and had little to say, down to the medical department very carefully in a Neil-Robertson stretcher. There now seemed to be about ten members of the family buzzing, and the boss daughter now had a deputy boss helping her with the questions. "Are you going to take an X ray?" Yes, as quickly as we can. "Will that do any good if you don't have a radiologist on board?"

"Can you give her anything for pain?"

Finally, out of innocent curiosity, I stopped what I was doing, looked up to stare at the boss daughter, and asked, "Are you from New York?"

She was offended by the question and yet not quite surprised that I would ask it. "Yes, I am. Why should you ask me that?"

"Just wondering," I said, but I wished I'd asked it sooner, because she slowed down the harangue a little after that. We never found any fractures in the mother's limb, but I missed the supersonic flyby.

We pulled back alongside Charlie pier about 1500. After the ship was all tied up, people were walking on and off, and we sent the large woman and her family off to the civilian hospital of her family's choosing. Shortly after liberty call around 1630, who should saunter down the starboard passageway but HMC Abercrombe!

"Chief, where have you been all day!"

"Down in chiefs' berthing. I was sick this morning."

"But the guys couldn't find you down there."

"Must have been while I was in the head. Bad diarrhea."

He was smooth. Like Rick Cox had said, "Better watch him." But even with watching him, he was going to be hard to catch.

I went out for a walk around the base to relax that night. I needed some fresh air and a walk on grass. When I passed the softball diamonds, I saw Tyrone Hill. He was playing third base, jumping around, moving his feet just fine. When he saw me he quit jumping and looked away, but he stayed in the game.

The next day Gary Pompadour officially reported for duty. He was different now, though. He wore a big white back brace on the *outside* of his uniform! And he wore an eye patch over his left eye.

"Oh, yeah, it's just that old back, you know."

That afternoon, he changed into civilian clothes after regular work hours. He was a little surprised that you had to wear a uniform all the time, even when you weren't at work. When he realized I wasn't joking that you're always at work while you're on the ship, he was even more surprised.

Gary had a very pleasing personality, and the guys liked his manner. Several people asked me during our last underway period whether the poor guy with that brace and eye patch should have to be on sea duty. Sometimes he would grope about with his arms as if trying to find his way. He didn't complain aloud at all, even though his condition seemed to worsen daily, and he was a good worker in sick call. I was still curious about why he hadn't closed out his rented apartment in Baltimore or moved his boat to Mayport, but I had to admit the crew and the corpsmen liked him. He made a lot of friends on our ten-day trip to St. Thomas.

When we were on the way back to Mayport one day, the 1-MC alarm called. "Medical emergency. Medical emergency. Hangar Bay I starboard side. Medical emergency." I ran up to the hangar as quickly as I could. In the dental passageway I passed Pompadour, who was walking down the passageway, holding his hand over his left eye, like Lon Chaney in the *Mummy* movies; I don't think he was even going toward the emergency. Up on the deck there was a gaggle of people kneeling over the patient. It was Tommy Cage. "Says he can't breathe, Doc."

"Feet. My feet are swollen again. I think I'm having a heart attack," he almost panted out.

He wasn't sweating. Pulse was normal at about eighty beats per minute. Although his chukka boots were slit up the sides, his feet weren't swollen at all. "Now, Petty Officer Cage, the specialist over at the hospital said he couldn't find anything wrong." The internist had done a stress test, checked a bunch of labs. "Your exam is normal now, too. I think you're just anxious. Try to calm down," I told him. There are litters everywhere in the hangar, so we put him on one and took him down to medical. His EKG was normal again.

This was one of the most fascinating cases of panic attacks I'd seen. Such attacks are uncommon among people his age, but I thought it showed how frightening, how extreme, the feelings can be. It also emphasized that they can happen to people who seem normal. The clinician has to remain vigilant. When Tommy calmed down, I reviewed this with him, and he agreed.

"If it's not physical, I sure feel terrible when that happens to me. If you say I need to see the psychiatrist, that's what I'll do."

He agreed too fast. That should have tipped me off. He rested for a while and then was able to go back to work.

My last order of business that day was being summoned down to the XO's office, where Master Chief Shapiro and FN Hill were waiting for me.

"Doc, Fireman Hill says you're keeping him from getting his disability."

"Disability?"

"Yeah, I got to leave because of a medical problem, that's supposed to be a medical discharge. In personnel they told me you were trying to make this just an administrative matter."

He had a letter from his congressman asking why he should be denied his rightful medical disability.

"Mrs. Hill called me this morning, Doc, and she was pretty upset," the XO said.

Once again, I explained about the feet. I brought them the podiatrist's note, explained that the sailor didn't have a disease, and that he had brought his flat feet with him when he came to the Navy, so this would be an administrative separation, not due to a disease.

"Oh, no!" Hill raised his voice in the anger that was by now becoming familiar to me. "My feet never hurt me until I came to this ship, and nobody here wants to help. They just treat you rough or try to kick you out."

I showed him and the XO his entrance physical. He had flat feet then. Still had them.

"OK," the XO said. "There's nothing we can do about this, Fireman. You can go back to see the specialist when we get back to Mayport, but I don't think this is going to qualify for a disability pension. Doc, I want you to call his mother when we get back and put her mind at ease." Hill was still not happy.

Later that night, lying awake, I reviewed something that had stuck in my mind—hadn't Gary Pompadour's *right* eye been the problem before?

The Deployment Nears

Van Hardy finally arrived in August. Somehow I'd expected not to like him, perhaps because he was uncertain about when he would arrive. When I first met him, though, I knew he was a keeper. Unassuming, affable, and pleasant, Van was a former nurse who had partly paid his way through medical school working as an RN. I hadn't been home for many months, so Van and Gary agreed to watch the department so I could spend a few days in Boston with Ann and our daughters.

My second day in Boston, I got a call from the ship. Gary fell down a ladder, couldn't move his left shoulder, and would have to be off sea duty permanently. He was alone when he fell, so there were no witnesses. The orthopedist at NH Jacksonville couldn't find anything torn or broken, but he said that without shoulder motion a man was unfit for sea duty, and he transferred Gary to the care of an orthopedist in Baltimore. "After all, he still has an apartment there," the Jacksonville orthopod said, "and since he can't be assigned to your ship, he might just as well recuperate in Baltimore as in Jacksonville."

I called Frank Trumble, the AIRLANT medical officer. "Gee, Terry, I wish you'd told me sooner you had problems with your staff. It's too late in the year for us to get a relief now. Sorry. You should have let me know before this."

"Come on, Frank, don't you remember you told me that I wasn't being fair about this! We've talked about Pompadour four times." In fact, Frank had even scolded me for doubting the young nurse's motives at one point.

"Funny," he said, "I just don't remember talking about it. Oh well, you'll have to do the best you can." So, we'd have to get along without a nurse. Once I thought just losing Don Kent was bad. Little had I suspected we might actually have to get under way without a nurse, too, as well as a GMO!

Finally, it somehow became late September, and the last in-port period was almost over. My phone call with Tyrone Hill's mother was generally unsuccessful. I was calm and tried to be helpful, but she remained convinced that her son had been cheated out of a Navy disability pension. At one point, I suggested that if he couldn't get a pension, perhaps he would like to stay in the Navy. She pondered that briefly but eventually ruled against it. Shortly Tyrone became a civilian, and we suggested he inquire about his disability from the VA. I never heard from him or the VA.

A few days before the deployment, Ann came down to visit and we had a picnic on the beach for the corpsmen and their families. While we were at the picnic that afternoon, I thought about Hugh Beaumont. Apparently his parents had been forced to ask him to move out. The psychologist decided Hugh's anxiety and his reactions were troublesome, all right, but not really psychotic. There hadn't been any more trouble from his hanging around. Still, the scene of this picnic with all the families touched me. Perhaps it touched me selfishly; my kids were older teenagers now, and they were up in Massachusetts. I missed them. It touched me for Hugh, too, though. I worried about his being alone.

It was eerie that I should have thought about Hugh that day, because when we came back to the department one of the corpsmen said, "Captain, HM1 Beaumont and his father are waiting for you."

The two of them were sitting in my office. Hugh had lost weight over the months. His eyes were red, and he sat expressionless but vaguely morose, just staring at a wrinkle in the bulkhead. His father, Bill, was a handsome man, and he looked a lot like Hugh. His outgoing charm reminded me of what had been so appealing in his son when we first met. "Captain, I don't think Hugh is in any shape to go on this deployment." Such a simple declarative sentence, yet I found myself preparing to debate.

I thought better of it, though, and looked at immobile, staring Hugh. "Petty Officer Beaumont, what do you think?"

"Tell you the truth, I'd rather go. Their transmitters can only reach a few miles. If I can just get away from here, she and her so-called friends will finally have to leave me alone."

"Your wife?"

"That woman. She calls herself my wife, but she's not, and she knows that I know it, too."

His father said, "A neighbor woman. Hugh has known her for years. Ask him her name."

"You can talk right to me, Dad. I'm right here," Hugh said. "Linda, Grindl, Lindl, Grinda. She uses them all. Sometimes they call her Elesandra, sometimes they don't use a name. They have their reasons."

Hugh's father was obviously right. Hugh had to go to the hospital. We were able to arrange it that afternoon.

Ann was able to stay another couple of days. The weather was good, we spent some time on the beach, had breakfast at the SunDog restaurant, just relaxed. I took Ann back to the airport the day before our departure. Since it would be six months before I'd sleep ashore again, I kept the room we had rented for one last night on land.

Besides the bedroom, another thing I wouldn't have for six months was a bathtub. Feeling a little lonesome, I climbed into the tub about 2200 that night for a long, hot soak. After about twenty minutes, though, just as my ligaments and muscles were sagging into warm laxity, the phone rang. In the distance I thought I could hear sirens, too.

"Uh . . . Captain Riley. This is HM3 Davis. There's been a fire on the ship, and we're vacating the medical department." I looked out the back window of the BOQ and saw smoke rising from Charlie pier.

Back at the ship, the smoke seemed to be coming only out of the island up on the flight deck and the starboard hangar bay doors. Hundreds of sailors were smoke stained and smaller numbers were coughing, but mobs and mobs of people were milling around. Water ran off the starboard side of the flight deck and the hangar deck, but there were no flames. The captain and the XO were there. Everybody was doing his job, and there was no shouting, but facial features were expressionless granite. Everyone remembered *Trial by Fire*. Every FID sailor remembers 29 July 1967. We remembered it that night, too. This time nobody was seriously hurt, and even the smoke inhalation wasn't severe for anyone.

It was a situation where somebody had to take charge, and nobody liked being in charge as much as SK3 Arden Womple. There he was up on the hangar deck barking orders, "Keep to your right, please! Don't go down there, you guys. What do you think you're doing? Let me see your ID."

Over the next several days the investigation showed that the fire had started in what was supposed to be an empty machine room on the starboard side, right under the island. We weren't told many details about the investigation, but most of us figured it must have been sabotage. One young sailor was escorted off the ship a few days later without explanation. Nobody died or was even badly hurt, but thousands of wires and cables leading from one important part of the ship to another were destroyed.

We couldn't get under way in the morning. In fact, it took a month with our own and extra contractor crews working around the clock to fix the FID so we could start our deployment. It felt like a new SRA on the second deck with hoses, welders, ropes, and barricades everywhere again.

In the first week of November, when it seemed as though we'd finally be able to start the deployment, we learned that one of the officers in the engineering department had nominated Womple for a Navy Achievement Medal for his role in fighting the fire. I called the new CHENG, Greg Sanford. "Hey Greg, Womple is a problem in our department. Don't your guys get a departmental endorsement for awards?"

He told me he'd look into the matter.

Two days later there was a formation in service dress uniform up on the flight deck for all the people getting awards. On my way up the ladder, Lieutenant Lucy stopped me. He was agitated. First his right shoulder, then his left, shrugged up and forward, and his left biceps lifted his left wrist. His neck and chin dipped to the right as the muscles on his neck stood out in photogenic relief. "Captain, Captain!" he almost shouted, then paused for a brief stare. "Captain, Petty Officer Womple has locked himself in the pharmacy and won't come out. He's drunk and he's threatening to eat a bunch of pills."

We ran back to the pharmacy, where the door was indeed locked. "Petty Officer Womple, are you in there?" I asked.

At first there was no answer. Lucy shrugged his back and thigh muscles anxiously. I wouldn't have suspected Womple would kill himself. Then from behind us, two doors aft, in one of the storerooms, came a muffled bass voice. "I'm not coming out!"

"Mr. Lucy, he's back there in a storeroom."

It took us two painful hours of negotiations to get Womple to come out. Only after being promised he wouldn't have to see me did he agree to leave the storeroom so he could be transported to the psychiatrist at NH Jacksonville. The psychiatrist said Womple was depressed. Although probably not suicidal, he'd need to stay in the hospital and could not deploy. We asked the ship's secretary to inform the hospital that when Womple recovered, he still should be separated from the Navy.

Gary Pompadour was off the crew a lot faster than he'd joined it, Arden Womple was admitted because of his frustration or depression, and Hugh Beaumont was being treated for a major thought disorder. This was not the right time for those three to go to sea, I decided, but it sure was for the rest of us. The team was short three players, but we needed to go.

Finally it looked like we might be able to get under way.

Chapter 12

Getting Under Way at Last

If God hadn't already created navies, the human race would have invented one for a day like that 5 November. The sky was so open you could see all the way to Nebraska, and it had just a few slashes of high cirrus clouds, like the marks Zorro used to zap into a silk curtain. It was definitely an aircraft carrier day. Charlie pier was crowded with a festive mass of TV news people, local politicians, and family members. A Navy band was playing, and people were waving banners. From the flight deck or the bridge, there were two views. Down on the pier, all the cheering people, dressed with lots of red, blue, and silver, looked like the crowd at a football game. There were even vendors selling Cokes, popcorn, and *Forrestal* souvenirs, just like at a stadium or a circus. From the nine stories up on the flight deck, or twelve up to the bridge, if you looked over to the port side, or aft, to the east, the sky and the spear clouds pulled your vision to the horizon, the ocean.

Down on the pier, an hour ago, all the sailors and officers had said their good-byes, had the long hugs, and, for the very young ones (likely who just met the girl this week), long, movie-like kisses. Then the brows had been pulled up, and everyone had to be on board in time to get everything ready. For final stragglers and any last-minute details, the last of about four brows waited until just before departure. Six months is a long time. Those who had never been through a prior deployment would fret about how a separation hurts, but those who had survived many before knew better all the pains and challenges ahead. The crying and working it out had been done over the past weeks for those who were able.

A lot of other veterans and their families just didn't indulge in the departure festivities. Too hard. They'd said good-bye at the house, did the crying there if they had to, and just drove to work. For those families, it wasn't a matter of ignoring the situation. They knew the pain too, usually from six or eight prior deployments. For the kids, it was better to start today knowing they were going to take on the routine, face every day ourselves and do it right, even if Dad wasn't there. Dad had probably cried on the way to the ship, and they all cried when they closed the door behind him. Even if they cried behind the door, they also started the coping right then. They didn't want to let the sailor or the strangers on the pier see them crying in public. Not that they had some phoney facade; they wouldn't deny the crying, they just didn't need to share it with strangers . . . and they didn't want to make the departure harder for him. (While at the same time, not always even knowing it, they were resentful at him for going. Again.)

Plenty did show up for the occasion, though. Departments and divisions had family groups with banners and signs painted on sheets. Lots of cameras. Many of the women were dressed up, although a lot less provocatively and wearing a lot less red than we all knew they would when we'd arrive in six months. Hundreds of crew members had ordered roses from the florists, who were there to deliver them to wives and sweethearts that day. Some of the small children were awestruck, as all small children had to be, by the size of the ship, but most especially by the gala, the motion, the noise. All of the excitement thrilled most children, especially those under four and over fifteen. But a lot of school-age youngsters had wet faces, clung anxiously to their mothers, and wanted either the day to go away or the whole idea to be a mistake. An hour before, a lot of "No, Daddy, don't go!" or "Daddy, we want you to stay, *please,*" were heard before everyone had to get on board. Now, scattered crying and shaking shoulders could be seen, but these were partly obscured or hidden among lots of crying babies (who were just tired of being held so long) and overshadowed by all the other youngsters caught up in the great patriotic spectacle.

Getting under way is a critical, busy, and dangerous time. Many people on the ship have a lot to do, especially those in the deck department. The bos'n's mates scurry from one sponson or station to the next. Line handlers and working parties on the pier and hangar wells throw and pull the eight-inch lines, always laying it in careful order so it can be moved and not be tripped over or caught in a knot by casual movement. Machinery and gear are everywhere, some of it whirring or moving, all of it skulking or sprawling someplace waiting to knock someone down, tear a trouser leg, or break an ankle. In the mass movement and activity, there's the danger of people falling off the ship or tripping on the pier. We had teams of corpsmen stationed with their Unit 1 first aid kits at critical places on the hangar deck and among the crowd until the brows came up, and the Mayport Clinic positioned an ambulance at the pier. Sure enough, one fortyish woman fainted and had to be carted off to the clinic, and forty minutes later a man in his sixties who had been warned twice not to smoke on the pier had sudden chest pain and was taken off, presumably to Dunes Hospital.

Running everywhere through all this were the two busiest men in the crowd, the XO and Ed DeMaestri, who was the first lieutenant now that Warner Hobs had moved on. Both were carrying on continuous discussions with their bricks, while their heads swiveled everywhere. The XO, with his dress-blue jacket bulging at the buttons and streaked tight across his waist and hips, searched for trouble from the crowds, looking to be sure everything was stowed and preparations were going well. His gaze was at eye level and often upward. Ed was responsible for the bos'n's mates and line handlers and all the sailor stuff. He, by contrast, mostly had to look down and sideways as he moved here and there, back and forth, pointing at things, yelling at some guy, speaking in the vernacular peculiar to bos'n's mates, longshoremen, and Marines.

Then somehow it was obvious, like the day your term paper came due, that it was time to go, and everybody seemed to know it and somehow everything was ready. All the activity didn't have any obvious connection to the being ready. The activity seemed kind of disembodied, like a ballet or something, and the ship just got ready by itself, like when a bud on a branch is ready to open. The time just arrives. First Ed, then the XO, came over the last brow, and the crane took the brow away. The crowd grew a little quieter. A few of the rent-a-cops moved among them, along with some shore patrolmen, and the margins of the crowd drew back a few feet. Some lines were tossed from the ship to the pier, and a few others slurped up into the ship like long strands of spaghetti. The rails were all manned, with sailors dressed for recruiting posters, at parade rest, all along the flight deck and up the walkways on the island. They looked just as you'd expect, only better. All straight, kerchiefs flying, hats whiter than if they were a thousand ivory teeth in the line. At the bow, in the straight line at the end of the flight deck, in front of the number 59, the place that only shipmates can call "the pointy end," it was Marines at parade rest in their dress blues with white gloves. The crowd on the pier got very quiet for some reason. Then, gradually, in a breath, you could tell why. The ship moved just a little, with a sideways sigh, not jerky at all.

Suddenly, next came the captain's music, first Willy Nelson singing "On the road again . . . I can't wait to be on the road again . . . Makin' music with my friends. I can't wait to get on the road again . . ." loudly on the 1-MC and on the speakers on the pier. Now the crowd was rowdy and every shipmate smirked a little, but at the same time he wondered, "How did the captain know . . ." The ship moved in earnest then, finally with a . . . a little shudder. The crowd whooped, and a few wives and children jumped up and down or did little dances while they waved.

The tugs pulled the ship out into the turning basin and started to turn her around to face the ocean. I scrambled up to get as high on the island as I could to take this all in. About the time I got up near the signal bridge, as high as you can go without going up a tower, the music stopped for a moment. From where I was you could see the swirls of sand bottom contours under the blue ocean in the St. Johns inlet. It kind of set off the paler cirrus slashes up in the clearer but paler sky. The crowd quieted now because we were about to leave. Music again. First a real short organ prelude. Then in a voice as clear as this day, and as rich as her memory, Kate Smith sang "God bless America . . ." The cliché says, "You really had to be there." Well, for those of us who were there that day, most would confide that it was probably a little like Fatima or Lourdes (of course, being there meant we were zealots already, so our objectivity as observers was tainted). By the time she reached "From the mountains . . . to the prairies," the *Forrestal* was turned, and if there had been a single communist in Florida, he would have converted and joined the rest of us in the orgy of patriotic tears. We were under way.

I stayed up on the signal bridge for about a half hour, watching Mayport shrink and fade. The view was hypnotic. Knowing there was going to be a steady diet of eighteen-hour days for the next six months, and that it was going to be worse without a GMO, I let myself linger for a while, enjoying the fine sea mist and the view from up there, about a hundred feet above the whitecaps. Finally, I decided I should go ahead and take my departure photos and get down to the medical department. No film in the camera. I'd forgotten to load it when I left the stateroom a couple of hours ago. Was that an omen? Oh, well, time to get to work.

On my way below, I got off on the O-3 level to cross over to the port side so I would pass my stateroom on the way to the department. There I could change from blues to khakis and drop off the camera. I could cross over on O-3, the hangar deck, or on the second deck, and it was more or less random which one I'd take any particular time. The O-3 level was pretty busy on departure day, with a lot of traffic coming and going from strike ops, where daily plans were organized, and a lot of business in the ship's office. Most especially, though, the O-3 deck was where the staff lived and worked. On departure day, the staff had reasons to be out bothering and bossing everybody.

I was greeting and glad-handing Tom Fitzgerald and Ed Dicey, a couple of the staff guys I liked, when suddenly there he was in all his six-foot, two-inch gaunt sobriety: Oliver Leen. My circuits erased. I was speechless. Tom and Ed must have wondered how I went from effusive camaraderie to abject catatonia in midsentence. They hadn't seen Leen, who came down the passageway behind them. Even if they had seen him, they probably wouldn't have known why I went into brain arrest. I tried to speak, to be confused, to be angry, to have an opinion or reaction of any kind at all. I think I said something along the lines of "b'duh . . . b'duh . . . b'duh." How did he get here? Almost a year ago, John Seibel, the head of internal medicine at NH Jacksonville, had signed his medical board to keep him off sea duty.

Commander Leen seemed a little bit startled, but a lot less befuddled than I was at the moment. He'd probably been expecting an encounter. He quietly turned and left, so Ed and Tom never knew he was there. They looked at each other and telepathically agreed that this conversation was not a rewarding one. We halfheartedly mumbled some platitudes about how nice it was to see each other again, and they quickly ducked back into the flag offices while I scrambled down to my office. I had to see Leen's medical record. If he was a stowaway or had altered his medical record, I was going to go straight to the admiral. His own health and the concern of a lot of other people were involved.

When I got to the department, there was a crowd in the amidships passageway between my office and the ER. A couple of MAAs with their big white belts and their bricks squawking were milling around with two chiefs and a jg. A seaman was sitting on the bench with a Jimmy Cagney half grin, *Forrestal* ballcap tilted back on his head, and a semidirty T-shirt wrapped around his forearm. "Don't tell me," I said. "You cut your wrist, right?" He nodded, and the half grin became a victorious but small smile. The seaman knew that we were within helo distance of the beach and that he'd be going back to Jacksonville before long. We would examine him and do a detailed medical history and psychiatric evaluation, all right. Yet, when we had finished, either he was earnestly suicidal and would need to go for treatment, or, even if he wasn't a likely risk, he knew we'd never gamble or play tough with these stakes. Either way, we'd have to send him back.

"It's his buddy I'm more worried about, Doc," his chief said. There was another seaman in the ER. Bob Willmore was with him. The second seaman had a characteristic stack of very, very superficial scratches on his left wrist, too. Since most people are right-handed, they hold the pocketknife or razor blade in the right hand and make the tentative slicing attempts on the left wrist. A little bit more blood on this guy than on Jimmy Cagney out in the passageway, but the marks were still way too superficial to require sutures. This guy was weepy, morose, incommunicative. He spoke only with semiaudible grunts. He'd only been on the ship a couple of months and didn't have any real friends. He did his work acceptably, but wasn't a standout. In fact, his chief had begun to notice a few weeks ago that he kept to himself a lot and didn't mix with others. When we'd started getting ready to go the day before, he was seen sobbing a little but refused to talk. Thinking he was alone outside a workspace after we got under way, he tried to cut himself, but a couple of friends—including the smart aleck on my bench outside—saw him.

They called the chief, who came right away and called medical and security. Just when the MAAs arrived, seaman number one took out his knife and said, "I know what he's going through. I can't take it either." Whereupon he made as many tiny little cuts on his left wrist as he could before the MAAs wrestled his knife away from him.

I asked Bill Kelly to help Willmore with the two cases for the present. Besides looking after the patients, there would be reports to the XO and the captain, notification of the sailors' department head, and arrangements for flying them off if the skipper would agree.

I ducked into my office and buzzed for Burt Rosen. He got me Oliver Leen's medical record. Both to my alarm and yet also a little to my relief, Leen was back on the ship legally! His record showed the medical board recommending permanent limited duty, which would have allowed him to stay in the Navy to complete his twenty years but prohibited duty at sea or in duty stations where a hospital was easily accessible. He had gone through the proper appeals route, rebutting the medical board to the central physical evaluation board (PEB). The rebuttal included a letter from his (civilian) endocrinologist saying that shipboard duty would be no problem for Commander Leen, who was very capable of managing his own insulin. In all these years, he said, the commander had not suffered any complications from his diabetes or insulin therapy. The PEB was persuaded by the rebuttal and determined he was fit for sea duty. I was chagrined, of course, that the near-coma ketoacidosis that almost killed him last year showed something that us old-fashioned GP types would have been tempted to call a complication. His hiding severe illness from us was still worrisome (worrisome, hell, it was infuriating) to me. Would it happen again?

Finally, I resolved my feelings this way: the central PEB knew that he had insulin-dependent diabetes, and they knew that a reliable board-certified internist, John Seibel, recommended he not go to sea because he'd had a serious case of pyelonephritis. If, after weighing all the evidence, the PEB would let him go to sea, the consequences were Leen's and the PEB's. We on the ship now knew we'd have to be very attentive, and frankly, now that we were on alert, I felt comfortable that we would be able to handle his diabetes. While the medical risks were manageable—especially since we knew about his propensity to cover up—he didn't really need to go to sea. There were other officers in his special field, and there were plenty of jobs available to him on shore duty. With the questionable premise that medical precaution could hurt his career or promotion opportunities, he was permitted to go into an environment with more risk than was necessary. But this time it wouldn't ruin my day. He'd followed the rules. I couldn't fault him for that. Ironic. I'd spent so much of my time the past many weeks with people looking for physical excuses to avoid going to sea. Here was the opposite, and I had resisted emotionally. I phoned Leen to tell him I was glad to see him back on the ship, and invited him to come down for a cup of coffee when he had the time.*

Bill Kelly came in to talk about our two suicidal sailors. One of them was almost speechless and couldn't express what he was anxious about, but Bill was worried about him. He might be depressed, Bill thought, but he might also be psychotic. Bill thought he would be safe as long as somebody stayed with him, but we had to get him to a proper suicide-proof environment and competent—probably inpatient—psychiatric care. The second character, the smart aleck, seemed to just want off the ship. We had no choice. Since HS-15, the H-3 helo squadron, flew on board the first day (while we were still within their range), we could send these two fellows back to NH Jacksonville. I talked it over with the XO. We now had a cellular telephone on the ship, so I was able to make arrangements with the psychiatrists at the hospital without using the red phone.

---

*Four years later, assigned to the bureau of medicine and surgery, I was jogging across the Memorial Bridge toward the Pentagon one sunny February day and I passed Ollie going the opposite direction. He was going a helluva lot faster than I was. The diabetes had obviously not done him in yet.

Flu Shots Again

The first day was still only in midafternoon. It was far from over. George Lucy brought the officers and chiefs of the department in for the 1600 meeting we'd scheduled to talk about flu shots. Everybody remembered that I'd sworn "No more mass immunizations!" but flu shots couldn't really be spread over the entire year. Influenza is predominantly a seasonal, winter illness, so immunizations should be given in the fall. Because the influenza virus undergoes antigenic evolution from one year to the next, the vaccine changes every year, and to be effective it must be given annually. Flu is a serious disease and can be savagely infectious in the confines of a ship, so we had to plan to give flu shots. Everybody on the ship would need them. The best time to do it would be while transiting the Atlantic, before operations became very busy. Therefore, we would have to make an exception to my "no mass programs" dictum.

"But I thought you didn't want to give shots anymore," Lucy said. He twitched his jaw to the right and his head to the left, flexed his pecs.

"No, Mr. Lucy. I said I didn't want to give *mass* shot programs again. Giving flu shots is not optional. We still have to do it. I just want to do it smarter. No lines, OK?" He gave me the blank expression.

We talked about how to schedule people in manageable small groups of about forty every fifteen minutes so nobody would have to stand around too long. We could keep the whole exercise down on the second deck, maybe entirely in the medical department. Bob Willmore suggested we keep the project going almost twenty-four hours a day so that people who worked night shift wouldn't have to interrupt their sleep schedule. We decided to schedule shots alphabetically rather than by workspaces so that the shops could spread out time away from work. It was my job to go to the department heads and the XO at eight o'clocks to clear it with the ship and all the departments.

That night at eight o'clocks I brought up the subject. Groans all around. "Hey, Doc, my grandmother's never had a flu shot in her life. She's ninety-seven years old and never had the flu. You tryin' to tell me healthy people our age need those shots?" A very popular complaint was this one: "Doc, I don't take flu shots anymore. They always make me sicker than hell. Ever since I quit takin' the shots, I've never had the flu. No thanks." I heard that one more than a dozen times every flu season. Another popular stanza was, "Why make us get these shots for the flu? I can see typhoid or yellow fever, but not a minor illness. Nobody ever dies from flu!" Of course, the general public doesn't understand influenza, so every year we had an educational program about it on the ship, with pamphlets, lectures on the closed-circuit TV, and sessions like this one.

The common, mostly trivial, respiratory or gastrointestinal short illnesses people catch from time to time are often, but erroneously, called "flu." Confusing those minor illnesses with influenza creates a serious misimpression. The real illness is caused by a very infectious virus and spread by close contact and moisture droplets in cough or breath particles. Of course, the elderly or people in crowded environments are the most vulnerable. In the world's worst epidemic, in 1918, millions died, more than a hundred thousand in the United States, in a single year. There is no cure. As with other viral infections, antibiotics have no direct effect. Although the vaccine isn't 100 percent effective, it prevents an outbreak from becoming an epidemic and significantly limits the severity of illness in those few vaccinated people who do catch the flu. If we had an influenza outbreak on the ship without immunizations, a conservative estimate might be that more than a thousand members of the crew would become sick, and at least two-thirds of those would be unable to work for a day or more. Case fatality rates vary among outbreaks, but were usually far more than one in a thousand. Influenza is not a trivial disease.

Once the department heads and XO heard this pitch, the moans subsided, even if they didn't go away entirely. The department heads would cooperate, and the XO would make the shots mandatory. The blackshoes always would have gone along. Once I announced that there was an instruction from the secretary of the Navy requiring flu shots for everybody, the shoes would comply immediately. No questions asked. Aviators were another matter. If something hurt, other than PT or an airplane crash, aviators were against it. They agreed now, after I spelled out the facts, and while their friends were watching. But when the time came to roll up the left sleeve, there would be sniveling, guys would suddenly remember allergies that weren't in their health records, and some would suddenly remember something they had to do immediately. Aviators hated shots. For now, though, I had everybody's consent for the program, and it would start the next day, the fourth day under way. Adm. Sweetcakes Barnes, our new battle group commander, he volunteered to go first. The skipper, the XO, and I would be next. By setting an example, we'd get more cheerful cooperation from the crew. (Being a flight surgeon, I didn't forget that Captain Louis and the admiral were aviators. The more senior they get, the more crafty aviators can be about dodging a needle.)

The fixed-wing aircraft from the air wing came aboard that morning. In its more private and military manner, this was as impressive for us as our getting under way had been a couple of days before. We had our planes now. The hangar bay filled, and the flight deck started teeming. The sleeping giant Admiral Yamamoto had spoken of forty-seven years ago stirred again.

Later that day we sent representatives around to all divisions to begin the education and information campaign and work out the scheduling. Chief Priggemeier down in the print shop made up hundreds of schedules so we could post them all over the ship. Even the captain consented to plug the flu shot program on his daily 1-MC address to the crew. He was getting to like the 1-MC—perhaps too much. It was getting to be a running joke how long he'd carry on. "Good morning. This is the captain." Who else would it be with that country accent? "We're 800 miles east of Norfolk, and 1,280 miles away from Mayport. The weather is clear and mild with a temperature of fifty-two degrees. We're makin' about sixteen knots and we should be near Rota in about five days. Today we're going to . . ." Then he would talk about the day's various activities. Next, he'd read the notices he had received in the day's message traffic, which included the two to four babies born to wives of FID crewmen every day. Then he plugged the flu shots for us. "Now I know you guys are like me in not liking to get shots, but Doc Riley and his gang down there in medical tell me that flu is a lot more serious than you might realize." Captain Louis, I thought, should consider a career in politics or radio if he ever retired from the Navy. He had a perfect touch with the crew.

Captain Louis then got on to the part of his daily fireside chat that made me cringe, the "Letters to the Captain" show. Ninety percent of the letters were complaints about either medical or supply, with another ten percent about personnel. The XO now and then gave me and the SuppO leadership pointers. Because of the disproportionate number of complaints we received, the XO saw these as his two "problem" departments. Medical was even one of what the XO called the "minor" departments, because we had so many fewer people than engineering, air, supply, AIMD, and weapons. The SuppO and I didn't take it personally, though. We realized that most complaints in all ships were about the service departments. Ours were the ones that touched everybody on the ship, regardless of his job. Since everybody was one of our consumers, everybody had an opinion about how well we did our jobs. They were less likely to have such an opinion about other departments. After all, what could the sailors complain about in the way the weapons or air department did their business? Medical and supply were the two departments most directly responsible for the sailor's quality of life. The crew loved it that the captain welcomed their input, and at the core, the SuppO and I liked it, too. We just didn't like what we considered a kind of capricious quality to the process.

On this particular day, medical escaped. The letter complained about the choice of breakfast cereals. Sure, the complainant said, you could always get eggs and a choice of cream of wheat or oatmeal, but nobody likes oatmeal and cream of wheat anymore. Those are old fashioned, he said. The selection of cold cereals was poor. How come we never ran out of cornflakes (almost as stodgy as oatmeal), and the Fruity Pebbles ran out every day before 0700? That wasn't fair. Remarkably, on this ship of war, this supercarrier with more bomb power than was used in all of World War II, the two most popular breakfast cereals were Trix and Fruity Pebbles. The captain promised the writer that he would look into the matter. The SuppO knew he'd be increasing the inventory of Fruity Pebbles.

While the captain finished up his 1-MC announcement, I was completing the day's reports in my office. When he signed off with his trademark "and above all, have a *fine* Navy day!" I left the office to check on something elsewhere in the department. I could scarcely get into the passageway. It was crammed too tight with sailors to permit any movement at all! There was a line stretching all the way down the starboard main passageway, back up our amidships passageway past my office door, doubled back on itself, then stretching all the way back down the starboard passageway up a dozen frames or more. What in the hell was this? I hated lines!

"Get me Warrant Officer Lucy!" I shouted, hoping some corpsman somewhere might be able to hear me.

When Lucy was able to squeeze through the crowd to find me, he must have known I was angry. Maybe he could tell by the red face or the steam streaking out of my collar or my ears. Perhaps my breathing rate or the foam at the edges of my mouth gave me away. I'm not sure. He knew, though. I knew that he could tell, because he was flexing and twitching a little more and a little faster than usual.

"Mr. Lucy, why are all these people standing in line outside my door? I hate lines, Mr. Lucy."

He said they had arranged to have forty men every fifteen minutes, just like I had instructed. He flexed his right thigh and left shoulder.

"But there are a couple of hundred people out here!"

"Well, yes, Sir. We told all the people from 1600 to 1730 to show up a little before 1600, so everyone could be in line and ready to go, then we could have a break at 1730 for dinner."

The plan had been for people to arrive in increments of forty, at fifteen-minute intervals. Apparently not everyone had understood. I got Burt Rosen and Rob Emerson to help us, and we all went up and down the line to work it out for people to come back in fifteen minutes, thirty minutes, forty-five minutes, and so on. Eventually we got rid of the line. I needed some exercise and a good hard run to cool myself off.

A Hatch

Flight quals were going on up on the flight deck, so I had to run in the hangar bay. In some ways, I preferred it there anyway. You had to keep your gaze alert and look everywhere, just like an aviator's scan on the control panel, to avoid banging into a wing or a drop tank. People pop out from behind yellow gear, bulkheads, and airplanes, and if you don't watch carefully you can collide with a shipmate. Periodically we had to treat a fractured arm from two-man jogging collisions on the hangar deck. The tie-down chains that held aircraft and yellow gear in place on the deck were sneaky, dark, and only ankle high above the deck. All these distractions slowed me down a little but added something to think about while I did lap after lap. The hangar is loud, though. I asked all the crew to wear earplugs when they worked there, so I wore mine when I was running.

Even with the earplugs, though, I heard the 1-MC: "Medical emergency. Medical emergency. Seven tack eighty-six tack sixteen. Medical emergency." They hadn't added "This is a drill." Still in my PT gear and sweating, I ran forward to the AIMD ladderwell as fast as I could, down one ladder, back through the port passageway, and to the ladderwell over the spot. I was the first medical rep there. Looking down the shaft from the second deck, I saw four open watertight hatches and one closed. I figured the sick guy was on the deck down there. I climbed through the hatch to the vertical ladder and started climbing down as fast as I could. I realized suddenly that I was going down the same hole where we'd found Jimmy Fulford less than a year ago. When I got to the last open hatch, I stopped and looked down. The hatch wasn't really closed. I could see some guy's dark hair and the top of his head sticking out. Was he helping out his buddy, who might be stuck on the ladder there? No, that couldn't be it, the hatch was mostly closed. They weigh close to five hundred pounds. When I climbed down closer, it was clearer. The head belonged to the injured guy. It wasn't moving, and he wasn't making any sound.

"This is Doc Riley up here. Anybody down there?" I hollered through what little opening there was.

Airman somebody was down there. He was the one who had called for help. Just then HM3 Ammerman and Rob Emerson came down the ladder. The hatch was just too heavy for one guy to lift by himself, and the job was made more difficult because of the trapped sailor. It looked as though he might be dangling by the top of his head. While we lifted the hatch, we had to make sure he didn't fall. Most of the vertical shafts like this one had canvas nets draped under the openings, so that if a guy fell, he would only go one level and not plummet straight down the sixty or seventy feet some holes dropped. With the hatch closed, though, we didn't know about this one. "Airman," I shouted through the crack, "we're going to lift the hatch. Please make sure he doesn't move. Most of all, for God's sake, don't stand where you can get hurt too if this thing slips. One injury is enough. Try not to let him move at all, but especially don't let him fall. Is there anybody else down there with you?"

"Yes, Sir, there are two of us."

I pushed my hands around both sides of the head below us, and Rob and Petty Officer Ammerman lifted the hatch. It was almost too heavy for two guys. We didn't know how it happened, so I warned them to be slow. An MAA arrived then and was able to help. When the hatch came up, we saw that we had an unconscious boy about nineteen years old. Both sides of his chest seemed pushed in. Blood was coming out of his ears and nose. Obvious multiple rib fractures. He wasn't breathing, but he wasn't cyanotic yet. There was indeed a canvas net slung under the hatch, and his right knee was braced against it. From somewhere on that lower deck, HM3 Brooks appeared, and he helped the two other guys down there slowly lower the patient to the deck while I tried to hold his head and neck. As soon as we had him on the deck, Rob Emerson came alongside. The medical response bags had been lowered down to us by rope. While I checked the guy over for other signs of injury, Rob started ventilating him with an ambu bag.

We learned that his name was Connor Bergen, a hatch repairman in the elevator department. He and a coworker had been doing preventive maintenance on a hatch just like this one and had needed a spare spring for the latch mechanism. This particular hatch was apparently out of order, so Bergen had come to take the spring out. You're never supposed to work on one of these alone, and there's a complicated procedure for getting permission. Also, the door was supposed to be "tagged out"—identified as out of order.

"Should we intubate him, Captain?" Rob asked. It was clear he was going to need ventilation for a while. A direct tube to his trachea could handle that far better than a facial mask. In the meantime, Rob kept his color up well with the ambu and mask.

"I don't know, Rob. Can you get a tube in?" We both agreed that with such a severe chest injury, any ventilation might be difficult. His upper airway seemed intact. Rob was able to slip in a normal endotracheal tube. Breath sounds into both lungs were barely detectable. We were able to stabilize his neck and fasten him to a rigid litter. By going just a few frames forward, we were able to get to one of the weapons elevators and take him up to the medical department on the second deck. As we rose, I kept listening to his chest with my stethoscope. A loud gallop and harsh murmur warned me that he probably had a heart injury too. The crush had fractured the base of his chest, probably lacerated his brain and the aorta.

We went straight to the ICU. Rob and Van Hardy looked after the necessary attachments to the ventilator and started IVs. I called the XO. In seconds, I told him the patient's name and told him to tell the captain it was very bad, a heart and lung injury. I'd get back to him as soon as I could. "Somebody quickly find out what his religion is." We tried to get the priest, Father Lynch, if a Catholic was dying.

We immediately gave him dexamethasone, a drug used to combat brain swelling. We couldn't use any anticoagulants, given his heart injury. How would we cope with blood loss and shock? I checked all the signs of brain-stem responsiveness that we neurologists use to determine brain death. He qualified, but right now we had our hands full to just keep his breathing and heartbeat going.

Rob and Van were busy with the necessary sustainment actions, but they had things under control. The seaman was a Catholic, reportedly a religious young man. Father Lynch came to give last rites.

I went up to the bridge to tell the captain. I described everything we had seen and done and explained the nature of the injury. "Captain, I'm afraid he's already brain-dead. Even if we could repair his heart, there's no way he could survive." The captain asked how we could know that this soon. I described the complicated heart injury and the significance of the brain-stem functions.

"Well, Doc, do all you can and let's hope for a miracle."

You never close out the hope for a miracle. Not with a family member or a shipmate. Yet, while leaving room for prayer and hope, it is irresponsible to contribute to false hopes. "Yes, Sir, but that is truly what it would take. I have to be clear with you about that."

At this time we were about midway across the Atlantic, a little bit closer to Rota, Spain, than to the States. It would be two days before we could get into range for fixed-wing flights to shore. He couldn't handle the G forces for a cat shot, though, and our H-3s wouldn't have long enough legs to reach Spain until even later. Realistically, it would be three days before we'd be in range of an H-53 helo to Spain.

With this injury and clinical brain death, if we were in most U.S. hospitals we'd talk to the family about the meaning of brain death and gently help them reach the most likely conclusion—terminating life support. None of us felt we should terminate life support while we were at sea. For one thing, the family has a right to participate in the decision. Also, we didn't want the family to have any doubt at all that their son had been given the fullest chance at survival. We resolved to keep him alive and in the best possible condition until he could be taken safely to the nearest hospital, which in this case would be NH Rota.

Word spreads quickly on the ship. The captain knew this better than anybody, so he talked to the crew on the 1-MC. "Good evening. This is the captain. Probably most of you know by now that we've had a shipmate injured. It's Seaman Connor Bergen from down in G-4. They're doin' all they can for him down in medical, but Doc Riley tells me he's in very serious condition." The captain said that everybody should pray for him, and then ended. That was the only short 1-MC announcement I recall from the captain, and one of only two that didn't end with "and above all, have a fine Navy day."

Rob and Van and I took turns staying with Bergen around the clock. Rob looked after the ventilator. The patient's arterial blood gases stayed good until the second day, when he became a little acidotic. Chest films showed some diffuse infiltrates. We had a hard time deciding whether he had pulmonary edema secondary to the cerebral injury, or was developing pneumonia. Van suggested we start high doses of a couple of antibiotics. In just a few days a resistant organism wouldn't be a concern, but if he had a fulminant pneumonia at this point he might not be alive in a few days to worry about it.

When we were a day out of port I went up to the CIC to get on the red phone to talk to a doctor at NH Rota. No radio at the hospital. We had to call a destroyer in the port there. They called the hospital, and a doctor came down to the destroyer to talk with me. It took a couple of hours to get it all hooked up, and then we waited for the nets to let us communicate. The doctor was a surgeon named Harris. I recognized the name. He'd just left NH Jacksonville a few months before. In fact, he'd been considered for Rock Tosser's relief before

Van Hardy was picked. I explained the patient's condition and that we expected to helo him over the next day. Harris was receptive and pleasant. We promised to send over our detailed notes about SN Bergen. Harris had no questions, and we signed off.

Making the connection between the ICU and the helo would be critical, so we started making arrangements right away. I recalled the time during workups when Captain Louis was irritated about our coordination for a medevac. This time we needed everything to go perfectly. Bergen was stable, all right, but very fragile. His shattered lungs were somehow taking the oxygen we were pumping to him. Everything had to be coordinated with the weapons department for Elevator 7 on the starboard side, beside one of the mess decks. The helo would call en route from about twenty minutes out, and we'd get everything set up. Bergen should be on the helo within five or ten minutes from when he left the ICU. I didn't want to use the deck-edge elevators to take him up to the flight deck. They were a little faster and could be used with less hoopla, but they were jerky and windy. Weapons Elevator 7 opened up by the after edge of the island, near what's referred to as the "bomb farm" on the starboard edge of the flight deck.

I insisted that we rehearse the transfer a few times that afternoon with HM3 Brooks in the litter. Petty Officer Brooks was about the right size. The first time we tried it, it took us fourteen minutes just to get the simulated monitors in the ICU moved and disconnected and the litter brought back to the mess deck. The second time, we got him back to the elevator in seven minutes, but there was a twelve-minute delay getting the elevator crew to crank up the elevator. Finally, on the third try, we got the litter up to the flight deck in eight minutes. "OK, guys, let's not tamper with a smooth system. It has to go at least this well in the morning. Everybody please remember your part."

Back in the department, Van was his usual well-composed, amiable self. I frequently was thankful to have him, and now was one of those time. It crossed my mind for one painful instant what it would have been like to deal with Rock at a time like this. Rob was quietly getting a little anxious about the trip. "Captain, I think I should go with him."

"Rob, I know you'd like to make sure his ventilation is maintained. He never would have survived until now without you, but you know we can't spare you." The helo ride would take more than two hours. For the round trip, including the transfer over to the hospital, he'd be gone for five hours. We really couldn't be without anesthesia coverage for that long.

The next morning at about 0800, the ATO called to say that the H-53 had departed Rota and was en route. At 0900, the pilot called to say they were twenty minutes out. The handler, Lt. Cdr. Tony McFarlane, had cleared a spot on the waist for the big helo and made sure there was a clear passage from the elevator to the deck. We started getting everything ready down in medical. George Lucy had gathered up SN Bergen's personnel and pay records from Lt. Max Small, the admin officer. All the litter bearers were standing by. George McDonough was the flight surgeon who would go. He already had his gear on and was standing by to help us move Bergen to the helo.

"Let's make sure he has enough oxygen," Rob pointed out.

It was all worked out. Last night Rob had computed the amount of oxygen that would be needed—a little over one standard bottle—and the helo crew would have twice that amount on board. Medical oxygen differs from aviation oxygen by the technique of preparation. They both have to be free of oil and other contaminants, but for flight ops more moisture is added, whereas in medical applications the amount and type of moisture may be adjusted. "What if they forgot it?" Rob said. "I think we should send a spare tank just in case." About then, the air boss called down to say the helo was overhead and would be on the deck momentarily. Once they unloaded the mail and refueled, they'd be ready to go. We should plan to be up on the flight deck in about twelve minutes.

OK, we had a few minutes. Before unhooking the monitors, one of the corpsmen ran back to the ER to pick up a spare oxygen tank. We carefully unhooked the monitors and attached the portable monitor. SN Bergen remained the same as he had been for four days—completely unresponsive. His color was still good, his face cleaned, his hair combed. The gun boss and a few of his shipmates asked to come in just to say good-bye to him. They all knew he couldn't hear them, but they needed to say it whether he could or not. The captain came in, too. Always considerate, he asked if time would permit him to say good-bye. It would. The unloading on the flight deck was taking a little longer than expected. He reached down and took Bergen's hand. "Be careful, shipmate. I wrote a letter to your mother, and I'll call her as soon as I can." That's all he said, unpretentious and genuine. We took Bergen down the passageway to the elevator.

The elevator operators made sure the elevators were running and waiting for us. When we got him loaded on, Rob and I were going to ride up with him, one of us working the ambu bag all the time, since he was detached from the big ventilator now. Before they could close the grate on the elevator platform, Rob ran off back to the medical department and asked HM1 Amstutz to help me on the elevator. "Where are you going, Rob?"

"I want to make sure he has enough oxygen. I'll meet you up on the flight deck."

"But they have plenty on the airplane, and we're bringing—" It didn't matter. Rob was already out of earshot and the elevator was taking us up.

When we arrived on the flight deck, they were just finishing unloading the mail and refueling. The H-53 is a huge helicopter, about the size of a very large mobile home or a boxcar. A huge tail door, about the size of a volleyball court, opens down like a ramp to permit entrance. It's big enough to let in a couple of jeeps. We stood there waiting in the wind for clearance to bring our patient on board. The crew was arranging the inside of the helo. I sent somebody into the flight deck BDS on the island to bring out an extra blanket for Bergen. Rob came panting up with another oxygen bottle. "Rob, for Pete's sake, you've brought enough!"

"Nothing wrong with being safe," was all he said.

George McDonough had gone up to talk to the pilots and check the situation in the back where he and SN Bergen would be going. "They're almost ready. They have two oxygen bottles in there."

"That's not enough!" Rob said.

"Jesus, Rob, you said two bottles would be enough last night, and besides, we have three more we're sending, thanks to you."

"How do you know theirs are all right?"

We were interrupted then by the loadmaster beckoning us on. We brought Bergen up through the back and secured his litter. Rob ran out to grab the spare oxygen bottle from the flight deck BDS.

"Just in case," he said. This was getting interesting. We now had six oxygen bottles on the aircraft.

Finally we had Bergen tied into the aircraft and we all exited and stood along the island, waiting for the big H-53 to be untied and depart. Rob grew nervous. "It took longer than we expected. He's been on that tank for almost twenty minutes. John, go get another tank!"

"Rob, cut it out. There are already six tanks on that helo. They're just going to Spain, not to Mars."

"If he runs out of oxygen he's going to die. It's that simple."

"Yeah, but that's not going to happen until April with that many tanks, Rob. Let it go."

"Be safe. Hurry, John." So, before we could let the helo lift off, HM3 Delrosario ran up and handed an aircrewman the seventh oxygen bottle.

Finally, they were gone.

We learned the next day that an EEG had been obtained, a flat line confirmed. The day of the injury, the Red Cross had notified Bergen's family in Vermont, and the Navy flew them to Rota. His father was a retired Marine, his mother a veteran of many deployments. They were there when Connor arrived, and after the EEG they asked that the ventilator be removed.

First the fire and now this. Not a great start to the deployment.

Chapter 13

The Med

■✚ The next day we arrived at Rota, the NATO base just south of Cádiz, right at the gate to the Mediterranean. Here we were going to "chop" with the *Eisenhower*, the carrier we were relieving in the Med. The *IKE* was a "nuke," one of the big *Nimitz*-class nuclear carriers. Although only about eight years old, she didn't have the maturity, dignity, and character of a ship like the FID. She was kind of arrogant with her higher-tech propulsion plant and bigger flight deck, but we on the FID knew that newer isn't by itself better, in fact often isn't better.

The *IKE* had extended her cruise by about three weeks because we were late. After our turnover, we'd have war games for about a week between our battle group and *IKE*'s. Ordinarily the turnover would take place inside the Med, and the departing ship wouldn't pass through Gibraltar until its replacement arrived. A combination of glasnost, reduced international tensions, and the pressures to get *IKE* home for the holidays led to our having a turnover in the Atlantic. It was the first time since World War II there wouldn't be an American aircraft carrier in the Mediterranean.

Helos flew parties between the ships. On the 1-MC, we heard Admiral Barnes and Captain Louis bonged off to meet with their counterparts on the *IKE:* "Carrier Group Six, departing. *Forrestal,* departing." Shortly, a couple of H-3s from *IKE* arrived on our flight deck with some of her department heads coming to give us turnover information. To our surprise, the SMO and MAO from the *IKE* were among them. The XO had told me earlier that there weren't going to be any medical reps. That had been unusual and irritating news, but not unexpected. Medical guys are accustomed to being thought of as expendable hangers-on by some "operators." That was never true on the FID—Mitchell didn't listen to my advice as often as I wanted,

256

but at least he respected and cared about the role of medical services.

So I was pleased that the *IKE*'s SMO had arrived. For business, of course, I wanted to get the information from the last SMO in the Med. The main reason was personal, though. Fred Spencer, the *IKE*'s SMO, was a friend. He hadn't been in the Navy very long, but already he was a lieutenant commander. Most SMOs were full commanders, or occasionally captains like myself, and usually had to have a lot of Navy experience to get a SMO's job. Fred, however, had come to the Navy as an experienced physician only a couple of years before. When he was given the opportunity to be a SMO he had resisted at first, even though he was confident of his medical and managerial skills. I was one of the people who had encouraged him to take the opportunity.

Our greetings were enthusiastic. Not only because we were good friends, but also because we both needed some ventilating. I reviewed our experiences in the past couple of weeks, including the loss of the young airman. Overall, I told him, I was glad we were under way; the ship is better when we're steaming. We talked about a few common clinical problems. One was the matter of suicide and what to do about suicide threats. Manipulative suicide threats were occurring frequently on the *IKE*, too, even more often than on the FID. In fact, on the *IKE* they'd had a psychologist embarked for a couple of months, but the number of threatening gestures hadn't decreased.

It seemed that Fred needed to ventilate more than I did, though. Both of my skippers had always listened to my input and trusted my judgments, and even if the XO gave me more direction than I wanted, I really knew, somewhere just below consciousness, that he was really on my side. This wasn't the case with Fred on the *IKE*. He was tired, quiet, less eager than usual.

"Maybe you're just overreacting because you're tired, Fred. This is new for you. Maybe you and your captain are just getting to know each other. Obviously he knows about your medical credentials. I'm sure he has more confidence in you than you think."

"No, Terry, this is different. It isn't working out." Fred had always been successful at everything he ever did. He had once run a state's emergency medical systems and had been a professor in a couple of medical schools. Apparently, a couple of times his department hadn't carried out some administrative functions the way the captain wanted, and on a couple of other occasions the captain questioned some diagnoses or some medevac decisions. Fred felt that the skipper didn't listen to him. It was frustrating for him to meet this kind of stone wall. Even worse, though, was not knowing how to fix it, how to win his captain's confidence.

A few hours after Fred's helo left we heard the ship's bell and the 1-MC, "*Forrestal,* arriving," and then four bongs and "Battle Force Sixth Fleet, arriving." That was Admiral Barnes's new title since taking over from the admiral in *IKE*'s battle group.

For the next three days and three nights we had war games against the *IKE*'s battle group. Except for an extraordinary attention to safety, we used all tactical tools, just like in a real war. The *IKE* was bigger and more modern in design, and she had more ships in her battle group. Her air wing had more airplanes, too.

News about the war games came two ways: the captain's reports on the 1-MC and, of course, the grapevine. While the grapevine messages may have been factually a little less accurate, they were surely more succinct. Captain Louis's reputation as a blabbermouth on the 1-MC continued to grow. Whenever he got that microphone in his hand, the disc jockey lurking inside just had to speak. Once or twice during the war games when Tommy Linker, the 'gator, made the 1-MC announcement, it would be just a brief comment about how many of *IKE*'s planes we shot down. I couldn't tell whether the cheering was for the news (because it was invariably good; we were clobbering the *IKE*) or for the brevity of the announcement.

The Hostage

Despite the operational tempo of the war games, the business of the ship still had to go on. All those things like mail, paychecks, and cargo had to come and go like always, squeezed in between the attacks and maneuvers. Among that business was the arrival and transfer of personnel. One day, a nervous young newcomer brought his orders down to the personnel office to check in after arriving on the COD. The personnelman who checked him in snickered and silently showed the orders to a coworker. The two salty veterans exchanged derisive glances and went immediately to a back office, snickering and joking in whispers as they went off. The other new guys behind our perplexed victim now joined in making him an outcast, because he was the cause of their being delayed, too. One more reason to stand in a line, one more delay from the predicted holdups of the day, one more space between them and dinner.

From the door in the back office, a few other faces peeked out, squinted or stared at the new guy, sometimes pointed at him when they laughed, and then ducked back into the office. About ten minutes later, the MAAs came for the new guy. Although they tried to look stern, the

MAAs chuckled and spewed half-suppressed laughs while they hand-cuffed him. "Seaman Snyder," one of them stammered, because every second or third word broke up, "come with me. Captain Louis wants you on the bridge."

Arriving on the bridge, he was greeted with a plate of cookies, a photographer, and a party atmosphere. "Sit right here in my chair, Seaman Snyder," Captain Louis told him, and then the captain keyed his 1-MC microphone. "Good afternoon, shipmates, this is the captain. I guess you know we've been waxing the *IKE* for the past couple of days, and up until now it's been a fair fight, even though we've been winning. Well, this afternoon they reached the lowest depths and we still beat them. The dastardly villains from the *IKE* tried to sneak a spy aboard, but don't worry. Thanks to quick thinking and an impenetrable intelligence system, we've caught him."

Poor Snyder had caught the wrong COD in Sigonella. He was supposed to report to the *IKE* and came to us by mistake. Later he rode over to the *IKE* with a basket of FID cookies as a condolence prize. The FID had humbled the big nuke, and even caught her in her feeble resort to crime.

After our war with the *IKE*, we steamed east and began to think about our first port call. The weather was cloudy, cold, and drizzly almost every day, and our moods matched the weather. Several flying days had to be canceled. The crew was ready for liberty. The fire, the delayed deployment, then the death of a young sailor. So far a hard cruise. Now the bad weather. The ship rolled more than we spoiled carrier sailors were accustomed to. I recalled Warner Hobs, the former first lieutenant, making jokes about the poor job my medical department did in tying down gear. Destroyer sailors, he reminded me, had to be much better at preparing for heavy seas; we spoiled Airedales had no idea, he said. Two days before pulling into Toulon, my TV tumbled off its shelf and shattered like a Christmas ornament—because I hadn't tied it down. We even had a few people who came to medical for seasickness, which is very rare on a carrier. Most of us had never visited Toulon, and a few days of liberty can be good for attitudes. Shift gears, get out of this bad weather, step into our *Forrestal* role.

There was also interesting news in the daily message traffic. One day I misjudged my timing for lunch and found myself trapped at the table when the XO came in. When he started to take over the conversation as usual, I thought, "Oh, no, another Australian sea story," but the subject was world events, and this time they affected us. Recently the Baltic states had been asserting their independence, and with surprisingly little rebuttal from the Soviets. Premier Gorbachev's glasnost was moving along much faster than almost any Americans had predicted. President Bush and the Soviet premier were hinting about a major summit meeting, even very soon—like this month— and the president might come to the *Forrestal!* From that day on, the subject grew and took up more and more of every conversation.

One day, the whole summit had been called off. Another day, it was going to be held in some neutral country rather than at sea. Well, the two of them wanted to capture some drama, some history. The last time a Soviet leader and an American leader had met as friends was when Truman and Stalin met in Yalta. To meet at sea, in the Mediterranean, would be symbolic, dramatic. The conference was back on, and it would be in November.

We began to plan. Painting got a little more vigorous. There were more meetings. The tempo picked up with all the preparations, which even competed with liberty for the crew's attention.

Liberty did finally come, though. On the first night at Toulon, boating was rough. The sea state was right on the margin of what would allow boating. It was drizzling or raining most of the night, and riding the boats into fleet landing slapped the bows up so high that a few guys got knocked down and a few others got pretty seasick. I came back to the ship around eight o'clock that night, right after my first meal in a French restaurant. It was good I did, because the camel off the fantail burst loose in the high seas, and boating had to be canceled. Everybody who was still ashore at that point had to stay ashore all night.

The Boxing Smokers

On the second day, the seas were still too high for boating, so liberty had to be called off—except for the guys stranded ashore. However, it was supposed to be a liberty port, and we had scheduled some recreation time, so we salvaged the situation with the first boxing "smokers." The name apparently came from back in the days when everybody could sit around and puff on cigars during the boxing match. There was, of course, no smoking any longer up in the hangar deck, but the name still seemed to fit.

Boxing is a worry to all ship's doctors. Fleet boxing programs have been around for generations, and traditions die hard in the Navy. The sailors love boxing matches and the competition between divisions, between ships, and even between battle groups or fleets, so it's tough for us doctors to prevent the matches, even though we all want to. As a neurologist, when I first heard about the idea of boxing on the *Forrestal* I was distraught. The American Academy of Neurology and most other medical groups have publicly condemned all forms of the sport for years. A couple of years before I arrived, Captain Guitar had agreed to having a boxing program, but John Busby was able to talk him out of it.

When I learned that Lieutenant Gines, the new ship's secretary and a former boxing champion himself, had already secured Captain Louis's permission for the boxing team, I resolved to put an end to it. Gines had circumvented me, knowing I would try to talk the captain out of a boxing program if I could. "You know how doctors are . . ."

I'd learned about Gines's boxing team plans before the deployment and gone straightaway to the XO. "Yeah, yeah, Doc, I know. Doctors are always against boxing tourneys. Let me tell you something. I've been on a lot of ships. Some allowed boxing and on some the doc was able to frighten the old man enough to prevent 'em. Never seen anybody hurt. These are healthy guys. It's a Navy tradition. You'll never talk this captain out of it."

"XO, that's just flat-out wrong. The facts are straightforward. Never mind the fact that guys die from boxing injuries, there are hundreds of vegetables in American hospitals from this so-called innocent sport. If you and the captain will just listen, the data will speak for itself."

"OK, I'll tell the captain we need to talk to him. But you're not going to change his mind."

Well, I'm a neurologist. This happened to be something I knew a lot about . . . I thought.

After gathering about thirty medical and epidemiologic articles, I found I had to revise my earlier conclusions. It is true that there are a number of deaths and brain injuries from boxing. However, I discovered that most of my prior information had overlooked some critical control factors. The most numerous and severe injuries occur when there are major disparities in the size or experience level of the boxers. Other major factors are poor conditioning, light gloves, and inadequate headgear. Professionals, for example, often use ten- or even eight-ounce gloves and almost never wear head protectors. The simple precaution of using sixteen-ounce gloves brings boxing down to a level of risk of injury similar to that for baseball and basketball. When, in addition, contestants are properly matched and in good condition and appropriate headgear is used, boxing produces fewer and less severe injuries than most other American sports. With proper screening of participants and exclusion of people with concussions, the risks fall to much less than unsupervised recreation.

Reviewing all this with Lieutenant Gines, I learned that he was much more knowledgeable about the subject than I was. He was a trained coach. He had purchased super headgear that wrapped all the way around the jaw, had cheek pads, and even protected the boxer's nose.

I found myself being the ringside doctor for FID boxing. The second night in Toulon, cheated out of liberty, we had the FID's first boxing smoker in years. Only a few hundred guys had been able to get out on liberty the first night, so there were over four thousand still left on the ship. Only about a thousand came to the matches, but probably just as many watched on channel 8.

Although Gines had been training them, amateurs is amateurs. Each bout lasted only two rounds for this first smoker. The crowd cheered just as enthusiastically as if the boxers had known what they were doing. These guys flailed around, elbows almost out at their sides, throwing roundhouse cannonballs at one another, even when they thought they were jabbing. Although they were in very good shape, when you're carrying around a sixteen-ounce glove at the end of your arm, you tire after a couple of minutes, especially if everything you throw is a haymaker.

After the matches broke up, the enlisted guys went back to their mess decks and lounges and the officers went to the wardroom. Everybody sat around eating popcorn for half an hour, discussing the bouts with the same enthusiasm they'd have after a Leonard/Hearns fight. They were all looking forward to the next series of smokers. Eventually, Gines was planning to invite boxers from some other ships in the battle group over for competition.

The next day the rain and drizzle continued, but the seas weren't as bad and boating did permit people to go ashore. We'd hired a couple of ferries in Toulon, as we often did, to augment the ship's boats. As it turned out, that was a good idea. Every battery on the ship's boats seemed to be dead. Ed DeMaestri was demoralized. When Admiral Barnes came down to get in his barge to go ashore, it wouldn't start. The flag lieutenant and the admiral's aide looked at one another conspicuously and then stared off to the horizon. The admiral wasn't upset. He just wanted to go ashore. Ed and the OOD were embarrassed, though. Ed called for one of the other personnel boats, made an apology to the admiral, and said he'd send the barge over to pick up the admiral as soon as possible.

The other boat wouldn't start either.

Ed sent down to the storeroom to have another battery brought up for the admiral's barge, but there weren't any down there that would fit his boat. Finally, they took the battery out of the captain's gig, put it in the admiral's barge, and, after only a fifteen- or twenty-minute delay, the admiral and his party went ashore. Twenty minutes later, the captain came down to go ashore in his gig. No battery, of course.

Captain Louis, in his typical manner, chided Ed about it a little bit, but enjoyed the laugh. At this point, Ed did not. By that time the utility boat was working, and the skipper just went ashore in that. You could see Ed was going to have a talk with Senior Chief Jones about the boats.

Since boating was open now, I needed to make my visit to the local hospital, so I went ashore the next day. When I got up to the quarterdeck, the boating officer said, "We're having some trouble with the boats, Doc. You may want to go back to the fantail and take the ferry. They're running every thirty minutes, and there should be one by in fifteen or twenty minutes. We're going to be without boats for a little over an hour." As I trudged back through the hangar bay to the fantail, I saw a lot of guys sniffling and blowing their noses. I made a note to myself that we'd be seeing a lot of guys in sick call the next couple of days, what with this foul weather and guys maybe staying out in the drizzle too late at night.

Toulon was a major port for the French Navy. At the pier we could see their aircraft carriers *Clemenceau* and *Foch* tied up. The *DeGaulle* was apparently going to be commissioned soon, but it wasn't around when we came to town. Some years ago, the French unified the medical departments of all of their military services, so they have just one military medical department, as do Canada and a few other countries. St. Anne's is no longer a naval hospital but is called "l'hôpital des armées," a hospital of the armies. Military medical people in France may wear the uniform of whatever service they have spent most of their career with, I guess. Most of the people at St. Anne's were in Navy uniforms, although when I went to meet the CO he wore the uniform of an Air Force general.

After I met the CO, the chief of the medical staff, Dr. Picard, took me around the hospital. Picard was a naval flight surgeon too, and he enjoyed talking about his experiences as a SMO. They were much like mine. He told me, in confidence, how much trouble he'd had with the XO on his last carrier. It seems the XO never listened to his advice and always told him how he thought a flight surgeon should practice medicine. I smiled and told him I was glad I never had that kind of problem. "Yes, you're lucky you don't," he said.

By this time the FID had been at sea for a little over three weeks, and we had accumulated a lot of plastic and medical trash. I discussed this with the folks at St. Anne's, and even before I could finish explaining the details, they nodded knowingly. Medical waste and plastic trash was a new problem for the French Navy, too. They agreed to take all of our medical waste and our plastic trash and to dispose of it in their system, which had national rules about the same as the United States'.

"You don't have any sharps, though, do you?"

"Yes, we have quite a few sharps." We'd done flu shots on the crossing. (A numbing recollection of the results of flu shot needles from eighteen months before crept over me.) Couldn't they take our sharps? After some deliberation, it turned out they could as long as they were in properly marked hard containers, which they were.

The next day I came back to St. Anne's with a couple of my petty officers, and we unloaded about a dozen large, plastic bags of trash from the medical department and five hard containers full of needles and other sharps. The clerk we handed them to was a little puzzled as to why we wanted a receipt for the trash. If he'd been in Mayport for the investigations a little over a year ago, maybe he would have understood a little better. At any rate, we made damn sure we had somebody sign a receipt for all of the bags and the sharps. When we got back to the ship, we put that receipt right in our disposal logs.

The final night in Toulon, all of the department heads went out to dinner with the skipper. Toulon is a beautiful, picturesque city. Winding streets of round cobblestones are lined with shops, houses, and restaurants right on the street. For some reason, all my life I'd heard the French were unfriendly. It certainly wasn't apparent anywhere I went that year in France, most especially not in Toulon. The French people were happy to see us, would cross a street to shake the hand of an American, always had a smile or a greeting. They seemed to enjoy it when an American tried to speak French. Whenever I stumbled, those who spoke English were happy to insert the missing part or would speak a sentence or two of English to get me back on track; but then they did expect to continue the conversation in French.

After dinner, knowing it was the last night in town, the captain wanted to walk around and visit with the FID sailors before they returned from liberty. We walked over to the part of town where the clubs and bistros were located. A ship with five thousand sailors can increase the nighttime population of any town, even one the size of Toulon. Business was good that night, and the French customers mingled eagerly with the FID sailors. All of our guys were behaving well, nobody was making too much noise or creating any problems.

When our party of twelve or thirteen older guys walked down the street, the sailors would see the skipper and ask him to join them for a drink. It reminded me of the way kids will clamor around a favorite teacher on the playground in grade school. The sailors loved Captain

Louis. He made them happy. A tall guy with silver hair, straight posture, shoulders back, almost always smiling, and with a ready joke for any sailor, he just made them like him. The captain's affection for his sailors was obvious, as was theirs for him.

"Hey, look. There's the skipper!" Five or ten of them would run out of the bar to shake his hand, and out of courtesy the hand of whoever was standing near him.

They wanted to introduce him to their new French friends, or to show him some curious thing in a shop or restaurant. Ten or eleven separate sailors offered to buy the skipper a drink that night, but he had to refuse them all since we were going to get under way the next morning. He always called people "shipmate."

"No, shipmate, thanks. You might have had enough tonight, too!" Laughs all around. I don't think we ran into a drunk guy that night, but the captain made little jokes with everybody about how much they'd had to drink. Everybody laughed at the jokes, but they knew they were being reminded not to overdo it.

By this time it was well past midnight, and the rest of us department heads wanted to get back to the ship. We wanted to make sure everything was OK in the departments and, for God's sake, get some sleep. The skipper was reveling in the company of his sailors, though. He had allowed liberty to continue until 0200 for second class petty officers and a little later (but not overnight) for first class petty officers and chiefs, so there were still a lot of sailors in town for him to mingle with. The rest of us were tired as hell, and we were hoping he'd finally run out of gas. Finally, a little after 0100, the captain decided to go back to the ship. I noticed he was sniffling, and a lot of the sailors we'd seen had been blowing their noses. It was still a little drizzly, but it wasn't raining.

It was pretty cold when we finally got back to the gig, and we noticed that the boat crew had the lid off the engine. Ed DeMaestri was there with them, looking a little bit flustered. The gig wouldn't start. It was 0130, we were all tired, and the ship was getting under way the next day. Ed had radioed back to the ship half an hour ago for a new battery, and it was reportedly on the way. Ed mumbled some kind of an apology to the captain, who just chuckled and made a halfhearted joke about it, but then we all just sat down on benches and waited for the new battery.

By the time we got back to the ship it was well past 0200, and we were due to get under way early the next morning. It had been a great port call. We were going to see more of France during the cruise, with port calls in Marseilles and Cannes, and just like the rest of the crew, I was looking forward to it.

On the way back to my stateroom, I passed by the ER and was sorry to see there were four or five guys standing around to be seen. They were all wiping their noses, and a couple of them were coughing. George McDonough was on duty, so I stopped in to help him.

"Seeing a lot of respiratory symptoms, Captain."

"Mostly just congestion?"

"No, a fair amount of bronchitis and a lot of systemic symptoms. It looks a lot like the flu to me."

Looking at the medical department logs, I noticed that more and more guys had come in with symptoms of sore throat, nasal congestion, or bronchitis that day. The "Toulon crud" was arriving. In sick call a couple of mornings later, we had over a hundred guys with a symptom complex that was going to be with us for the next three or four weeks. The symptoms were a raspy and slightly painful cough, not a lot of phlegm, usually some congestion of the ears and nose, but most especially a general sensation of fatigue. About a third of the cases had sore muscles and a low fever, seldom over 100 degrees.

On the first week out of Toulon, we saw two or three hundred cases of this illness in sick call. We knew by taking surveys on the ship that over six hundred people had symptoms of at least a mild degree but not bad enough to seek treatment. Only 65 guys had fevers, and a little over 120 had sore muscles. Over the course of the next two or three weeks, fewer than a hundred had to miss any work because of illness. During that entire month, we didn't have a single case of pneumonia as a complication, but fifteen guys had to be admitted to the ward so we could keep their hydration up and look after them.

It was the right time of year for influenza, which was also going around Europe at about that time. We weren't able to get immunologic studies to determine the agent of the Toulon crud. However, if this was the influenza, having no pneumonia and only fifteen guys who required admission was the best proof you could ask for the value of the vaccine. Left unchecked, influenza could devastate a closed population of five thousand people locked together on a ship. Even counting the people who had mild symptoms and didn't come for treatment, fewer than 20 percent of the ship caught the crud. The shots helped.

Sweetcakes Barnes, the Red Rotator

Admiral Barnes had voluntarily been one of the first guys to get his flu shot, which I had greatly appreciated at the time. When he got the crud, I made it a point to go up and see him every day in his cabin, almost feeling guilty that he even caught it.

Sweetcakes Barnes was called the "Red Rotator" by people who had worked for him before and by some of the senior officers in the ship's company. A man with an immense capacity for facts and details, he got his nickname because of his hair color and for his reputation for spinning up action from the people who worked for him. As the ship's doctor I never saw that. Sweetcakes always went to church services on Sundays, where he made it a point to meet everybody on the fo'c'sle. He had an outgoing personality and a ready smile. Admiral Barnes's staff didn't invite the medical department to their morning meetings like Admiral Kohl's staff had, so I didn't get to know Sweetcakes as well as I did Sniffles. I liked him as much for what I knew of his background as I did for his friendly personality, though.

Admiral Barnes had started out as a NavCad, a Navy cadet. Years ago, when the Navy really needed pilots, young hotshots could go down to the Navy recruiter and apply for flight training. If they passed all the IQ and physical tests, they could get into flight training, but as cadets, not commissioned officers. Those who washed out of aviation training simply became sailors. Without a college degree, most weren't likely to have very successful military careers, and when their flying days ended they usually didn't go very far—except for a few of them, like Sweetcakes, who went ahead and finished college.

I always enjoyed speaking with aviators about their flying experiences and training. Sweetcakes kind of looked out toward the distance, although we were sitting in some small room, and said, "Yeah, that was quite an adventure for a young man. I liked it a lot." He flew A-4 Skyhawks for a while, and during the late sixties he switched over to the A-6 Intruder, which was becoming more and more important for naval air warfare. He must have been recognized as a promising young officer, because the Navy sent him to college for a engineering degree in 1969. When he returned to flying, some flight surgeon noticed that Sweetcakes needed glasses, so he switched over from pilot to BN. That was kind of an unusual transition, since most pilots in that situation just take up some other kind of specialty, such as aircraft maintenance, intelligence, or operations. I was always fascinated by his ability to make that transition. He obviously did it well, too, because he became not only a squadron CO but a wing commander and a very successful flag officer.

When Admiral Barnes healed up after a few days, I was much relieved.

About the second day out of Toulon, Bob Willmore asked me to see a quartermaster who had been in twice that day. He came in for sick call because of pain in his abdomen after he fell down a ladder. Bob couldn't find anything wrong on examination and thought he'd reassured the sailor. He came back around noontime, saying he'd been a little bit nauseated and didn't feel like he could work. Once again, Bob found his examination normal. The quartermaster was a pretty squared-away guy, but he had kind of a long, sad face. Bob was troubled about the story, so he asked me to examine him, also.

"Good afternoon, Petty Officer Wolff, I'm Dr. Riley. What's the problem?"

"I still have this pain right here in the middle of my stomach, Doctor." He pointed just to a place well above the belly button, a little bit off to the left—not where the spleen is, usually. He wasn't tender there. I began poking gently, and pushed harder, watching his face to see his reaction. Usually, with real tenderness, the patient will wince, hiccough, or something, to give you some sign of the real pain they're having. He showed no sign of discomfort.

"Does that hurt?"

"Yeah, that's pretty uncomfortable, Doc." When the patient's report and his facial expressions don't match, the doctor is usually concerned.

I was a little concerned, but I really didn't think anything was wrong. Even so, we had to take abdominal complaints pretty seriously. It took us an hour to get X rays and lab tests done. By then he said his abdomen was more tender, but his examination remained normal. This just didn't fit, and I found myself getting a little bit suspicious about whether this was a guy who just wanted some time off from work. I think I was a little bit snappy with him.

"Petty Officer Wolff, everything looks normal. If there were any damage inside your abdomen, it ought to show up on either the examination, the lab tests, or the X ray. Why don't you go lie down for a couple of hours and check back with us after dinner? Don't take any solid foods, and let me have a look at you around 1830, all right?"

That sounded OK to him. That was another reason for me to worry. Usually a sailor who's looking for a way out of work wouldn't be satisfied if you told him you thought he was going to be all right and asked him to check back later. He'd usually want you to write a note to his chief or admit him to the ward. Wolff was cooperative at all points and just looked a little bit sad.

Van Hardy was out in the passageway, so I nabbed him then to talk over the case.

"I sent him back to his rack to check with us in a few hours, Van, but I wonder if we should tap his abdomen."

Van was so much easier to talk to than Rock had been. "No, I think you did the right thing. If he has normal bowel sounds and his abdomen isn't rigid, you can watch him for a while."

"Well, I really don't think this is anything serious, but I'm a little worried about him. Do you have time to see this guy now?"

I don't think Van ever said no the whole time he was on the ship. He didn't find anything different on examination, either. However, Van said he could have a perforated viscous.

"Without any rebound? Without a rigid abdomen?"

"I've seen that sometimes," Van said. He agreed, though, that we didn't need to tap the guy right away, but should watch him for another couple of hours.

Wolff was still tender after dinner, though. "Are you having any nausea?" I asked. He wasn't.

It was getting to be nighttime, and the guy was still tender. We repeated his X ray, and it was still normal. Even so, Van thought we should tap his abdomen.

We found blood in the abdomen, so we had to operate. I trudged up to talk it over with the captain. Like Captain Guitar, Captain Louis was always behind us. He never hassled me when I told him we needed to operate.

To my surprise, Van found a perforation in the proximal ileum! It was a contusion that opened a tiny window into the small intestine. When Petty Officer Wolff fell against the brace on the ladderwell, it hit that part of the abdomen just enough to bruise and tear the ileum at that point. The reason his symptoms were so mild was that there had been no significant blood loss and only microscopic leaks of intestinal juices. A tear in the bowel would usually make a person much sicker than Wolff had been. The peculiar combination of circumstances could have continued to hide this injury from us until it gradually reached a dangerous stage. It scared me to realize that in doubting the severity of his symptoms I could have let him get much worse. Van was able to repair the perforation without an ileostomy, and the sailor healed up fine in a week or so, but for the rest of the cruise I was a little sheepish every time I saw him because I'd doubted his symptoms.

While the Toulon visit had been good for the crew, as I'd hoped, the crud played itself out pretty slowly over the next four weeks. We didn't let it dampen our spirits, though. We didn't have time. Thanksgiving was coming, then a short visit to Naples, and in the first week of December the president would come aboard.

One morning after sick call, Bob Willmore asked me to see a patient. "I think you've seen him before, Dr. Riley. He's got some kind of attacks. He went to see the psychiatrist for them back in Jax and just flew out to the ship this week."

"Oh, Tommy Cage," I guessed. I had grown fond of him, so it would be good to see him and check his progress. When Bob brought him into the office, though, I almost gasped. How could we have missed it! The man was gaunt. He had a tiny little tremor, bulging eyeballs, and his now-thin skin was a little moist. His pulse was around 105. He was the most florid example of thyrotoxicosis I'd ever seen, certainly the most florid case I'd ever missed! To think I had called his problem panic attacks!

I tried to stay calm as I greeted him, but I don't think it worked. "Petty Officer Cage, have you lost some weight since I saw you a couple of months ago?"

"Oh, yes, Sir. My wife noticed it, too."

While we talked I leafed through his health record. It didn't comfort me too much to note that several of us didn't make the diagnosis of his thyroid disorder. We had at least checked screening levels for two thyroid hormones twice. He was florid now, though, and this condition could be fatal. We should have been seeing him more often. Then he told me he'd just come back to the ship this week. He'd been back in Jacksonville for the last month, and several doctors had seen him for months. How he reached this stage before we recognized his condition still puzzles me.

We went to Naples for a couple of days at the end of November, so we sent PH1 Cage to the NH Naples, where they started his treatment and sent him home to recover.

While we were in Naples, I paid a preemptive visit to Bullis Butts, the CO of the hospital. Remembering last year's visit, I decided it would be a lot easier for me to visit him this time. To my surprise, the visit went so well that I invited him and his wife, along with Capt. Gil Paseo, the Sixth Fleet surgeon, to come to dinner on the ship when we would return in January.

That morning on the ship there was a message from Cdr. Jesse Hill at AIRLANT that I should call him as soon as I could get to a telephone, so they let me use one at the hospital.

"Captain, I'm sorry to tell you this," Jesse said after the requisite opening pleasantries, "but it looks like SK3 Womple has a malignant tumor on his scrotum, and he's going to need an amputation."

My heart sank. Poor Arden. Why couldn't we have been more gentle with him, I thought. But I hadn't heard the worst yet . . .

"He says he went to see you about it and you told him it was nothing."

What!?

"He says he was doing a lot of sit-ups because you were harassing him about his weight. When he showed you the mass on his scrotum, he says you told him it was just new muscle tissue."

I immediately hung up and called NH Jacksonville. The surgeon there said, "Yup, we biopsied the mass and it was a sarcoma, but we sent him up to Charleston for oncology. Do you remember how big the mass was when you examined him?"

"I never examined him. I try not to treat the guys who work for me. You probably noticed there was no note from me in his chart."

"Well, that's part of the problem. He says some people from the ship tore out parts of his health record to protect themselves."

I was beginning to lose part of my sympathy for Arden. How could we have tampered with his record? It stayed with him when he left the ship before we deployed.

We had to get under way the next day, so I couldn't track it down any further for a couple of weeks. It worried me every day, though.

Once we got under way, planning for the president's visit dominated every moment outside of flight ops. The visit affected everybody a little differently. All the young guys wanted to see the president and maybe get their faces on the news back home. All the aviators were basking in the arrival of the first president who had been a carrier pilot. The captain was probably going to escort him around. It was fun for all of them. For us department heads and the XO, though, it was another story. We had hoops to jump through and official inquiries to write.

If we ever thought conventional VIP visitors required our attention, they paled by comparison to a presidential advanced party. As demanding as some of the younger staffers could be—and the younger they were, the bossier they were—they were simply cherubic compared to the press. One well-known network anchorwoman stepped off the H-3 with an open umbrella, which she had been told was very dangerous and strictly forbidden on the flight deck. She was wearing high-heeled shoes, which the press had also been warned would be dangerous on the ship. Kevin Millet was assigned to escort her. When she tripped leaving the helo, Kevin asked, "Do you have a pair of flats?"

She retorted, "No. Do you have a pair of heels?"

It may be that the staff caused more excitement about this than the White House, though. Here we were in the Mediterranean with just a couple of weeks to plan for the president's visit, flying jets off the deck every day, and our CO, XO, and SuppO had to answer a new question every day about the size and tint of the red carpet. Thirty-six inches isn't wide enough. No, not crimson. Red. No, thirty feet isn't long enough, has to be forty or more.

Then there had to be rehearsal after rehearsal for the president's arrival. Was it a visit or a coronation, I started to wonder.

Finally, after the long wait, the day arrived. In the back of my mind I remained troubled about Petty Officer Womple, but like everybody else I was excited about having the president on board.

President Bush had been the pilot of the huge TBM Avenger torpedo bomber when he was a very young man. Before giving us a speech, he went down to the mess decks to have an uninterrupted lunch with the enlisted guys. They locked the place up. Just George Bush, the sailors and Captain Louis. They tell me he enjoyed it even more than the sailors. He took off his jacket, rolled up his sleeves, and relaxed. He stayed forty-five minutes longer than scheduled, so somebody from his staff had to go down to get him.

When he came to talk to us in the hangar bay, he called us "fellow Navy men" and used words like "grape" and "midrats." He said the ship looked good, but added tartly that he still could recognize "the smell of new paint." Oh, we loved him. Even though I'm an old-fashioned New Deal Democrat, that day I loved George Bush as much as everyone else. When he walked through the hangar after his talk, I stretched out as far as I could to shake his hand. Every day I still wear the presidential tie bar his medical staff gave me when we worked together.

After the president and the press left, the glow lingered for a few days for most of us. What he and the premier had worked out transformed our world, and we on *Forrestal* felt that our ship had played a big role in it for years, and most especially that week.

The glow wasn't as bright for me. One of my corpsmen was about to lose his privates to a cancer I may have failed to find, and he was accusing me of neglecting it.

We were steaming to the island of Majorca for a port call in a couple of days while I read the request for a quality assurance investigation about Womple's arm. Rob Emerson and Van Hardy were trying to cheer me up.

"Captain, everybody knows you have a policy that the other doctors are supposed to treat members of the department," Rob told me. "Our medical records will stand up to anybody. Nobody took anything out of that record."

Warrant Officer Lucy came in just then with a stack of bills the ship's secretary had sent us. It seems that NH Naples was putting people in local hotels at a cost of around $180 per day, rather than admitting them. "They say these guys can be treated outpatient," George explained. Tommy Cage was one of the patients. The bills totaled over $3,000, and the ship had to pay them.

"Mr. Lucy, can you compare this to what happens to our guys if they go to Rota?"

"I already have, Sir," he said with a coordinated flex of his right thigh and right forearm that reminded me of a classic Charles Atlas photo. "No charge. In Rota they usually admit them or put them up in the barracks."

"We also get nice discharge summaries from Rota, and either nothing or sloppy, handwritten notes from the docs in Naples," Van added.

"Arrogant, too," Rob reminded us about Naples.

Palma

As soon as we got to Palma, I went straight to a phone to call Jesse Hill. "Anything new on Womple's tumor, Commander?"

"Maybe some good news, Captain," Jesse answered. "It may be a benign tumor. They say Womple wants an operation, but the docs say it may not be so bad."

Apparently, Womple first showed the lump to his psychiatrist at NH Jacksonville. The psychiatrist called one of the general surgeons to do a needle biopsy. The pathologist called it a malignant fibrous sarcoma, and the doctors told Womple it was a very malignant cancer, that he would lose the whole scrotum and still maybe not survive. They sent him immediately to the oncologist at Charleston. Since the radiation unit at Charleston was under repair, Womple was sent to NH Philadelphia, where the pathologists and oncologists thought the mass was a benign tumor called a teratoma and had probably been present for fifteen or twenty years, maybe his whole life.

Womple was so angry that he called his congressman and forced the doctors at Philadelphia to send him to the Army hospital in Pittsburgh, where the pathologists and oncologists reached the same conclusion. Inquiries from Arden's congressman and lawyer finally forced a repeat of the biopsy, which supported the later finding. They told him to ignore the mass because it would never bother him, whereas cutting it out could require amputating his scrotum and penis. Arden said he wanted it cut out anyway. The doctors refused and tried to discharge him from the hospital, but he wouldn't budge for a few weeks.

Finally, one day I was able to reach Dr. W. Hudson Barney, the orthopedic urologist in Pittsburgh who was treating Womple. His tribulations with Arden seemed to have been as difficult and lengthy as mine. He said the tumor was benign and didn't need to be cut out.

While a part of the guilt and worry were off my shoulders, I was still concerned. What if Arden could eventually find somebody to cut his tumor out? What could we have done earlier to give Arden more than the hope of a malignant cancer to make him feel important?

The next day, Father Steve Lynch and I went on a tour of the island, including the abbey where Chopin and George Sand lived. That night some of the crew bought tickets for dinner at a big tourist nightclub. I was sitting with the captain and some other old guys over in one corner, laughing and relaxing as we recalled the work of the last month. A patch of red hair off to the left caught my attention. It was Billy Dorsey . . . and there was a bottle of wine in front of him.

"Airman Dorsey," I said with as much supportive enthusiasm as I could muster. "Good to see you!"

Billy kind of looked down. At any rate, no eye contact. He just mumbled a quiet, inarticulate hello.

"How did Level II go?" I asked him.

"OK."

"You better not be drinking, do you think?"

"I can do what I want here. I'm not on restriction. You're not in charge of me."

His tablemates didn't seem like long-time acquaintances, but they also seemed a little defiant. "If you guys are real shipmates, you won't let him drink tonight." They all just shrugged. I didn't want to make a scene for Billy in front of the captain, so I left him alone then and decided I'd talk to his chief or DivO in the morning.

As the evening wore one, Billy grew more effusive. Every time he saw me looking at him from across the room, he toasted me with his wineglass and took a big gulp.

When we left, Billy was passed out on his table. Only one of his new buddies was still there. He and I carried Billy back to the bus.

The next week we sent him to rehab again.

Chapter 14

End of the Tour

Shortly after we left Palma we had another boxing smoker. For this one we hosted a team from one of the cruisers in the battle group. Their skipper came over, so Admiral Barnes and our chief of staff, Captain Lane, attended. The captain was always present for the boxing. Lieutenant Gines's training was starting to bring about a little improvement in our guys, and they had a little better showing than the other team. One of our guys, Bos'n's Mate Woods, was turning into a pretty poised heavyweight.

Somehow, George Lucy talked Gines into allowing a comic wrestling demonstration with the Red Pharaoh and some hapless volunteer dressed up in cowboy gear. George wore his professional Red Pharaoh outfit: red leopard leotard tights, a skintight red spandex tank top, and a red silk head and face mask.

I wondered if anybody would recognize who the Pharaoh was, and when he started prancing and flexing his well-formed muscles, everybody knew instantly. Suddenly, the context for his familiar muscle flexing was evident. Prancing around the ring with his high steps, he flexed one arm, then both, turned this way and that to ripple his muscles for the audience. Same as in professional wrestling on TV, but it didn't seem as funny or as entertaining here.

Then it got gruesome. The Red Pharaoh reached around one corner of the ring and brought out two pies, one whipped cream and one blueberry. A thousand spectators suddenly realized the tragedy that was inevitable at this point. Oh, why didn't the Red Pharaoh just stop? Or maybe couldn't time just skip ahead about twenty minutes and leave this out? The Pharaoh awkwardly stalked the hapless cowboy around and around the ring too darned many times, his hands holding the pies above his head. The cowboy . . . the *cowboy* was supposed to be the stooge! They

275

knew that, they'd allegedly even practiced it. We all cried out internally, "Please don't!" But sure enough, the whipped cream pie hit the visiting CO right on his shiny black shoes, and the tragic blueberry pie splattered across the faces and chests of the admiral and Captain Louis.

It was so quiet.

Should've been funny, you know. Blueberry pie right in the admiral's kisser . . .

The admiral just got up quietly and went away. Captain Louis pointed to Lieutenant Gines, who ushered the Red Pharaoh away. The rest of us just looked down at our shoes until the boxing started back up.

We arrived in Marseilles two days before Christmas, ready for a long port call and the holiday season. We were still basking in the fun and warmth of the president's visit, and although we'd been busy, the last three weeks hadn't been overwhelming. Everyone was looking forward to plenty of rest, some sightseeing tours, and, for many, trips to Paris. Some had arranged, as I had, for their families to fly over to meet them at Christmastime.

Marseilles lived up to all of our expectations. It was winter, after all, not the time you expect to come to the Riviera for a holiday, yet the Christmas and New Year's weeks in Marseilles are at least as balmy as they are in Jacksonville. In fact, there was snow that week in Jacksonville, while in Marseilles the temperature ranged from forty-five to sixty-five degrees. The commercial harbor in Marseilles is deep and huge. We tied up right on the pier, so sailors could come and go without boating, just like in Mayport, but here there were buses that could take them straight into town or to the picturesque "old harbor," full of sailboats, brasseries, bakeries, and shops.

The day after Christmas, the MWR department had arranged a bus tour of some of the picturesque landscape and countryside around Aix, including some of the vintners and a few historic caves. I arranged to have the day off so I could take my family on the tour. Two hours before the trip, though, the XO called me to his office. A FID sailor had been murdered the night before, and the XO wanted me to coordinate the investigation with the local coroner. "Doc, they're going to do an autopsy this morning, and the captain wants you to be there."

My initial reaction was that the skipper and the XO didn't realize how high French medical standards are. To think I would have anything to add to the work of a skilled forensic pathologist was naive. (I also wanted to go on that trip.) This was one of the few times I was circumspect enough to keep my mouth shut and listen to the XO, though. "You speak French, don't you, Doc?"

"Yes, but not well enough to follow complicated medical studies like a postmortem."

"We know that, Doc, but there are no other American medical reps in town. If this should later have any important ramifications—FBI, NIS [Naval Investigative Service], national security—we need to be sure there's a member of the service there. Didn't you tell me you studied pathology and even did autopsies for a while?"

"Well, yes, XO, but that was almost twenty years ago . . ." Reluctantly, I was beginning to understand that the XO was right. I needed to be there.

So I sent Ann and my daughters off to the tour, where they had a great day. I learned all I could about the murder before I went over to the city morgue for the autopsy. The victim, though an American sailor, had been raised in Sierra Leone, and he had friends who had come to the growing Sierra Leone community in Marseilles when he went to the States. Sitting in a bar with his countrymen that night, he was mistaken for a local drug dealer and shot dead in the back with two shotgun blasts.

Launching an A-6 from the Thunderbolts. I am the "shooter"—launching officer—in this shot. The red cross on the cranial is worn by all members of the medical department on the flight deck. *Courtesy of Lt. Cdr. Ron Eslinger*

My French, it turned out, was entirely adequate for the autopsy. The forensic pathologist's techniques were almost identical to those I'd learned back at the University of Missouri. In fact, during the procedure, when it was difficult to find the precise mechanism of death, I found the pellets and aortic tears that had killed him. One can't say that we "enjoyed" working together, I guess. Notwithstanding the ugly circumstances, however, my French colleagues and I recognized that we had shared a meaningful day's work.

When I gave the XO my report about the autopsy, it was evident as usual that he couldn't wait for the talking to stop so he could get on with some other work, but naturally he wanted a written report first thing the next morning.

"By the way, Doc, how come it costs so much for our guys to be treated at the Navy hospital in Naples?"

"It's a little convoluted and complicated, XO. Some of it has to do with lack of barrack space in Naples, and some of it has to do with command policies there. We have a plan—"

I was going to explain that we were going to try to send most of our consultations and transfers to Rota, but the XO broke in first, "Wouldn't it be better for us to send our guys over to Rota? With the log flights, I can get them there from any place in the Med usually."

"Good idea," I said. "Rota's got a beautiful new hospital, too." Well, that was good. Not only did I have the XO's backing for our new plan, but he thought it was his idea.

Even with the autopsy and the paperwork, I was able to take a week's leave with my family. We drove over to Monte Carlo, spent a couple of nights in Nice, and took the train up to spend New Year's Eve in Paris. It may have been winter, but it was still Paris. When I put them on the plane in Paris, the deployment was almost half over.

A few nights after we left Marseilles, Douglas Williams came to see me. He had been letting me look at his rhymes and ventilating a little. Without pushing him too much, I encouraged him to read some poetry we found in the ship's library, but he didn't like poetry that didn't rhyme or "have a beat," so I let him go at his own pace. He had been letting his blond hair grow a little longer, but he was keeping it combed. His appearance was better, and he was a little more positive.

"Doc, why do you suppose they make people who have other talents stay on the ship? You know I got friends back home who can't get a job, you know. They'd be glad to work. This isn't right for me, you know."

We talked about obligations, what Douglas's earlier expectations had been, what they were now.

"See, Doc, I got this agent back in Jacksonville. I think I got what it takes, you know, for like show business. I think I can make it in country western."

"Douglas, we'll be back in Jax in just about four months, man. If you start polishing up your material, you might be ready for a couple of bookings on the weekends when we get back."

That wasn't what Douglas had in mind, exactly. He pouted a little. "No, Doc, that ain't it." He didn't want to talk any more, so he left, shoulders hunched down a little.

A couple of weeks later we came to our next port call, the big industrial city of Valencia. No American carrier had been to Valencia for more than ten years. We heard the city was looking forward to our visit, but there were reports that the Greenpeace organization might picket us, alleging that we might have nuclear weapons aboard. Most of us didn't know whether we did or not, of course.

The port in Valencia seemed to me to be even larger than the one in Marseilles. They were both large enough for us to tie up right at the pier. When we pulled into the harbor, a few Greenpeace inflatable boats tried to block us, but the Spanish Navy and police gently guided them away.

People lined up by the thousands to see the ship, and we sold even more *Forrestal* ball caps than we did in New York City. Thousands of friendly Spaniards crowded up to see the ship and tried to meet Americans. Because of the reports of the Greenpeace demonstrations, though, we had to be careful. Extra shore patrolmen, Marines, and MAAs wandered up and down the pier, trying vainly to look inconspicuous and unconcerned.

Finally, on the third day in port, the protests started. A truck drove up in the parking lot with about half a dozen young people in the back. Two of them stood in the bed of the truck and started to give speeches—one in English and the other in Spanish—about nuclear weapons. Before they could finish two sentences, a squad of Spanish policemen appeared from nowhere, ripped their bullhorns away, and carted them off in a paddy wagon that materialized as mysteriously as the police had. Twenty other protestors suddenly appeared down by the fantail. They threw big balloons at the ship that burst open with fluorescent chartreuse and yellow stains. A bos'n's mate up on the catwalk drove the balloon painters away with a fire hose, knocking one of them down.

My worst fear was that an angry American sailor or Marine would punch one of the young protestors or strike someone with a club, thus aggravating a mob. Our guys had been well coached, though, and maintained an almost amused aloofness and calm. The Spaniards who had come to see the ship and meet the Americans were more angered by the protestors than we were.

On the third night in Valencia, I was awakened well past midnight by the OOD. A FID sailor was injured and had been brought to the university hospital downtown. There were no details at first; it might have been an auto accident. I had one of the corpsmen wake up Pablo Santez, the nurse commander who'd relieved Rob Emerson, to come down to the hospital with me and find out about the sailor. As usual, the ship had rented a handful of cars for official business during the port call, so we were able to drive down to the hospital. Pablo and I had been down to visit the hospital the day we arrived, something I liked to do in every port call. I was glad we knew the place already.

My impressions of Spanish medicine were already favorable from my visits to the small hospital in Benidorm over a year ago and the community hospital we'd visited in Palma a few months ago. The university hospital in Valencia was very impressive. The magnificent structure had wide hallways with pretty columns and sweeping stairwells, a proud grandeur just in the building. The main buildings of the medical school had been built in the thirties. There was a seven-foot bust of General Franco in the main entrance foyer of the medical school. We wandered down past the anatomy wing and some of the lecture halls, impressed all the way by how much cleaner and neater the surroundings were in this academic part of the institution than in most American universities.

To get to the ER, we had to go back out the other side of the wing we were in, cross a courtyard, and then step into a busy ward indistinguishable in every respect from an American ER. A clerk greeted us none too friendly and said something unenthusiastic. When Pablo smiled his characteristic smile and started to answer, a supervisor intervened. Even though I don't speak Spanish, I know the supervisor said, basically, "For God's sake, look at their uniforms! They're obviously here to see the American. Let them in!"

Our sailor was in a cubicle, his leg elevated in a traction splint. With the fracture immobilized, he had very little pain. He'd obviously been medicated, too. A friend was with him. They were a couple of guys from the air department. "Hey, Dr. Riley! We're glad to see you."

"Broke his leg, Doc," the friend said, in a classic recapitulation of the obvious.

When the doctor came to talk to us, it was clear that he was finishing a long shift from the preceding night. He had bags under his eyes and was sipping a cup of coffee. Very friendly, though. I probably didn't need Pablo as a translator—at least right then—because the doctor wanted to practice his English, which seemed to be at a level very near my own ability in French, which I considered pretty good.

"He has a mid-shaft femoral fracture, as you can see," he said as he showed us the X rays. "Did not break the skin and the bone is not . . ."

"Not comminuted, not shattered," I inserted.

"Yes, comminuted, thank you. It is not comminuted. Our orthopedists have seen him, and they say he can go back to the ship."

Back to the ship!

"Oh, I'm afraid you may not understand, we can't really treat him on the ship."

"But don't you have a surgeon? An operating room?"

This was kind of hard to explain. In absolute terms, or in wartime, all of the doctors on the ship could put a pin into or through the bone and place the femur in traction. The young man would probably heal with the treatment we could give, especially with Van's direction, at about a 90 percent cure rate. We could meet the standards of, say, 1955. However, if there would then ever be an emergency on the ship, we might not be able to get such a guy in traction off in a hurry, or into a survival raft. Besides, in this day and age, in peacetime, 90 percent was just not acceptable, especially since the patient was right here in a thoroughly competent university hospital with a full orthopedic department, which could give him definitive treatment and prepare him for proper transport over to NH Rota.

We discussed this with the ER doc, who seemed perplexed. When he learned that we had all those doctors on the ship, he wanted to know why we couldn't just put the pin in and keep him in traction on the ship? I did feel a little guilty, momentarily, when he asked me that, but I explained our concerns about safety and the importance of considering whether a sailor could escape in an emergency. OK, then we summoned the orthopedic doctor.

This doctor spoke even better English. He had studied in Cleveland and once toured an aircraft carrier. "But I've seen your departments on those ships. You have a good ward, no? I'll show your surgeon how to handle it." I explained again that we couldn't keep a guy on board who wouldn't be able to escape in an emergency. Like a footnote in my frustrated thinking, I reflected on how difficult it sometimes was to explain these same points even to our U.S. Navy doctors. The escape issue isn't so far-fetched, and it's something we never forget on the *Forrestal*. July 1967 had been vividly reinforced in all our minds with the fire just a couple of months ago.

The Spanish orthopedist wanted to go home. It had been a long night for him, too. "OK," he said, "we can set the thigh properly in a traction cast that will give him excellent, perfect stability. Then he will be safe to return to the ship, and moderate movement will not be a problem. After a month or two, if he is not healing well, you can reevaluate whether he will need an operation."

"Thank you, that is the most important, of course, to get him the treatment he needs. However, even if stabilized, if he has a cast, especially on a lower extremity, he wouldn't be able to escape in the event of an emergency!"

"Ah, escape! Now I understand." Finally.

We agreed that the orthopedic department at the hospital would treat him and we would arrange for him to be flown to NH Rota. The orthopedist went off to get some of the orthopedic residents and begin arranging for the case. I had to speak with one of the hospital administrators.

"How are you feeling, Airman?" I asked, as much to hear how sober he was at this point as to know the answer.

"Hey, great, Dr. Riley, considering how lucky we were!" He was absolutely sober, even with the pain medicine on board. I figured the alcohol must have worn off. By now we'd learned that he and his buddy were walking in town after dark and had been struck by a railroad locomotive on the tracks downtown. He apparently had been thrown to one side a distance of about twelve feet. To only break one thigh rather than be cut in half or lose a leg was remarkable. The buddy, too, had been thrown aside, but, remarkably, had only mild injuries.

I stood by while the patient called his parents so I could tell them what to expect, and Pablo went to an adjacent room to interview the friend. We were surprised to learn that these two young sailors had consumed no alcohol that day or that night. At first I was skeptical. How can a healthy young man be run over by a train in the middle of a clean city without being drunk . . . or deaf. Yet it was clear. There were witnesses who had seen them around town. The two were beginning to be offended by our questions about alcohol. They had *not* been drinking!

Eventually the sailor went to the OR, where they put a pin through the end of the femur, which was held in place in traction by a big cast that extended from his hips down to his ankle.

We came back the next day to arrange to transport the patient to the airport so he could fly to Rota. It seems that in Spain, ambulances are still independent, private businesses. They aren't owned by the hospital, although the hospital calls them. So the driver met us on the ward, and he knew immediately how to get to the medevac plane at the nearby airport. No problem. He wanted cash first, though. But our ship was going to pay the hospital, and the hospital would pay the driver.

No, not in Valencia. Cash first, in pesetas, please.

"But we don't have a way to do that." And the plane would be ready to leave shortly. "Wait here," I asked, and I ran off to make arrangements with the administrator. To avoid a confrontation, we were able to agree on a way for the hospital to pay the driver, but when we got back he was gone. He put out the word that this trip was not a cash deal, and none of the ambulance drivers in Valencia were willing to come. Finally the Spanish Navy arranged transportation for us, and we got our sailor to the plane two hours late.

When it was all over, the cost of excellent medical care, even if we had calculated a price for the airfare to Rota, was less than comparable treatment would have been in an American hospital, and much less than the various related and peripheral costs of treatment, lodging, and logistics at Naples.

After another week we were back in Naples. We had a rash of guys who needed outpatient evaluations by specialists, but, by prior arrangement, anybody who would need an operation or admission to hospital was going to fly to Rota.

On the sea and anchor detail, while pulling into the molo, our star boxer, BM3 Woods fractured his right ring finger across a joint surface. Burt Rosen escorted him over to the clinic at the hospital, and one of the orthopedists pulled them out of the line and scheduled Woods for an operation to pin the finger the next week, then a month of therapy in Naples.

When they got back to the ship, Rosen and Woods came to see me. If the big bos'n's mate was going to be off the ship for a month or two, he might as well be back in the States in his own home. It would cost us thousands of dollars to put him up in Naples. The only worry was that there was a narrow window of about four days during which the operation had to happen. If it were delayed beyond that, the likelihood of contractures and nonunion went way up. We discussed it with the patient, the XO, and the ATO. We knew we could carry it off, so I called over to the hospital and asked them to cancel the operation scheduled for four days hence. Less than five minutes later, the orthopedic surgeon was yelling at me on the phone. "If this guy doesn't get his operation in the time window, I'll see you get kicked out of the Medical Corps. Do you have any idea what you're doing!" My goodness, he was angry. I have to admit that it sometimes amuses me when other people—especially surgeons—get mad.

That evening, the Paseos and Buttses came for dinner and a tour of the ship, as we'd arranged a month ago. Hard as I tried to be the knowledgeable host, it became apparent even to me that Gil Paseo knew a lot more about aircraft carriers—this one included—than I did. Whenever I stammered or was uncertain about any question during the tour, he would gently, even unobtrusively, ask a kind of reminding sort of question that would hint to the answer that I could slip in. I began to appreciate some of the differences between him and Captain Butts, who never seemed to defer on any subject.

We ended our tour up on the flight deck. It was a classical Naples early spring evening. With shades of purple and yellow streaming over the harbor at dusk, Naples took on all the grand beauty that history intended. Looking across from our elevation to the evening traffic and building lights, and then to the dusky silhouette of Vesuvius, it felt as though the cool spring breeze had been ordered for the occasion. The careful angles and sweeps of the airplanes posed against this setting seemed surprisingly fitting. It was a very harmonious evening, and I was enjoying the company of our guests. They thanked me for the evening, and Mrs. Paseo surprised me with an invitation to bring a bunch of my guys to dinner a couple of days later.

A Quiet Evening in Napoli

Rob had departed back in Marseilles. Although I would miss him much, Lt. Cdr. Pablo Santez promised to leave his own colorful stamp on the department. So, for the dinner trip to the Paseos we had Pablo, George Lucy, Bill, Van, George McDonough, and Will White, our recently acquired temporary GMO. Dress was discussed a good deal that day. I requested ties and jackets, although one of the guys suggested that Navy people in Naples seemed to favor a more leisurely style. No, I said, we wouldn't be overdressed with a sportcoat, and coming to the home of a senior officer called for a level of decorum. So, the evening of the dinner, we all assembled at the quarterdeck for a drive to the other side of town, where we would watch the sunset from the Paseos' balcony.

After the brief ferry ride over to fleet landing, we turned to George Lucy, who was to have arranged for the van we'd drive over to the

Paseos' house. "Sir, we just go over to the beach guard office and sign up for it." My heart sank. Sign up? We were expected for dinner in less than an hour, and we were just going *now* to sign up? "No problem, Sir, there are plenty of vans."

We walked the two blocks over to the transport desk that the beach crew had set up. Nobody there. Warrant Officer Lucy walked the two blocks back to the main beach detachment office while we waited. When he returned ten minutes later, he showed us the keys with an attached license number and said, "It's a white Fiat, supposed to be out here on the back lot." Good, ready to go. We looked for about twelve minutes, beginning now to be concerned about being late for dinner. Finally I took the keys back to the main desk to tell them we just couldn't find the van.

"Doc, they're back over at the transport desk now. They were just out for dinner before. You'll have to check with them." Dinner break, eh? I was wondering if we were going to make it to dinner. "I don't know why he gave you those keys. That van's not even *around* here. What you have are the spare keys. The XO and some other guys have that van. We just don't have any transportation for you, Doc."

I looked at Lucy. "Mr. Lucy, I asked you to arrange for a vehicle for this two days ago." Deer in the headlights. Flex left shoulder, twitch chin to left.

He was going to remain stunned and paralyzed for the present, so I tried to negotiate. "Isn't there anything we can drive? We're late for an invitation from the head doctor on the Sixth Fleet staff. How about a supply vehicle?"

"Well, if you want, we have a cargo van, but there aren't any seats except the two in front." We had no choice.

Pablo volunteered to drive. He said, "Captain, you don't want to drive, and these people are like my people. I can get us there faster."

Will and George McDonough were a little hesitant to get in. No seats, no seat belts. Two wooden pallets on the deck, bits of cabbage, and little metal parts, like wing nuts and angle irons, rattling around in the dusty rear of the van.

Driving in Naples is like a bumper car concession in double speed. It would be a painful cacophony of horns and shouting if those noises weren't drowned out by worn-out mufflers and the sound of collisions. Add to that Pablo Santez, who, for all his personal charm, goes into a cinematic trance whenever there's a steering wheel in his hands. I guess he can't help it. It seems automatic whenever he drives, even in normal settings. His eyes take on a flaming glint, his left eyebrow rises, and his head jaunts forward just so. That day, the opportunity to enter the great Neapolitan traffic adventure overtook his very being, and Pablo became one with the passion. Darting a Lamborghini or Alfa Romeo in and out may be artistic, but such wizardry is wasted on a big commercial Toyota van.

In the back of the van, the young officers were being thrown around like dice in a cup. George McDonough was getting irritated. Bill, when he could catch his breath, called, "Pablo, can you make those turns a little more grad . . . [banged his head] ouch . . . more gradually!?" I looked back now and then to ask if the guys were OK. When their bodies were stationary enough for me to focus on a facial expression, I could see grim resolve on Van's and Will's faces. Those two always made the best of any situation. George McDonough and Bill were starting to get angry. Lucy was using this adventure as an opportunity to do some novel isometric contortions. He wedged a shoulder against one bulkhead and a knee against another and then tightened his muscles to anchor himself in.

"Pablo, maybe we ought to take it a little easier."

He made a characteristic, and I must say very winsome, shrug of his shoulders, turning both palms up. (Turning both palms up in this traffic melee, of course, left his hands off the wheel for a moment. That added a certain flair to the gesture, but a bit of anxiety for me. I was glad the guys in the back couldn't see it.) "Captain, there's nothing I can do about it. This is just Naples." Just then I felt the vehicle lurch to the left with a bang, and, looking back, I saw Will actually inverted bouncing off the left wall. Will's and George McDonough's Navy-blue blazers were beginning to get some dusty marks.

About this time, we departed the busy urban traffic and got to the outskirts near the Paseos' house. Now, however, the roads took on a romantic, almost sinusoidal curve pattern, going up and down the hills, back and forth from one valley to another. Evening was coming, casting beautiful shadows on the gnarled Italian trees and shrubs on these lovely hills. Pablo hopelessly succumbed to the devil inside him, which made him attack the curving, narrow roads as if in a grand prix or a James Bond movie. Now it wasn't quite as rough as it had been in the heavy traffic, but, in this big van, I saw the tires bite tauntingly over the edge of the cliff now and then. The undulating turns rolled the guys around in the back more than before, and I thought they might be getting sick. Also, we were climbing at a pretty steep angle. Suddenly the back door popped open from their weight against it. Van slid out, hanging onto the wooden pallet as his feet dangled out. George McDonough or Will vomited, somehow missing Van with the load.

"Stop, Pablo, they're falling out," I told him.

"They're just teasing you, Captain."

"Pablo, I'm not kidding."

About that time a big dog—it looked like a cross between a police dog and a retriever—started chasing us. At first it was barking at Van's dangling legs, then it caught up and jumped into the open back door. George Lucy reached back to try to pull Van in, but when he did that the other wooden pallet slid out to the road, knocking Van's left hand loose. The dog leapt up to the front, barking loudly, as though enjoying this immensely. It took a sudden interest in Pablo, jumped up to his lap, and wedged against the steering wheel just as we entered another sharp bend in the climbing road.

With the door flapping in the back and the dog barking into my left ear, I couldn't hear the conversation very well, but it sounded like George Lucy was calling some instructions to Van. Suddenly the van lurched forward a little faster, and then Pablo finally threw on the brakes.

Looking back, I saw what had happened. Following Lucy's advice, Van fell out, followed by Warrant Officer Lucy. Seeing that in the rearview mirror, Pablo slammed on the brakes, breaking the windshield when he slammed forward. On the hill behind us was the record of our accomplishments. A quarter mile back were the splintered remains of the wooden pallet. Stalled behind it was a small collection of traffic. The pallet had fallen into the grill of a truck full of dogs. I still don't know if it was a dogcatcher or what, but about twenty dogs of various sizes were running all over the neighborhood. Two tiny little terriers and a lumbering, big sheep dog were now coming up to meet their scout friend from our vehicle, who in turn was now running down to give them a report. They were all yelping and barking excitedly. Assorted motorists were yelling and making Neapolitan gestures behind the blocked truck.

Van was back there fifty yards or so, somehow being his unflappable gentlemanly self, now with holes in the knees of his trousers and not-quite-tattered sportcoat. He was dusting off his sleeves as though there had merely been a spilled saltshaker. Somebody else vomited again out the back.

Oblivious to the entire scene, Pablo looked at the map in his hand and said, "We're almost there. Just two more blocks." Everybody filed back in without a comment, and we drove up to the Paseos' villa.

Gil greeted us warmly at the front door, in an open-collar shirt and short sleeves. "Oh, you guys didn't have to dress up to come over here. I told you 'casual.'" The five guys from the back of the van glanced down at their variously dusty, rumpled, or torn sportcoats. They all made prim little smiles and then menacingly made eye contact with me one at a time.

"I hope you had no trouble finding the place or getting here," Mrs. Paseo said.

"No, none at all," Pablo told her. "It was a lovely drive."

The evening at the Paseos' home was wonderful. Mrs. Paseo is an accomplished linguist and, like her husband, is conversant in a wide range of literary and artistic subjects. Everybody truly enjoyed the conversation and an elegant meal. Of course, knowing that a trip back to the pier in that van would come next, they could have enjoyed a night in Newark.

Thanking our host and hostess on my way out the door, I was handed an envelope by the captain. "This is from Bullis Butts. Don't read it until you get back to the ship."

Van offered to drive back.

Before Pablo could protest, George McDonough and Bill Kelly hooked his elbows and threw him in the back.

Back at the ship, I opened the letter from Butts. It was handwritten, and on the surface simply a collegial letter of advice. "In these troubling times," he wrote, "we always have to be concerned about the costs of medical care." Then he talked of the line dividing quality care for our patients from fiscal constraints. In the case of BM3 Woods, Butts said, "I think you crossed that line." He understood the need to "satisfy your XO," but it would be wrong to let "a few bucks" get in the way of treatment for a patient. He closed by saying he was worried for my career if I kept making patient judgments based on cost.

At first I was infuriated by the letter. He had clearly not understood anything of what I had told him and seemed not to understand the way his doctors acted toward the patients and the rest of us. Was the hospital there to serve the fleet, or was it the other way around?

Gradually, I grew more philosophical. It was at the least considerate of him to take the time to give me what he considered good advice and warning. Finally, I just let it go. I thought that Dr. Butts and his orthopedists had no idea what the needs of the fleet were, and no real grasp of the situation for BM3 Woods, either. They were just in a different navy. I threw his letter away and forgot about it.

A couple of weeks later, just after flight ops ended, Van and I were inspecting some of the gear in the OR when the 1-MC called "Medical emergency. Medical emergency. Engine Room Two." Van ran to his post in the

ER, and I ran out to the port side passageway and aft to the special doors down to the engineering spaces, about halfway to the wardroom.

In the engine room, back on one of the grated false decks in behind the top of a stack of pipes and machinery, a gaggle of snipes in blue coveralls were standing around a guy blond on his back. None of them were kneeling, though, like people usually do around a fallen person. As I ran up closer, I could see why. He was having a seizure. Seizures frighten and confuse onlookers. They often stand by more as sentinels, rather than touching the patient the way they might for other conditions. Which is just as well, since there's not much a layperson can or should do until the seizure stops, anyway.

At first I couldn't see the person's face, but I saw the arms and legs shaking. This would be a pretty long grand mal seizure, I thought. Allowing for the alarm, the announcement, and my response, it had probably been five minutes or more.

When the witnesses saw me, they stepped back and uncovered the patient. It was Douglas Williams, the unhappy would-be country star. Above him there was an open high-power junction box, but there was no toolbox nearby.

Douglas's seizure was not a typical tonic-clonic convulsion. He looked more like a fluttering catfish on the bank. His hands and wrists were slapping up and down, a little bit like he was slapping out a rhythm on the grate. His knees and heels were kicking up and down, but reciprocally, not synchronously: right, left, right, left. His eyes weren't just closed, they were clenched, and yet his face was expressionless.

Speaking loudly, so Douglas would know I was there, I asked, "Who saw it happen?"

"I did!" one of the frightened sailors said. "He just walked right up to that junction box and stuck his hand right on those wires. I'm telling you he did it on purpose sure as hell. There's something like 400 volts in that thing, Doc. He works with electricity. Knew what he was doing. Did it on purpose!"

Douglas's right eye opened for an instant, and I thought the shaking paused briefly while I caught him glancing at me.

"All right, everybody, he's going to be OK. You guys leave us here for now." Just then a couple of corpsmen arrived.

I kneeled down to be close to him. "You can stop now, Douglas. This is not a convulsion," I said as quietly as one could say anything in the ninety-decibel engine room.

SN Williams stopped shaking, but his eyes stayed clenched.

"You're fine, Douglas. It's over now. I'm a neurologist, shipmate, and

I can tell this is a fake." He stuck to his performance, but his eyes opened.

"Where am I?" he asked, as naively as if in a B-movie script, I thought. "Who are you?" he asked slowly and sluggishly, although he had seen me daily for the past several weeks.

While I examined him for any trauma and checked his vital signs and his neck, I asked HM3 Brooks to have somebody from E Division come to check the junction box. Douglas was fine. He was still acting groggy, but not shaking.

"There aren't any lines connected to that box at all, Captain," said the electrician's mate chief who came to check it. "No telling how long it's been unhooked, but it doesn't even show on the current diagrams." Only an electrician could have known that.

"Did you put your hand in that box to kill yourself, Williams?" his DivO asked just then.

Williams's stupor appeared to worsen momentarily, and he nodded yes slowly.

"Well, since there's no juice in the box, we know you didn't get shocked, and I can tell the seizure is a fake, so let's go on back to medical, OK, Douglas?" I suggested.

"Not . . . fake . . . really tried . . . ," Douglas haltingly groaned out. When we tried to help him to his feet, he swooned and flailed out his arms. I didn't think Douglas was a very skillful thespian, but I was afraid that in his acting out he might injure himself or somebody else, so we brought him up to medical in a litter.

The electricians verified that there was no power to the box. Douglas had no burns on his hands or his shoes. As the night went on, his speech was inconsistently telegraphic, but he continued trying, as I saw it, to convey a slowly recovering encephalopathy.

As hokey as we thought it was, we had to be as careful with this apparently fake suicide attempt as we would with a more sincere one. I went down to see the XO to plan to fly Douglas off as soon as we could.

"But that's just what he wants, Doc!" the CHENG said. He was right, of course. Douglas probably wanted to hurry back to Jacksonville to the country music career he thought was waiting for him.

"This is as clear a case of malingering as you can get," the lawyer said. We could do a summary court-martial.

"What if he raises the ante next time?" I asked. "Whether he's faking or not, the next time he might really hurt himself, or even really die trying to convince us."

The XO agreed. Douglas's apparent performance was a little sillier, a little more flagrant, than most, but the majority of our suicide gestures were just acting out. They were usually pitiful scratches on the left wrist that didn't even draw much blood, and they were usually made by some of the more immature troublemakers. I was becoming convinced that this was a different phenomenon from the rising numbers of suicides among young males in American society. These futile threats differed in degree and in the entire setting, and yet the whole spectrum, from the feeble gestures to the real suicides, had something in common. The pernicious and growing respectability or acceptability of the idea of suicide was somehow at the base of both. At any rate, they all had to be dealt with surely and safely. If Williams—or any other sailor—felt his first attempt didn't win our attention, if this was how he wanted to win it, the next try might be worse.

That week, Douglas flew off the ship with a friend and went to the psychiatry department at a U.S. Army hospital in Germany. Eventually he returned to Florida . . . five weeks after we did. He never was charged, but he also never staged a suicide act again. The psychiatrist said he had a personality disorder and an adjustment reaction. I don't know if his music career ever took off. I wish we could have persuaded him to stay out the cruise.

Crossing the Atlantic

The translant return trip seemed a little less hectic than the one eighteen months ago. No flu shots or catch-up immunizations this time, and the 3-M inspection had been done a few months ago. I'd been on the job for a while now, too, so I knew what to look out for every day. We still had a gaggle of politicians, VIPs, and reporters coming to the ship for "fact-finding" trips across the Atlantic, and they required attention and escorting. In general, though, the tempo was slowing just a little.

I took advantage of the respite to get up to the flight deck a little more. The fly-off was even more impressive to me than last year's, perhaps because I knew more of the people now. When the Red Rippers zoomed past at deck level, we all squared up a little. At this point, though, the main benefit of the fly-off was that it liberated the flight deck for joggers. Running was now unrestricted—no tie-down chains, taxiing aircraft, or rolling tractors. A fellow could finally have a good run, so there were dozens of us up there most of the time—whenever we could fit it into our schedules.

The hangar bay was busy, though. Since the fly-off there were no airplanes left in the hangars, so the supply, AIMD, and air department guys were turning the hangars into huge industrial warehouses. With their forklifts and tractors pushing tons and tri-walls of industrial volume into staging corridors for the coming off-load, the cavernous bays became more crowded than they were when full of airplanes. Like a maze in a Kafka story, a person could be lost among the stacks if he wasn't very careful.

One afternoon when we were about three days away, I ambled off the flight deck, happily fatigued from a windy run. After peeking in to chat with the corpsman in the flight deck BDS, I stopped for a moment to watch the frenetic shuffle of forklifts and materials in Hangar Bay II and then went down the starboard ladder to the second deck. It was about 1700, and I had to get ready for dinner.

About the time I stepped on the ladder, the 1-MC said, "Man overboard. Man overboard. Starboard side . . ." I didn't have to hear the rest of the announcement. The captain and XO came running past me up the ladder, elbows in front of them to get to the bridge as fast as they could. I hurried to Ward II to check in and get the medical department ready in case we'd have work to do.

All our drilling on man overboard was finally effective. Within six minutes, all but one member of the crew was accounted for. The lookout stationed on the fantail who called in the alarm had a strange report. He saw a guy in the wake waving to him, as though just waving farewell. The guy had a purple shirt, which meant he was a "grape"—one of the guys who worked in fuels. That he was in the wake at least meant he hadn't been sucked into the screws, one of the main worries about falling overboard.

His name was Johnnie Travis, an airman who had been on the ship about two years. He was due to leave the Navy in a few months and had been a lackluster performer his entire time. One of his buddies, a forklift operator, had seen him up on the starboard deck-edge elevator in Hangar Bay III a little earlier. At first he thought it was a little curious, but then he thought Johnnie was kidding around somehow. Johnnie was standing on the edge of the elevator, like he was staring at the ocean going past. Not looking upset, just transfixed. He waved to his buddy and stepped behind a stack of gear. The buddy didn't think any more about it and went on about his work.

You're not allowed on the elevators under way without a flotation vest. Had Johnnie been wearing his? His buddy and several witnesses said they thought they recalled seeing it on him.

We launched the rescue helo within about fifteen minutes. The marker buoy thrown by the lookout was found quickly, but no sailor.

We checked the water temperature. He should be able to survive almost forty minutes without special protective garments. A second helo went up within another ten minutes, and a third one shortly thereafter. The ship came almost to a stop. Besides the helos flying carefully designed search grids, every pair of binoculars on the ship was being used on the signal bridge or the captain's bridge, and hundreds of us were searching from the flight deck.

An hour went by, and the first helo, not topped off when it launched, had to refuel. After checking on the water temperature, I called the bridge. "Captain, if he hasn't drowned, we're passing survivable hypothermia." The skipper knew that, of course, but survival data was part of my job.

There shouldn't have been much of a shark threat in this area. Some garbage had been thrown out just before he went over, and the helo crews reported it was still floating and there were no sharks seen. No purple shirts, either.

Travis's bunkmates were rounded up and interviewed. No, most of them said, this guy would never kill himself. His chief pointed out, though, that Johnny had just been disciplined an hour earlier—his flight deck qualifications had been yanked. He had a weird sense of humor, one buddy said . . . he *might* do something like this on a lark. Somebody heard him say just before he stepped off, "I can't believe I'm going to do this." Could that be why he waved to the forklift operator and to the lookout?

The XO pointed out how pilots sometimes become so fixated on another airplane while flying in formation that they just fly into it. Could Travis have become hypnotized by the rushing water as he stood on the elevator edge?

Two hours went by, then four. Then it was dark. It was three hours beyond his survival time just by temperature alone. We recovered the helos. The captain sent a message to the fleet and prepared a letter for Travis's mother. Our quiet ship headed back to Florida.

When we got back to Mayport, we found that BM3 Woods's finger had healed up fine. Petty Officer Womple didn't have cancer; he finally left the Navy a year later. I still get inquiries periodically from a surgeon or oncologist about a new workup for Arden's mass. He nearly had one surgeon persuaded to amputate his scrotum, but the doctor was sent to jail for doing too many operations on old people in a nursing home, so the operation was canceled that time. As far as I know, Arden is still looking for a surgeon. George Lucy returned to the Coast Guard the next year, but you can see him selling a tool for building shoulder muscles late at night on cable TV sometimes.

A month after we got back to Mayport, Tommy Linker fleeted up from 'gator to XO, and Mitchell Vaughan left the ship. About a month after that it was my turn. Somebody told me later that they bonged me off, but I didn't hear it. When I saluted the ensign, I didn't turn around to look back at the ship. After I drove off Charlie pier, though, I got about a mile away and had to stop and look back for a few minutes. My desk was cleared and I had completed a good turnover with Bruce Bohnker, my relief, but somewhere under the stack of the day's thoughts it felt like I'd left some unfinished business somehow. No, I guess I felt as though I'd left something back on the ship.

In October 1993, Ann and I went to Philadelphia for the decommissioning ceremony for the USS *Forrestal.* We didn't find Captain Guitar, but Captain Louis, now working for McDonnell Douglas, was there, along with five or six other former skippers. Six months later, I learned that Captain Guitar had been there, too. He wouldn't have been hiding, of course, but I suspect the Cajun was as distracted that morning as the rest of us. There were several hundred FID sailors there from all across the country. Their memories and sea stories about the First of the Supercarriers covered thirty-eight years.

Not many of us had been in the ship's company at the same time, but even a stranger could tell we were all shipmates. That day I realized what it was I'd left on the ship back in Mayport, and I knew I wasn't supposed to have it back.

After the ceremony, I walked back to the fantail where I'd finished a lot of days the way Monty told me to. Maybe there were only fourteen people in the world who had my job. Maybe when we have fewer carriers, there will only be twelve.

But I will always be one of them.

About the Author

Terrence Riley was born in St. Joseph, Missouri, in 1947. A graduate of Harvard College and the University of Missouri Medical School, Dr. Riley did his residency in neurology at the National Naval Medical Center in Bethesda, Maryland, and completed a postdoctoral fellowship in electroencephalography at Johns Hopkins University in Baltimore.

Dr. Riley left the navy in 1980 to join the faculty at Boston University, where he rose to the rank of associate professor. As a naval reservist from 1980 to 1987 he became a pilot, eventually earning instrument, multiengine, and instructor ratings and licenses.

He returned to active duty in 1988 and in July became senior medical officer on the USS *Forrestal*. Since June 1994 he has served as executive officer of the Cherry Point Naval Hospital in North Carolina. Dr. Riley has written more than forty papers and edited two books on sleep disorders and other medical topics. He and his wife, Ann, have three daughters, Mary, Abigail, and Deirdre.

The **Naval Institute Press** is the book-publishing arm of the U.S. Naval Institute, a private, nonprofit society for sea service professionals and others who share an interest in naval and maritime affairs. Established in 1873 at the U.S. Naval Academy in Annapolis, Maryland, where its offices remain, today the Naval Institute has more than 100,000 members worldwide.

Members of the Naval Institute receive the influential monthly magazine *Proceedings* and discounts on fine nautical prints, ship and aircraft photos, and subscriptions to the bimonthly *Naval History* magazine. They also have access to the transcripts of the Institute's Oral History Program and get discounted admission to any of the Institute-sponsored seminars offered around the country.

The Naval Institute's book-publishing program, begun in 1898 with basic guides to naval practices, has broadened its scope in recent years to include books of more general interest. Now the Naval Institute Press publishes more than seventy titles each year, ranging from how-to books on boating and navigation to battle histories, biographies, ship and aircraft guides, and novels. Institute members receive discounts on the Press's nearly 400 books in print.

Full-time students are eligible for special half-price membership rates. Life memberships are also available.

For a free catalog describing Naval Institute Press books currently available, and for futher information about U.S. Naval Institute membership, please write to:

Membership & Communications Department
U.S. Naval Institute
118 Maryland Avenue
Annapolis, Maryland 21402-5035
Or call, toll-free, (800) 233-USNI.